Paying for Care Handbook

6th edition

Helen Winfield

Gary Vaux

Counsel and Care

Child Poverty Action Group

CPAG promotes action for the prevention and relief of poverty among children and families with children. To achieve this, CPAG aims to raise awareness of the causes, extent, nature and impact of poverty, and strategies for its eradication and prevention; bring about positive policy changes for families with children in poverty; and enable those eligible for income maintenance to have access to their full entitlement. If you are not already supporting us, please consider making a donation, or ask for details of our membership schemes, training courses and publications.

Published by Child Poverty Action Group
94 White Lion Street
London N1 9PF
Tel: 020 7837 7979
staff@cpag.org.uk
www.cpag.org.uk

A CIP record for this book is available from the British Library

ISBN: 978 1 906076 20 7

Child Poverty Action Group is a charity registered in England and Wales (registration number 294841) and in Scotland (registration number SC039339), and is a company limited by guarantee, registered in England (registration number 1993854). VAT number: 690 808117

Cover design by Devious Designs
Typeset by David Lewis XML Associates Ltd
Printed in the UK by CPI William Clowes Beccles NR34 7TL
Cover photo by Duncan Phillips/Photofusion

The authors

Helen Winfield is Principal Welfare Rights Officer for Wolverhampton Social Care Services. She is a trainer on benefits in care homes and writes on these issues in the *Disability Rights Handbook*.

Gary Vaux is Head of Advice (Benefits and Work) for Hertfordshire County Council, as well as being a regular columnist in *Community Care* magazine and a freelance trainer for CPAG and others. He is also chair of the Social Security Advisers Group at the Local Government Association (LGA), and represents and advises both the LGA and the Association of Directors of Adult Social Services on social security matters.

Counsel and Care is a national charity providing advice, information and support for older people, their families and carers. Gill Coombs is the Advice Service Manager and Garry Macdonald the Senior Advice Worker.

Acknowledgements

The authors would like to thank Geoff Tait, Pauline Thompson, David Simmons, Michael Roche, Jane Hayball, Jenny Hambidge and Carolyn George for their contributions to the checking of this *Handbook*.

Thanks are also due to Nicola Johnston for editing and managing the production of the book, and to Alison Moore for compiling the index and Sara Carbone and Kelly Wilson for proofreading the text.

We would also like to thank staff at the Department for Work and Pensions, the Revenue, Department of Health, Welsh Assembly Government and Scottish Government for their co-operation.

The authors have made their best endeavours to try to ensure that the law covered in this *Handbook* was correct as at 1 February 2009.

Contents

How to use this *Handbook*

This *Handbook* aims to provide all the information you will need about claiming practical and financial assistance in meeting your care needs from adult social care services, health authorities, the Revenue and the Department for Work and Pension. It aims to give practical help in the areas where disputes are likely to arise between those who need assistance and those who are responsible for administering and providing it. If you are not satisfied with the help you are being offered, the *Handbook* aims to guide you in challenging decisions made about you.

The organisation of the **contents** is explained in the introduction (Chapter 1). The main subjects in each chapter are also summarised in the contents page at the front of the *Handbook*. The main subject heads and page numbers are repeated at the beginning of each chapter.

It is often helpful to refer to the sources from which the information in the text is drawn, which is the relevant law and official guidance, as well as caselaw which often clarifies what the law and guidance should mean in practice. **References** to these are given in the notes at the end of each chapter and are numbered in the order in which they appear in the text. The references are usually to Acts or Regulations, but sometimes they are to formal guidance issued by government departments (or the Scottish Government or Welsh Assembly Government), and sometimes to caselaw. The notes are in abbreviated form and the abbreviations used are explained in Appendix 6.

Abbreviations are often also used in the text to save space, but an abbreviation is always given in full the first time it is used in a chapter or section (followed by the abbreviation in brackets).

The **index**, like the contents, will also help you to find the information you are looking for. Entries in bold type direct you to the general information on the subject, or where the subject is covered more fully. Sub-entries under the bold headings are listed alphabetically and direct you to specific aspects of the subject.

There are many **cross-references** in the text which are also designed to assist you in finding other relevant information about a particular topic. They give either the chapter or page number(s), as appropriate.

Whereas many of the sources of information about social security benefits will be familiar to readers of other CPAG Handbooks, the main **sources** of legislative powers and duties of adult social care services departments (social work departments in Scotland) may be less familiar, and for ease of reference these are set out in full in Appendix 4 (followed by a list of key guidance circulars in Appendix 5).

The *Handbook* covers the law and practice which applies in England and Wales (and includes references to some differences in sources of guidance and terminology). The different provisions which apply to Scotland, but which more often than not are of similar effect, have also been covered. Although much of the law relating to social security is similar in effect in Northern Ireland, the very different arrangements for health and social welfare generally (although also sometimes similar in effect) are such that it has not been possible to cover them in this *Handbook*.

Because the areas of policy, practice, law, caselaw and guidance covered in this *Handbook* are notoriously the subject of constant change, readers are urged to use the *Handbook* in conjunction with other sources which may provide regular updates or may provide more extensive detail on particular aspects which are beyond the scope of this *Handbook* (such as those sources referred to in Appendix 3).

Although the authors have made their best efforts to ensure that the information contained in this *Handbook* is correct or at least represents a reasonable interpretation, the authors readily acknowledge that, in view of the pace of change in an emerging and contentious area of law and the complexities and uncertainty of some of the issues analysed, some errors or omissions may be inventible, or else will become apparent over the course of time. Any comments from any readers which may be considered to improve the text or the structure of the *Handbook* in future editions would be gratefully received (and should be sent c/o CPAG).

Abbreviations used in the text

AA	Attendance allowance
BL	Budgeting loan
CA	Carer's allowance
CAB	Citizens Advice Bureau
CCG	Community care grant
CL	Crisis loan
COSLA	Convention of Scottish Local Authorities
CQC	Care Quality Commission
CSSIW	Care and Social Services Inspectorate Wales
CTB	Council tax benefit
CTC	Child tax credit
DLA mobility	Disability living allowance – mobility component
DLA care	Disability living allowance – care component
DWP	Department for Work and Pensions
EC	European Community
ECJ	European Court of Justice
ESA	Employment and support allowance
EU	European Union
FNC	funded nursing care
FSA	Financial Standards Authority
GP	General practitioner
HB	Housing benefit
IB	Incapacity benefit
IS	Income support
MP	Member of Parliament
MS	Medical Service
MSP	Member of Scottish Parliament
OFT	Office of Fair Trading
PEA	Personal expenses allowance
PC	Pension credit
PCT	Primary care trust
PC	Pension credit
SDA	Severe disablement allowance
SERPS	State Earnings-Related Pension Scheme
SSP	Statutory sick pay
WTC	Working tax credit

Means-tested benefit rates

Income support/income-based jobseeker's allowance

Personal allowances		April 2009 to April 2010 £pw
Single	Under 25	50.95
	25 or over	64.30
Lone parent	Under 18	50.95
	18 or over	64.30
Couple	Both under 18	50.95
	Both under 18, certain cases	76.90
	One under 18, one 18-24	50.95
	One under 18, one 25 or over	64.30
	One under 18, certain cases	100.95
	Both 18 or over	100.95

Premiums		
Carer		29.50
Disability	Single	27.50
	Couple	39.15
Enhanced disability	Single	13.40
	Couple	19.30
Severe disability	One qualifies	52.85
	Two qualify	105.70
Pensioner	Single (jobseeker's allowance only)	65.70
	Couple	97.50

Children	(Pre-6 April 2004 claims with no child tax credit)	
Child under 20 personal allowance		56.11
Family premium		17.30
Disabled child premium		51.24
Enhanced disability premium (child)		20.65

Capital limits	Lower	Upper
Standard	6,000	16,000
Care homes	10,000	16,000

Tariff income £1 per £250 between lower and upper limit

£pw

Pension credit
Guarantee credit

		£pw
Standard minimum guarantee	Single	130.00
	Couple	198.45
Severe disability addition	One qualifies	52.85
	Two qualify	105.70
Carer addition		29.50

Savings credit

Threshold	Single	96.00
	Couple	153.40
Maximum	Single	20.40
	Couple	27.03

Capital disregard

Standard	6,000
Care homes	10,000
No upper limit	

Deemed income £1 per £500 above disregard

Income-related employment and support allowance

	Assessment phase	Main phase
Personal allowances		
Single		
Under 25	50.95	64.30
25 or over	64.30	64.30
Lone parent		
Under 18	50.95	64.30
18 or over	64.30	64.30
Couple		
Both under 18 (max)		
Both 18 or over	100.95	100.95
Components		
Work-related activity	–	25.50
Support	–	30.85
Premiums		
Carer	29.50	29.50
Severe disability (one qualifies)	52.85	52.85
Severe disability premium (two qualify)	105.70	105.70
Enhanced disability		
Single	13.40	13.40
Couple	19.30	19.30

		£pw	£pw
Pensioner			
Single, no component		65.70	65.70
Couple, no component		97.50	97.50
Single, work-related activity component		40.20	40.20
Couple, work-related activity component		72.00	72.00
Single, support component		34.85	34.85
Couple, support component		66.65	66.65

Capital limits
As for income support

Housing benefit and council tax benefit
Personal allowances

		£pw
Single	Under 25	50.95
	Under 25 (on main phase ESA)	64.30
	25 or over	64.30
Lone parent	Under 18	50.95
	Under 18 (on main phase ESA)	64.30
	18 or over	64.30
Couple	Both under 18	76.90
	Both under 18 (claimant on main phase ESA)	100.95
	One or both 18 or over	100.95
Dependent children	Under 20	56.11
Pensioner 60 or over	Single under 65	130.00
	Single 65 or over	150.40
	Couple both under 65	198.45
	Couple one or both 65 or over	225.50

Components

	£pw
Work-related activity	25.50
Support	30.85

Premiums

		£pw
Carer		29.50
Disability	Single	27.50
	Couple	39.15
Disabled child		51.24

		£pw
Enhanced disability	Single	13.40
	Couple	19.30
	Child	20.65
Severe disability	One qualifies	52.85
	Two qualify	105.70
Family	Ordinary rate	17.30
	Some lone parents	22.20
	Baby addition	10.50

Capital limits	Lower	Upper
Standard	6,000	16,000
Care home (housing benefit only)	10,000	16,000

Tariff income £1 per £250 between lower and upper limit£1 per £500 for those aged 60 or over

No upper limit or tariff income for those on PC guarantee credit

Social fund payments

Maternity grant		500.00
Cold weather payment		25.00
Winter fuel payment	60–79	250.00
	80 or over	400.00
	Care home (60–79)	125.00
	Care home (80 or over)	200.00

Non-means-tested benefit rates

	Claimant £pw	Adult dependant £pw
Attendance allowance		
Higher rate	70.35	
Lower rate	47.10	
Bereavement benefits		
Bereavement payment (lump sum)	2,000	
Bereavement allowance/widow's pension (55 or over)	95.25	
Bereavement allowance/widow's pension (45–54)	28.58-88.58	
Widowed parent's allowance/widowed mother's allowance	95.25	
Carer's allowance	53.10	31.70
Child benefit		
Only/eldest child	20.00	
Other child(ren)	13.20	
Child dependant (some existing claimants only)		
Only/eldest child	8.20	
Other child(ren)	11.35	
Disability living allowance		
Care component		
Highest rate	70.35	
Middle rate	47.10	
Lowest rate	18.65	
Mobility component		
Higher rate	49.10	
Lower rate	18.65	
Contributory employment and support allowance		
Assessment phase		
Under 25	50.95	
25 or over	64.30	

	Claimant £pw	Adult dependant £pw
Main phase		
16 or over	64.30	
Work-related activity component	25.50	
Support component	30.85	
Guardian's allowance	14.10	
Short-term incapacity benefit		
Lower rate	67.75	41.35
Higher rate	80.15	41.35
Lower rate (over pension age)	86.20	51.10
Higher rate (over pension age)	89.80	51.10
Long-term incapacity benefit	89.80	53.10
Age addition (under 35)	15.65	
Age addition (35–44)	6.55	
Industrial disablement benefit		
Under 18	20%: £17.61 to 100%: £88.05	
18 or over	20%: £28.72 to 100%: £143.60	
Contribution-based jobseeker's allowance		
Under 25	50.95	
25 or over	64.30	
Maternity allowance		
Standard rate	123.06	41.35
Retirement pension		
Category A	95.25	57.05
Category B (widow(er)/surviving civil partner)	95.25	
Category B (spouse/civil partner)	57.05	
Category D	57.05	
Severe disablement allowance	57.45	31.90
Age addition (under 40)	15.65	
Age addition (40–49)	9.10	
Age addition (50–59)	5.35	
Statutory maternity, paternity and adoption pay		
Standard rate	123.06	
Statutory sick pay	79.15	

	Claimant £pw	Adult dependant £pw
National insurance contributions		
Lower earnings limit	95.00	
Primary threshold	110.00	
	11% of	
Employee's class 1 rate	£110.01 to	
	£844	
	1% above £844	
Class 2 rate	2.40	

Tax credit rates

		£ per day	£ per year
Child tax credit			
Family element	Basic	1.50	545
	Baby element	1.50	545
Child element		6.13	2,235
Disability element		7.32	2,670
Severe disability element		2.95	1,075
Working tax credit			
Basic element		5.18	1,890
Couple element		5.10	1,860
Lone parent element		5.10	1,860
30-hour element		2.13	775
Disability element		6.94	2,530
Severe disability element		2.95	1,075
50-plus element	Working 16–29 hours	3.57	1,300
	Working 30 hours or more	5.31	1,935
Childcare element	80% eligible childcare costs to a weekly maximum of:		
	One child		weekly maximum 175
	Two or more children		weekly maximum 300
Thresholds			
First income threshold	Working tax credit only or with child tax credit		6,420
	Child tax credit only		16,040
First taper			39%
Second income threshold			min. 50,000
Second taper			6.67%
Income disregard			25,000

Part 1

Introduction

Chapter 1

Introduction

This chapter covers:
1. The purpose and scope of this *Handbook* (below)
2. What is community care (p4)
3. Systems to deliver services and benefits (p5)
4. Arrangements to fund care yourself (p9)

1. **The purpose and scope of this *Handbook***

Nearly all individuals at some time in their lives will come into contact with the social security and/or care system. Often it is at a stressful time, and many people find it difficult to know what help could be provided, and where to go to get help.

This *Handbook* draws together the effects of the laws relating to social security and community care and considers how they work in practice and how they could work better within the existing limitations. It provides a guide for adults in need of care and support, their carers and relatives, and professionals involved in administering or advising on the effects of each scheme.

Some people are fortunate not to require any financial assistance from adult social care services or the NHS or the Department for Work and Pensions even if they have significant personal care needs due to old age, health problems or disabilities. More commonly, however, many will need at least some assistance, whether by way of care, or by cash, or in kind. This applies whether they live at home in the community or in a care home.

This *Handbook* explains what services and help people can expect from the state, both to remain in their own home or if they need any form of residential care. It covers the social security benefits you can receive, the help you can get from the NHS (which is largely free) and the help you can get from local authorities' housing and adult social care departments (which is normally charged for). An understanding in some detail of both what the state *has to* or just *may* provide, can help you to know whether you are likely to have to arrange your own care or meet some or all of the cost yourself.

For reasons of space, there are a number of areas which are beyond the scope of this *Handbook.* In particular, it does not attempt to cover in any significant detail the very different responsibilities of welfare agencies which may apply in respect of young people (under the age of 18) and children in need. Nor does it cover the different private financial or insurance arrangements which individuals may have the opportunity to make so that they do not require state assistance for their care needs (although some of these are briefly referred to at the end of this chapter). Where appropriate, however, references are made in the text to other sources of information on particular aspects which may be of interest but which are not covered in this *Handbook*.

2. **What is community care**

Although community care (or care in the community) is a term which has a common usage, it can mean different things to different people. Some think of it as excluding care in a care home, although many care home owners go to considerable lengths to ensure that their care home is part of the local community and that residents can make use of local facilities. Equally, staying long term in hospital does not necessarily mean you are no longer part of the community. The hospital itself may be a vital part of the community, employing local people and utilising local services.

Others take the view that community care encompasses *anything* which helps older or disabled people remain in their homes for as long as possible. In addition to the services described in this *Handbook* they include all the informal care that goes on as part of everyday life. Community care could, therefore, encompass help from friends, relatives and neighbours. It would include the role of local facilities such as pubs and hairdressers in welcoming older or disabled people. It could also include ways that the local environment supports all people, such as paths being in a good state of repair, accessible transport and buildings, and actions which ensure people feel safe to go out – eg, adequate policing and lighting.

The working definition

The previous government in its 1989 White Paper gave the following definition of community care:

> Community care means providing the right level of intervention and support to enable people to achieve maximum independence and control over their own lives. For this aim to become a reality, the development of a wide range of services provided in a variety of settings is essential. These services form part of a spectrum of care, ranging from domiciliary support provided to people in their own homes, strengthened by the availability of respite care and day care for those with more intensive care needs, through sheltered housing, group

homes and hostels where increasing levels of care are available, to residential care and nursing homes and long-stay hospital care for those for whom other forms of care are no longer enough.[1]

The White Paper went on to recognise that in reality most care is not provided by statutory bodies but by family, friends and neighbours, so the right level of support for them at the right time is vital. It also confirmed the important role of health care, and the role of the benefits system in providing financial support. With the introduction of direct payments, in addition to having services provided for them, people were given the ability to purchase their own services.

A further White Paper issued in 1998 outlined the changes which it proposed to make to community care provision. The aims of community care remained broadly the same and the proposals again emphasised the desirability of enabling people to retain their independence for as long as possible, wherever possible remaining in their own homes. Health and adult social care services were to target support especially at those in danger of losing their independence. Direct payment schemes were to be made available to a wider group of service users to give them control over their care. More support was to be given to carers to enable to them to continue in that role where both carer and cared for person wanted this.[2]

These ambitions were also expressed in equivalent White Papers for Wales and Scotland.[3]

Since 1998 there have been numerous initiatives, frameworks, strategies and targets set to try to achieve these aims. How far the practice of community care lives up to these aims is a source of debate. There is no doubt that some individuals receive excellent services which provide them with the care they need when they need it. Equally, the measures that authorities have adopted due to resource constraints (described in Chapters 2 and 9) and the extent to which the social security system supports people in need, can leave individuals and their families in a state of high anxiety about whether they will get the services they need and whether they will be able to afford them. There has been much debate about whether the funding for community care is sufficient to achieve the policy objectives and a Green Paper on the future funding of social care is expected from Government in 2009 as part of the push for the right care and the right deal for those in need of care.

3. **Systems to deliver services and benefits**

If you need help in the form of services or benefits you should normally first contact your local adult social care services, housing department or Jobcentre Plus, depending on the nature of your need. If you have a health need you should see your GP or practice nurse.

This section briefly describes the role of central government departments in providing services, and the structure of local services. Chapter 2 describes in more detail the individual responsibilities of health, housing and adult social care services and where those responsibilities overlap.

Please note that the term 'adult social care services' has been used throughout this *Handbook*. Different names are used in different areas, such as social services or community care services. However, they are normally still part of the local authority and undertake adult social care services functions. In a few areas care trusts have developed (see p18). The use of the term 'NHS body' covers the many different names that are currently being evolved in England, Wales and Scotland for the providers or commissioners of health care at a local level.

Health services

Responsibility for the overall policy for health services lies with the Department of Health (England), the Welsh Assembly Government and Scottish Government. They set the framework of policy objectives and resources for the delivery and administration of health services. They issue directions and circulars to the appropriate NHS bodies and independent contractors such as GPs and dentists. In relation to community care, the same guidance is often issued to adult social care services.

Local NHS bodies set policies at a local level for the resident population and are responsible for commissioning an appropriate range of health services to meet local needs. These include hospitals and community nursing and pharmaceutical services, GPs, dentists and opticians.

In England, primary care trusts (PCTs) commission all local health services. So, for instance, the PCT would commission your care if you needed to go into hospital, and also ensure that there are enough local GPs, opticians, dentists, patient transport, etc. Some PCTs can also take on the status of 'care trusts', which can also commission social care services (see p18). There are also 10 Strategic Health Authorities which manage the NHS locally and are a key link between the Department of Health and the NHS.

In Wales, local health boards, which match local authority areas, have control over commissioning and delivering health care. Some have joined together in local partnerships. Three regional directorates ensure co-ordinated provision at a regional level. The Wales Centre for Health is responsible for seeking to improve public health in Wales.[4]

In Scotland, provision of healthcare is the responsibility of 14 geographically-based local Health Boards and a number of National Special Health Boards. In Scotland, the NHS was subject to reorganisation under the National Health Service Reform (Scotland) Act 2004. The changes included the dissolution of NHS Trusts and the establishment of 'community health partnerships'. Health Boards are now duty bound to involve the public in the design and delivery of services and the Act extended the powers of the Scottish Ministers to intervene to ensure appropriate health care provision. At the time of writing, MSPs voted through the general principles of the Health Boards (Membership and Elections) Bill. The Bill proposes to introduce direct elections to local health boards so that members of the public can stand for election. Two pilot schemes will be set up and evaluated, before MSPs decide if they should be rolled out across Scotland.

Although currently not democratically elected, health bodies are accountable locally and are required to consult their local community. In England, Patient Advice and Liaison Services provide information and support to patients and their families. There should also be an Independent Complaints Advocacy Service which can help you to pursue a complaint against the NHS. In Scotland, the Scottish Health Council offers support to patients and in Wales community health councils perform this function.

Local authorities have been given money to fund local involvement networks (LINks). These are made up of individuals and community groups who work together to develop and improve local health and social care services. LINks consult local people about local health and social care services, and suggest improvements directly to the people who deliver those services. They also conduct spot checks on services to check performance. LINks can refer unresolved issues to a local 'Overview and Scrutiny Committee' if it seems that effective action is not being taken. To become involved in your local LINk contact your local authority or call the NHS Centre for Involvement on 024 7615 0266.

Local authority services (adult social care services and housing)

Two different government departments in England are responsible for policy making in the areas of adult social care services and housing: the Department of Health for adult social care services and the Department for Communities and Local Government for housing. In Wales, the Welsh Assembly Government is responsible for policy development and implementation. The Scottish Government's 'Healthier Directorate' combines strategies for health and housing. These departments issue guidance, circulars and letters to inform or, in some cases instruct, local authorities. Legislation sometimes states that the Secretary of State for Health, the Welsh Assembly Government or the Scottish Secretary for Health and Wellbeing can issue mandatory directions to adult social care services. Guidance can also have considerable force if it is issued under section 7 Local Authority Social Services Act 1970 in England and Wales or section 5 Social Work (Scotland) Act 1968 (see Appendix 1). The housing department can also be issued with directions (such as the Code of Guidance on Homelessness).[5]

Central government funding for all services provided by local authorities comes from the Revenue Support Grant and other grants such as Supporting People (see Chapter 3). The amount each local authority receives is calculated using the formula grant system, which considers demographic factors in the area and is used to calculate the formula spending share (FSS) for each area. The FSS for adult social care services includes factors such as the number of older people in receipt of income support and attendance allowance. It is advantageous to local authorities to encourage the take up of these benefits, as it can mean they receive a greater proportion of the Revenue Support Grant. However, the total amount remains the decision of government.

The local authority can decide how it will divide the money it receives from government between all its departments (although some amounts are ring fenced – eg, the grant for mental health). Some spend less on adult social care services than would be expected from the FSS while others spend considerably more.

In addition to government money, local authorities top up their funding through locally raised council tax, housing rents and charges for services.

Local authority officers are responsible for the day-to-day running of services, but it is elected council members who are responsible for the policies and quality of the services provided. This is why it is sometimes useful to bring your case to the attention of a councillor (see p44).

Different types of local authority

Not all local authorities have both housing and adult social care services functions, although the majority now do. There are four types of local authority:
* county authorities based on fairly large geographical areas, often reflecting historical shires (eg, Lancashire). There are adult social care services in county authorities and they normally have a number of offices so that you do not have to travel too far to the nearest adult social care services office;
* district or borough authorities within a county area. They do not have any adult social care services functions but provide housing services;
* metropolitan district authorities and London borough councils are based in urban areas and have responsibility for both housing and adult social care services;
* unitary authorities were created out of some county and district/borough authorities. They are responsible for both adult social care services and housing. Some still retain the title district or borough in their name. All authorities in Wales and Scotland are unitary.

Some authorities which are responsible for both housing and adult social care services have combined their committees and have just one director responsible for both adult social care services and housing.

Social security benefits and tax credits

The government department responsible for the overall administration and policy work for most social security benefits, other than housing benefit(HB) and council tax benefit (CTB), is the Department for Work and Pensions (DWP). Tax credits, child benefit and guardian's allowance are dealt with by Her Majesty's Revenue and Customs (referred to in this Handbook as 'the Revenue'). HB and CTB are administered by local authorities.

See p91 for the agencies that make up the DWP.

DWP staff are responsible for making decisions on claims for benefits and are issued with guidance on the interpretation and application of the law. This is called *The Decision Makers Guide*. Although this guidance is usually strictly adhered to, it is not binding on DWP staff, and certainly not binding on higher authorities such as the First-Tier Tribunal.

4. **Arrangements to fund care yourself**

Many people pay for their own care. This means buying your own help or paying the fees for care in a care home directly to the home. You may have too much money to qualify for adult social care services help in a care home, or you may not come within adult social care services eligibility criteria for needing help (see p38), or the sort of help you want is not provided – eg, gardening or housework. This section looks briefly at ways of using your money to pay for your care. However, it is always wise to check whether or not you should get state help before arranging to pay for your own care. In addition, it is helpful to get an assessment of your needs by adult social care services or the NHS in order to be sure of the type of help you do need and to talk through the various options you may have.

Using your money to pay for care

If you only need small amounts of care you may be able to pay for it without too much difficulty. This *Handbook* describes the various benefits to which you might be entitled and also the powers and duties of the various statutory agencies. Before you arrange to pay for your own care you should check whether it should be provided for you, if this is what you would prefer. Local authorities cannot refuse to arrange your care at home just because you have resources of your own.[6] In Scotland, local authorities must arrange your care in a care home regardless of your ability to pay[7] although they can take your resources into account at the earlier stage of deciding how best to meet the need.

The care you need can sometimes be very expensive, especially if you want to remain at home but need a lot of care. Care homes can also be very expensive. Therefore, if you have capital which you want to preserve you might want to think of ways to make it last longer and you should get independent advice about how best to invest it.

There are two main ways of using your capital to pay for care: equity release and long-term care insurance.

Equity release

The most common form of equity release scheme is a 'home reversion scheme' which involves selling your home or part of your home to a 'reversion company'. In return you receive a cash sum (with which you could buy long-term care insurance) or a monthly annuity income. You can remain in the house rent-free or for a nominal rent for the rest of your life. When the property is sold, the reversion company receives a share of the proceeds. For instance, if you sold a 50 per cent share then the reversion company will receive 50 per cent of the proceeds. However, when you sell your home (or a share of it) to the reversion company you will not receive the full open market value because you retain the right to live there for the rest of your life. The value you receive depends on your age and sex. Older people will get more than younger people and men get more than women.

There are also 'home income plans' where you take out a mortgage loan against your home, usually up to a specified amount, and the money is used to buy an annuity which pays you a regular income for life. The interest payments on the loan are deducted from this monthly income.

Long-term care insurance

Some insurance companies offer schemes to help pay for long-term care, either in your own home or in a care home. Pre-funded long-term care insurance, where regular premiums or a lump sum are paid against possible future care needs, is now very rare. The main type of financial product currently available to help meet the cost of long-term care is an immediate needs plan, where a lump sum is paid to purchase care immediately.

The cost of the plan will depend on your age, sex and state of health when you purchase it.

Getting advice

It is very important to get independent advice when thinking about any scheme which involves your capital. Seek advice on the way payments from either equity release or an immediate needs plan might affect your entitlement to benefits or care services from either adult social care services or from the NHS. Financial advisers should be aware of the benefits you could claim or when the NHS or local authority will fund services, but there is no guarantee they will be aware of all the benefits and services described in this *Handbook*.

The schemes described above are not yet all subject to financial regulation. Firms selling or advising on long-term care insurance and mortgage-based products such as home income plans (subject to meeting certain requirements) are regulated by the Financial Services Authority (FSA). The Government intends to bring home reversion schemes under FSA regulation but at the time of writing it was not known when this will be implemented. Some companies have signed up to a voluntary code of practice (eg, safe home income plans) and the Association of British Insurers encourages its members to belong to the Insurance

Ombudsman, the Personal Insurance Arbitration Service or the Personal Investment Authority Ombudsman Bureau. Always be clear about what you hope to achieve through equity release or long-term care insurance, then check if those requirements will be met by a particular product.

Notes

2. What is community care
.1 *Caring for People: Community Care in the Next Decade and Beyond, 1989,* HMSO, para 2.2
2 *Modernising Social Services, Promoting Independence, Improving Protection, Raising Standards,* 1998, DoH, p21
3 *Social Services: Building for the Future, A White Paper for Wales,* National Assembly for Wales 1999; *Modernising Community Care: An Action Plan,* the Scottish Office, 1998

3. Community care changes in 1993
4 Health (Wales) Act 2003
5 s182 HA 1996

6. Arrangements to fund care yourself
6 *Fair Access to Care Practice Guidance 2003 Q 8.5*
7 HLD (2003)7 Annex D

Part 2

People living at home

Chapter 2

• •

Community care services at home

This chapter covers:
1. What are community care services (below)
2. The responsibilities of adult social care services, health and housing (p17)
3. Getting the services you need (p34)
4. How far the authority's resources can be taken into account (p38)
5. How to complain (p40)

---

1. **What are community care services**

Although all services helping you remain in the community could be described as 'community care services', they are defined in legislation. The services covered in this *Handbook,* however, are not limited strictly to these services because other services, such as those you can get from the NHS and housing, are equally vital in helping you remain at home.

The legislation

• •

England and Wales

The services defined in the National Health Service and Community Care Act 1990[1] as 'community care' services are those which local authorities may provide or arrange under any of the following enactments:

- Part III of the National Assistance Act 1948 (ss21 and 29);
- section 45 of the Health Services and Public Health Act 1968;
- section 21 and Schedule 8 to the National Health Service Act 1977;
- section 117 of the Mental Health Act 1983.

• •

Scotland

The National Health Service and Community Care Act 1990 defines community care services as those provided by local authorities under Part II of the Social Work (Scotland) Act 1968[2] or sections 25 to 27 of the Mental Health (Care and Treatment) (Scotland) Act

2003. The National Assistance Act 1948 mainly applies to England but it provides the legal basis for charging for residential care (see p19). The Community Care and Health (Scotland) Act 2002 introduced free personal care and also enhanced individual rights to direct payments and carers' assessments.

The legislation is explained in more detail on p19 where it relates to services which are provided in non-residential settings and in Chapter 9 where it relates to residential services.

Note that although we do not cover the legislation relating to residential services in this chapter, as this is covered in Chapter 9, sections 3, 4 and 5 of this chapter apply equally to care at home and care in a residential setting.

The non-residential provision which counts as community care services within the legislation spans a wide variety of services, including: practical assistance in the home (home help); respite care to give you or your carer a break; equipment to help your daily living; adaptations to your home; telephones, televisions, radios; help with travel; facilities for rehabilitation; meals-on-wheels, day centres, recreational activities, outings and wardens in sheltered housing. It also includes adult social care services advice, support and information.

In some cases adult social care services have the *power* to provide services and in others they have a *duty* to provide services. Sometimes this duty is a *general duty* to ensure that services are available for the local population, and sometimes it is a *specific duty* to you as an individual to provide services you have been assessed as needing.

Sometimes a service is provided by the NHS (eg, a laundry service or incontinence pads), but in the event of it not providing the service or only providing it inadequately, you may find that adult social care services make these provisions. The social fund (see p182) has made a payment for incontinence pads when an applicant failed to meet the health authority's stringent criteria.[3] With the NHS and adult social care services increasingly using 'pooled budgets' it is often difficult to know which organisation has the responsibility.

There might be confusion over who is responsible for adaptations to your home. Assistance in carrying out works of adaptation is listed as a community care service and as such could be the responsibility of adult social care services. Grants for facilities to improve housing for disabled people (see p82) are normally the responsibility of the housing department, but adult social care services have a duty to assist where the local housing authority refuses or is unable to approve the application even if the housing department has established that you need the adaptations.[4] In England, community equipment, provided you are assessed as needing it, is free as are minor adaptations of up to £1,000.[5] In Scotland, guidance produced by the Confederation of Scottish Local Authorities suggests that local authorities should consider not charging for equipment and adaptations or only charge a maximum of £20.

Chapter 2: Community care services at home
2. The responsibilities of adult social care services, health and housing

2

Who your services are arranged by can be important for a number of reasons.

- Charging – you will probably be charged for a service if it is supplied by adult social care services rather than by the NHS.
- Your rights – it is important to know when there is a duty to provide you with a service, and how far you can choose the way that service is provided.
- Knowing which department to go to or where to complain – it is sometimes not clear which department has responsibility for a service and it is not uncommon to have to complain to more than one department.

In England there is a joint charter for social services, health and housing which may help you through the community care maze.[6] There are national guidelines for local charters which should indicate how long you may be expected to wait for an assessment or a service and how to complain to each of the departments. There is a similar charter in Wales called the *Health and Social Care Guide*.

---

2. The responsibilities of adult social care services, health and housing

Adult social care services, health and housing authorities each work to different statutes and their respective responsibilities have been the subject of an increasing amount of caselaw in the courts. The responsibilities of adult social care services, health and housing departments are constantly evolving, with changes being driven by government and caselaw. Not all the changes need legislation and departments are often informed by circulars about changes in the interpretation of the law or about conditions attached to the money they are allocated.

In England, the Care Quality Commission (CQC) is responsible for performance indicators. Up to 2008, it gave local authorities a 'star rating' based on their performance and their ability to improve. From April 2009, the star ratings are replaced by the Comprehensive Area Assessment (CAA – see below). The CQC also gives all registered care services and care homes a 'quality rating' which compares services against national standards. Three stars means than the services are excellent; two stars good; one star adequate; and zero stars poor. Following its key inspection, every care home or care service will have a published quality rating (unless it is being disputed).

CAA is the new joint assessment framework for local authorities in England and their partners. It is the first independent and joint inspectorate assessment of local areas and the quality of life for the people living there. So health and social care services will be assessed alongside, for example, community safety, sustainable communities and children's and older people's services. The first CAA reports, expected around November 2009, will include an assessment of

2

Chapter 2: Community care services at home
2. The responsibilities of adult social care services, health and housing

performance and prospects for improvement in local areas against Local Area Agreement targets and a wider set of the national indicators.

In addition to the responsibilities to people with disabilities listed in this chapter, there is a general power for local authorities in England and Wales to take any action they consider will promote or improve the economic, social or environmental wellbeing of their area.[7] This can include action to help individuals. One case held that this power was broad enough to enable local authorities to provide financial assistance to secure accommodation. If the only way to avoid a breach of the European Convention was to invoke this power, then the authority was bound to invoke it.[8]

Responsibilities of adult social care services

The prime responsibility for ensuring that community care services are provided rests with adult social care services. In some areas of England, 'care trusts' have been set up which commission and provide both health and social care services. Care trusts are responsible for providing services under the legislation listed in this chapter as if they were adult social care services and local authority councillors are still ultimately responsible for the service. You can be charged for these services in the same way as if adult social care services had provided them.

Adult social care services decide, through the assessment process (see p34), who receives care services. The assessment is part of what is known as 'care management'. A decision that you need services leads on to the design and setting up of a 'care package' to meet your identified needs. This may include a range of services provided by adult social care services, health or housing departments, independent providers or family and friends. The care package should be monitored and reviewed to ensure it continues to meet your needs, and changed if necessary.[9]

Adult social care services and care trusts work to acts, regulations and directions (which have the force of law) and to guidance from the Secretary of State for Health, or from the Welsh Assembly Government, or the Scottish Ministers in Scotland. Guidance can be:

- formal (often called policy guidance);[10] *or*
- general (often called practice guidance).

Formal guidance should be followed and deviation from it without good reason is unlawful.[11] Practice guidance is not issued under the same legislation, but even this should not be disregarded by local authorities on a regular basis.[12]

Increasingly in England the Department of Health (DH) and the Department of Communities and Local Government use their websites to disseminate information in the form of notes rather than guidance. Advisers should be aware of this and check the websites frequently if possible. Each Thursday there is a *Chief Executive's Bulletin* placed on the DH website which summarises recent

Chapter 2: Community care services at home
2. The responsibilities of adult social care services, health and housing

2

information. There is a similar weekly bulletin on the Scottish Government website (see Appendix 3).

Community care services provided or arranged by adult social care services

Community care services have a specific legal meaning and have been provided under various Acts of Parliament since 1948 (see p15). The terms used in regulations are therefore often outdated and can be offensive to modern thinking.

This section looks at the legislation under which domiciliary services are provided. Appendix 4 gives the legislation in full. The brief summary here outlines the powers and duties to provide particular services to particular groups.

Help if you are disabled: Part III National Assistance Act 1948, section 29 (England and Wales)

Section 29 underpins the provision of non-residential care if you are disabled. Although s2 of the Chronically Sick and Disabled Persons Act 1970 (see p20) gives you stronger rights, it is linked to s29 of the National Assistance Act.[13] Section 29 gives adult social care services duties in relation to people who are:

* ordinarily resident in the local authority's area (see p242);[14]
* are 18 or over, 'blind, deaf or dumb, or suffer from a mental disorder' or are 'substantially and permanently handicapped by illness, injury or congenital deformity or such other disabilities that may be prescribed'. This includes partial sight and hearing.[15]

The *general duties* (which are only powers if you do not ordinarily live in the adult social care services area) are to:

* compile and maintain registers of disabled people (you do not have to be on the register to get a service);
* provide a social work service and such advice and support as are needed for people at home or elsewhere (this can include benefits advice);[16]
* provide, at centres or elsewhere, facilities for social rehabilitation and to help you adjust to disability, including assistance in overcoming limitations of mobility or communication;
* provide, at centres or elsewhere, facilities for occupational, social, cultural or recreational activities and, if appropriate, payment for work you have done.

These are not individual duties arising from your assessed needs, but just general duties towards the local population.

In addition there are *powers* to provide holiday homes, travel (free or subsidised if you do not get other travel concessions), help in finding accommodation, contributions to the costs of wardens, information about services available under s29, instruction in overcoming your disability, workshops or work you can do at

2

Chapter 2: Community care services at home
2. The responsibilities of adult social care services, health and housing

home.[17] These powers cover you whether or not you are ordinarily resident in the adult social care services area.

Adult social care services may not make cash payments (other than for work you have done) under s29. But see p69 for direct payments.

Help if you are disabled: Social Work (Scotland) Act 1968

In Scotland, the Social Work (Scotland) Act gives local authorities the duty to 'promote social welfare by making available advice, guidance and assistance on such a scale as may be appropriate for their area'. These duties relate to people who are:

- ordinarily resident in the local authority area (see p242);[18]
- 'persons in need',[19] which includes the elderly, physically or mentally disabled people or those with a limiting illness (disabled is not defined in the legislation).

The social work department has a general duty to promote social welfare by providing:

- advice, guidance and assistance to help promote social welfare;
- services in the home to enable a person to maintain as independent an existence as is practicable.

The social work department can give help in the form of practical assistance or cash (see also p69 for direct payments). Under s12 of the Social Work (Scotland) Act, cash can only be given in circumstances which amount to an emergency. Practical help can be given in circumstances which do not amount to an emergency – eg, paying a bill. Section 12 payments are used widely, as the only criterion set down by the Act is that the giving of assistance in either form would avoid the local authority being caused greater expense in the future.[20]

Help if you are disabled: Chronically Sick and Disabled Persons Act 1970 (England, Wales and Scotland), section 2

Although not listed as a community care service, s2 of the Chronically Sick and Disabled Persons Act 1970 links to s29 of the National Assistance Act (and s12 of the Social Work (Scotland) Act). The Act places a duty on adult social care services to make arrangements for specific services for individuals. It has been the subject of important community care legal cases, in particular in relation to whether adult social care services can take their own resources into account when deciding whether you need services, whether they will provide services to you, and if so what services[21] (see p38).

You can get any or all of the services listed in s2 if:

- you are defined as disabled by adult social care services (see p19) or as a person in need in Scotland (see p20). But note s2 does not specify you have to be over 18;

- you are ordinarily resident within the adult social care services area[22] (see p242); *and*
- adult social care services are satisfied that they need to make arrangements for you to meet your needs.

There is a specific duty on adult social care services to establish the number of people who are disabled within their area, to publish what services they provide for them and to give to existing service users information about other services.[23]

The services listed in s2 are wide ranging and must be provided if you have been assessed as needing them. They include:
- practical assistance in the home – this can range from housework to personal care tasks. Many adult social care services have concentrated on personal care tasks in recent years and moved away from basic household tasks;
- provision of or assistance in obtaining radio, television, library or similar recreational facilities;
- lectures, games, outings or other recreational facilities outside the home or assistance for you to take advantage of educational facilities;[24]
- facilities for or assistance with travel to and from services;
- assistance in carrying out adaptations to your home or the provision of any additional facility designed for your safety, comfort and convenience. This is a separate duty from that of the housing department to provide grants for facilities to improve housing for disabled people. The guidance makes it clear that adult social care services have the lead role and that the duty to act remains regardless of the housing department's actions. Additional facilities include fittings such as handrails, alarm systems and hoists;[25]
- help for you to take a holiday. Caselaw has established that adult social care services cannot restrict to only providing holidays they have arranged. It has also been found that to assist only with the extra costs caused by disability, not with the ordinary hotel and travel costs, had fettered the authority's discretion and was not consistent with the Act;[26]
- meals either at home or elsewhere;
- provision of, or help in getting, a telephone or any special equipment to use the phone.[27] Since the Act came into force, technology has changed so it may be possible to consider items such as modems and wireless networks.

Help if you are an older person: Health Services and Public Health Act 1968, section 45 (England and Wales)

If you are an older person who does not fit into the definition of disabled (see p19) but still need services because of frailty due to old age then you may be able to make use of the general provision which s45 gives to 'promote the welfare of old people'. Directions by the Secretary of State explain that its purpose is to promote the welfare of older people and as far as possible prevent or postpone personal deterioration or breakdown.[28] The directions merely *empower* adult

2

Chapter 2: Community care services at home
2. The responsibilities of adult social care services, health and housing

social care services to provide the following services, some of which are *duties* under s2 of the Chronically Sick and Disabled Persons Act. If you are an older person who is also disabled, your services should be provided under s2 and so you will have some additional rights. The services listed for older people are:

- meals and recreation in the home and elsewhere;
- information on services for the elderly;
- assistance with travel to s45 services;
- assistance in finding boarding accommodation;
- social work support and advice;
- home help and home adaptations – including laundry services;
- wardens.

If adult social care services want to provide services outside of the directions, they can do so provided they gets the specific approval of the Secretary of State.

Help from adult social care services – National Health Service Act 2006, section 254 (England) and National Health Service (Wales) Act 2006, section 192

Most of these Acts relate to services provided by the NHS, but there are specific responsibilities for adult social care services to make arrangements for:[29]

- pregnant and breast feeding mothers;
- the prevention of illness and the care and aftercare of adults suffering from illness; *and*
- the provision of adequate home help services in the area for households with a person who is ill, is pregnant or has recently given birth, is aged, or disabled by illness or congenital deformity. It is linked to laundry services which can include the provision of washing machines. As with most community care legislation, it is subject to the Secretary of State's directions. However, the provision of adequate home help and laundry services is not subject to direction and therefore is a *duty*, although it is only a *general duty* to provide for the area.

Adult social care services have *powers* to provide services for pregnant and breast feeding mothers of any age; centres or other facilities with a view to preventing illness or for aftercare; meals at such centres or at home; social work services, advice and support; night sitter services; recuperative holidays, social and recreational facilities; and services specifically for those dependent on alcohol or drugs.[30]

Adult social care services have a *general duty* to those who are, or who have been, suffering from a mental illness to make arrangements:

- for centres for training and occupation;
- for sufficient approved social workers to act under the Mental Health Act 1983;
- to exercise the functions of the authority for those received into guardianship;

Chapter 2: Community care services at home
2. The responsibilities of adult social care services, health and housing

2

- for the provision of social work services to help in the identification, diagnosis, assessment and social treatment of mental disorder and to provide social work support at home and elsewhere.

In recent years, the Government has been developing its 'personalisation' agenda. The culmination of this is the extension of the existing direct payments scheme into a system of individual and personal budgets. An individual budget is a sum of money allocated to an individual who is assessed as needing personal assistance services. Like a direct payment, it is a method of self-directed support designed to allow the individual service user as much choice and control as possible over how their support needs will be met. However, an individual budget can include funding from more than just social care services, which direct payments presently cover. For example, it may be possible to receive funding from sources such as the Supporting People scheme. It can be a cash payment, arranged services or a combination of both.

Putting People First – a shared vision and commitment to the transformation of adult social care[31] refers to personal budgets. Personal budgets are similar to individual budgets. However, they are an upfront and transparent allocation of predominantly social care funding rather than funding from a potentially broad range of funding streams. This funding can be managed by a local authority or another organisation on behalf of an individual should they choose, or paid as a direct payment, or a mixture of both. As a result personal budgets are a potentially useful option if you do not want to take on all of the responsibilities required to receive a direct payment.

There is no new legislation underpinning either individual or personal budgets, so the way the local authority determines what support you are entitled to must still follow the existing guidance. However, the new process may appear very different. A local authority may ask you to complete a questionnaire, either on your own or with help. This is then used to determine an 'indicative budget', which should be a reasonable estimate of how much your care is likely to cost. There will then be a more detailed process of considering your needs and how they can best be met. This results in an agreement about how you will spend your budget. If, after more detailed consideration, it emerges that you cannot meet your needs from the 'indicative budget' then a request for a higher budget should be submitted and considered by a panel.

A number of pilot sites have been run since 2005, focusing on different client groups and these have been evaluated. Targets for the implementation of personal budgets have been set by the Government for all local authorities. By 2011, the Government expects all publicly funded service users to be offered a personal budget, except in urgent cases.

For further information about using direct payments, see p69.

2

Chapter 2: Community care services at home
  2. The responsibilities of adult social care services, health and housing

Help from adult social care services in Scotland

Local authorities in Scotland have a duty to provide a home help service to 'persons in need' and to women who are pregnant or have recently given birth; and a laundry service to people receiving this service. This is a general duty to provide for the area.[32]

Under the personal care duties contained within the Mental Health (Care and Treatment) (Scotland) Act 2003 social work or local authorities have a duty to provide aftercare for people who have or have had a mental illness or a learning disability. They must also provide habilitation and rehabilitation services including; social, cultural and recreational activities, training to persons over school age and assistance in obtaining and undertaking employment.[33] The local authority must provide (or assist in providing) transport so you can participate in these services.[34]

Aftercare if you have previously been detained in hospital: Mental Health Act 1983, section 117 (England and Wales)

Health and adult social care services both have a responsibility to provide aftercare services if you have been detained in hospital for treatment.[35] This is an individual duty and remains until both health and adult social care services are satisfied that you no longer need such aftercare services (you must be fully re-assessed before a decision is taken to withdraw aftercare services).[36] Some people are subject to aftercare under supervision which may impose conditions on where you live, your attendance at a set time and place for medical treatment, and the person supervising your care having access to your home.[37]

Aftercare services are not defined in the Act. They would normally include social work support and help with employment, accommodation or family relationship problems, the provision of home care services and the use of day centre and residential facilities.

Adult social care services have no power to charge you for these services (see p59).[38] This is discussed in more detail in Chapter 9 (see p242). Seek advice if you are told you will be charged, or if you have been charged in the past for these services.

Aftercare in Scotland: Mental Health (Care and Treatment) (Scotland) Act 2003

The Mental Health (Care and Treatment) (Scotland) Act 2003 places a legal duty on social work departments (personal care duties) to provide 'aftercare' for people who are, or have been, suffering from a mental disorder. This means a mental illness, personality disorder or learning disability[39] and includes someone with dementia. In providing aftercare services the local authority must co-operate with the relevant health board. The powers apply regardless of whether the person is, or has been, in hospital. Aftercare is not defined in the Act but could include similar services to examples given for England and Wales (see above). There is currently no provision to charge for services provided under the Act.

Chapter 2: Community care services at home
2. The responsibilities of adult social care services, health and housing

2

Services if you are a carer: Carers and Disabled Children Act 2000 (England and Wales)

If you are a carer, you *may* have services in you own right if:

- you are 16 or over;
- you are providing or intending to provide a substantial amount of care on a regular basis to someone aged 18 or over; *and*
- an assessment leads to the decision that you have needs in relation to the care which you provide or intend to provide.[40]

There is no restriction on the services that adult social care services can provide, but they must, in the local authority's view, help you to care for the person cared for. Service to you could take the form of a service delivered to the person cared for, as long as you both agree and it is a community care service (see p15). However, it may not, except in prescribed circumstances, include anything of an intimate nature.[41] This is so that services which should really be provided to the cared for person are still given directly to her/him. The Carers (Equal Opportunities) Act 2004 requires local authorities to inform you of your right to be assessed and to take account in the assessment of your work, education or leisure commitments or desire to develop these. Guidance on this Act was issued to local authorities in August 2005.[42]

You can receive direct payments for these services (see p69).[43] 'A voucher scheme has been introduced in England to help carers access short-term breaks.[44] Voucher schemes have also been piloted in Wales.

If you are a parent of a disabled child, you may also ask for an assessment for services to help you provide care for your child.[45] This could also be in the form of direct payments or vouchers. The Work and Families Act 2006 extended the right to request flexible working to employees who care for adults.

Services if you are a carer: Community Care and Health (Scotland) Act 2002

Local authorities and NHS boards have a duty to inform you (including if you are under 16) that you have a right to be assessed independently and there is a duty to take your views into account when constructing a care plan for the person you care for. There are, however, no plans to provide direct services to carers as you are regarded as key partners in providing care, not service users. However, you may have the right to a community care assessment if you are in need yourself. If you are a parent of a disabled child, you can receive direct payments to purchase services for your child (see p70).[46]

Equipment that you can get from adult social care services

Equipment can often be just as vital as services in helping you stay independent and remain at home. The legislation described above gives adult social care services the duty or the power (see p16) to provide equipment. Adult social care services can provide an extensive range of equipment that includes help with:

2

Chapter 2: Community care services at home
2. The responsibilities of adult social care services, health and housing

- getting off the toilet – eg, a raised seat or rails;
- getting in and out of the bath – eg, bath boards, rails or hoists;
- getting in and out of a chair – eg, high-backed chairs or riser chairs;
- dressing – eg, stocking aids and long-handled shoe horns;
- cooking and eating – eg, safety pans, cooker guards, special cutlery;
- reading – eg, magnifiers and page turners.

There are many other ways in which equipment can help. You could be provided with ordinary equipment such as a microwave, washing machine or TV remote control, although in practice this is fairly uncommon.

New and improved equipment for people with disabilities is always being developed. It is important, therefore, to ask someone who is knowledgeable if there is a new gadget available which will exactly meet your needs.

There are about 50 Disabled Living Centres in the UK (see Appendix 1) which display and demonstrate a wide range of equipment and give advice. They are open to the public and to professionals and may give advice by phone or letter if you cannot visit. If you are buying equipment it is very important to make sure you get the item that suits your needs.

Adult social care services have a duty to provide general information about the services they provides under the Chronically Sick and Disabled Persons Act. If you are receiving services under this Act, adult social care services must also inform you of other services you might need (see p20). This includes providing information about equipment provided by adult social care services, the NHS, housing or voluntary organisations.

Generally, equipment from adult social care services is arranged by occupational therapists (OTs), although it may be arranged by physiotherapists, rehabilitation workers for people with sight problems and social workers for people with hearing problems.

In order to get equipment you often need to be assessed (see p34) by qualified staff such as OTs. Adult social care services should have adequate staff to enable them to carry out that function,[47] but a shortage of OTs is a common problem. If the problem has been acknowledged but not been tackled, contact the Local Government Ombudsman who may find maladministration.[48] In England, once it has been decided that you need equipment adult social care services should aim to get it delivered within three weeks if it is less than £1,000.[49] From 2004 all equipment needed should be in place within a week.[50]

In England, you should not be charged for community equipment or for 'minor' adaptations of £1,000 or less which you have been assessed as needing.[51] In Scotland, equipment that is defined as coming within 'free personal care' such as personal reminder systems for taking medicines, or sound/movement alarms are free. Also any equipment that is installed within four weeks of you coming out of hospital is free. Guidance issued by the Confederation of Scottish Local

Chapter 2: Community care services at home
2. The responsibilities of adult social care services, health and housing

2

Authorities recommends that local authorities should not charge for equipment and if they do, they should only do so for small items up to £20.[52]

In England, there is funding for adult social care services and health departments to provide integrated community equipment.[53] There are proposals in Scotland for an integrated community equipment service. In Scotland, direct payments can be used to buy equipment or adaptions directly from a local authority (where the equipment or adaptions are deemed to come under community (social work) care legislation.

The Department of Health has launched a *Transforming Community Equipment and Wheelchair Services Programme* which aims to allow more choice and control over equipment provision for service users and their carers. As part of the programme, a 'retail model' for the provision of community equipment in England has been developed. This involves a 'prescription' being issued to you or your carer, where there is an assessed need, that can be exchanged for free equipment at an approved retailer.

Equipment can be obtained from a national catalogue containing a basic range of products. If you wish to obtain an alternative piece of equipment not in the national catalogue, you can 'top-up' the 'prescription' with your own money.

The model is intended to cover equipment provided as part of the hospital discharge process and local authority community services. It is also intended to provide equipment if you choose not access state provided community equipment services or if you are ineligible for local authority provision. You can use the model if you are entitled to free equipment by adult social care services but wish to access products not provided by them.

The new model is not mandatory for local authorities and their health partners. The model does not affect your entitlement to receive equipment free of charge under *Fair Access to Care Services* criteria.

The model includes the planned creation of Independent Needs Assessors who will assess equipment needs and make recommendations and who can also provide other related services – eg, additional therapeutic interventions and advice. These will be appropriately qualified professionals such as OTs and physiotherapists. They will carry out assessments with individuals who either choose not to or who are ineligible to access state provision. The Government would like to see these professionals linking with other service providers, such as third sector organisations, to meet the range of needs identified in the assessment.

Adult social care services responsibilities for planning and providing information

As most people only approach adult social care services for help at a time of great need and they do not know what to expect, information is vital. This was recognised when community care was reformed and various duties were placed on adult social care services to plan services and inform people about them.

2

Chapter 2: Community care services at home
   2. The responsibilities of adult social care services, health and housing

Planning

Each local authority must prepare and publish a plan outlining community care services to be provided[54] and this must be updated each year. In England this does not have to be a stand alone document, but can be part of the overall plans produced jointly with health bodies for the area.[55] In drawing up plans, adult social care services must consult with health, housing and voluntary organisations which represent groups likely to need services. If a provider organisation writes to ask to be consulted then it must be.[56] Guidance tells adult social care services to identify the following:

- assessment – the care needs of the local population, how those care needs will be assessed, and how identified needs will be incorporated into the planning process;
- services – how priorities for arranging services are made, how it intends to offer practical help and how it intends to develop domiciliary services;
- quality – how service quality is monitored, the role of the inspection unit, and the role of complaints procedures;
- choice – how it intends to increase consumer choice and develop a mixed economy of care;
- resources – the resource implications of planned and future developments and how it intends to improve cost effectiveness;
- consultation – how it intends to consult;
- publishing information – how it intends to inform service users and carers about services, and how and when it will publish the plan for the following year.[57]

The duty to inform

Apart from having to publish its plan and complaints procedures the only other duties to inform people of the services they can get are set out in the legislation described on p22. Policy guidance states that local authorities must have published information accessible to all potential service users and carers, in formats suitable for those with communication difficulties or differences in language or culture. The information should set out the types of community care services available, the criteria for the provision of services, the assessment procedures and the standards by which care management will be measured.[58]

Local authorities in England and Wales are also required to produce charters based on a national framework.[59] These should give an indication of the services people can expect to receive, and how quickly they will be provided. Charters do not have any legal effect, but it is possible to complain if standards in a charter are not met. In one case the Local Government Ombudsman found maladministration when a community care charter gave misleading timescales for assessment.[60] In England, community care charters are now replaced by joint local long-term care charters covering health, social care and housing called *Better Care, Higher Standards*. There is a similar charter in Wales, *The Health and Social Care* Guide. In

Chapter 2: Community care services at home
2. The responsibilities of adult social care services, health and housing

2

Scotland new 'Single Outcome Agreements' detailing services provided and the impact they will have are being agreed between the Scottish Government and all local authorities.

Responsibilities of the NHS

Health services, which are an essential element of community care, are not classified as community care services and are provided under different legislation. Unlike adult social care services, there are no specific duties to individuals who need health care services. If when assessing you (see p34), adult social care services think you have a health care need, then in England and Wales they must notify the appropriate health body and invite it to assist in the assessment. The health body has no duty to respond or co-operate. In Scotland, the social work department must notify the health board and ask what services it is likely to provide and then take this into account in the completed assessments.[61]

In England, NHS bodies have a duty to inform the local authority of a hospital inpatient's possible need for community care services when s/he is discharged.[62]

Health bodies have only a broad duty to provide services to the extent the Secretary of State (or Scottish or Welsh Ministers) considers necessary to meet all reasonable requirements. Such services include:

- medical, dental, nursing and ambulance services;
- hospital and other accommodation for services provided by the NHS; *and*
- facilities for the prevention of illness, care of those suffering an illness and aftercare for those who have suffered an illness which are appropriate for a health service to provide.[63]

Health bodies, therefore, have wide discretion in deciding what meets 'all reasonable requirements', even to the extent of deciding that a particular service will not be provided at all. As long as a decision about the level (or non-provision) of a service is justifiable on the grounds of local priorities and resources, then it would be difficult to challenge.[64]

There is guidance about NHS responsibility for continuing health care needs.[65] NHS continuing care can be provided in any setting, including your own home, and should not be restricted to hospitals or care homes.[66] The previous national guidance was criticised for not being sufficiently clear and local eligibility criteria for continuing NHS services based upon it were found to be unlawfully restrictive. This is discussed in more detail in Chapter 9. The Government stated its commitment to the development of a national continuing care framework which was subsequently implemented in October 2007 and sets out national eligibility criteria. It is intended to make the process fairer and more transparent. New guidance on NHS continuing healthcare eligibility has been issued in Scotland and includes a commitment to produce clearer national guidance to complement local criteria. A similar process is underway in Wales and is likely to be similar to the developments in England.[67]

The current national guidance in each country allows health bodies to decide (in agreement with adult social care services) what health services will be provided. In each of the Strategic Health Authority areas in England, one set of eligibility criteria should be used throughout the whole area. Local policies must be published. The following services must be available in each area:

- specialist medical and nursing care;
- rehabilitation and recovery services. Local policies should prevent premature discharge and should agree with local authorities any additional social or educational support required as part of an agreed package of rehabilitation;
- palliative health care including support for people in their own homes;[68]
- continuing inpatient care in hospital or a home providing nursing care;
- respite health care;
- specialist health care support for people in care homes or in the community – eg, specialist palliative care, incontinence advice, stoma care, diabetic advice, physiotherapy, speech and language therapy, or chiropody. It should also include specialist equipment;
- community health services (eg, district nurses) for people in care homes (see p250);
- primary health care (ie, health care from GP surgeries, district nurses, dentists and opticians);
- specialist transport services to and from hospital or other health care facilities, and where emergency admission to a care home is necessary.

While wide differences remain between local criteria in different areas, it is important to find out what is available in your area and to challenge it if you consider it to be too restrictive (see p40). The *Better Care, Higher Standards* charter should provide information about health services in each area in England.[69]

Hospital discharge

It is very important that any stay in hospital has a planned discharge so that you do not go home without the services you need. The consultant will normally decide (but should do so in consultation with others) whether or not you continue to need acute care. If your needs are such that you may need intensive support there should be a multi-disciplinary assessment. You, your family and your carer should be kept fully informed so that you can make decisions, and you should be provided with written details of the likely cost of any option you are considering. If the NHS is arranging services you should receive information in writing describing what aspects of your care the NHS is funding.[70]

Once adult social care services have been notified that you are ready to be discharged, they assess you and arrange suitable services for you within strict time limits and are fined if these are not met. In England, directions on hospital discharge[71] have been issued under the Community Care (Delayed Discharges etc) Act 2003. A Department of Health workbook, *Discharge from Hospital: pathway, process and practice,* covers points of good practice in hospital discharge.[72] Guidance on hospital discharge has also been issued in Wales and Scotland.[73] In all three countries the guidance emphasises the need for the different agencies involved in the discharge process to work together. You, your family and carers should be given information about the process and be actively involved in it.

There is a right of review of discharge decisions (see p42).

Equipment you can get from the NHS

As well as providing services, the NHS is responsible for providing certain equipment. In England, this may be through the integrated community equipment service. You should talk to your doctor, district nurse or health visitor first about any equipment you might need.

The sort of equipment you may be able to get includes:
* wheelchairs;
* commodes (normally for short-term use);
* bathing equipment including hoists (if your need is for a medical bath);
* eating and drinking equipment if there is a medical need. This can include food preparation equipment such as a liquidiser;
* bed equipment such as a cradle to keep the bed clothes off you, a back rest, raising blocks and bed rails if your need is defined as a health need rather than a social need. It may include the bed itself if you need a special bed;
* environmental control equipment (on loan);
* walking aids;
* artificial limbs;
* hearing aids;
* low vision aids;
* TENS machines for pain relief;
* special footwear;
* incontinence pads and other equipment.

As with all services provided through the NHS it will depend on the resources available as to whether particular equipment will be supplied in your area. If your local area does not supply the item you need, you should complain (see p40).

Equipment issued on prescription

GPs can provide a range of appliances on prescription. These include incontinence devices (this includes pads in Scotland), stoma care appliances, oxygen cylinders, diabetes equipment and elastic stockings.[74]

Home care equipment

Your GP may be able to help you get orthopaedic footwear, breast prostheses, cervical collars, communication equipment, nebulisers, supports for limbs or trunk, hoists, special beds and mattresses, and walking aids.

2

Chapter 2: Community care services at home
2. The responsibilities of adult social care services, health and housing

Help with incontinence

Some equipment for incontinence is issued under prescription including catheter bags, catheters, male urinals and night drainage bags. Incontinence pads can be supplied by the NHS and usually are, but sometimes their supply can be limited.

Pad disposal services are often jointly run by the NHS and adult social care services. Laundry services are usually run by adult social care services but the NHS may have a local laundry service. Some areas have neither service.

Incontinence advisers are available in many areas and it is important to seek advice about incontinence, which is only a symptom of a variety of physical or mental conditions. In England, the DH has published a good practice guide on continence services.[75]

Wheelchairs

In addition to a range of ordinary wheelchairs, the NHS provides outdoor/indoor electric wheelchairs[76] if you are assessed as needing one because you are unable to walk or propel an ordinary wheelchair. Each health authority has its own criteria within the national guidelines, but if you move to another area your wheelchair should not be taken from you without good clinical reason. In Scotland, the criteria are set nationally and if you move to a different area then you can take your wheelchair with you. In March 2009, the Scottish Government published an Action Plan setting out plans for modernising wheelchair and seating services over the next three years.

In England, there is a voucher scheme which allows you to put extra money towards a more expensive wheelchair than the NHS will provide.[77]

As outlined on p27, wheelchairs have been included in the new 'retail model' of equipment provision in health and social care in England.

Intermediate care services

As part of the National Service Framework for older people and the National Plan for the NHS, there are intermediate care services in England and Wales. The responsibility is shared between the NHS and adult social care services and the services are aimed at enabling people to leave hospital earlier than they otherwise would, or preventing hospital admission. In order to count as an intermediate care service it must involve cross-professional working, provide active therapy, treatment or opportunities for recovery and be short term, lasting normally not more than six weeks and often one to two weeks. Where such services are being provided as intermediate care they should be free. They can be in a step downward of a hospital, in a care home or in your own home.[78] You should not be charged for intermediate care services provided by adult social care services.[79] In Wales, there is also guidance on free home care for up to six weeks following a hospital stay (see p58).[80] In Scotland you may, if you are not entitled to continuing care or intermediate care, receive four weeks free care at home following discharge from hospital if you are eligible. After those four weeks, a financial assessment will be

Chapter 2: Community care services at home
2. The responsibilities of adult social care services, health and housing

2

carried out to decide how much you can contribute to the cost of any care you need at home (care that is not already covered by free personal care for those over 65 at home).

Responsibility of housing departments

Housing is a vital part of community care, but like health services it is not listed as a community care service within the legislation. If, when assessing you, adult social care services find that you need housing services, they can invite the housing department to assist, but there is no duty for housing to respond.[81] In Scotland, the social work department can notify the housing authority and request information as to what services are likely to be made available.[82] However, the housing department may be under a duty to make enquiries if you are homeless and in apparent priority need.[83] **'Priority need'** is defined as being vulnerable due to old age, mental illness, or handicap or physical disability, or other reason such as pregnancy or where there are children. It will then have a specific duty towards you as long as you are not intentionally homeless.

Guidance stresses the important role of housing departments and suggests they should be involved in:
- community care planning;
- community care assessments;
- local housing strategies involving co-operation with housing associations and considering special needs housing;
- provisions for homeless people;
- home adaptations.[84]

Different types of housing

Housing departments may assist you in getting accommodation with a housing association or provide the following:
- housing designed to give you access at all times to all principal rooms if you need a wheelchair to get about;
- sheltered housing. This is mainly intended for older people and there is usually a minimum age (often 60). There is almost always an alarm system linked to a 24-hour control service. Some schemes have a resident warden; others have a mobile warden who visits the scheme regularly. Charges for these support services may be included in the rent. These services now come under Supporting People services (see p52);
- extra care sheltered housing that offers extra care such as help with bathing or dressing, and often has a dining room where meals are available. They can be run jointly with adult social care services;
- lifetime homes. A few councils and housing associations build homes which are adaptable to changing needs, including level access and downstairs toilet facilities, a wide front door, a living room that can take a bed, kitchens designed for easy use and safety.

Chapter 3 explains in more detail about supported housing and Supporting People services and Chapter 4 explains the charges for these services.

Houses in England and Wales built after October 1999 must have basic accessibility features such as a level threshold and downstairs toilet.[85] In Scotland, Scottish Homes, the national housing agency, requires all housing it funds to incorporate barrier free standards. Unfortunately, most older homes do not have these features so you may need adaptations or assistance with repairs. See Chapter 5 for the financial assistance you can get to help make your home easier for you to live in.

3. Getting the services you need

If you have difficulties managing everyday tasks, or are in hospital and think that you will need some help when you leave, you need to ask adult social care services for a care assessment. Someone else can refer you, although it should always be with your permission unless you are unable to give it because of your mental condition. In England and Wales the NHS has a duty to notify adult social care services if you are an inpatient and likely to need community care services when you leave hospital. It must consult you (or your carer) before it notifies adult social care services.[86] The care assessment is important as it is the first stage of getting support from adult social care services.

Once you have come to the notice of adult social care services, they have a duty to assess and make a decision about whether or not you are entitled to services. If you are, then a care plan will be drawn up, with your agreement, put into place and reviewed on a regular basis to make sure it continues to meet your needs. The care plan could include care in a care home, or a wide range of services to help you stay at home.

The assessment of your needs

Adult social care services must assess you if:
- you appear to be in need of a community care service – ie, those listed on p15;[87]
- you are disabled;[88]
- you help look after someone else.[89]

You are entitled to such an assessment irrespective of your level of savings, capital or income.

Assessment is a service in its own right.[90]

Most adult social care services operate a screening process to decide who is eligible for an assessment, how quickly it will be provided and the type of assessment you will get. In England, your local long-term care charter, *Better Care, Higher Standards,* should give you an indication of how the assessment will be done and how long you should expect to wait. If your need is urgent, adult social care services can provide the services first and assess you as soon as possible afterwards.[91] A single assessment process (SAP) has been introduced for older people in England. It aims to save you having to repeat basic information to a number of different professionals, and should mean that you get the right level of assessment depending on the complexity of your needs.[92] It applies to both the NHS and local authorities. Local assessment processes should have been SAP compliant by April 2004. Similar processes have been introduced in Scotland (known as the single shared assessment) and Wales (unified assessment).[93]

Screening for assessment

The practice of screening referred to in policy guidance[94] has been questioned, in particular when it screens people out of an assessment. Local authorities have been told to set a low threshold for assessment.[95] Even if adult social care services think there is no prospect of providing a service because of lack of resources (see p38), they should still assess you.[96]

Sometimes screening takes place over the phone, and you may have been deemed to have had an assessment without ever seeing anyone or even realising that the phone call was the assessment. Complain if you feel that you have not been given a proper opportunity to be assessed.

How quickly will the assessment be carried out?

There are no national rules about how quickly an assessment should be carried out. Many local authorities set their own timescales. You should be told in your local *Better Care, Higher Standards* charter the maximum time you will have to wait for an assessment. An Ombudsman has found maladministration in a case where the local charter set unrealistic timescales.[97]

In England all assessments of older people should start within 48 hours of referral and finish within 28 days.[98] For hospital patients, assessment for your discharge plan should start before admission to hospital in the case of elective treatment and very quickly after an emergency admission. Strict time limits have been placed on the time local authorities have to do the assessments and get services in place. Once you are ready for discharge, adult social care services can be fined if they have caused any delay.

Waiting lists for assessments have been the subject of numerous investigations by the Local Government Ombudsman, especially in relation to assessments for equipment, which require the intervention of an occupational therapist. Due to the large number of complaints in relation to disabled facilities grants, the Local Government Ombudsman has previously suggested what s/he considers to be 'reasonable times' for awaiting an assessment – ie, two months for urgent cases, four months for serious cases and six months for non-urgent cases.[99] However, two months may be too long if your need is very urgent.

If you are in need of drug and alcohol services, there has been guidance on assessment and 'fast track' assessment.[100]

The fact that adult social care services are permitted to prioritise the waiting time for your assessment presupposes it has enough information to make a judgement on how long you should wait. It is therefore important when you first contact adult social care services that you make clear the exact nature of your needs and whether your situation is urgent.

The nature of the assessment

The type of assessment you get depends on the nature of your needs. Assessments vary from 'simple assessments' (eg, for bus passes and disabled car badges) to 'comprehensive assessments' if you have needs which cut across departments and which are likely to lead to intensive support. Under the single assessment process for older people there are four types of assessment:

- a contact assessment which takes basic details, explores whether you have wider health and social care problems, and deals with simple requests;
- an overview assessment, where your needs are such that various aspects of care need to be explored;
- a specialist assessment to explore specific problems by an appropriate member of staff such as occupation therapists, geriatricians or old age psychiatrists;
- a comprehensive assessment, if your needs are such that you are likely to be offered intensive or complex support which may involve a range of different professionals.

You should be encouraged to contribute fully to your assessment. There is similar guidance about assessment in England, Wales and Scotland.[101] Directions have been issued in support of existing good practice and guidance in England.[102]

If, during the assessment, a need for health or housing services becomes apparent, adult social care services have a duty to notify the relevant department and invite it to assist in the assessment.[103] There is no duty on either of those services to respond, although in practice it is rare for them to refuse.

The assessment could take place in your own home or in hospital. You should be fully involved in your assessment, which should look at all of your needs as a whole.[104] This should include your social and psychological needs.[105]

Carers' assessments

A '**carer**' is defined as someone who provides or is about to provide a substantial amount of care on a regular basis.[106] It is left to adult social care services to decide what constitutes a substantial amount of care. If your carer is not thought to provide substantial amounts of care, s/he should still have a role in your assessment.[107] Paid carers and volunteers cannot have a carer's assessment.

There is a duty to assess your carer if s/he requests it, at the same time as your assessment.[108] This is not a freestanding assessment but is done in conjunction with your own assessment. In England, Wales and Scotland, carers aged 16 years or over are entitled to be assessed in their own right independently of the cared for person if that person is someone for whom adult social care services may provide or arrange community care services.[109]

The Carers (Equal Opportunities) Act 2004 requires local authorities in England to inform carers of their rights to an assessment. A similar duty to inform exists in Scotland. New guidance on carers' assessments is being drafted in Wales.

The result of your carer's assessment must be taken into account when making a decision about services. The object of the assessment is to identify your carer's ability to provide and continue to provide care. Practice guidance has made it clear that in assessing your carer's ability to care, adult social care services should not assume her/his willingness to continue caring or to continue to care at the same level.

Recording the assessment

You should be told the outcome of your assessment and the decision on service provision.[110] Guidance suggests you should get a written record of your assessment which will normally be combined with your care plan. In England the *Better Care, Higher Standards* charter states that you should be given a decision in writing.

If you have difficulty in getting a copy of your assessment (or care plan), request a copy of your file under the Data Protection Act 1998. If you are requesting a copy on behalf of a person who does not have mental capacity, speak to a solicitor about common law rights and rights under the Human Rights Act 1998 if a copy is denied due to a 'duty of confidentiality owed to the incapacitated person'.

Your care plan

If, having assessed your needs, adult social care services decides that you need services, they should give you a care plan giving details of:
* overall objectives;
* specific objectives;
* the services that will be provided and by who;
* the cost to you;
* other options considered;
* any point of difference between you and the care assessor;
* any unmet needs;
* who will be responsible for monitoring and reviewing; *and*
* the date of the first planned review.

This should have been discussed with you and have your agreement. There is no statutory duty for adult social care services to provide a written care plan, and you may find that you are not offered one. However, the single assessment guidance for older people makes it clear that you should get a written copy of your care plan. If you are a younger person and want to see your care plan then you could ask for access to your file.

Your care plan can include a wide range of services, with a mix of adult social care services help and care from the NHS and your carers. Services can be provided directly by adult social care services or from an independent provider. You could, as an alternative, receive a payment from adult social care services to arrange your own care (see p69).

How soon should services be provided?

The law is silent on how soon services should be provided (except in the case of disabled facilities grants in England and Wales, where it can be up to 12 months). Whether or not the delay is excessive will depend on your particular circumstances. In England a performance indicator sets a target of services being provided within four weeks of the assessment being completed. If you are in an acute ward in hospital it is likely that you will get services put in place quickly, in order that the local authority avoids being fined (see p30).[111] If you feel that you have been kept waiting too long for your services you should complain (see p40).

Monitoring and reviewing your services

There should be regular reviews to ensure that the objectives of the care plan are being met and whether any changes are required because of changing needs or service delivery policies. In the case of older people under the single assessment guidance it is made clear that a review should be held within three months and from then on at least every 12 months. This is also specified in *Better Care, Higher Standards*. If you are discharged from hospital (or intermediate care) with a home care package the suitability of your care should be checked within two weeks.[112]

The review should also monitor the quality of the services provided, taking account the views of you and your carer. If you have concerns about the quality of your care (eg, the manner, the reliability and trustworthiness of a carer provided via the local authority) you should raise this without waiting for a review.

---

4. How far the authority's resources can be taken into account

For housing and adult social care services, there are specific duties that arise and there have been various legal challenges to establish whether the local authority's resources can be taken into account.

This section looks at how local authorities try to manage their resources. It also looks at eligibility criteria, when resources can be taken into account in an assessment, and ceilings on home care services. Local authorities often use waiting lists to manage finite resources.

Eligibility criteria

After you have been assessed, adult social care services must make a decision about whether your needs are eligible for services.[113] To determine who should get services, adult social care services uses 'eligibility criteria', often using a banding system. Any 'banding' should not, however, be rigidly applied (councils should not 'fetter their discretion') as account needs to be taken of individuals' circumstances'.[114] The *Fair Access to Care* guidance, states that councils should 'assess an individual's presenting needs, and prioritise their eligible needs, according to the risks to their independence in both the short- and longer-term were help not to be provided.'[115]

Where resources are scarce, the eligibility criteria may be tightened so that people who may have been receiving a service are now defined as no longer needing that service. If a local authority tightens its eligibility criteria (eg, it will only now meet critical or substantial care needs) because of lack of resources, it must assess you against these new eligibility criteria before withdrawing any services you already receive.[116]

Your local authority's plan should give a description of its eligibility criteria. The criteria might also be described in leaflets about community care in your area. Different local authorities have different criteria, so you could get a service in one area, but if you move to another you might not be eligible.

In England and Wales, guidance (*Fair Access to Care* – England; *Creating a Unified and Fair System for Assessing and Managing Care* – Wales) sets out the principles which authorities should follow when devising and applying eligibility criteria.[117] In Scotland, the *single shared assessment – indicator of relative need* (IoRN) is a measurement of resources tool that is intended to enable older people to have equitable access to services.

When resources can be taken into account

Adult social care services cannot take their own resources into account when deciding whether you are entitled to an assessment.[118]

Once adult social care services have decided that you need services under the eligibility criteria, lack of resources is not a valid reason for failing to provide those services. There is a duty to do so.[119] It is likely that the same principles would apply in a community care assessment under s12 of the Social Work (Scotland) Act 1968. This is equally true of education services[120] and housing services for disabled facilities grants.[121]

Where there is a choice of care packages under consideration, adult social care services can only choose the cheaper option if it will meet your assessed needs as well as the more expensive one would have.[122]

Practice guidance for *Fair Access to Care* makes it clear that just because you have your own resources you should not be denied services. Local authorities should arrange services at home irrespective of your resources or capacity, if that is what you want them to do.[123] Complain if you are told to arrange your own care because you have enough money to pay for it.

Ceilings on home care services

You may find that there is a financial ceiling on the amount of home care provided, particularly for older people. Sometimes this is expressed in hours – eg, you may find that the maximum adult social care services will provide is 10-15 hours service, as any more would make care in a care home a cheaper option. The ceiling may be equivalent to the net or gross cost to adult social care services of providing residential care.

Ceilings are more likely to affect older people, with many authorities imposing no ceilings (or setting very much higher ones) on support packages for younger people. The National Service Framework for Older People and the guidance in *Fair Access to Care*, which are statutory guidance, state that decisions about eligibility criteria should be made without reference to age, and not stick rigidly to predetermined cost ceilings. Seek advice if your services are being restricted because of your age (you have a right to refuse a care home placement as an alternative to home care if you have the mental capacity to do so).

If you are told that you need services beyond those that adult social care services is prepared to pay for, seek advice. It may also be possible to use the European Convention on Human Rights (in particular Article 8) (see p46).

5. How to complain

Complaining about health and social services

From 1 April 2009, social care and health complaints are dealt with as part of the same complaints system in England.[124] From that date if you are not satisfied with the way a local NHS body or practice has dealt with your complaint, you can ask the Health Service Ombudsman to look into it. Social care complaints that are not resolved locally will need to be brought to the Local Government Ombudsman.

The new approach focuses on you as the complainant and enables health/ social care bodies to tailor a flexible response to resolve your specific concerns. It is based on the principles of good complaints handling, published by the Parliamentary and Health Service Ombudsman[125] and endorsed by the Local Government Ombudsman:

Principles of good complaint handling

1. Getting it right
2. Being customer focused

3. Being open and accountable
4. Acting fairly and proportionately
5. Putting things right
6. Seeking continuous improvement

The new complaints procedure has two stages: local resolution and the Ombudsman.

The legislation uses the term 'responsible body' which includes local authorities, NHS bodies and certain other providers who provide services under arrangements with NHS bodies.

The first stage – local resolution

You should try to resolve the complaint locally on an informal basis. Each 'responsible body' must make information available its arrangements for dealing with complaints and how further information about those arrangements may be obtained.[126] This could be via leaflets or on its websites. There should be a complaints manager who is responsible for ensuring complaints are responded to and that this first stage is properly carried out.[127]

Your complaint must usually be made within 12 months, or later if there are good reasons for doing so.[128] It can be made orally, in writing or electronically.[129]

If the complaint is made orally you will receive a written record of the complaint. The 'responsible body' should acknowledge (orally or in writing) your complaint within three working days after the day it received the complaint. At the time it acknowledges, it must offer you the chance to discuss how the complaint is to be handled, the likely period for investigating the complaint and when it will respond to you.[130]

If the complaint involves two or more organisations, you should get one, co-ordinated response.[131]

Every NHS trust and primary care trust (PCT) in England should have a Patient Advice and Liaison Service to provide on-the-spot help, support and information about how to complain. If you are considering making a complaint, you may also find it helpful to speak to your local Independent Complaints Advocacy Service which can help you make a formal complaint about NHS services. Community health councils in Wales offer advice and support on complaints in their areas. In Scotland, each Health Board should ensure the availability of independent advocacy, advice and support.

The second stage – Ombudsman

If your complaint is not resolved locally, you can take it to the Health Service Ombudsman or Local Government Ombudsman. In Wales, the Public Services Ombudsman deals with complaints about local government. In Scotland a Public

Services Ombudsman deals with complaints about the Scottish Government, other public bodies and their functions, including health and social care.

The Ombudsman will not usually investigate a complaint unless you have first exhausted the local resolution procedure. However, if the authority is not acting upon your complaint, or there are unreasonable delays, this delay may also form part of your complaint. The time limit for lodging a complaint with the Ombudsman is 12 months from the date you were notified of the matter complained about. This time limit can be extended if it is reasonable to do so.[132]

An investigator will examine your case, look at the relevant papers, interview you if necessary and interview the officers. Sometimes the investigations are discontinued either because it becomes apparent there was no maladministration or because the authority settles the dispute.

Some cases are reported. If that is to be done, you and the local authority or health authority will have an opportunity to comment on the report for factual correctness before it is finalised. If the case is reported, the authority will be named, but your name will be changed and the officers identified by a letter of the alphabet. Although Ombudsman decisions do not have the force of law, some can be very influential and become well known throughout local authorities and health services. They can occasionally lead to changes in law or to guidance. Sometimes they can influence practice not only in your area but others.

Complaints to the Ombudsman have the advantage of being free, so can be very useful if you cannot get legal aid to pursue your complaint through the courts.

Requesting a review of a discharge from hospital decision (England and Wales)

There is a separate procedure[133] if you think you should not leave hospital, or your care in a care home providing nursing should continue to be fully funded by the NHS (see p241).

You, your family or any carer have the right to ask for a review of the decision that you no longer need inpatient care. This can give some breathing space as during the review you should remain as an inpatient, although the request should be dealt with urgently and you should have an answer within two weeks. This can be extended if there are exceptional circumstances which make the timescale impossible.[134]

In reaching a decision the NHS body should seek advice from an independent panel which will consider your case and make a recommendation. The NHS body has the right not to convene a panel if your need falls well outside the eligibility criteria for continuing inpatient care. If it is decided not to convene the panel you should be given the reasons in writing. The Ombudsman has criticised a health body which refused to hold a panel hearing on the grounds that the patient did not meet the eligibility criteria. S/he interprets the guidance as meaning that only where there is no doubt whatsoever that the eligibility criteria would not be met should the possibility of not convening a panel be considered.[135]

This review procedure cannot be used to challenge the content of the eligibility criteria, only the way the criteria have been applied to you. Neither can it be used to review the type of inpatient care and where it is offered, the content of any alternative care package or any other aspect of your treatment in hospital. It cannot be used for resolving funding disputes between the NHS body and local authority. In all these cases you can use the complaints procedure, and there is nothing to stop you using both procedures at the same time.

The review procedure can only be used to:
- check that the procedures have been followed correctly in reaching the decision; *and/or*
- ensure that the eligibility criteria have been properly and consistently applied.

Appealing against a discharge decision (Scotland)

If you are in hospital in Scotland you have the right to appeal against the clinical decision to discharge you from continuing NHS care.[136]

Information on this procedure and any advocacy services must be available from hospital staff on request. The appeal is in two stages. Once the consultant has decided that you can be discharged, you or your carer/advocate have ten days to request a review of the decision by the Director of Public Health. This should be completed within two weeks. If it is decided that you should be discharged, you have the right to request a second opinion from an independent consultant from another health board area.

You cannot be discharged during the appeal process. The aim of this appeal process is to ensure that the criteria set out in the guidance have been correctly applied. It cannot be used to complain about the content of the criteria. The appeal procedure is separate from the NHS complaints procedure and there is nothing to stop you using both procedures at the same time.

Reviews against other decisions about the need for NHS services and NHS funding of nursing care (England and Wales)

In England and Wales the type of review explained on p121 for hospital discharge can also be used to question about the need for continuing NHS health care or continuing NHS services contributing to a health and social care package (see p29).[137] It can also be used for any complaints about the NHS funding of registered nursing care in a home providing nursing (see p29).

The procedure is the same as that described on p40. Any existing care package, whether hospital care or community health services, should not be withdrawn in any circumstances until the outcome of the review is known.

Complaints about the standard of care provided

If you have a complaint about the care that is provided by a regulated provider, complain to the provider under the complaints procedures that it must have in place as part of being regulated. It is part of the regulatory process that you should have details of the complaints procedure and how complaints are dealt with. You should also be made aware that if you are dissatisfied with the outcome of the complaint you can take up the matter with the Care Quality Commission (England), the Scottish Commission for the Regulation of Care or the Care and Social Services Inspectorate Wales.

Other remedies

At the same time as, or instead of, a complaint to health, housing or adult social care services you may want to think of other action you can take. Sometimes it is difficult to decide which course of action will have the best outcome. It is useful to talk this over with someone experienced in community care issues. Most national organisations for older or disabled people have helplines and they may be able to suggest the options you could consider to remedy your situation (see Appendix 1).

Local action

There are other actions which could be pursued at the same time as a formal complaint or as a way of attempting to resolve your situation without recourse to the complaints procedure.

Local advice groups, your councillor or MP

Sometimes you can get help in resolving your problem with the authority by contacting a local advice group, your councillor or MP/MSP. In Wales, you can also write to your National Assembly Member (AM). Some gentle querying of a decision by a knowledgeable adviser may get to the root of the problem far faster than the complaints procedure. Councillors and MPs will often take up your case. Sometimes your MP/MSP/AM will pass your complaint to the minister responsible for health. This can sometimes lead to resolution, as officials will look at the complaint and, where necessary, take it up with the local authority or health service, although this is only likely to happen where the authority is clearly outside the law.

Local (or national) newspapers

Although you may want to think twice about going to the papers (as you may lose control of the nature and detail of the complaint), sometimes in an urgent or very difficult situation it can resolve your problems. It has proved quite an effective remedy against waiting in hospital for funding for a care home, or against withdrawal of services.

Contacting the local authority monitoring officer

This is one of the lesser-known remedies which can at times be very speedy and effective. Each local authority is required to have an officer (often the chief executive) to ensure that the authority's policies and decisions are within the law.[138] If you think that a decision has been made which does not follow the law then a letter to the monitoring officer will ensure that the legal department looks at it. It may be worth making sure you are right before taking this action, but in an emergency it can produce a very swift response.

Secretary of State's default powers

If either adult social care services or the NHS fail to carry out their duties the Secretary of State can declare them to be in default of their duty[139] and direct them to do so. In Wales these powers have devolved to the First Secretary. In Scotland these powers have now transferred to the First Minister. In practice that step has never been taken, but if you write to the Secretary of State asking her/him to use her/his default powers, an investigation by officers of the relevant department may informally resolve your problem if the facts show that the authority is clearly in breach of the law.

Judicial review

The main legal remedy in cases which involve public bodies such as local authorities and the NHS is judicial review. Until recently rarely used, there is now an increasing body of caselaw and there have been some very important test cases addressing some of the most contentious community care issues.

The most common grounds for judicial review are:

- the decision is illegal (*ultra vires*);
- the authority has misunderstood the relevant law;
- the decision is unreasonable given the facts;
- the decision shows an improper exercise of discretionary power – eg, that the authority has fettered its discretion;
- the authority has taken into account an irrelevant consideration.

To take your complaint to judicial review you will need to seek legal advice and in particular discuss the costs, as it can be very expensive if you are not eligible for legal aid. Judicial review can be a lengthy process, but at times, when your situation is very urgent, action can be taken within days and sometimes on the same day.

There are strict time limits and you must start your case within three months of the decision relating to your complaint. Normally your solicitor will write a 'letter before action' which tells the authority the grounds of the complaint and indicates that unless it is resolved, an application will be made to the courts to grant leave for a hearing.

Sometimes this letter itself will resolve the problem (often because the authority's legal department sees the case for the first time and realises there are flaws in the decision, or because a decision is made not to get involved in litigation). Courts are increasingly keen that disputes are settled by local resolution wherever possible.

If this does not happen you must seek leave from the High Court for a full hearing. Sometimes your case will still get settled before the full hearing. The Court can:

- overturn the decision and order the authority to take the decision again (*certiorari*). This can sometimes mean the authority could still make the same decision, but this time may make it correctly;
- forbid the authority to do something (*injunction*). This is often used as an interim way of making sure services are put back in place while waiting for the hearing by forbidding them to be withdrawn;
- oblige the authority to take positive action (*mandamus*);
- forbid the authority from doing something inconsistent with its legal power (*prohibition*);
- make a statement about your rights and the general legal position (*declaration*).

Your case may go on to the Court of Appeal either on the grounds that there is a realistic prospect of success on a point of law or that the case is of public interest and so merits a hearing in a higher court. Eventually your case could go to the House of Lords.

In Scotland, a similar process for judicial review exists through raising action in the Court of Session in Edinburgh. There are other (seldom used) remedies under Scottish law: consult an adviser or a lawyer for details.

European Court of Human Rights and Human Rights Act 1998

The European Court of Human Rights and Human Rights Act 1998 are beginning to have a direct effect on decisions made in community care. The Human Rights Act means that the same basic set of rights, which you used to need to take to Europe under the European Convention on Human Rights, are considered in UK courts. Even prior to the Act coming into force there was evidence that the courts were taking it into consideration in their decisions.[140] There have been a number of cases since the Act came into force, including cases on home closures and the independence of complaints panels.

The Articles in the European Convention on Human Rights that are of significance in community care are:

- the right to life (Article 2);
- the right not to be subject to torture or degrading treatment or punishment (Article 3);
- the right to liberty and security of the person (Article 5);
- the right to a fair hearing by an independent and impartial tribunal (Article 6);

- the right to respect for family life, home and correspondence (Article 8).

The Convention includes the right to an effective remedy if a violation of any right has been committed by a public body. It also requires that your rights and freedoms are secured without discrimination.

Local authorities and health services should scrutinise decisions on the basis of whether they impinge on any of these rights.

This is a remedy which is likely to become increasingly common over the next few years and the extent of these rights will be tested in the courts.

Disability Discrimination Act

If you are disabled the Disability Discrimination Act 1995 (DDA) makes it unlawful for you to be discriminated against in access to services. Service providers include healthcare services, adult social care services and housing authorities.

It is also unlawful for landlords (private, local authority and housing associations) to treat you less favourably than someone else for a reason relating to your disability and the reason cannot be justified. Landlords must make reasonable adjustments to practices, policies and procedures, and take reasonable steps to provide additional services and aids.

Seek advice if you think you have been discriminated against (see Appendix 3).

The Equality and Human Rights Commission provides free information on the DDA: see www.equalityhumanrights.com or call 0845 604 6610 (England), 0845 604 5510 (Scotland) or 0845 604 8810 (Wales).

Notes

1. **What are community care services**
   1. s46(3) NHSCCA 1990
   2. s5A(4) SW(S)A 1968
   3. *R v Social Fund Inspector ex parte Connick*, 8 June 1993
   4. DoE Guidance 17/96
   5. CC(DD)(QS)(E) Regs
   6. *Better care, higher standards a charter for long term care: a summary for users and carers*, DH/DETR, December 1999

2. **The responsibilities of adult social care services; health and housing**
   7. s2 LGA 2000
   8. *R on the application of J v Enfield LBC* CCLR, September 2002

9. *Community Care in the Next Decade and Beyond – Policy Guidance*, 1990. Assessment and care management SWSG11/1991
10. s7(1) LASSA 1970; s5(1) SW(S)A 1968
11. *R v North Yorkshire County Council ex parte Hargreaves* CCLR, December 1997 and *R v Islington LBC ex parte Rixon* CCLR, March 1998
12. *R v Islington ex parte Rixon* CCLR, March 1998
13. *R v Powys CC ex parte Hambidge* Court of Appeal CCLR, September 1998
14. LAC (93)7; WOC 41/93
15. LAC (93)10; WOC 35/93 Appendix 4

16 There have been a number of Ombudsman Reports on the extent of advice and the accuracy of such advice. LGORS 91/C/1246, 94/B/2128 and 93/A/3738
17 LAC (93)10; WOC 35/93 Appendix 2
18 SWSA 1968; SWSG 11/96
19 s94 SW(S)A 1968
20 s12(2) SW(S)A 1968
21 *R v Gloucestershire CC ex parte Barry* CCLR, December 1997
22 LAC (93)7; WOC 41/93
23 s1 CSDPA 1970
24 *R v Haringey ex parte Norton* CCLR, March 1998. Because these words are in the Act social services has to assess you for them if you are a disabled person.
25 LAC (90)7; SDD40/1985
26 *R v Ealing LBC ex parte Leaman* (TLR), 10 February 1984 and *R v N Yorkshire ex parte Hargreaves* (No.2) CCLR, June 1998
27 The AMA/ACC issued a joint circular in 1971 but there has been no government guidance.
28 DHSS Circular 19/71 is the only and still current circular.
29 s254 and Sch 20 NHSA 2006; s192 and Sch 15 NHS(W)A 2006
30 LAC (93)10; WOC 35/93 Appendix 3
31 *Putting People First – a shared vision and commitment to the transformation of adult social care*, DH, December 2007
32 s14 SW(S)A 1968
33 s26 MH(CT)(S)A 2003
34 s27 MH(CT)(S)A 2003
35 Under ss3, 37, 47, or 48 MHA 1983
36 s117(2) MHA 1983 and *R v Ealing District Health Authority ex parte Fox* 1993, All ER 170 QBD
37 LAC (96)8/HSG (96)11, WHC (95)6
38 *R v Manchester CC ex parte Stennett* HL, CCLR, September 2002
39 s328(1) MH(CT)(S)A 2003
40 s1 CDCA 2000
41 s2(3) CDCA 2000
42 *Carers and Disabled Children Act 2000 and Carers (Equal Opportunities) Act 2004 Combined Policy Guidance*
43 s5 CDCA 2000
44 CDC(V)(E) Regs
45 s6 CDCA 2000. Local authorities must take the assessment into account when deciding what, if any, services to provide under s17 CA 1989.
46 Draft CCD 10/2002
47 s6 LASSA 1970; s3 SW(S)A 1968
48 LGOR 92/A/4108
49 *Better care, higher standards a charter for long term care: a summary for users and carers*, DH/DETR, December 1999
50 Speech by Secretary of State 23 July 2002
51 CC(DD)(QS)(E) Regs
52 *Guidance on charging policies for non-residential services that enable older people to remain in their own home*, COSLA 2002
53 LAC (2001)13; HSC 2001/008
54 s46 NHSCCA 1990; s5(A) SW(S)A 1968
55 Community Care Plans (England) Directions 2003
56 LAC (93)4; WOC 16/93/SW4/93
57 *Community Care and the Next Decade and Beyond – Policy Guidance* 1990 para 2.25; SWSG 11/1 para 7
58 *Community Care and the Next Decade and Beyond – Policy Guidance* 1990 para 3.56; SWSG 11/91
59 LAC (94)24; WDC/6/92
60 LGOR 97/A/4069
61 s47(3) NHSCCA 1990; s12A(3) SW(S)A 1968
62 CC(DD)A 2003
63 s3 NHSA 1977 and Part III NHS(S)A 1978
64 See *R v N and E Devon ex parte Coughlan*, (CA) CCLR, September 1999 which discusses the duties of the Secretary of State to provide nursing
65 HSC 2001/015; LAC (2001)18; (2004)54; CEL 6 (2009) 22
66 LGO report 02/B/10226, Cambs CC 2004 (Pointon case)
67 *Response to Health Select Committee Report on Continuing Care*, 2005, CM 6650
68 Further guidance on palliative care is found in EL (93)14 and EL (94)14; MEL (94)104
69 *Better care, higher standards a charter for long term care: a summary for users and carers*, DH/DETR, December 1999
70 The Delayed Discharges (Continuing Care) Directions 2007
71 The Delayed Discharges (Continuing Care) Directions 2007
72 *Discharge from hospital: pathway process and practice*, DH, March 2007
73 WHC (2005)035; CEL (2008)6
74 NHS (GPS) Reg 1992
75 *Good practice in continence services*, DH 2000
76 HSG (96)34; MEL 92/67
77 HSG (96)53 and HSC 1998/004

78 LAC (2001)1; HSC 2001/001; NAFWC 43/02; WHC (2002)128
79 LAC (2003)14
80 NAfWC 05/02
81 s47(3) NHSCCA 1990
82 s12A(3) SW(S)A 1968
83 Part VII HA 1996; Part II H(S)A 1987
84 DoE Guidance 10/92 SWSG 7/94
85 Part M Building Regs 1991 – Access and facilities for disabled people. Approved document 17 1999.

3. Getting the services you need
86 CC(DD)A 2003
87 s47(1) NHSCCA 1990; s12(A) SW(S)A 1968
88 s47(2) NHSCCA; s12(A) SW(S)A 1968; s4 DPSCRA 1986
89 ss4 and 8 DPSCRA 1986; s1 CRSA 1995, s2 of this Act added a new s3A into SW(S)A 1968
90 *Community Care in the Next Decade and Beyond – Policy Guidance* 1990, para 3.15
91 s47(5) NHSCCA 1990; s12(5) SW(S)A 1968
92 LAC (2002)1
93 CCD8/2001; NAfWC 09/02
94 *Community Care into the Next Decade and Beyond – Policy Guidance* 1990 para 3.20; *Assessment and Care Management* (SW11/1991) para 5.2
95 LAC (2002)1; CCD8/2001; NAFWC 09/02
96 *R v Bristol ex parte Penfold* CCLR, September 1998
97 LGOR 97/A/4069
98 PSS PAF Indicator 2004/05
99 LGOR 94/C/1165 and 94/C/0805
100 LAC (93)2 SWSG 14/93
101 LAC (2002)1; NAfWC 09/02; CCD8/2001
102 Community Care Assessment Directions 2004
103 s47(3) NHS and CCA 1990; s12A(3) SWSA 1968
104 *Community Care into the Next Decade and Beyond – Policy Guidance* 1990 para 3.9; *Assessment Care Management* (SW11/1991) para 5
105 *R v Haringey ex parte Norton* CCLR, March 1998 and *R v Avon CC ex parte M* CCLR, June 1999
106 s1(1)V CRSA 1995; s1 CDCA 2000
107 *Policy Guidance* 1990 para 3.27-3.29
108 s1(1)A CRSA 1995
109 s1 CDCA 2000; CCH(S)A 2002

110 *Community Care into the Next Decade and Beyond – Policy Guidance* 1990 para 3.56 EW.S; SW11/1991 para 5.9
111 CC(DD)A 2003
112 DD(CC) Directions 2007
113 s41(1)(b) NHSCCA 1990; s12A(b) SW(S)A 1968
114 CI (92)34 known as the Laming letter. Although cancelled in 1994 this letter is still used and quoted in legal judgments.
115 LAC (2002)13
116 *R v Gloucestershire ex parte Barry* CCLR, December 1997
117 LAC (2002)13; NAfWC 09/02; WHC(2002)32
118 *R v Bristol ex parte Penfold* CCLR, September 1998
119 *R v Gloucestershire ex parte Barry* CCLR, December 1997
120 *R v Sussex ex parte Tandy* CCLR, June 1998
121 *R v Birmingham ex parte Mohammed* CCLR, September 1998
122 *R v Lancashire ex parte Ingham (R v Gloucestershire ex parte Barry* (CA)) CCLR, December 1997
123 Q and A 8.5 *Fair Access to Care Practice Guidance*

5. How to complain
124 LASSNHSC(E) Regs
125 *Principles of Good Complaint Handling*, Parliamentary and Health Service Ombudsman, 28 November 2008
126 Reg 16 LASSNHSC(E) Regs
127 Reg 4 LASSNHSC(E) Regs
128 Reg 12 LASSNHSC(E) Regs
129 Reg 13(1) LASSNHSC(E) Regs
130 Reg 13(6) and (7) LASSNHSC(E) Regs
131 *Listening, responding, improving: a guide to better customer care*, DH, 26 February 2009
132 s26 LGA 1974; s9 HSCA 1993; s25 LG(S)A 1975
133 *The National Framework for NHS Continuing Healthcare and NHS funded Nursing Care*, DH, 26 June 2007; WOC 16/95; WHC (95)7
134 *The National Framework for NHS Continuing Healthcare and NHS funded Nursing Care*, DH, 26 June 2007; WHC (95)7
135 Case E1626/01-02 Annex E of the Special Report *NHS funding of long-term care*, Health Services Ombudsman 2003
136 NHS MEL (96)22

137 The National Framework for NHS
Continuing Healthcare and NHS funded
Nursing Care, DH, 26 June 2007; LAC
(2001)26; HSC 2001/17
138 s5 LGHA 1989
139 s7D LASSA 1970; s85 NHSA 1977; s211
LG(S)A 1975
140 *R v N and E Devon ex parte Coughlan*
CCLR, September 1999

Chapter 3

Supported housing and Supporting People

This chapter covers:
1. Supporting People (p52)
2. Sheltered housing and floating support (p53)
3. Hostels and other supported accommodation (p54)
4. Adult placement schemes (p55)
5. Abbeyfield Homes (p55)

Even though you may encounter difficulties in trying to live independently in your own home, your personal care and support needs may not be so great that residential or nursing care would be a desirable, appropriate or available option. There are many different types of supported accommodation schemes which aim to meet different needs. Some offer accommodation which has been specially adapted or designed to suit particular physical needs. Others offer services with the support of wardens or other support/care staff and additional facilities, which may sometimes be supplemented by community care services arranged by adult social care services (see Chapter 2).

Some supported housing schemes offer so much care and support that it can be difficult to distinguish them from care homes. The different terms used in this chapter to describe different types of supported housing do not necessarily have any particular significance in themselves for social security (or community care) purposes. The effect of a stay in supported housing on your entitlement to certain social security benefits will depend less on how your accommodation is described by your landlord or the provider of the accommodation than on any combination of the following factors:

- whether it is registered as a care home;
- whether the accommodation is owned or managed by a local authority;
- the extent to which adult social care services or NHS powers and duties have been applied in accommodating you, or in assisting you with the costs of your accommodation;
- how long you have been living in your accommodation and any previous arrangements that may have been made to accommodate you.

These factors will determine whether or not your accommodation will be classed as a care home for the purposes of determining your entitlement to housing benefit, council tax benefit, attendance allowance or disability living allowance (see Chapter 7).

For further details of how your benefit may be affected by a stay in accommodation classed as a registered care home, and for definitions of registered care homes, see Chapter 16.

The accommodation discussed in this chapter is not treated as registered accommodation. If you are resident in such a supported accommodation scheme, you can usually therefore claim social security benefits in much the same way as if you were living in ordinary accommodation. There will often be no need for adult social care services to be involved in making any arrangements for you to live there. Registration requirements are applied by the Care Quality Commission (CQC), the Scottish Commission for the Regulation of Care (SCRC) or the Care and Social Services Inspectorate Wales (CSSIW). These specify that establishments must be registered if they provide accommodation together with nursing or personal care (which includes assistance with bodily functions such as feeding, bathing and toileting, if required) for people who are or have been ill, disabled, infirm, mentally disordered or dependent on drugs or alcohol.[1] Establishments are no longer exempted from the registration requirements just because they do not also provide board.

The registration status of the accommodation you live in or are considering moving into will affect which benefits you can claim or which charges you may have to pay. If you are unsure of the registration status, you should check with the accommodation provider, with your local adult social care services, CQC, SCRC or CSSIW, or seek independent advice (see Appendix 2).

1. **Supporting People**

'**Supporting People**' is a government programme to ensure supported housing services are funded from one single budget, monitored for quality and take into account local need. It requires the administrators of the Supporting People programme to consult with service users, providers and others involved in supported accommodation when developing their local Supporting People Strategy.[2]

The Supporting People scheme is administered locally by the 'administering authority' on behalf of all the Supporting People partners. The administering authority is the local authority (for the different types of local authority, see p8). 'Partners' include health trusts, probation services, adult social care services and local housing departments.

The Supporting People programme only funds housing support services aimed at facilitating and enabling independent living. It does not aim to provide assistance with personal care needs, which are the responsibility of adult social care services (see Chapter 2). Housing support services include advice to enable you to maintain your accommodation and advice in using domestic appliances safely, or checking and advising on general health and safety problems.

In Scotland, since April 2008 there has been no Supporting People budget.[3] Instead the funds have been absorbed into the main local government settlement to allow more flexible support packages to be developed and reduce administrative and accounting functions. Funding for housing support services still exist, it is simply absorbed within the main local government settlement rather than being a separate grant.

Information on Supporting People is available from your local authority and at www.spkweb.org.uk (England) and http://new.wales.gov.uk/topics/housingandcommunity/housing/supportingpeople (Wales).

2. Sheltered housing and floating support

The term **'sheltered housing'** (or very sheltered housing, depending on the level of support provided) is commonly used to refer to groups of flats usually supported by a warden and mainly intended for occupation by older people in an establishment which does not have to be registered as a care home. Sheltered housing schemes are commonly provided by local authority housing departments or housing associations, although many are also provided by profit-making bodies.

Sheltered housing schemes vary from services where an emergency alarm is provided and linked to a mobile on-call warden, to services termed as 'extra care' where higher level housing support is provided with a personal care package.

If you live in sheltered or very sheltered housing you can claim social security benefits in the same way as if you were living in ordinary accommodation or your own home. For example, you could claim all appropriate income support/pension credit, personal allowances and premiums, attendance allowance or any care/mobility component of disability living allowance for your own needs. If you pay rent you can claim housing benefit to meet eligible housing costs (for the accommodation and for certain services which may include those provided by the warden) and council tax benefit to meet any council tax liabilities. Exemptions or relief (following a financial assessment) from Supporting People service charges may also apply. If you have personal care needs which the housing scheme cannot provide, additional community care services may be provided by adult social care services, although you may be charged for them (see Chapter 4).

A sheltered housing scheme will, therefore, usually be more financially attractive both to you and to adult social care services than a care home. You will also have greater security of tenure in a sheltered scheme (where you will usually be a tenant) than in a care home (where you will usually only have a licence to occupy). The introduction of Supporting People has required service providers to be subject to quality monitoring and review as a condition of receiving Supporting People grants

The level of support in some very sheltered (or 'extra care') housing schemes may be as great as, if not greater than, that provided in some registered care homes. The distinction in treatment for social security purposes will depend on whether the accommodation needs to be registered as a care home.

If you are considering sheltered housing, check with the landlord or seek independent advice to see what arrangements will apply.

Housing support in your own home ('floating support')

'**Floating support**' services are housing support services that are delivered into your own home to help you remain independent. This may be as a result of a crisis – eg, returning home after a stay in hospital. These services do not include help with personal care but are aimed at providing low-level support to enable you to return or remain home. These services can be delivered whether you live in rented or owner-occupier accommodation. You may be charged for these services if they are intended to provide you with support for more than two years – the arrangements will depend on the administering authority where the service is provided, the service provider will be able to give you more details.

---

3. Hostels and other supported accommodation

Support services are provided in a range of designated 'supported accommodation' providing a wide range of services from single units to multi-occupancy with the tenants having entitlement to the full range of benefits. Some schemes which may be described as care homes or hostels do not have to be registered as care homes because they do not provide the necessary degree of personal care.

A wide variety of hostels offer support for those with a broad range of different needs (eg, for those with mental health difficulties or drug/alcohol dependencies) and the extent of the support available varies widely from hostel to hostel. Residents of hostels are normally licensees rather than tenants, but group homes are normally covered by tenancy agreements.

Some accommodation in certain parts of some registered care homes may be exempt from the registration requirements – eg, because no (or insufficient) personal care is provided. This may be because certain units of accommodation attached to the home are sometimes used for less dependent residents (or for staff). Sometimes these are self-contained units or bungalows in the grounds of the core home and are often referred to as 'cluster' homes. Similarly, some self-contained units may be clustered around the grounds of a core local authority care home or even in the grounds of a hospital. Units are often used to accommodate a number of residents together for mutual support and to encourage independent living.

If you are resident in a hostel or other supported accommodation hostel or similar accommodation, you can claim benefits in the same way as if you were living your own home (see Chapter 7). You can also claim council tax benefit to meet any council tax liabilities and housing benefit to meet eligible housing costs. Exemptions or relief (following a financial assessment) from Supporting People service charges may also apply. Additional community care services may be provided to meet personal care needs not provided in your accommodation – eg, help with getting up in the morning or provision of a day centre although you may be charged for them (see Chapter 4).

4. **Adult placement schemes**

Adult placement schemes (sometimes called Shared Lives) are similar to fostering arrangements. An adult placement scheme (often run by adult social care services) will place a vulnerable or disabled adult in the care of an approved adult placement carer. This could be, for example, for a short stay when leaving hospital before returning home.

Placements may be arranged on a long-term basis, or for short-term breaks, or for regular (sometimes even non-residential) befriending purposes. Such accommodation arrangements have the advantage of offering a home environment in the community and a greater degree of individual care and attention, which will have been considered more appropriate for a person's needs than a care home. Such arrangements are most commonly used to accommodate adults with severe physical disabilities, learning disabilities, mental health issues or drug/alcohol problems .

The schemes are regulated by Care Quality Commission in England,[4] Care and Social Services Inspectorate Wales[5] and the Scottish Commission for the Regulation of Care.[6]

Visit www.naaps.co.uk for more information on adult placement schemes.

5. **Abbeyfield Homes**

Special arrangements apply to residents of homes provided by the Abbeyfield Society. Most Abbeyfield Homes are not required to be registered as care homes. Some of the services they provide are likely to be covered by the Supporting People programme. However, a small number are registered and some provide nursing care.

Residents of Abbeyfield Homes usually have their own room, although they may share communal facilities and meals, and are generally more independent than those who need residential care (residents are often moved into care homes when they become more dependent). All Abbeyfield residents are treated in the same way, as if they were in sheltered accommodation (see p53), except that residents in Abbeyfield Homes are treated as licensees rather than tenants. They can therefore claim social security benefits as if they were in ordinary accommodation or in their own homes (see Chapter 7), which may include income support, pension credit, attendance allowance, disability living allowance, council tax benefit and housing benefit or any eligible housing costs. Residents may also be provided with community care services but may be charged for them.

Notes

1 s3 and s121(9) CSA 2000

1. Supporting People
2 Annex B Supporting People Programme
   Grant (England); s8 Supporting People
   Strategic and Interim Guidance
   (Scottish Executive); s3 Arrangement for
   the Implementation of Supporting
   People in Wales
3 Concordat between the Scottish
   Government and local government,
   November 2007
4 Reg 3 Adult Placement Schemes
   (England) Regulations 2004
5 Reg 33 Adult Placement Schemes
   (Wales) Regulations 2004
6 Reg 2 The Regulation of Care
   (Registration and Registers) (Scotland)
   Regulations 2002

Chapter 4

Paying for services at home

This chapter covers:
1. Charges for care services at home (below)
2. Charges for housing support services (p64)
3. Buying your own care (p65)

1. Charges for care services at home

Not many care services you receive either at home or in day centres are free. Local authorities have the discretion to charge for most care services to help you remain in your own home, and most do charge.[1] Services provided as NHS health services are free. Personal care is free in Scotland for those 65 or over, but local authorities can still charge for other aspects of your care such as shopping and housework. Charges for housing support services are based on both national directions and local discretion. There are national rules to calculate charges for housing grants for people with disabilities (see p82) and national charges for health items covered by health benefits (see p76).

At the time of writing, the personalisation of services is becoming a key part of many government policies, and does not just refer to social care. 'Personalisation' is a general term used to describe how individuals should be supported to shape their own lives and the types of services they receive. Self-directed support is a new approach in the social care system that aims to put service users in control of the services they use. Direct payments, personal budgets, individual budgets and self-assessment are examples of self-directed support. Although different streams of funding may be utilised to meet the individuals needs (eg, Supporting People funding, disabled facilities grants, etc) the service user may still be subject to a means test to establish how much s/he can afford to pay towards services that s/he needs.

Services for which charges cannot be made (England and Wales)
- You cannot be charged for aftercare services provided under s117 of the Mental Health Act 1983 (see p24).

- If you have any form of CJD and use home care services you should be treated as automatically exempt from charges.[2]
- In England, you should not be charged for 'intermediate care', which is aimed at helping you leave hospital earlier or avoid having to go into hospital.[3] Such care is normally only expected to last for up to six weeks and will often be for a shorter time. It can be at home or in residential settings.
- In Wales, there is a similar scheme for home care aiming to help vulnerable people to have the care they need either on return from hospital or to prevent inappropriate admission. It is normally for six weeks, although it may be more.[4]
- In England, if you have been assessed as needing community equipment it will be free. Minor adaptations of £1,000 or less are also free.[5]

Services for which charges cannot be made (Scotland)

- You can get four weeks' free care (including tasks such as shopping and housework) following a stay in hospital for more than 24 hours or for surgery as a day patient.[6]
- No charges can be made for day centres or travelling to day centres if you have a mental illness, personality disorder or learning disabilities.[7]
- Local authorities should not charge for services if you have a mental health condition and are subject to a community care or supervision order.[8]
- Personal care is free if you are 65 or over. See Appendix 4 for the definitions of personal care, support and social care that should be free under the Community Care and Health (Scotland) Act 2002.[9]
- If you are 65 or over, local authorities should consider not charging for day care, aids and adaptations.[10] Minor equipment or adaptations should be free if supplied within four weeks of discharge from hospital.[11]

How charges are decided (England and Wales)

It is up to each local authority to decide for what, if anything, it considers reasonable to charge.[12] If you can show that it is not reasonable to expect you to pay that charge then it can be waived or reduced to what is considered reasonable for you to pay.[13]

When setting their charging policies, local authorities in England have to follow certain minimum requirements set out in the guidance *Fairer charging policies for home care and other non-residential social services*.[14] In Wales, similar guidance was issued but authorities have only been required to partially implement it.[15]

The question of reasonableness has been raised in the courts. In one case the 'overriding criterion of reasonableness' enabled adult social care services to make charges long after the person had finished receiving services (in this case when compensation came through).[16] Another case found that it was not necessary to consult about raising charges or when formulating a charging policy as difficulties in paying charges can be taken up individually.[17] However, a High Court judgment concluded that when a local authority, which had consulted when first introducing its charging policy, later made some fundamental changes to this policy, 'fairness required that there should be proper consultation before they were introduced'.[18] *Fairer Charging* guidance makes it clear that consultation about charges and any increases or changes in charges is routinely expected. There is a requirement in the guidance that local authorities should specifically consult users on whether to take disability expenditure into account for users not in receipt of disability related benefits, whether to set an overriding maximum charge, and on their policies in relation to savings.

Which services are charged for?

Most authorities charge for home care, and nearly all charge for meals on wheels and meals in day centres. An increasing number charge for day care, and some charge for the transport to day care.

Who should be charged?

The legislation implies that only the service user should be charged. The *Fairer Charging* guidance confirms this by saying that the legislation envisages that councils will have regard only to a service user's means in assessing the ability to pay a charge. Family members should not be required to pay unless they are acting on your behalf and are responsible for your finances because you are unable to manage them, and so paying out of your money (see p257). However, there may be times when you could have a beneficial interest in the value of an asset – eg, a bank account, even though it is not in your name.[19] It is for the council to decide in the light of its own legal advice whether a request might reasonably be made for the partner to disclose such resources. Practice has varied considerably around the country regarding spouses/partners who may be asked for information about their finances, and their income and capital may be included in the calculation of how much you have to pay. If your spouse/partner's resources are being taken into account, or if you are charged the full cost if your spouse/partner refuses to give information about her/his resources, seek advice (see Appendix 2). This question has been the subject of an Ombudsman investigation, and it was found that the council's inclusion of a spouse's invalid care allowance (now called carer's allowance) and carer's premium in the initial assessment was wrong. However, it could take into account a spouse's means in deciding whether to reduce the charge because of hardship.[20] A Court of Appeal judgment found that the financial resources of a disabled child's parents could be a relevant factor in a local authority's decision whether or not it should make arrangements for a child under the Children Act 1989.[21]

Taking account of benefits

The *Fairer Charging* guidance offers a framework for local authorities to use for people in receipt of benefits such as income support (IS), attendance allowance

(AA) or incapacity benefit. Your income should not be reduced below 'basic' levels of IS, income-based jobseeker's allowance (JSA), income-related employment and support allowance (ESA) or the guarantee credit of pension credit (PC) plus a buffer of not less than 25 per cent above the basic IS/PC (guarantee credit) level. This does not include any additional amount paid due to severe disability so the basic level plus 'buffer' may still be less than the benefit you actually receive. Local authorities should exempt from charging anyone whose overall income does not exceed the defined basic levels.

Adult social care services cannot charge against the mobility component of disability living allowance (DLA) or the war pensioner's mobility supplement.[22] However, the guidance allows charges to be made against what are known as disability related benefits: the severe disability premium of IS and additional amount for severe disability under PC (guarantee credit); attendance allowance; DLA; constant attendance allowance and the exceptionally severe disablement allowance. It is open to local authorities to decide whether to take these benefits into account subject to the overriding principles that charges do not reduce a user's net income below basic levels of IS/PC (guarantee credit) plus a 25 per cent buffer and they do not result in the user being left without the means to pay for any other necessary care or support or other costs arising from disability. Where disability benefits are taken into account, local authorities should assess your disability related expenditure (see below). In Wales, the authority must ensure that your net income is not reduced below the level of the basic income level plus a buffer of 35 per cent and a flat rate disability related disregard of 10 per cent.[23]

Fairer Charging guidance also refers to a case[24] where it was found to be wrong for an authority to charge more for daytime services because the person received the higher rate AA/DLA which included an amount for night time care. The guidance states that if the council purchases no element of night care, then the night care element (ie, the difference between the middle and higher rate) should not be taken into account as income in the assessment.

In both England and Wales, any PC savings credit should be disregarded from the calculation of your income.[25]

Taking account of your extra disability related costs

Most local authorities take disability benefits into account and so also have to allow for your extra costs of disability. Even if you do not get a disability benefit (eg, because you are in the six-month waiting period for AA), there is nothing to stop you asking for your disability related costs to be taken into account. It is worth thinking about all the costs that you have that you would not have if you were fit and well. Some authorities list the typical items on their financial assessment forms, but you should mention other costs that you have. This could include a gardener, taxis, extra heating, special diet, hairdressing if you cannot wash your hair or the cost of maintaining equipment. If you need to buy extra care because some services are no longer offered by adult social care services, or because a ceiling has been imposed (see p40), ask that this be taken into account when assessing your charge. You may have significant extra costs in these circumstances.

The guidance lists examples of typical extra costs of disability, and there is also practice guidance to help local authorities decide in individual cases. If you think that not all your extra costs are being considered, ask to see both the policy guidance and practice guidance.[26] The High Court found that a local authority did not have to include the cost of care provided by a family member as disability related expenses. However, the Court of Appeal subsequently found that the authority's inflexible policy of always disregarding such payments was unlawful. The authority had fettered its discretion by refusing to consider whether the circumstances of individual cases might constitute an exception to its usual policy.[27]

Some local authorities have chosen to allow a standard amount for disability related costs in order to avoid intrusive questioning. The amount allowed varies between authorities, but in all cases if your costs are more than the standard allowance, you should be given an individual assessment of your costs.

Complain if adult social care services refuse to take your extra costs into account (see p40).

Taking account of other income and capital

Other income you receive such as pensions (either state or private), incapacity benefits or private income can be taken into account. However, earnings must be disregarded. This is to avoid a disincentive to work. On the same principle, tax credits should also be disregarded, although at the time of writing there has been no guidance on this.

Most local authorities take your capital and savings into account. The *Fairer Charging* guidance stipulates that those that do should not set limits lower than those used for charges for residential accommodation when deciding if you should pay the full cost for your services or working out tariff income from your savings. For 2009/10, the upper limit is £23,000 (£22,00 in Wales) and the lower limit is £14,00 for (£20,750 in Wales). Local authorities can set more generous limits if they wish.

Local authorities should review cases regularly where savings are being used up by charges. The current legislation and guidance on home care charges do not contain any provision to apply rules on deliberate deprivation of assets in this context. If adult social care services tries to treat you as having notional capital as a result of deliberate deprivation, ask them to confirm their authority for doing so.

How charges are decided (Scotland)

Guidance on charges for non-personal care services for older people in Scotland has been produced by the Convention of Scottish Local Authorities (COSLA).[28]

The Scottish Government has the power to regulate home care charges but has not as yet chosen to exercise it. See p58 and the list in Appendix 4 for the services that should not be charged for. The Scottish Government has revised previous guidance and has now explicitly advised local authorities that assistance with the preparation of food should not be charged for.[29]

As yet there is no new guidance in Scotland for charging people under 65 for care which also includes personal care. Guidance which was issued in 1997 therefore should still be followed for people under 65.[30] However, the COSLA guidance states that some of the principles and practice of its guidance may be equally applicable to charging for other care services and other user groups. If you are a younger service user and think your charges are unfair it may be worth checking the COSLA guidance.

The COSLA guidance on charging for non-personal services provides a framework that aims to maintain local accountability and discretion while encouraging best practice. The guidance recommends the following:

- Charges should not take single older people and couples below the standard minimum guarantee level for PC plus a buffer of 16.5 per cent – ie, £151.45 a week in 2009/10 for a single person and £231.19 for a couple.
- If income is above this level, charges should be based on a percentage taper, but charges should not exceed the cost of providing the service. The guidance gives a range of examples of different tapers.
- There should be a common approach to the treatment of income which would take into account net earnings, all social security benefits (with the exception of the DLA mobility component) and be net of housing and council tax costs. Authorities should exercise discretion to disregard some forms of income – eg, war pensions and industrial disablement benefits. The guidance goes on to say that authorities may wish to include other disregards such as household insurance and water costs, or disability related costs. It reminds authorities of the caselaw about night time AA/DLA (see p121).
- In the case of couples, both partners' income should be taken into account 'as both partners would benefit from domestic services provided to them'.
- Where the service user has dependant child(ren) there is a recommended fixed disregard for each child.
- Day care and aids and adaptations should be free, although a suggested compromise is that a charge of up to £20 could be made for small items.
- The upper capital limit in Scotland is £22,500 and the lower limit is £13,750.

Information you should receive (England, Wales and Scotland)

You should receive information about your authority's charging policy. You will normally be asked to fill in a financial assessment. This should be done after your needs assessment (see p34) although often the two are often done at the same time. You should also receive benefits advice at the time of your financial assessment, either by the person who is working out your charge or, if you prefer, from an independent source. In Scotland, local authorities are encouraged to be proactive in benefit maximisation and that there should be dedicated staff for this.

Once your charge has been worked out, you should get a written statement explaining how much you need to pay and how to pay it. It should also explain how you can ask for your charge to be waived or lowered. Charges should not be made for any period before an assessment has been communicated to you. You should also not have any increase in charges before you have received notification of the increase.

Adult social care services should offer you a choice of how to pay your charge.[31] If adult social care services are not providing the service but are using an independent provider, they may ask that you pay the charge directly to the provider. You should not be required to do this as, depending on the way your authority's charging system works, the provider could obtain knowledge of your finances, which raises issues of confidentiality.

If you have not received a service for any reason you should not be expected to pay for it unless you have received clear information about notifications of changes that will affect your charge – eg, you should know how much notice you need to give in order not to pay if you are on holiday. You should not have to pay if your carer does not turn up. Some computer systems have difficulty in dealing with all the changes that can occur in a care plan. Complain if you think you have been charged for services you have not received.

If you cannot afford your charge

Ask adult social care services to look at your situation again and give as much detail as possible to support your case – eg, extra costs you have because of disability or whether capital is earmarked for a purpose.

Adult social care services cannot withdraw your service if you are unable, or refuse, to pay the charge. As adult social care services have a duty to provide the service you need, this cannot be overruled by the power to charge. Services should not be withdrawn.

If you are getting a direct payment or have a personal budget, the local authority should pay gross if you are arguing about the amount of the charge so that you can be sure you can afford your care in the meantime.

Some people stop their services because of the cost. Before you do this, make sure the local authority will not waive the charge. Failing that, ask for a reassessment of your needs to establish that you will not be left at severe risk if you no longer receive, or have fewer, services. The Ombudsman has previously found maladministration where a local authority allowed a service user to withdraw from services because of the cost without explaining that it would not be able to cancel services on these grounds itself.[32]

Adult social care services can, however, recover the charge as a civil debt through the Magistrates' Court (or Sheriff Court in Scotland).[33]

2. Charges for housing support services

Supporting People is a fund administered by the local authority which covers housing support. A list of the types of services you get under Supporting People are explained on p52. You may be able to get housing benefit (HB – see p163), income support (IS – see p147), income-related employment and support allowance (ESA – see p156) or the guarantee credit of pension credit (PC – see p158) for other housing costs that do not come under Supporting People services. This section explains how you will be charged for your housing support services. In most cases you will pay your charge directly to the provider of the housing support services. If you are a tenant, the local Supporting People team will pay a subsidy to your provider to cover the difference between your assessed contribution and the cost of the service. If you receive both home care and Supporting People services for which you are charged then it will depend on local arrangements whether you pay via your landlord or directly to the local authority.

People who do not have to pay for Supporting People services

You do not have to pay for your Supporting People service (or get full help towards the cost) if you:
- get HB;
- get IS/jobseeker's allowance (JSA)/PC (guarantee credit) and prior to April 2003 used to have an amount paid in your IS/JSA for services that are now included in Supporting People services, or if you are a new owner occupier getting IS/JSA/ESA/PC (guarantee credit) and are receiving housing support services and this receipt is included in the title deeds. As an owner occupier you will have an agreement to meet the charges for these services, and so you will be paid an amount to cover your supporting charge by your local Supporting People team, rather than receive it through your IS/JSA/ESA/PC (guarantee credit). In England you will be paid in a lump sum for the year, and in Scotland and Wales paid on a monthly basis;
- are in a short-term scheme aimed at bringing about or increasing the capacity for independent living in less than two years (note that in Wales such schemes are funded directly by the Welsh Assembly Government rather than locally under Supporting People and cannot be charged);
- get support services as part of your package of care under s117 Mental Health Act 1983;
- in Scotland, up to and including 31 March 2003, had your housing support services funded in full or in part by the special needs allowance package;

- in Scotland, are a 'protected tenant' (or the successor of a protected tenant) and you were occupying and receiving housing support services for at least one month prior to 1 April 2003 (this just applies to services which were part of the rent pool for tenants in local authority housing or tenancies where the landlords used rent pooling). This protection lasts as long as you are a tenant in the same service. If you need to increase your Supporting People services then you will have to pay for the extra (but see p65 for getting help with these charges).

Getting help from the local means test

If you do not get HB or IS/JSA/ESA/PC you can apply for help under the *Fairer Charging* guidance (see p58) or in Scotland the guidance issued in 1997 and if you are 65 or over the COSLA guidance (see p61). When Supporting People was introduced in 2003 local authorities were told they must try to avoid a 'cliff edge' whereby someone who is only just above HB thresholds would be liable to pay the full support charge without any taper. Your housing support provider should tell you about your right to apply for help. If you think you need help towards paying the costs of your support services you could ask to be assessed using the local authority means test. Complain if you are refused an assessment to see if you can get help with your Supporting People charges.

If you get home care services as well as Supporting People services, the local authority should financially assess you under its *Fairer Charging* policy (although if you get HB your Supporting People charge will still be nil as you are exempt from charges for your 'housing support'). If you live in an authority which does not charge for home care services, the authority could still decide to charge for Supporting People services and in this case it should use the *Fairer Charging* or COSLA guidance.

If you think your Supporting People charge is wrong you can complain to your Supporting People team. If your support charge has been worked out by using *Fairer Charging,* use the complaints process that has been set up to deal with these complaints.

3. Buying your own care

If you are unable to get help with your care from the state, you need to consider other ways of obtaining help. You may have relatives and friends who will undertake caring tasks or do some gardening for you. However, you may need to pay someone to do these jobs. Sometimes you need to buy in extra care over and above that supplied by adult social care services. The points to take into account if you pay for your own fees in a care home are described on p69.

This section looks at some of the practical issues of buying your own care. It applies equally whether you receive direct payments, a personal budget (see p69) or money from the Independent Living Fund (see p73), or whether you are buying care yourself with your own money. See p9 for a brief description of ways in which you might raise money to pay for care. This *Handbook* describes the various benefits to which you may be entitled and the powers and duties of the various statutory agencies. Before you arrange your own care, check whether it should be provided for you if this is what you would prefer.

Note that adult social care services cannot refuse to provide you with the services you need just because you are able to afford to pay for your care. If you are assessed as needing a service, it must be provided if this is what you wish.[34]

Finding a carer

If you have been assessed by adult social care services but found not to need the type of care they offer, they may be able to give you information about local schemes which offer the service you need. Voluntary organisations sometimes provide domestic care, or have gardening or handy-person schemes, so may be a good place to start. Adult social care services may also be able to give you a list of private and voluntary agencies in the area which provide care.

Agencies which provide personal care are subject to regulation so you may prefer to use them rather than find your own worker. As well as the safeguard of having an organisation to complain to if things go wrong, you should be assured of getting the service even if the person who normally comes to you is unable to do so. If possible, try to use an agency which has been personally recommended. The United Kingdom Homecare Association (see Appendix 1) is the umbrella group for homecare agencies that meet certain standards of home care provision and it can direct you to local private care agencies.

Agencies providing home care in England are inspected by the Care Quality Commission. Its reports say what the service provider does well and what needs to be improved. A staring system is used to rate providers and make it easy to compare the quality of different services.

You may need to advertise for your own carer. You can do this in a Jobcentre Plus even if you only want someone a few hours a week, or in local papers, or on a noticeboard. If you advertise you may want to consider how prospective applicants contact you – eg, think about using a PO box number, or asking a relative or friend if you could use her/his address or phone number.

Points to consider when paying for your own care

There are national and local organisations which help people who buy their own care using direct payments from adult social care services (see p69) or the Independent Living Fund (see p73). There is also published information to help, particularly about employing your own staff. The National Centre for Independent Living may be able to give you details of this literature (see Appendix 1) and direct you to a local organisation that provides practical support with advertising for and employing a carer, drawing up contracts and administrative tasks connected to payroll, national insurance and income tax returns.

The following are a few considerations to take into account if you are paying for your own care:

- if you are employing your own carer, it can be useful to have someone with you when you are interviewing applicants;
- always take up written references on someone you plan to employ;
- if you are using an agency or employing someone yourself, be very clear exactly what you expect, the number of hours to be worked, and how much you are willing to pay;
- if you are employing your own staff and do not know how much to pay, the local Jobcentre Plus will be able to tell you how much is usually paid for such work;
- if you have not employed people before, it is important to seek advice about your responsibilities as an employer and to check carefully what insurance cover you might need;
- put everything in writing before the person starts working for you so you are both clear about the conditions;
- if you use an agency, ask for a contract (although most agencies will offer you one and those agencies providing personal care will have to provide you with a clear statement of what you are getting and the fees that you will be paying as part of their registration requirements).

Notes

1. **Charges for care services at home**
   1. s17 HASSASSAA 1983
   2. *Fairer Charging Policies for Home Care and other non-residential Social Services*, DH 2001
   3. LAC 2001(1); CC(DD)(QS)(E) Regs
   4. NAfWC 05/02; NAWC 43/02
   5. CC(DD)(QS)(E) Regs
   6. CCD 2/2001
   7. s27 MH(CT)(S)A 2003
   8. MH(CT)(S)A 2003 and SWSG 1/97
   9. *See also* CCD 4/02 which gives guidance on the implementation of free personal care
   10. Guidance on charging policies for non-residential services that enable older people to remain in their own home; COSLA 2002
   11. CCD 2/2001
   12. s17(1) HASSASSAA 1983; s87(1A)(6) SW(S)A 1968, this was inserted by s18 HASSASSAA 1983
   13. s17(3) HASSASSAA 1983; s87 SW(S)A 1968
   14. *Fairer Charging Policies for Home Care and other non-residential Social Services,* DH 2001; LAC (2001) 32
   15. NAfWC 17/03; NAfWC 10/04
   16. *Avon CC v Hooper* (CCLR), September 1998
   17. *R v Powys CC ex parte Hambidge (2)* (CCLR), September 1999
   18. *R v Coventry City Council ex parte Carton and Others*, QBD(Admin), CCLR, March 2001

●●●

19 para 59 *Fairer Charging Policies for home
    care and other non-residential Social
    Services*, DH 2001
20 LGOR 99/C/1983 Durham City Council
21 *R(Spink) v Wandsworth LBC* [2005],
    EWCA Civ 302
22 para 25 *Fairer Charging Policies for home
    care and other non-residential social
    services*, DH 2001
23 NAfWC 17/03; NAfWC 10/04
24 *R v Coventry City Council ex parte Carton
    and Others*, QBD(Admin), CCLR, March
    2001
25 LAC(2003) 32; NAfWC 32/03
26 Para 41 *Fairer Charging Policies for home
    care and other non-residential social
    services* and see also practice guidance
    available at www.dh.gov.uk.
27 *R (on the application of Evelyn
    Stephenson) v Stockton-on-Tees BC*, CA,
    26 July 2005
28 *Guidance on charging policies for non-
    residential services that enable older
    people to remain in their own home*;
    COSLA 2002
29 DKT/1/16/21
30 SWSG 1/97
31 The Local Government Association has
    produced a *Good Practice Guide for
    Discretionary Charges*
32 LGOR 99/C/1983 Durham City Council
33 s17(4) HASSASSAA 1983; s87 SW(S)A
    1968

2. **Charges for housing support services**

34 Q85 *Fair Access to Care Practice Guidance*

Chapter 5

Financial assistance for services at home

This chapter covers:
1. Direct payments and 'personal budgets' from adult social care services (below)
2. The Independent Living Funds (p73)
3. Special funds for sick and disabled people (p76)
4. Health benefits (p65)
5. Housing grants in England and Wales (p82)
6. Housing grants in Scotland (p86)
7. Transport concessions for disabled people (p87)
8. Charities (p89)

1. Direct payments and 'personal budgets' from adult social care services

Instead of having the services you need provided or arranged by adult social care services, you can choose to have a 'direct payment'. This means that adult social care services pays you an amount of money equivalent to the amount it would have cost to provide the service, so that you can choose how best to meet your needs. It is also possible to have some services provided by adult social care services and some which you buy using your direct payment.[1] The Green Paper on adult social care proposes increased use of direct payments and, by 2012, individual budgets for care services to increase service users' choice and control over their care.

Who can get a direct payment?

Once you have been assessed as needing community care services, you can get a direct payment if you are:
- 16 or over;
- a 'disabled person' (see p19) or in Scotland any person aged 65 or over who requires community care services;

5

Chapter 5: Financial assistance for services at home
1. Direct payments and 'personal budgets' from adult social care services

- a carer (which includes parents of a disabled child) for whom the local authority has decided to provide services.[2] The ability to make direct payments to carers only applies in England and Wales. In Scotland, carers do not receive services in their own right (as they are considered to be partners in care rather than service users), therefore they will not normally receive direct payments. Local authorities in Scotland have a duty to offer direct payments to parents of disabled children to purchase services their children require;
- an attorney or guardian (see p257) in Scotland (only) who can set up, alter and receive direct payments on someone's behalf.[3] Amendments to the existing direct payments regulations under the Health and Social Care Act 2008 will enable direct payments to be made to a 'suitable person' on behalf of a person who lacks capacity from 2009. The Act seeks to ensure that those lacking capacity are not excluded from the options available to others, including direct payments;
- willing to manage your direct payment;
- able to manage your direct payment either by yourself or with assistance[4] (although note above the different provisions in Scotland). In England this could be a 'nominee'.

The High Court has decided that it is lawful to pay an independent trust that has been set up for the service user. In this case an independent trust had been set up comprising trustees who are the parents of the disabled person, representatives of a disability organisation and the local authority. The Court held that this fell within the meaning of a 'voluntary organisation' within the terms of the legislation and so it was lawful for the local authority to pay the trust to provide the services needed.[5]

If your liberty to arrange your care is restricted by certain mental health or criminal justice legislation, you cannot receive direct payments. This will apply if you are:
- on leave of absence from hospital under mental health legislation;
- conditionally discharged but subject to restrictions under criminal justice legislation;
- subject to guardianship or supervised discharge under mental health legislation;
- receiving any form of aftercare under a compulsory court order;
- under a probation order or you have been conditionally released on licence with a requirement to undergo treatment for a mental health condition, or for drug or alcohol dependency.

Guidance stresses that adult social care services should consider what assistance would enable a prospective direct payment user to manage, rather than assuming the person cannot manage. This is particularly important if the person has a learning disability, and may be able to manage with some help. It suggests that

Chapter 5: Financial assistance for services at home
1. Direct payments and 'personal budgets' from adult social care services

5

someone with a fluctuating condition may be able to manage if there is greater assistance during the time when the condition has worsened. The guidance also suggests that if you receive a direct payment and have expressed a preference for this to continue when setting up an enduring power of attorney then it can continue.[6]

Adult social care services are required to offer you direct payments if you meet the requirements set out above. If you are not offered a direct payment or it seems adult social care services are restricting those it offers them to on grounds other than those above, this may be grounds for a complaint.

There are guidance and regulations covering direct payments paid to carers under the Carers and Disabled Children Act 2000.[7] Carers in England also receive vouchers for short-term breaks.[8] Vouchers have also been piloted in Wales.

What a direct payment cannot be used for

Direct payments cannot be used to pay:
- your partner living in the same house;
- a close relative, or her/his partner, if s/he lives in the same house as you (close relative has the same meaning as for benefit purposes – see p151).[9]

  In England and Wales, if the authority is satisfied that securing the services from a partner or close relative, regardless of where s/he lives, is necessary to meet your need, then the above restrictions do not apply.[10] In Scotland, authorities can, in exceptional circumstances, make payments to close relatives who live elsewhere or non-relative members of the same household;
- for residential accommodation for any period of more than four weeks in a 12-month period. Within this time, periods of less than four weeks separated by periods of more than four weeks will not be added together;[11]
- for purchasing services from adult social care services in England and Wales. In Scotland, you can purchase services from the local authority.[12] Personal budgets in the form of a direct payment cannot be used to purchase services from the local authority but a 'virtual' personal budget (where no money is transferred to you from the council but the money still exists in a virtual personal budget for you to meet your care needs) can be used to purchase services from the local authority.

The level of your direct payment

The direct payment should not normally be more than it would have cost adult social care services to provide (or arrange) the service itself. It should be enough for you to cover all the legal costs of being an employer – ie, national insurance contributions, annual leave, sick pay, employers' liability insurance. If circumstances warrant it, adult social care services should be prepared to go above the cost they normally incur in providing the same services.

5

Chapter 5: Financial assistance for services at home
1. Direct payments and 'personal budgets' from adult social care services

If you manage to buy services more cheaply than expected, your direct payment may be reduced to that level rather than allowing you to use what is left over to buy in other services that are not specified in your care plan.

Any charges you would have had to pay if you had been receiving services from the authority are normally be deducted from direct payments. It is possible, however, for the payment to be made in full and for you to pay any required charges back.

Monitoring and support

Adult social care services have to monitor the direct payment to make sure you do not misuse it and that your needs are being adequately met. Money can be recovered if it has not been used for the services for which it was paid, or if you have not kept to conditions that may have been imposed.[13] Honest mistakes should not be penalised.

When setting up direct payment schemes, adult social care services should ensure there is a support group to provide appropriate information, advice, training and peer support. Such groups often produce leaflets about recruiting someone to care for you (often known as personal assistants), dealing with the administration of the direct payment, being a good employer, and dealing with emergencies. Ask adult social care services or the National Centre for Independent Living (see Appendix 1) to put you in touch with a local support group.

Putting People First

Putting People First introduces the concept of 'personal budgets' and is a joint initiative from central government, local government, the NHS and various partners. The intention is to have one large community-based care system for those who are eligible for council services. Different funding streams will be drawn together to produce one large support system and these may include: disabled facilities grants, welfare benefits, social care, independent living fund etc. A local authority circular[14] sets out how the Government intends to support local authorities to deliver this by changing current service provision models.

If you are eligible for council services (ie, you have capital under the upper limit and have eligible care needs) you can have a **'personal budget'** in the form of a direct payment if you choose to. The amount of money in this budget will depend on the resource allocation calculation carried out by the council in accordance with your assessed care needs. In theory, you should be able to use your personal budget to purchase a wider range and type of services than was previously available, as long as it is legal and meets your care needs. Over 6,000 people have a 'personal budget' at the time of writing and this will grow over the next few years.

2. The Independent Living Fund

The Independent Living Fund makes cash payments to you so you can employ carers to help you live independently in your own home. This is a government funded, independent and discretionary trust fund managed by a Board of Trustees. Awards are discretionary, but the trustees must follow basic eligibility criteria and guidelines.

The Independent Living Fund (2006) replaced the Independent Living (Extension) Fund and the Independent Living (1993) Fund in October 2007.[15] The new fund has two groups of users:

- former Extension Fund users. This maintains the pre-1993 system and no new applications are accepted. The maximum award payable is £785 a week. If you go into a care home or hospital, your payments may be suspended. However, if you employ a carer a retainer may be paid for up to four weeks.
- former 1993 Fund users and new applicants. The Fund works in partnership with adult social care services to devise 'joint care packages' combining services and/or direct payments from adult social care services (see p69) with cash payments from the Fund. The Fund then arranges for one of its own social workers to discuss your care needs with you and negotiate an appropriate joint care package (and provide advice and assistance with meeting the duties you will have as an employer of your carers). The maximum payment is £455 a week.

To be eligible for help from the Independent Living Fund (2006) you must be:

- so severely disabled that you need help with personal care or household duties to maintain an independent life in the community; *and*
- living alone or with people who are unable to fully meet your care needs. No payments will be made in respect of paying a partner or close relative who lives with you but payment may be made to those who do not. In such cases, your carer may also be able to claim carer's allowance for looking after you, although this means that your contribution may be reduced if you are no longer entitled to the severe disability premium; *and*
- be at least 16 and apply before your 65th birthday; *and*
- be receiving the higher rate care component of disability living allowance (DLA – see p121); *and*
- have less than £23,000 in savings including the savings of your partner; *and*
- be receiving direct payments or services costing at least £320 a week (after any charge you pay for them) from adult social care services. The cost to adult social care services for providing home care, day centre care, supervision, regular respite care and meals on wheels, for example, *less* any charge you pay for such services, will count towards the £320, but capital or running costs of any equipment, social work salaries, services provided by the NHS and

childcare costs, for example, do not count. The costs of any services provided under the Supporting People programme (see p52) also do not count;[16] *and*

- expect that the cost, to the Fund and adult social care services together, of meeting your support needs for the first six months will be less than £785 a week; *and*
- have care needs that are generally stable and will be met by the joint care package for the following six months.

This last condition means that some terminally ill people may not qualify. The requirement that you must be getting DLA may cause practical problems if there is any delay in processing your claim as no retrospective awards are ever paid and adult social care services may be reluctant to arrange care packages costing over £320. Applications can be accepted where DLA or attendance allowance has been awarded under 'special rules'. It may also cause practical problems if your award is terminated or reduced. Although the Fund will continue to make payments provided you are seeking a review of or appealing against the decision to stop or reduce your benefit until any appeal has run its course, you are still expected to pay your contribution to the care package based on the award of DLA you will no longer have (see below).

You do not have to be receiving income support (IS) to qualify for assistance from the Fund but your income (and that of your partner) will affect how much you have to contribute towards the cost of your care.

In April 2008, the Fund introduced budgetary measures and applications are being prioritised. Priority is being given to:

- existing users already receiving payments; *and then*
- new applicants working or self-employed for at least 16 hours a week provided the eligibility rules (see above) are met; *and then*
- new applicants with a total care package which is expected to be at least the minimum package cost (currently £500) and getting IS, PC guarantee credit, income-based JSA, income-related ESA, or have an income at a similar level even if you do not receive benefit.

Contributions toward your Independent Living Fund payments

If you meet the eligibility criteria, you will usually be expected to make a contribution to the fund towards the cost of your care. It will be half of your DLA care component plus all your severe disability premium if it is payable with any IS/JSA/ESA you receive (see p151). The guarantee credit of PC is treated in the same way. If you do not get IS/JSA/ESA/PC you are expected to contribute any income in excess of the amount you would get if you did qualify. However, earnings of either you or your partner are disregarded. If you do have other excess income, the calculations are based on IS rates, except that most housing costs (including all mortgage payments and endowments or rent, and council tax and water rates liabilities) and child support maintenance payments are usually allowed. Tariff income is assumed on capital above £13,500. The Fund will also usually refuse to become involved if a substantial sum is held in a trust fund for you. However, there is discretion to ignore capital which is intended for imminent major purchases, and in line with IS/JSA/ESA/PC capital from lump sum payments for CJD, vaccine damage and former Far Eastern prisoners of war are disregarded (see p209).

If you are paying charges to adult social care services for care they provide, this may also be taken into account. This means that if adult social care services expect you to contribute all or part of your award of DLA and/or severe disability premium, the Fund may treat this amount as already being used towards the cost of care and the assessed Fund charge may be reduced accordingly.

If your needs change

If there is a significant change in your circumstances the Fund will reassess, and may increase, your award if appropriate and if there are sufficient funds in its budget. The Fund will not, however, increase its own contribution if the change is due to any reduction in care provided by adult social care services or to a new or increased charge payable to it for its services.

If any services provided by adult social care services in respect of your increased needs are subject to a charge; the Fund may offset this charge from any contribution you would otherwise be expected to make.

Awards are suspended if you go into hospital or a care home. However, if you privately employ a carer or personal assistant, you can apply for an appropriate retainer to be paid for up to four weeks to avoid potential disruption of care. Your case is kept open for 13 weeks (or up to 26 weeks at the Fund's discretion) and payments are reinstated if you return home within that time.

For more details contact your adult social care department or the Independent Living Fund (see Appendix 1 and www.ilf.org.uk).

3. Special funds for sick and disabled adults

The Macfarlane and Eileen Trusts

The Macfarlane Trust, the Macfarlane (Special Payments) Trust and the Macfarlane (Special Payments) (No.2) Trust make payments to haemophiliacs who contract HIV through blood transfusions or tissue transplants.

The Macfarlane Trust also administers the Eileen Trust which helps people infected with HIV through NHS blood transfusions or transplants.

For further information visit www.macfarlane.org.uk or contact the Macfarlane Trust, PO Box 627, London SW1H OQG (tel: 020 7233 0342).

The Skipton Fund

The Skipton Fund makes payments to certain people who were infected with Hepatitis C through NHS blood or blood products prior to September 1991 and other eligible people. For further information, visit www.skiptonfund.org or call 0207 808 1160.

4. Health benefits

This section deals with the following areas of provision under the NHS:
* prescriptions;
* dental treatment and dentures;
* sight tests;
* glasses;
* wigs and fabric supports;
* fares to hospital.

Although the NHS generally provides free health care, there are charges for the items listed above. You are exempt from these charges, however, if:
* you, or a member of your family, are receiving income support (IS – see p147), income-based jobseeker's allowance (JSA – see p158), income-related employment and support allowance (ESA – see p156) or the guarantee credit of pension credit (PC – see p158); *or*
* you, or a member of your family, have an annual income of £15,050 (£15,276 in England, other than for sight tests) or less (for tax credit purposes) and get:
  – both working tax credit (WTC) and child tax credit (CTC); *or*
  – WTC with a disability element paid in it; *or*
  – CTC but are not eligible for WTC as you work less than 16 hours;
* you have an NHS tax credit exemption certificate; *or*
* you are a permanent resident in a care home and adult social care services are assisting you with the costs of your accommodation (if you are not receiving adult social care services funding, you may get help under the low income scheme – see p79); *or*
* you are under 16; *or*
* you are under 19 and in full-time education; *or*
* you are a war disablement pensioner and you need the item or service because of your war disability; *or*
* you, or a member of your family, are an asylum seeker (or the dependant of one) who is receiving asylum support; *or*
* you are aged 16 or 17 and receiving support from a local authority after being in local authority care; *or*
* your income is low enough (see p79).

You may also be exempt from some charges because of your age or health condition. If you are not exempt on any of the above grounds, you may be entitled to remission of charges under the low income scheme (see p79).

Prescriptions

Prescriptions are free in Wales (in Scotland it is proposed that free prescriptions will be available from 2011 and charges are being phased down yearly). Otherwise you qualify for free prescriptions if you:[17]

- are in one of the exempt groups listed on p76; *or*
- are aged 60 or over; *or*
- are pregnant or have a child under the age of 1; *or*
- have one or more of the following conditions:
  - a continuing physical disability which prevents you leaving your home except with the help of another person;
  - epilepsy, requiring continuous anti-convulsive therapy;
  - a permanent fistula, including a caecostomy, ileostomy, laryngostomy or colostomy, needing continuous surgical dressing or an appliance;
  - diabetes mellitus (except where treatment is by diet alone);
  - diabetes insipidus and other forms of hypopituitarism;
  - myxoedema, hypoparathyroidism or myasthenia gravis;
  - forms of hypoadrenalism (including Addison's disease) for which specific substitution therapy is required.
  - (in England, from 1 April 2009) cancer for which you are undergoing treatment.[18]

If you are diagnosed with one of these conditions you need to get a form FP92(A) in England or EC92(A) in Scotland, from your GP or hospital to get your exemption certificate.

If you do not qualify for free prescriptions, and you need more than three prescription items in three months (four months in Scotland) or 14 items in a year (10 in Scotland), you can save money by buying a pre-payment certificate. You apply for a certificate on Form FP95 in England or EC95 in Scotland, which you can get from chemists, some doctors' surgeries and relevant health bodies. In England, you can also apply using a credit or debit card on 0845 850 0030 or via the Prescription Pricing Division website at www.ppa.nhs.uk. You can also pay in monthly instalments by direct debit. A refund can be claimed in certain circumstances – eg, if you buy a pre-payment certificate and then qualify for free prescriptions.

Dental treatment and dentures

You qualify for free NHS dental treatment (including check-ups) and appliances (including dentures) if you are:

- in one of the exempt groups listed on p76; *or*
- aged under 18 (in Wales, for an examination only, you are aged under 25 or over 60); *or*
- pregnant or have a child under the age of 1.

Sight tests

Sight tests are free in Scotland. Otherwise you qualify for a free NHS sight test if you:[19]
- are in one of the exempt groups listed on p76; *or*
- you qualify under the low income scheme (see p79); *or*
- are aged 60 or over; *or*
- are registered blind or partially sighted; *or*
- have been prescribed complex or powerful lenses; *or*
- have diabetes or glaucoma or are at risk of getting glaucoma; *or*
- are aged 40 or over and are the parent, brother, sister or child of someone with glaucoma; *or*
- are a patient of the Hospital Eye Service; *or*
- in England, you are on leave from prison or a young offender institution.

If you cannot get to the opticians for a sight test you may be able to arrange for an optician to visit you at home. If you are entitled to a free NHS sight test, you will not have to pay for the visit.

Glasses

You qualify for a voucher which you can use to buy or repair glasses or contact lenses if you:[20]
- are in one of the exempt groups listed on p76; *or*
- are a Hospital Eye Service patient needing frequent changes of glasses or lenses; *or*
- qualify under the low income scheme (see p79);
- have been prescribed complex or powerful lenses;
- in England, are on leave from prison or a young offender institution.

You must need these for the first time or because they have worn out through fair wear and tear, or your new prescription must differ from your old one.

Wigs and fabric supports

You qualify for free wigs and fabric supports if:
- you are in one of the exempt groups listed on p76; *or*
- you are a hospital inpatient when the wig or fabric support is supplied.

Fares to hospital and other medical establishments

You qualify for help with your fares to hospital and other NHS establishments if you:[21]
* are in one of the groups exempt from charges under the rules set out on p76; *or*
* qualify under the low income scheme (see below);
* live in the Isles of Scilly or the Scottish Islands or Highlands and have to travel more than a specified distance for hospital treatment.

You are entitled to payment for the cost of travelling by the cheapest means of transport available and, in Scotland, overnight accommodation where necessary. This usually means standard class public transport. If public transport is available but you go by car or taxi, fuel costs to the value of standard class travel should be paid. If you cannot use public transport due to your disability or if it is not available, your fuel costs or taxi fare will be covered. The travel expenses of a companion can also be met if you need to be accompanied for a medical reason.[22]

You can get help to pay for fares to NHS establishments (not just a hospital) if a referral is made by a doctor or a dentist as well as a consultant.[23] However, you are not eligible if it is for primary care medical or dental treatment or if the appointment is in the same visit to or the same building as the person making the referral.

In England and Wales, if you are travelling abroad to receive NHS treatment, you are entitled to payment for the cost of travel to and from the airport, ferry port or international train station if you are in one of the above groups. You are also entitled to payment or repayment of onward travelling expenses to the treatment centre, whether or not you fall within one of the above groups. The amount and mode of transport is determined prior to travel by your health authority).

You should claim at the hospital or establishment. You may be able to request payment in advance of travelling, where this is necessary or, alternatively, you could apply for a social fund crisis loan from the DWP (see p188). If you are receiving IS, income-based JSA, income-related ESA or the guarantee or savings credit of PC and are visiting a close relative or partner, you may be eligible for a social fund community care grant to help with your fares (see p185).

The low income scheme

You may be entitled to full or partial help with NHS charges under the low income scheme if you are not already exempt on other grounds.

To qualify for help under the low income scheme you must have less than £16,000 capital. If you live in a care home and are not receiving adult social care services funding (and so entitlement to full help), you may be entitled to help under the low income scheme based on the capital limits in the country in which you live (£23,000 in England, £22,000 in Wales and £22,500 in Scotland) (see p291). See Chapter 12 for details of how your capital is calculated. A calculation is then carried out to compare your 'income' with your 'requirements' (see below). If your income is less than your requirements, you are exempt from health charges. If your income exceeds your requirements, the amount of your excess income determines how much help you get with health charges.

Income

Your income is calculated in the same way as for IS (see Chapter 8) except that:
- your income is normally only taken into account in the week in which it is paid;
- regular maintenance payments count as weekly income and irregular payments are averaged over the 13 weeks prior to your claim;
- insurance policy payments for housing costs not met by IS count as income but payments for unsecured loans for repairs and improvements (including premiums) are ignored;
- the capital limit for tariff income (see p216) is based on the lower capital limit of the country where you live (see p291) if you are permanently in a care home;
- student loans are divided by 52, unless you are in your final year or doing a one-year course, in which case the loan is divided by the number of weeks you are studying (a £10 disregard from loans applies if you are eligible for a premium or you receive an allowance for deafness);
- the savings credit of PC is ignored.

Requirements

Your requirements are the same as your IS applicable amount would be (see p151) except that:
- you are entitled to normal allowances, whatever your immigration status is;
- the disability premium (see p152) is included after 28 (instead of 52) weeks of incapacity;
- your housing costs include interest and capital payments on all loans secured on your home, any loans to adapt your home for the needs of a disabled person, any council tax liabilities (less council tax benefit), and any rent (less housing benefit). Deductions are made in respect of any non-dependants (see p169).

Excess income

Your '**excess income**' is the difference between your income and your requirements.
- The amount of help you can claim for hospital fares is reduced by the amount of your excess income.
- The cost of a sight test is reduced to the amount of your excess income if lower, plus the amount by which the cost exceeds the NHS sight test fee.

- The value of a voucher for glasses or lenses is reduced by twice your excess income.
- Charges for dental treatment and for wigs and fabric supports which are higher than three times your excess income are remitted.
- You cannot get partial remission of charges for prescriptions.

Claiming health care costs

- If you are exempt because of **age or receipt of a qualifying benefit**, you need to complete the declaration on the back of the prescription form, or complete a form provided by your dentist, optician or hospital receptionist before you receive treatment.
- If you are exempt because you **receive tax credits** (see p175), you should be sent an exemption certificate (normally valid for up to 15 months) automatically.
- To claim **free prescriptions** because you have a prescribed condition, you should apply for an exemption certificate (see p77).
- If you are **pregnant**, or have a **child under 1**, you should apply for an exemption certificate on form FW8, obtainable from your doctor, midwife or health visitor.
- For free treatment for **war pensioners** contact the Service Personnel and Veterans Agency for details (tel: 0800 169 2277).
- If you are an **asylum seeker** receiving asylum support, a certificate is issued by the Border and Immigration Agency. If you have queries, telephone 0845 602 1739. Certificates last for six months from the date of claim.
- To apply for help with charges under the **low income scheme**, you need to complete form HC1. You can get this from Jobcentre Plus offices or NHS establishments. You can also request a form at www.ppa.nhs.uk. If you live in a care home, you can use a special short form HC1(SC). If you qualify for free services you will be sent a certificate HC2. If you qualify for partial help you will be sent certificate HC3 which tells you what your contribution towards the charges is. Another person can apply on your behalf if you are unable to act for yourself. Certificates are normally valid for a year.[24]

If you pay a charge for an item or service which you could have obtained free or at reduced cost, you can obtain a **refund** by applying within three months or longer if you have good reasons – eg, you were ill. Apply for a refund of a prescription charge on Form FP57 (EC57 in Scotland), which you must obtain when you pay as one cannot be supplied later. For other items and services, apply for a refund on Form HC5. You can get the forms by telephoning 0845 850 1166, or from a Jobcentre Plus office or NHS establishment. You must submit a receipt or other documents to show that you have paid the charge. If you need an HC2 or HC3 certificate and have not applied for one, you should also send a Form HC1 with your application for a refund.

Health care equipment

Health care equipment such as special footwear, leg appliances, wigs, surgical supports, wheelchairs, incontinence pads, hearing aids and low vision aids can be provided by health authorities, hospitals and GPs, either free of charge or on prescription.

---

5. **Housing grants in England and Wales**

This section briefly covers the availability of housing grants in England and Wales. A similar system exists in Northern Ireland. See p86 for grants in Scotland.

Local authorities in England and Wales have the power to determine their own policies and procedures to improve living conditions in their areas. Assistance can be given in the form of a grant, loan, materials, labour or advice (or any combination of these). Each local authority must adopt and publish a local policy.[25] Contact your local housing department to find out what is available in your area.

Disabled facilities grants

The disabled facilities grant (DFG) is the only mandatory grant which local authorities have a duty to make available. It is available to help with the costs of adapting a property (including some mobile homes and houseboats) for the needs of a disabled person. It also covers common parts of a building (eg, a staircase) containing one or more flats and access to gardens.

You can apply for a DFG if you are:[26]
- an owner occupier; *or*
- a private tenant; *or*
- a local authority tenant – check first if the council will carry out the work under it's own adaptations programme; *or*
- a landlord with a disabled tenant; *or*
- a housing association tenant.

You are treated as disabled if:[27]
- your sight, hearing or speech is substantially impaired; *or*
- you have a mental disorder or impairment; *or*
- you are physically substantially disabled by illness, injury, or impairment present since birth, or otherwise; *or*

- you are registered (or could be registered) as disabled with adult social care services. If you are not registered disabled an occupational therapist or disablement assessment officer will usually assess your needs.

Grants of up to a maximum of £30,000 in England and Wales can be awarded for:[28]
- facilitating disabled access to and from a dwelling or a room and garden;
- provision of a bedroom, toilet, bathroom, shower or wash basins;
- making a dwelling safe;
- facilitating a disabled occupant's use of a source of power, light or heat, or food preparation facilities;
- improving or providing a suitable heating system; *or*
- facilitating access and movement around the home to enable the disabled occupant to care for someone dependent on them who also lives there.

The means test is similar to that which applies to housing benefit (HB – see p163) or, if you are over 60 pension credit (PC), except that:
- there are no non-dependant deductions;
- the applicable amount is increased by £56.40 (the means test for disabled children has been abolished – the DFG for children is now free);
- if you are on income support (IS), income-based jobseeker's allowance (JSA), income-related employment and support allowance (ESA) or the guarantee credit of PC the applicable amount is automatically £1 and your income and capital are disregarded, giving a zero contribution;
- there is no maximum capital limit and the first £6,000 is disregarded (with tariff income applying on capital above this);
- if you are disabled or a carer, the earnings disregard is £20;
- there is a system of stepped tapers on excess income which is used to calculate how much you would be able to repay on a notional loan to pay for the work over a period of 10 years for owner-occupiers and five years for tenants. The national means test does not apply to applications from landlords;
- working tax credit and child tax credit are disregarded as income;[29]
- if you are on HB, council tax benefit (CTB) or tax credits due to low income, you will be fast tracked through the means test and not be required to provide any further information.[30]

Applications should be made to your local housing department, which must then consult with adult social care services. In practice, people are commonly referred first to adult social care services who then arranges for an occupational therapy assessment. Your application must be supported by a certificate stating that you intend to live in the property for at least five years after the work is completed or a shorter time if there are health or other special reasons.[31] Applications should be determined within six months and if approved, the work should normally be carried out within one year.[32] Housing departments have a discretion to approve a grant but stipulate that it will not be paid for up to a year after the application was made, and may revise their decision if your circumstances change before the works are completed.

If you do not get a decision within six months of applying, contact the housing department to determine why and request that a decision be made. Seek advice if you still do not get a decision (see Appendix 2).

From April 2008 in England, if your DFG exceeds £5,000 your local authority may place a charge against your property.[33] The maximum charge is £10,000 and would apply for 10 years – ie, if you sold the property within 10 years the value of the charge would be repayable. This charge is discretionary and should be determined on a case-by-case basis.

Warm Front grants in England

The 'Warm Front' scheme offers grants for improvements in energy efficiency and heating systems to owner-occupiers and tenants in England.[34]

You can qualify for a 'Warm Front' grant of up to £2,700 (£4,000 if oil central heating is installed or repaired) if you or your partner:

- are aged 60 or over and in receipt of any of the following benefits:
  - PC or IS;
  - income-based JSA;
  - income-related ESA;
  - HB;
  - council tax benefit (CTB);
- have a child under 16 or are at least 26 weeks pregnant (and have a MAT B1 certificate) and are receiving any of the following benefits:
  - IS or PC;
  - HB;
  - CTB;
  - income-related ESA;
  - income-based JSA;
- own or privately rent your home and receive one or more of the following benefits:
  - WTC (with a household income less than £15,460 a year, this must include a disability element);
  - CTC (with a household income less than £15,460 a year);
  - disability living allowance (DLA);
  - attendance allowance (AA);
  - IS (which must include a disability premium);
  - HB (which must include a disability premium);
  - CTB (which must include a disability premium);
  - war disablement pension (which must include the mobility supplement or constant attendance allowance);

– industrial injuries disablement benefit (which must include constant attendance allowance).

For more details call freephone 0800 316 2805 or go to www.warmfront.co.uk.

Home Energy Efficiency Scheme in Wales

The Home Energy Efficiency Scheme (HEES) offers grants for improvements in insulation and heating systems to owner-occupiers and tenants in Wales.[35]

To qualify for a grant of up to £2,000 you must be pregnant (and have a MAT B1 certificate) or have children under 16 and getting one or more of the following:

* IS;
* WTC (with a household income less than £15,460 a year); *or*
* HB; *or*
* CTB; *or*
* CTC (with a household income less than £15,460 a year); *or*
* income-based JSA; *or*
* income-related ESA.

You can qualify for an **'HEES Plus'** grant of up to £3,600, if you are:

* 80 or over;
* 60 or over and receiving:
  – PC; *or*
  – CTB; *or*
  – HB; *or*
  – income-based JSA; *or*
  – income-related ESA.
  Note: if you are over 60 but not in receipt of qualifying benefits you may still be eligible for a grant of up to £500 towards energy efficiency measures;
* a lone parent with a child under 16 who is getting:
  – PC or IS; *or*
  – CTB; *or*
  – HB; *or*
  – income-based JSA; *or*
  – income-related ESA;
* disabled or chronically sick and receiving:
  – IS (which must include a disability premium); *or*
  – WTC (which must include a disability premium); *or*
  – HB (which must include a disability premium); *or*
  – CTB (which must include a disability premium); *or*
  – AA; *or*
  – DLA; *or*

- war disablement pension (which must include the mobility supplement or constant attendance allowance); *or*
- industrial injuries disablement benefit (which must include constant attendance allowance).

For more details, call freephone 0800 316 2815 or visit www.heeswales.co.uk.

6. Housing grants in Scotland

Improvement and repairs

The Housing (Scotland) Act 2006 provides for a new scheme of assistance for housing repairs and improvements. The aim is to give householders access to a wider range of advice, information, practical assistance and financial assistance (eg, grants, loans and subsidised loans) to help with repairs and improvements to their homes, and to make properties suitable for occupants with disabilities.

Contact your local authority to find out when the new powers will be implemented in your area. When it starts to implement the new powers, your council will publish its 'Scheme of Assistance' setting out how it will help householders in your area.

Improvement grants for people with disabilities

If you are registered disabled, or could be registered disabled, you have a right to an assessment of your needs by the social work department, including your needs for 'adaptations to your home, or equipment for your use for your greater safety, comfort or convenience'.[36] Following assessment, the social work department should either provide what is needed or provide assistance, including financial assistance to help with the cost of the adaptation. The housing department may offer a discretionary improvement grant towards the costs of the works.[37] The grant may cover:
- alteration or enlargement; *or*
- making the house suitable for your accommodation, welfare or employment.

Mandatory grants are available to all households for the provision of standard amenities. Even if the house already has one of these amenities, you may still be entitled to a grant for another if this is essential to her/his needs – eg, a further toilet on the ground floor.

Financial assistance from the social work department is separate from and can be paid in addition to any improvement grant for adaptation.[38]

For further details contact your local council housing and social work departments.

The Energy Assistance Package

From April 2009, the Energy Assistance Package will replace the Central Heating and Warm Deal programmes. It is an holistic package to help maximise incomes, reduce fuel bills and improve the energy efficiency of homes. The package has four stages.

- **Stage 1** – an initial energy audit available to anyone who phones the Energy Savings Scotland Advice Centre (0800 512 012). Those at risk of fuel poverty continue to Stage 2.
- **Stage 2** – help with improving incomes and reducing energy bills.
- **Stage 3** – a package of standard insulation measures (eg, cavity wall and loft insulation), as part of the energy companies' obligation under the carbon emission reduction target.
- **Stage 4** – more enhanced energy efficiency measures (eg, heating systems and insulation measures for hard to insulate homes).

7. **Transport concessions for disabled people**

In addition to any help with travel costs which you may be entitled to from adult social care services (see Chapter 2) or from the social fund (see p182) or from the NHS (see p79), you may also be entitled to:

- help under the Motability scheme;
- road tax exemption;
- blue badge parking concessions;
- disabled person's railcard concessions.

Motability

Motability is a registered charity that runs a scheme to help you lease or buy a car if you receive the higher rate mobility component of disability living allowance (DLA) or war pensioner's mobility supplement for a period of 12 months or more.

DLA mobility is paid direct to Motability.[39] You may also have to make a down payment on the cost of an expensive car and further payments may be necessary if you drive more than 12,000 miles a year. For information, visit www.motability.co.uk or call 01279 635 666. Motability produces leaflets on its schemes for car leasing and hire purchase of new/used cars and powered wheelchairs/scooters.

Road tax exemption

If you get the higher rate mobility component of DLA (or war pensioner's mobility supplement) you are also entitled to exemption from road tax (vehicle excise duty) for one car if it is being used solely by you or for your benefit. Contact the

Disability Contact and Processing Unit (see Appendix 1) for an application form. Road tax exemption cannot be backdated even if there is a delay in processing your claim for benefit.

Blue badge parking concessions

The blue badge scheme[40] provides parking concessions for disabled people (or people who are driving them) to park (either in specially reserved parking bays or in other restricted parking areas) near shops, public buildings and other places, usually for extended periods and without charge. The scheme applies throughout Great Britain and in the European Economic Area (with certain local variation).

You are entitled to a blue badge if you are over 2 years old and you:

- receive the higher rate mobility component of DLA (or war pensioner's mobility supplement); or
- are registered blind; or
- have a 'permanent and substantial disability which causes inability to walk or very considerable difficulty in walking'; or
- drive regularly and have a severe disability in both arms so that you cannot turn a steering wheel by hand (even if the wheel is fitted with a turning knob).

Contact your local authority for further information. Note that you may be charged up to £2 for a badge. If you are a blue badge holder, you can get 100 per cent discount on the congestion charge in London.[41]

Disabled Persons Railcard

The Disabled Persons Railcard entitles you (and an adult companion) to one-third off the cost of most train journeys. For details, see www.disabledpersons-railcard.co.uk or call 0845 605 0525 (0845 601 0132 textphone). Your local station may have details of other fare concessions offered by train operators and about assistance with access. You are entitled to the railcard if you:

- receive AA; or
- receive the middle or higher rate care component or higher rate mobility component of DLA (or war pensioner's mobility supplement); or
- receive severe disablement allowance; or
- receive 80 per cent or more war pension; or
- are registered as visually impaired or are deaf; or
- have recurrent attacks of epilepsy or cannot drive due to epilepsy; or
- are leasing or buying a car through the Motability scheme.

Other travel concessions

As well as the above concessions there are a number of other concessions for rail and bus travel, in particular for older people. Senior Railcards available to anyone

60 or over provide fare reductions for train travel (see www.senior-railcard.co.uk). All local authorities must offer free or reduced bus fares to people over 60. In Scotland, if you are over 60, you are entitled to free off-peak travel within the bounds of the local authority, although reciprocal arrangements mean cross boundary travel is possible. In Wales, bus travel within Wales is free for the over 60s and disabled people.

If you are disabled and cannot use public transport there are a number of locally operated door-to-door transport schemes. Contact you local council for more details.

8. Charities

There are hundreds of local and national charities that provide a wide range of help to people in need. Your local adult social care services may know of appropriate charities which may be able to assist you, or you can consult publications such as the *Guide to Grants for Individuals in Need* or the *Charities Digest* in your local library.

Notes

1. Direct payments from adult social care services
1. CCDPA 1996, s57 HSCA 2001; s7 CCH(S)A 2002
2. s5 CDCA 2000
3. s7 CCH(S)A 2002
4. Reg 2 CCSCCSDO(E) Regs
5. *R (And B, X and Y) v East Sussex CC*, CCLR, June 2003
6. *Direct Payments Guidance – Community Care, Services for Carers and Children's Services (Direct Payments) Guidance*, DH 2003
7. *Policy and Practice Guidance*, CDCA 2000; *Direct Payments for Young People*, 2000, DH; NAfW 2000; CCSCCS(DP)(E) Regs
8. CCSCCS(DP)(E) Regs
9. Reg 3 CCDP Regs
10. Reg 2 CCSCCS(DP)(E) Regs
11. Reg 4 CCDP Regs; reg 7 CCSCCS(DP)(E) Regs

12. CCD 4/2003
13. s2 CCDPA 1996; in England reg 9 CCSCCS(DP)(E) Regs

2. The Independent Living Fund
14. LAC(DH)(2008) 1
15. The Independent Living (2006) Fund Order 2007
16. ILF Newsletter January 2003

4. Health benefits
17. **E** Regs 7, 7A and 7B NHS(CDA) Reg and regs 4 and 5 NHS(TERC) Regs;
W NHS(FP&CDA)(W) Regs and regs 4 and 5 NHS(TERC)(W) Regs;
S Reg 7 NHS(CDA)(S) Regs and regs 3 and 4 NHS(TERC)(S) Regs
18. The National Health Service (Charges for Drugs and Appliances) Amendment Regulations 2009 SI No.29

19 **E** Reg 3 POS Regs and regs 3 and 8
NHS(OCP) Regs;
W Reg 13 NHS(GOS) Regs and regs 3
and 8 NHS(OCP) Regs
20 **E&W** Regs 8 and 9 NHS(OCP) Regs;
S Regs 8 and 9 NHS(OCP)(S) Regs
21 **E** Regs 3 and 5 NHS(TERC) Regs;
W Regs 3 and 5 NHS(TERC)(W) Regs;
S Regs 3 and 4NHS(TERC)(S) Regs
22 *Healthcare Travel Cost Scheme:
Instructions and guidance for the NHS,*
DH, October 2008
23 *Healthcare Travel Cost Scheme:
Instructions and guidance for the NHS,*
DH, October 2008
24 **E** Reg 8 NHS(TERC) Regs;
W Reg 8 NHS(TERC)(W) Regs;
S Reg 10 NHS(TERC)(S) Regs;

5. Housing grants in England and Wales
25 The Regulatory Reform (Housing
Assistance)(England and Wales) Order
2002
26 s19 HGCRA
27 s100 HGCRA
28 s23 HGCRA
29 *Lifetime Homes, Lifetime Neighbourhoods:
A National Strategy for Housing in an
Ageing Society,* Department for
Communities and Local Government,
DH and DWP February 2008
30 *Lifetime Homes, Lifetime Neighbourhoods:
A National Strategy for Housing in an
Ageing Society,* Department for
Communities and Local Government,
DH and DWP February 2008
31 ss21 and 22 HGCRA 1996
32 ss34 and 37 HGCRA 1996
33 *Lifetime Homes, Lifetime Neighbourhoods:
A National Strategy for Housing in an
Ageing Society,* Department for
Communities and Local Government,
DH and DWP February 2008
34 HEES(E) Regs
35 HEES(W) Regs

6. Housing grants in Scotland
36 s2 CSDPA 1970
37 H(S)A 1987 Part XIII
38 Scottish Office Circular SDD 40/1985

**7. Transport concessions for disabled
people**
39 Regs 44, 45 and 46 SS(C&P) Regs
40 DP(BMV) Regs 1982
41 www.tfl.gov.uk

Chapter 6

••

Claiming social security benefits and tax credits

This chapter covers:
1. The administration of benefits and tax credits (below)
2. Claims and decisions (p92)
3. Payments (p101)
4. Challenging decisions (p104)
5. Common problems (p111)

This chapter briefly explains the administration of the system of benefits and tax credits and covers general issues relating to making claims. For more details, see CPAG's *Welfare Benefits and Tax Credits Handbook* (see Appendix 3). If you need advice and assistance to make a claim or deal with a problem, see Appendix 2.

Chapter 7 sets out the rules for the individual benefits and tax credits you can claim.

1. The administration of benefits and tax credits

Department for Work and Pensions

Most social security benefits are administered and paid by the Department for Work and Pensions (DWP) via the following services.

- **Jobcentre Plus** deals with most benefits for people under the age of 60 through a network of local offices. The service is heavily 'work focused', in that most claimants are required to attend regular work-focused interviews (WFIs) aimed at helping them find work as a condition of claiming benefit. The service also acts as an employment agency, linking claimants with job vacancies. Disabled claimants can access specialised help to find work through disability employment advisers and job brokers (as part of the 'New Deal' for disabled people). The various New Deal programmes (lone parents, disabled people, young people, etc) are to be merged into a new Flexible New Deal from October 2009. Jobcentre Plus also manages the social fund.

- **The Pension Service** deals with most benefits for people aged 60 and over, including state retirement pension, pension credit and winter fuel payments, through regional offices (accessed by post and telephone) and a network of local personal access points.
- **The Disability and Carer's Service** deals with disability living allowance (DLA), attendance allowance (AA), carer's allowance (CA) and vaccine damage payments. AA and DLA are administered by a central office in Blackpool and regional disability centres (see Appendix 1). CA is administered by a central office in Preston.

Managerially, the Pension Service and the Disability and Carer's Service have been combined into a single organisation – the Pensions, Disability and Carers Service – but operationally, they remain distinct.

The DWP also runs the **Child Support Agency** (CSA) which administers the system for pursuing child maintenance from non-resident parents. The CSA is being wound-down and its functions are being taken over by a new **Child Maintenance and Enforcement Commission**.

Other benefit authorities

- **HM Revenue and Customs** ('the Revenue') deals with tax credits, national insurance contributions, child benefit, guardian's allowance and the health in pregnancy grant. It also has responsibility for resolving disputes over statutory employer-paid schemes (sickness, paternity, maternity, adoption).
- **Local authorities** (councils) administer and pay housing benefit (help with rent) and council tax benefit and discounts (help with council tax) as well as educational benefits such as free school meals and school uniform grants. However, educational maintenance allowances (up to £30 a week for people aged over 16 who stay on in education beyond Year 11) are the responsibility of the Learning and Skills Council.
- **The Service Personnel and Veterans Agency** (Ministry of Defence) is responsible for war pensions and compensation.

2. Claims and decisions

Who can claim

Chapter 7 sets out who is eligible to claim each benefit and tax credit.

If you are claiming a means-tested benefit (see Chapter 7) and you have a partner (see below):
- you must make a claim for both of you;
- in some cases, both of you will be eligible to be the claimant and you may be better off if one partner is the claimant rather than the other;

- you and your partner must make a 'joint claim' for jobseeker's allowance (JSA) if you do not have children.

If you are claiming tax credits (see Chapter 7), you and your partner must make a joint claim.

For means-tested benefits, **'partner'** means a husband or wife or civil partner with whom you are living in the same household, or another person aged 16 or over with whom you are living in the same household as if you were husband and wife or civil partners.[1]

Since 5 December 2005, two people of the same sex who share a household are treated as partners if they are registered as **'civil partners'**, or if they are living together as if they were 'civil partners'.[2]

Whether you are living together as partners in the same household depends on the details of your living arrangements – eg, how you pay bills, organise cooking and shopping, socialise, etc. 'Household' is not defined in the law but involves people living together in a domestic establishment that has some degree of independence and self-sufficiency. Seek advice if you disagree with any decision made by the benefit authorities about this (see Appendix 2).

For tax credits, **'partner'** means a spouse or registered civil partner (unless, in either case, you are separated under a court order, or likely to be permanently separated), or another person with whom you are living as if you were husband and wife or civil partners.[3]

Appointees

If you are 'unable for the time being to act' for yourself (eg, because of ill health or disability), someone else can be authorised by the benefit authorities to act as your 'appointee' and deal with your benefit claims on your behalf (unless someone has already been appointed by a court to look after your affairs).[4] Under the Mental Capacity Act 2005, you are deemed to be capable of handling your own affairs unless it can be shown otherwise and the fact that you may spend your money unwisely is not proof that you are incapable of handling your own affairs. Complain if you think an appointeeship has been granted or refused when it shouldn't have been.

Anyone aged 18 or over can be an appointee, including a partner, friend, relative, carer, solicitor, or in some cases an official from your local adult social care services. DWP guidance advises that owners or managers of care homes should only be made appointees as a last resort, if nobody else can be appointed (eg, a adult social care services official).[5] An appointee takes on all your rights and responsibilities as a claimant. S/he can claim benefits and receive payments on your behalf, must provide any evidence or information required in support of your claim, report any relevant changes in your circumstances, and may have to repay any benefit or tax credit which has been overpaid (see p113). Normally this will only apply from the date your appointment has been agreed, but if someone acts on your behalf before officially becoming your appointee, her/his actions can be retrospectively validated by the appointment.[6] Complying with the responsibilities of an appointee can sometimes cause problems because the appointee has no rights to obtain information from bank accounts and occupational schemes which may be needed as evidence in connection with benefit claims. An appointeeship does not give authority to spend the claimant's benefit income or capital, which, if it accumulates, may affect entitlement to means-tested benefits over a period of time.

In the past, it was common practice for a separate appointment to be required for each benefit administered by the DWP, but common rules now apply to all appointments and it is arguable that one appointment should cover all benefits. Local practice varies, however, and you should always clarify the scope of an appointment with the DWP. In some cases, you may only want an appointee to deal with some of your benefits and will need to negotiate clear and suitable arrangements with the DWP. A separate appointment is technically necessary for housing benefit (HB) and council tax benefit (CTB), but in practice the local authority will usually simply confirm an existing DWP appointment. If you are claiming tax credits, you will need to arrange a separate appointment with the Revenue.

Applications to become an appointee must be made in writing to the appropriate benefit authority (ie, the DWP, Revenue or local authority). The DWP will often arrange to visit both the claimant and the prospective appointee before deciding whether an appointment is appropriate, but some local offices are prepared to accept the opinion of adult social care services (eg, in a community care assessment) that a claimant is 'unable to act'.

An appointee is expected to give a month's written notice if s/he no longer wishes to act as appointee. An appointment can, however, be terminated at any time by the benefit authorities where, for example, they consider that it is no longer necessary, or no longer in the claimant's best interests, and someone else should be appointed instead – eg, another person or a social work department official).

If you are an appointee for a claimant who dies, you must re-apply to be an appointee in order to settle any outstanding benefit matters.[7] An executor under a will can also pursue an outstanding claim or appeal on behalf of a deceased claimant even if any decision on the claim in question was made before the formal grant of probate (confirmation in Scotland).[8]

Note that an appointee is different to an '**agent**', who is merely a person you authorise to cash or collect any payment of benefit for you.

For further information on the different options available to people who cannot manage their financial affairs, see p321.

Making a claim

In order to qualify for a benefit or tax credit, you must normally make a claim[9] for it in writing, usually on an appropriate form. In practise, however, many benefits can be claimed by telephone or online at www.dwp.gov.uk. For example, you can claim retirement pension and pension credit (PC) by telephone, and in addition, you will then be able to make a HB and CTB claim as well. Carer's allowance (CA), attendance allowance (AA) and disability living allowance (DLA) can all be claimed online.[10] Except for income support (IS) and jobseeker's allowance (JSA), any letter or other written communication may be accepted as a valid claim,[11] but in practice it is best to use the proper form if possible. Separate claims are normally required for each benefit. In a few cases, a claim for one benefit (eg, IS) can be treated as a claim for another benefit (eg, CA)[12] – see CPAG's *Welfare Benefits and Tax Credits Handbook* for the full list. Social fund applications are mainly made by phone as administration of social fund payments, even crisis loans, is carried out in regional centres not at the local DWP office.

Most claim forms should be available from your local DWP office (see p91). In some cases, claimants have had difficulty getting paper claim forms, allegedly because these claims don't get entered into the computer system in the same way that telephone claims are entered. That is not a reason for you to be denied one however, as paper claims are still valid and may be necessary – eg, if you are unable to use a phone to make a claim or need assistance in providing certain information.

Claim forms for HB and CTB are available from your local authority. There are also various helplines you can telephone to get forms. Details of how to get the appropriate form and submit a claim for each benefit or tax credit are given in Chapter 7.

You can download many of the claim forms from the DWP website. You can also download the form for child benefit and claim it online (www.hmrc.gov.uk). You can download tax credit claim forms from the same site but you can't apply for them online due to security problems.

If you request a claim form by telephone, the claim may be registered from the date of the request, and provided you then complete and return the form within a specified time (one month for most benefits, or six weeks for AA and DLA – although this six-week backdating may be withdrawn in 2009/10) the claim is treated as if it had been made on the date you first requested the form. If your claim is incomplete, you are usually given a month to complete it properly. See p96 for the circumstances in which your claim can be backdated.

If you are **aged under 60**, you are normally required to claim IS, JSA, employment and support allowance (ESA), bereavement benefits, CA, industrial injuries benefits and maternity allowance (MA) by telephoning a contact centre, on 0800 055 6688, which will take the claim over the phone or send you the appropriate claim form, or send you a written statement with your personal details obtained during the call. Unless you are only claiming industrial injuries benefits, CA or MA, you are normally required to attend a 'work-focused interview' (WFI) with a personal adviser to discuss your work prospects and finalise your claim for IS or JSA. ESA claimants have their own process after the initial call, involving supplying medical certificates, attending various assessments and also attending a series of WFIs.

If you are **aged 60 or over**, you can claim most benefits by sending your completed claim form to the relevant DWP office. Alternatively, in some areas, you may be able to submit your claim at a 'designated' local authority office or an 'alternative' office, which may be based in a local voluntary organisation.

Information and evidence to support your claim

For all benefits and tax credits, you are expected to provide information and evidence to support your claim.[13] The type of information and evidence you need is explained on the claim form or accompanying notes. You are usually given a month to provide any missing information without it affecting the date of your claim. You (and your partner if s/he is included in your claim) also need to provide your national insurance (NI) number or sufficient information for a number to be traced or allocated.[14] If you do not have a NI number, you have to apply for one by attending an interview at a DWP office and providing evidence of your identity.

If you are claiming IS or JSA, your claim is not valid and you are not entitled to any benefit if you do not provide the information and evidence required on the claim form, unless:

- you could not complete the form or get the evidence required because of a physical, mental, learning or communication difficulty and it was not reasonably practicable for you to get help (you do not have to show that it was not reasonably practicable for another person to take the initiative to help you[15]); or
- the information or evidence does not exist, or you could not get it without serious risk of physical or mental harm, or you can only get it from a third party and it is not reasonably practicable to do so.[16]

Inform the DWP as soon as possible if you think one of the above exemptions applies to you.

Backdating your claim

There are strict time limits for claiming some benefits (see Chapter 7). You can claim some benefits in advance if you know you will shortly become entitled but you will not receive any payment until your entitlement begins.

You are not usually entitled to any benefit or tax credit for any day before your claim is received by the relevant benefit authority. In some cases, however, your claim can be backdated, normally for a maximum of three months – see below for details. Note, however, that claims for AA and DLA cannot be backdated in any circumstances (but you will be given six weeks to complete the claim forms without losing any money although this may be withdrawn during 2009/10).

Benefits which can be backdated without condition

Claims for state retirement pension can be backdated for up to **12 months** without condition (ie, regardless of the reasons you did not claim earlier).[17]

Claims for the following benefits can be backdated for up to **three months** without condition:[18]

- ESA;
- industrial injuries benefits;
- bereavement benefits;
- PC;
- HB and CTB if you are 60 or over (for those under 60, it is six months and you have to show 'good cause' for not claiming);
- CA (and longer in some circumstances – see below);
- child tax credit;
- working tax credit (WTC);
- child benefit and guardian's allowance;
- MA;
- additional amounts of non-means-tested benefits for adult dependants.

Note: backdating is only possible if you ask for it, from the day you request it, and if you would have been entitled to the benefit for the relevant period had you claimed it.

Backdating claims for income support and jobseeker's allowance

Claims for IS and JSA can be backdated for up to **one month** if you could not reasonably have been expected to claim earlier because:[19]

- the office where you are supposed to claim was closed (eg, due to a strike) and there were no other arrangements for claims to be made; *or*
- you could not get to the office due to difficulties with the type of transport you normally use and there was no reasonable alternative; *or*
- there were adverse postal conditions – eg, bad weather or a postal strike; *or*
- you or your partner stopped getting another benefit but were not informed before your entitlement ceased; *or*
- you claimed IS or JSA in your own right within one month of separating from your partner; *or*
- a close relative (ie, your partner, parent, son, daughter, brother or sister) died in the month before your claim; *or*
- you were unable to notify the DWP of your intention to claim because the telephone lines to the office were busy or not working.

Alternatively, your claim can be backdated for up to **three months** if you can show that it was not reasonable to expect you to claim before you did for one or more of the following reasons.[20]

- You have learning, language or literacy difficulties, or are deaf or blind, or were sick or disabled (unless you are claiming JSA), or were caring for someone who is sick or disabled, or were dealing with a domestic emergency which affected you *and*, in each case, it was not 'reasonably practicable' for you to get help from another person to make your claim. The DWP should not assume that you cannot satisfy this provision if you have support available to you (eg, from family or adult social care services), as the test is whether it is reasonably practicable for you to seek help, rather than whether another person could take the initiative to offer help.[21]

- You were given information by an officer from the DWP or the Revenue which led you to believe that you were not entitled to benefit. This may include misleading information about your entitlement to benefit, a previous decision refusing the same or a different benefit which led you to believe you were not entitled, or where you are given the wrong claim form.[22]

- You were given advice in writing by a Citizens Advice Bureau or other advice worker, a solicitor or other professional adviser (eg, an accountant), a doctor or a local authority which led you to believe that you were not entitled to benefit (this could include oral advice which is subsequently confirmed in writing[23]).

- You or your partner were given written information about your income or capital by your employer or a bank or building society and as a result you thought you were not entitled to benefit.

- You could not get to your local DWP office because of bad weather.

Note: backdating under the above rules is only possible if you ask for it and if you would have been entitled to IS or JSA for the relevant period had you claimed it.

If a person is acting as your appointee, then s/he, rather than you, must satisfy the above rules.[24] If someone is acting on your behalf on an informal basis, you have to satisfy the rules, unless you can show that it was reasonable for you to delegate responsibility for your claim and that you took care to ensure that the person helping you did it properly.[25]

Backdating claims following the award of a qualifying benefit

Special rules[26] apply on backdating claims if your entitlement to one benefit (other than HB or CTB) depends on the outcome of a claim for another benefit. This commonly occurs where you can only gain entitlement to IS or income-related ESA if you are awarded DLA (which may entitle you to a premium within those benefits). The rules are designed to ensure that you do not lose entitlement to one benefit because of delays in getting a final decision about another benefit. The delays may occur in processing a claim, or because benefit is only awarded after a revision or an appeal (see p104).

The rules apply where:
- your claim for a benefit is refused because you have not been awarded a qualifying benefit; *and*
- a claim for the qualifying benefit was made before, or not later than 10 working days after, your claim for the original benefit (or, for IS/JSA only, after the termination of an award); *and*
- the qualifying benefit is then awarded (on the initial claim, or on revision or appeal by the First-tier Tribunal, Upper Tribunal or a court); *and*
- you reclaim the original benefit within three months of the decision to award the qualifying benefit.

Your claim for the original benefit is then backdated to the date you originally claimed it, or the first date of the period for which the qualifying benefit is payable (if later).

A similar rule applies if you are refused WTC because you are waiting for a decision on a claim for a qualifying benefit.[27]

The above rules mean that you should not delay making a claim for any benefit until you receive a decision on a claim for a qualifying benefit. You should instead claim both benefits together and reclaim the original benefit when the qualifying benefit is awarded. For more details about backdating after the award of a qualifying benefit, see CPAG's *Welfare Benefits and Tax Credits Handbook*.

There is no equivalent provision which allows for the backdating of HB/CTB claims on the basis of a subsequent award of a qualifying benefit, but you may be able to argue that delays in dealing with a qualifying benefit constitute good cause for backdating a claim for HB/CTB (see above).

If you are entitled to an increased amount of a benefit (including HB or CTB) you are already getting following the award of a qualifying benefit, you should request a revision or supersession (see p107) to get the full arrears.

Backdating claims for carer's allowance

If the person you look after is in the process of applying for AA or DLA you should claim CA anytime within three months of the date the cared-for person gets her/his DLA or AA decision letter. Your CA will then be backdated to the date s/he was awarded the qualifying benefit. In any other circumstances, CA can only be backdated for three months.

Backdating claims for housing benefit and council tax benefit

Your entitlement to HB/CTB normally starts from the first Monday following the week in which your claim is received by the local authority, unless:[28]
- you have just become liable to pay rent or council tax on your home because, for example, you have just moved in, in which case your entitlement will start from the beginning of the week in which you make your claim; *or*

- you claim HB/CTB within four weeks of claiming IS, PC, ESA or JSA, in which case your HB/CTB claim is treated as made on the same day as your IS/PC/JSA/ESA claim; *or*
- you are receiving IS/PC/JSA/ESA when you become liable to pay rent, in which case you will be allowed four weeks to make your claim for HB/CTB without losing benefit; *or*
- there is a delay in your local authority fixing its council tax rate, in which case your claim for CTB can be backdated to when you first became entitled as long as you claim within four weeks of being notified of the rate.[29]

A claim for HB/CTB can be backdated for up to three months if you are 60 or over or six months if under 60 – but for the latter, you have to show good cause. There is no definition of 'good cause' in the regulations but it has been held to mean 'some fact which having regard to all the circumstances (including the claimant's state of health and the information which he received and that which he might have obtained), would probably have caused a reasonable person of his age and experience to act (or fail to act) as the claimant did'.[30] This could cover situations where you failed to make a claim because of ill health, disability, language problems and misleading advice or information.

Decisions

Decisions about benefits and tax credits are made by 'decision makers' from the relevant benefit authority – ie, the DWP, Revenue or local authority. Decisions are sometimes based on medical evidence provided by doctors acting on behalf of the DWP. Note, however, that doctors have no decision-making powers relating to benefit clams.

You are entitled to written notification of all decisions, which must include notification of your right to appeal against the decision where appropriate.[31] In most cases, you are entitled to request a written statement of reasons for the decision within a month, which should be provided to you within 14 days (this, however, does not apply to tax credit decisions).

Decisions should be made and notified within a reasonable timescale. If there are long delays, make a complaint (see p111).

Changes in your circumstances

Once you are awarded a benefit or tax credit, payment will continue until you are no longer entitled (DLA and AA are normally awarded for a fixed period). Your award can only be terminated or changed if the benefit authority properly carries out a revision or supersession (see p104).

For most benefits, you must notify changes of circumstances which may affect your entitlement to the office handling your claim.[32] If you do not promptly report such changes, any resulting overpayment of benefit may be recoverable from you (see p103) and if you are considered to have acted dishonestly, you may also be guilty of an offence. For PC (see p158), you may not be required to report increases in certain types of income for a fixed period (see p162). For tax credits some changes must be reported within one month but others need not be reported until the end of the tax year (see p180.) However, this may lead to overpayments or underpayments so it is usually advisable to report those changes to the Revenue when they occur – do this in writing and keep a copy.

If you are entitled to an increased award of benefit because of a change in your circumstances, you should request a supersession or, in the case of case tax credits, a revision. If you are refused benefit and your circumstances change, make a fresh claim. You should do this even if you have appealed against the refusal of benefit, because the First-tier Tribunal cannot take into account any change of circumstances that occurs after the decision you are appealing about was made.

3. **Payments**

Method of payment

Most benefits are paid by direct payment into a bank account by credit transfer. There are a number of accounts you can have your benefit paid into, including:

- an ordinary bank or building society account;
- a 'basic bank account', which can be opened at most High Street banks and which allows cash to be withdrawn at post office counters;
- a post office 'card account', which can only be used for receiving benefits and tax credits and making withdrawals using a plastic card and personal identification number (PIN).

You can arrange for someone to collect your benefit for you by authorising her/ him to have access to your account (ask your bank about this). If you have a post office card account, you can ask for a second card to be issued to the person who regularly collects your benefit.

If you have difficulty opening or using an account, inform the DWP who can, at its discretion, pay you by cheque. It is understood that the Government intends to phase out the use of cheques by 2010 but, at the time of writing, details of what will take their place were not available.

Payment into an account, however, is a condition of entitlement to tax credits and failure to notify an account within eight weeks can result in the stopping of entitlement.[33] Housing benefit (HB) is normally paid to you (not your landlord) by cheque or credit transfer if you are a private tenant, or by reducing (rebating) your rent if you are a council tenant. If you are a private tenant, your HB can be paid to your landlord if you are vulnerable or if you have rent arrears of at least eight weeks. Council tax benefit (CTB) is paid by reducing (rebating) your council tax.

Most benefits are weekly benefits and are awarded and paid in respect of your entitlement for a whole week. Some benefits, such as incapacity benefit (IB), are daily benefits and may be awarded and paid for periods of less than a week. Certain weekly benefits, such as attendance allowance (AA), disability living allowance (DLA) and income support (IS), can be paid at a daily rate if you spend part of a week in hospital or in a care home.[34]

Most benefits are usually paid so that they can be cashed every week, but some benefits are paid fortnightly (eg, jobseeker's allowance (JSA) and IB), and some are paid four-weekly (eg, AA/DLA unless they are paid together with a weekly benefit such as IS). Some benefits are paid in advance, some in arrears, and some partly in advance and arrears.[35] Between April 2009, and April 2011, the DWP is phasing in the payment of most benefits two weeks in arrears. There will be a transition phase for some claimants which may cause temporary hardship as people move from payment in advance to payment in arrears. Seek advice if this affects you. Payments of tax credits into an account are paid either weekly or four-weekly in arrears.

Payments to other people

Payments may sometimes be made to someone else on your behalf, for example:
- your 'appointee' (see p93);
- for HB, your landlord if you are a private tenant;
- for IS housing costs, your mortgage lender;
- for DLA mobility component, the Motability scheme (see p87).

Some of your IS, income-based JSA, income-related ESA, or pension credit may be deducted and paid direct to:[36]
- certain creditors (eg, if you are in debt for fuel charges, water rates or council tax or rent arrears);
- a care home, or to a local authority as your contribution towards the costs of the care home, *if* it is decided that you have failed to budget for the costs and it is in your interests for the payments to be made in this way, *or* you are in a home run by a voluntary organisation for people with alcohol or drug dependency;
- certain hostels, where HB is payable but does not cover all of your charges (eg, for meals, fuel, water charges and other services).

Some, or all, of any of your benefit(s) may also be paid to another person if this is considered to be necessary to protect your interests (or those of any member of your family)[37] – eg, if your partner is failing to support you, all or part of her/his benefit(s) may be paid to you.

Interim payments

An interim payment of benefit can be made to you if it seems that you may be entitled to benefit but it is not possible for your claim (or revision, supersession or appeal) to be dealt with immediately.[38] Local authorities **must** make an interim payment of HB to you if you are a private tenant and your HB claim cannot be dealt with within 14 days, unless it is clear that you will not be entitled to HB or you have failed, without good cause, to provide any necessary information or evidence in support of your claim.[39] An emergency payment of tax credits can sometimes be made via a local tax credit office. Any overpayment of benefit resulting from an interim or emergency payment is recoverable from you. There is no right of appeal against the refusal of an interim payment (you will have to complain and if necessary, threaten judicial review – see p111).

Suspension of payment[40]

Even if a benefit has been awarded to you, payment may be suspended if:
- a question has arisen about your entitlement while information is being gathered; *or*
- your award may be superseded (p106) or revised (see p104); *or*
- it appears that you may be being overpaid (see below); *or*
- you are not living at the address you notified; *or*
- you have failed to provide information or evidence (or failed to submit to a medical examination); *or*
- the DWP or local authority is considering appealing against a decision made by the First-tier Tribunal, Upper Tribunal or court to award benefit to you, or even to award benefit to someone else if the issue in the appeal could affect your claim (eg, in a 'test case').

You cannot appeal to the First-tier Tribunal against a decision to suspend your benefit but you can make representations that the suspension should be lifted because, for example, you will otherwise suffer hardship. You could also threaten judicial review (see p111) if you believe that there are no grounds to suspend your benefit or that your individual circumstances have not been properly considered.

Overpayments

If you receive an overpayment of benefit or tax credit, you may have to repay it. The rules about overpayments are extremely complex and vary according to the benefit concerned. Always seek advice (see Appendix 2) if you receive a decision stating that an overpayment is recoverable from you. You can appeal against most benefit decisions about whether and how much you have been overpaid and whether the overpayment is recoverable.

Most overpayments can only be recovered if they resulted from a misrepresentation or failure to disclose a material fact.[41] All overpayments of HB and CTB are recoverable, however, unless they resulted solely from an official error made by a local authority or DWP official and the claimant could not reasonably have known they were being overpaid.[42] Overpayments of tax credits are always recoverable.[43] Overpayments can be recovered by weekly deductions from most benefits. Even if an overpayment is recoverable from you, you can argue that it should not be recovered because, for example, this will cause you exceptional hardship. You can also negotiate how you will repay an overpayment. If you are an appointee (see p93), you may be liable to repay an overpayment if you misrepresented a material fact without using due care and diligence.[44]

The DWP will sometimes ask you for repayment of an overpayment even though it was not caused by misrepresentation or a failure to disclose and was in fact due to its error, such as failing to act on information that it has been given. Seek advice if that happens as it is probable that you are not liable to repay the money. For further details about the rules on overpayments, see CPAG's *Welfare Benefits and Tax Credits Handbook*.

You cannot appeal against a decision relating to recovery of an overpayment of tax credits but you may be able to dispute recovery if the overpayment was caused by official error (ie, if the Revenue have failed to meet its responsibilities) or if recovery will cause you hardship. For further information, see the Revenue Code of Practice – COP 26.

4. **Challenging decisions**

Most decisions can be challenged by **revision, supersession or appeal** (supersession does not, however, apply to tax credits). Decisions about social fund community care grants (see p185), budgeting loans (see p187) and crisis loans (see p188) can be challenged by requesting an **internal review** within 28 days. If you are dissatisfied with the outcome, you can request a **further review** within 28 days by an independent Social Fund Inspector. Always consider challenging a decision if you think that it is wrong and get advice (see Appendix 2) about the merits of your appeal, particularly if you are seeking an increase of a benefit you are receiving. This is because a decision maker or the First-tier Tribunal can decrease or remove your entitlement altogether when dealing with a revision, supersession or appeal, so you could end up worse off than before.

Revisions

Revisions are designed to be a quick and easy way of getting an incorrect decision changed. You can ask a decision maker to reconsider a decision by requesting a revision. A decision maker can also undertake a revision on her/his own initiative. Alternatively, you can appeal against most decisions to the First-tier Tribunal (see p109). It is sometimes simpler and quicker to get a decision changed by revision, however, particularly if you have new evidence to support your case. Further, if your application for revision is unsuccessful, you get a fresh decision against which you can usually appeal.

There are two types of revision:

- For benefits (but not tax credits), a revision can be requested on **any grounds** (apart from a change of circumstances – see below) within a 'dispute period' of one month from the date the decision was issued.[45] The time limit can be extended up to 13 months if your application was late because of 'special circumstances' (eg, illness or wrong advice).[46] If you requested a statement of reasons for a decision, the dispute period for requesting a revision of most benefits is extended by a further 14 days.[47] In the case of housing benefit (HB) and council tax benefit (CTB), days between your request for a statement and its provision are ignored when calculating the time limit.
- A revision can also be requested at **any time** if:
  - there has been an official error[48] (ie, a mistake or omission by an official working for the benefit authorities, such as a failure to act on information s/he had about your claim) which you or somebody acting on your behalf did not cause or contribute to; *or*
  - you have misrepresented or failed to disclose facts and as a result, the decision is more favourable to you than it would otherwise have been;[49] *or*
  - the decision is about tax credits; *or*
  - a decision would have been made differently had the result of an appeal you made about a different decision been known; *or*
  - you have been awarded benefit, but are now entitled to it at a higher rate from the first day of the award because you, or a member of your family, have now been awarded another benefit (see p107).[50]

Decisions (apart from those relating to tax credits) can only be revised on the basis of your circumstances at the time the decision took effect.[51] If your circumstances have changed, you should ask for a supersession (see p106) of any award you are getting, or make a fresh claim if you not receiving the benefit concerned.

Except for HB/CTB,[52] you do not have to apply for a revision in writing but it is always best to do so (and to keep a copy), to ensure that there is a written record of your application. Any issues not raised by your application for a revision do not have to be taken into account.[53] Provide as much detail as possible in your application to ensure that anything that may be relevant is taken into account.

You will be issued a new decision following a revision, which either confirms or changes the original decision. You can generally appeal against the new decision, but there is no right of appeal if a decision maker decides there are no grounds for an 'any time' revision (unless the revision is about an HB or CTB decision).[54]

A revised decision normally takes effect from the date on which the original decision took effect.[55] This means that you can normally get arrears of benefit going back to that date. For tax credits, you are only entitled to up to three months' arrears from the date you notify a change in your maximum entitlement (see p180),[56] unless you are entitled to arrears of the disability or severe disability element after being awarded a qualifying benefit (see p107).

Supersessions

Supersessions are a way of getting a decision (apart from a tax credit decision) changed at any time on prescribed grounds, the most common of which is a change of circumstances. If, for example, you are getting attendance allowance (AA) or disability living allowance (DLA) and your care or mobility needs increase, you can request a supersession to get onto a higher rate of benefit. A decision can be superseded on application, or on the initiative of a decision maker if:[57]

- there has been, or it is anticipated that there will be, a relevant change of circumstances since the decision took effect (a decision to refuse benefit cannot be superseded on this ground – you will have to make a fresh claim for benefit if your circumstances change); or
- the decision was made in ignorance of relevant facts or there was a mistake about the facts of your claim; or
- the decision was made by a decision maker and was legally wrong; or
- you have attended a medical examination relating to the personal capability assessment (see p143) or work capability assessment; or
- you have been awarded benefit, but are now entitled to it at a higher rate because you, or a member of your family, have now been awarded another benefit (see p107).

Except for HB/CTB,[58] you do not have to apply for a supersession in writing but it is always best to do so (and to keep a copy), to ensure that there is a written record of your application. You are usually required to complete a new application form when seeking a supersession of a DLA or AA award. Any issues not raised by your application for a supersession do not have to be taken into account.[59] Provide as much detail as possible in your application to ensure that anything that may be relevant is taken into account. An application for a revision or a notification of a change of circumstances can be treated as an application for supersession.[60]

You should be issued with a new decision following a supersession which either confirms or changes the new decision (unless your application for supersession was completely hopeless, in which case the decision maker may refuse to consider it). You can generally appeal against the new decision.[61]

A supersession generally takes effect from the date you applied for it, or the date it was undertaken on the initiative of a decision maker.[62] This means that no arrears are normally payable on supersession. If, however, you report a change of circumstances within a month, you can get up to one month's arrears of benefit. The time limit can be extended up to 13 months if there are special circumstances.[63] For AA and DLA, the time limit runs from the date you qualify for a higher rate of benefit. The 13-month rule means that considerable arrears could be payable – eg, where you were unable to notify a change in your circumstances earlier because of illness or disability. If you are entitled to less benefit following a change of circumstances, a supersession will generally take effect from the date of the change.[64]

Revisions and supersessions following awards of another qualifying benefit

The rules on supersessions and revisions described above allow for any award of benefit to be increased from the start date of any subsequent decision to award a qualifying benefit on which your entitlement depends. If, for example, you are awarded income support (IS), and you are later awarded DLA or carer's allowance (CA), your IS award can be revised or superseded to include a disability, severe disability or carer's premium from the start date of your award of DLA or CA. A similar rule in relation to working tax credit allows the disability and severe disability elements to be backdated on the award of a qualifying benefit.[65]

If your claim for a benefit is refused because you have not yet been awarded a qualifying benefit, see p99.

Appeals to the First-tier Tribunal

Right of appeal

You have the right of appeal to the First-tier Tribunal (Social Security and Child Support) against most decisions relating to benefits and tax credits made by decision makers (including revision and supersession decisions.[66] Appeals about statutory sick pay, statutory maternity pay, statutory paternity pay and statutory adoption pay and some decisions about your national insurance contributions, however, can be decided by either a Revenue review or by the First-tier Tribunal (Tax Chamber). There is no right of appeal against certain types of decisions including:[67]

- the suspension of benefit;
- whether a claim for one benefit should be treated as a claim for another benefit;
- whether to make an interim payment;
- whether to appoint someone as an appointee (see p92);
- whether to accept a late appeal (see below);
- decisions about community care grants, budgeting loans and crisis loans (but you can request a review and further review by a Social Fund Inspector);
- decisions about recovery of an overpayment of tax credits.

Time limits

An appeal against a decision must be received by the office that issued the decision within one calendar month of the date the decision was issued.[68] For most benefits, the time limit is extended by 14 days if you have requested a statement of reasons.[69] In the case of HB and CTB, days between your request for a statement and its provision are ignored when calculating the time limit.[70] The time limit for appealing against a tax credit decision is 30 days.[71]

If you miss the time limit for appealing, a late appeal can be accepted within 13 months of the notification of a decision. There are no specific grounds for admitting a late appeal but it is advisable to clearly state your reasons for doing so. Seek advice if this applies to you.

There is no right of appeal against a refusal to admit a late appeal although you can ask for such a decision to be reconsidered, or you may be able to apply for a judicial review (see p111) if the decision is clearly unreasonable.

How to appeal[72]

You must appeal in writing, preferably using the appropriate appeal form, and submit the appeal to the office that issued the decision you are appealing against.

The appeal must be signed by you, or by a properly authorised representative, and must include enough information to enable the decision in question to be identified and must state the grounds for your appeal. If the appellant dies, some other person may apply to be her/his appointee to proceed with the appeal on her/his behalf.

You (or your representative) may withdraw your appeal at any time before it is decided by giving notice in writing.[73]

What happens after you appeal

On receipt of your appeal, the relevant office prepares a set of appeal papers, which includes a submission by a decision maker explaining why the relevant decision was made and copies of all the evidence. This is sent to you (and your named representative if you have one). You are also sent an 'enquiry form' asking whether you want an oral or 'paper' hearing of your case (see below). Always opt for an oral hearing because your chances of success are much greater. You must complete and return the form to the Tribunals Service (TS) within 14 days, or your appeal will be 'struck out' (see below). It is advisable to prepare a response to the appeal papers and this must be returned within one month.

Hearings are arranged at local venues. If you opt for an oral hearing, you are entitled to attend to present your case in person. Paper hearings are decided on the basis of the appeal papers only.

An appeal may not proceed for a number of reasons.

- Appeals can be 'struck out'.[74] This **must** happen where the appellant has failed to comply with a direction that states such failure would have this result or where the First-tier Tribunal has no jurisdiction. Appeals **may** be struck out where the appellant has not complied with a direction which stated that striking out was a potential consequence, where the appellant fails to co-operate with the tribunal to such an extent that the case cannot be dealt with fairly or justly or where the tribunal considers the case has no reasonable prospect of being successful. You can ask for an appeal to be reinstated within 28 days of being sent the notice if it has been struck out for failure to comply with a direction. All other powers to strike out can only be exercised when you have been given the chance to argue why this should not happen before the decision is taken.

- The decision under appeal can be revised in your favour before the appeal is heard. If this happens, the appeal lapses.[75] Note, however, that the appeal will lapse even if the decision is only partially revised in your favour. If you are still dissatisfied with the new decision, appeal again – eg, if you appeal against the refusal of AA and you are then awarded the lower rate on revision, your appeal will lapse and if you believe you are entitled to the higher rate, you will have to appeal again. For tax credits, the Revenue will contact you to try to 'settle' your appeal, which will lapse if you reach an agreement before the appeal is heard.
- If the outcome of your appeal could be affected by a test-case pending before the courts, the appeal can be postponed until the test case is decided.[76]

First-tier Tribunal hearings

The First-tier Tribunals consist of up to three members drawn from a panel of people with a range of different experience.[77]

- Three-member tribunals (a tribunal judge, who is legally qualified, a doctor and a person with experience of disability) hear appeals about DLA/AA, and entitlement to the disability elements of tax credits.[78]
- Two-member tribunals (a tribunal judge and one other person) hear appeals about whether:[79]
  - you are incapable of work; *or*
  - the extent of your disability for industrial injuries benefit.
- Two-member tribunals (a tribunal judge and a financial expert such as an accountant) hear complex appeals about relevant financial issues – eg, the accounts of trust funds and profit and loss accounts.[80]
- One-member tribunals (a tribunal judge) hear all other appeals.[81]

The First-tier Tribunal may also invite another panel member to assist as an 'expert'. The expert can attend, give evidence or provide a report, but may not take part in making the decision.[82]

The TS will convene 'paper hearings' in the absence of appellants.

Hearings take place at a range of local venues, which should all be accessible for people with disabilities (complain if they are not). You can apply for an oral hearing to be postponed if you cannot attend on the date arranged. A hearing can also be adjourned at the discretion of the tribunal.[83] If it is impossible for you to get to an appeal venue (eg, because you are housebound), you can request the appeal to be heard in your home (a domiciliary hearing). You will need to provide medical evidence of your inability to travel to a hearing.

The procedure at oral hearings is up to the tribunal chair but it must be fair and impartial. You must be given the opportunity to state your case, give evidence, call witnesses and ask questions. You are also entitled to be represented by anyone you choose.[84] A Presenting Officer from the authority that made the decision may be present to explain and argue its case. The tribunal cannot carry out a physical examination (unless the appeal relates to the assessment of disablement for severe disablement allowance or industrial injuries benefits) and therefore has to rely on the written and oral evidence in reaching its decision.[85]

The First-tier Tribunal can also make consent orders which dispose of the proceedings and makes other appropriate provision. At the time of writing, it was not know how these new powers, from November 2008, may operate.

Determination of appeals

The First-tier Tribunal must determine a case completely afresh and arrive at a new decision which replaces the original decision. It must look at all the evidence and reach a decision on the 'balance of probabilities'. It is not obliged to consider issues that are 'not raised by' your appeal and in the case of tax credits, can ignore any wilful or unreasonable omissions from the notice of appeal.[86] It can also only look at the circumstances which existed at the time the decision in question was made, and not any subsequent changes (such as a deterioration in your health), which may have occurred by the date of your hearing.[87] You should, therefore, ensure that the evidence you are relying on relates to the period preceding the decision and that you make a fresh claim for benefit (or seek a supersession of an existing award) if your circumstances change while you are waiting for an appeal.

First-tier Tribunal decisions

The First-tier Tribunal must issue you with a written notice of the decision after a hearing. This is sometimes given to you in person at the end of an oral hearing. You can request a full statement of the tribunal's decision and the reasons for it, within one month of the date of the decision notice. This time limit may be extended, but there is an absolute limit of three months.[88]

You may apply for a decision of the First-tier Tribunal to be set aside within a month (13 months in special circumstances). Decisions may be set aside on grounds of procedural irregularity – eg, a hearing proceeded in your absence even though you wanted to attend, but you were not given notice of the hearing, or relevant documents were not received by the tribunal.[89]

Appealing against First-tier Tribunal decisions

You can appeal against a decision of the First-tier Tribunal to the Upper Tribunal on the grounds that it is erroneous in law. Seek specialist advice to do this (see Appendix 2). There are strict time limits for pursuing an appeal. You should first obtain a full statement of the First-tier Tribunal's decision and reasons (see above). You must then apply for leave to appeal within one month of being sent the statement (although the First-tier Tribunal has the power to extend the time limit to 13 months). The tribunal must consider whether to exercise its power to perform a review before considering whether to grant permission to appeal to the Upper Tribunal.

Preparing for appeals

Bear the following points in mind when appealing against a decision.

- Always seek advice about appealing. The law and procedures are complex and your appeal will be much more likely to succeed if you have expert help and advice. In particular, you should get advice about the strength of your appeal, as the First-tier Tribunal will decide your case completely afresh and you could end up losing rather than gaining benefit.
- Always opt for an oral hearing, as this will allow you to explain your case in person and greatly increase the chances of a successful outcome. If possible, arrange for an expert representative to attend the hearing with you.
- The key to a successful outcome is evidence which shows that you satisfy the relevant legal conditions. Your own oral evidence to the tribunal will be important but independent written evidence which supports your case is also crucial. This particularly applies in appeals about AA, DLA, ESA or incapacity for work, where your appeal is unlikely to succeed without supporting medical evidence from your GP, consultant or other healthcare professional.

Judicial review

Where there is no right of appeal against a decision (see p107), or in certain circumstances where a benefit authority is refusing to make a decision, or to exercise its discretion properly, you may be able to threaten and pursue judicial review proceedings in the High Court (Court of Session in Scotland). You will need to consult a solicitor or law centre about this. There is a three-month time limit for making an application (in Scotland, an application must be made as soon as possible).

---

5. **Common problems**

This section alerts you to some of the problems you may encounter when claiming social security benefits and tax credits. Many of the issues are complex and you should always seek advice if you are unsure about anything (see Appendix 2).

Delays and maladministration

Unfortunately, delays and maladministration are prominent features of the benefit, tax credit and appeals systems. Inadequate resources, poor training, heavy reliance on computerised systems and constant changes in legislation can result in long delays in processing claims, payments and appeals, and poor standards of service. This frequently results in hardship and frustration for claimants, particularly as there is no right of appeal until a decision is issued.

There are, however, a number of remedies open to you, depending on the nature of the problem (often the threat of action results in the problem being resolved).

- All DWP, tax credit, local authority and Tribunal Service offices should have a customer services manager or section to whom you can complain if a problem is not resolved by staff dealing with your case. Although there is no statutory duty on the DWP or the Revenue to process claims within a set time, they set targets and can pay compensation if they are responsible for long delays.[90] You could also ask your MP to intervene on your behalf and/or refer your case to the Ombudsman, who can investigate complaints of maladministration and award compensation where appropriate.

- For tax credits, you can complain to the Adjudicator, if your complaint is not resolved by the tax credit office. If you are still not satisfied, complain to the Parliamentary Ombudsman.

- If your complaint is about the administration of housing benefit (HB) or council tax benefit (CTB), you should use the local authority's formal complaints procedure. Local authorities have a statutory duty to pay you any HB or CTB you are entitled to within 14 days of receiving your claim, or as soon as reasonably practicable thereafter, and they cannot refuse to issue a decision because you have not provided all the information they have requested.[91] You can also complain to a local councillor and/or to the councillor who chairs the committee responsible for administering HB/CTB. If your problem is not resolved, you can make a complaint of maladministration to the Local Government Ombudsman, or to the council's Monitoring Officer.

- If there is a delay in payment following a decision to award you benefit (eg, by the First-tier Tribunal), you may be able to take recovery proceedings in the county court (sheriff's court in Scotland). Seek advice about this (see Appendix 2).

- In certain circumstances, if a benefit authority is refusing to deal with a claim, you may be able to threaten and pursue judicial review proceedings (see p111). This tactic has been used successfully to deal with delays and refusals to issue a national insurance number to claimants.

Negligent advice

If you are given wrong or misleading advice by the benefit authorities, you can complain, refer the matter to the Ombudsman or Revenue Adjudicator, or make a claim for compensation (you may need legal advice to do this). If you are given wrong advice by an advice agency or solicitor, you may be able to claim compensation from them.

Underclaiming and underpayments

Many people do not claim all the benefits and tax credits to which they are entitled.

Even if you claim all the benefits which you are entitled to, you may be entitled to a higher rate of benefit. For example, you may claim attendance allowance (AA) but not declare all your personal care needs so that only the lower rate instead of the higher rate is awarded to you. There are very restrictive rules on the backdating of claims for all benefits (see p96) so you may lose money if you do not claim at the earliest opportunity. Always check that you are receiving all the benefits you are entitled to (most advice centres will undertake a benefit check for you).

A common cause of underclaiming is the failure to appreciate that the award of one benefit ('qualifying benefit') can entitle you to another benefit (or an increased amount of another benefit). If you claim AA, for example, you may be able to claim the severe disability addition with your pension credit. A person caring for you may be able to claim carer's allowance (CA) and the carer premium/addition and you may be able to keep your severe disability addition if s/he also claims a benefit which 'overlaps' with CA (eg, employment and support allowance or retirement pension – see p131). If an award of a qualifying benefit stops, this conversely could also result in the loss of other benefits and services (eg, the loss of your DLA could result in the loss of premiums, CA, assistance from the Independent Living Fund and access to the Motability scheme), making it extremely important to challenge the decision.

Special rules allow a claim for a benefit to be backdated when you are awarded another qualifying benefit (see p99). You must, however, ensure that you claim both benefits within the prescribed time limits. Although special rules allow the amount of a benefit to be increased on the award of another qualifying benefit, you must ensure that notification of the award of the qualifying benefit (eg, AA) is notified to (and acted on by) the office dealing with the other benefit (eg, HB or income support (IS)), so that the award can be superseded and increased.

Overclaiming and overpayments

Although it is normally best to claim all the benefits to which you may be entitled, there are occasions where this could make you, or another person, worse off.
- Claiming CA can sometimes adversely affect the benefit entitlement of others, so, between you, you may lose more than you gain (see p131).
- If you try to claim extra benefit (eg, a higher rate of AA of DLA) by requesting a supersession or appeal, you could end up worse off if a decision maker or the First-tier Tribunal decides that you are not entitled to any benefit at all.

Overpayments of benefit and tax credits are very common and may arise because of innocent or deliberate failures by claimants, or errors and inefficiencies by the benefit authorities. The rules on the recoverability of overpayments are extremely complex (see p103). Always get advice if you are told that an overpayment is owed by you or is recoverable from you. If you deliberately mislead the benefit authorities or fail to notify a change in your circumstances in order to qualify for more benefit or tax credits, you are committing fraud and may be prosecuted, or asked to pay a penalty, as well as repaying any overpayment. Seek specialist advice, if you are being investigated for possible fraud.

Notes

2. **Claims and decisions**
   1 s137(1) SSCBA 1992
   2 CPA 2004
   3 s3(5) and (6) TCA 2002; CPA 2004
   4 Reg 33 SS(C&P) Regs; reg 82 HB Regs;
      reg 63 HB(SPC) Regs; reg 68 CTB Regs;
      reg 52 CTB(SPC) Regs; reg 18 TC(CN)
      Regs
   5 *Agents, Appointees, Attorneys and
      Deputies Guide,* DWP, August 2008
   6 R(SB) 5/90
   7 CIS/642/1992
   8 CIS/379/1992
   9 s1 SSAA 1992; s3(1) TCA 2002
   10 Reg 4D SS(C&P) Regs
   11 Reg 4 SS(C&P) Regs; reg 83 HB Regs;
      reg 64 HB(SPC) Regs; reg 69 CTB Regs;
      reg 53 CTB(SPC) Regs; reg 5(2)
      TC(C&N) Regs
   12 Reg 9(1) and Sch 1 SS(C&P) Regs
   13 Reg 7(1) SS(C&P) Regs; reg 86 HB Regs;
      reg 67 HB(SPC) Regs; reg 86 CTB Regs;
      reg 57 CTB(SPC) Regs; reg 5(3)
      TC(C&N) Regs
   14 s1 SSAA 1992; reg 5(4) TC(C&N) Regs
   15 CIS/2057/1998
   16 Reg 4(1A) and (1B) SS(C&P) Regs
   17 Reg 19 and Sch 4 SS(C&P) Regs; reg 6
      SS(C&P)A Regs; reg 64(1) HB(SPC)
      Regs; reg 56 CTB(SPC) Regs
   18 Reg 19(2) and (3) and Sch 4 SS(C&P)
      Regs; reg 7 TC(CN) Regs
   19 Reg 19(6) and (7) SS(C&P) Regs
   20 Reg 19(4) and (5) SS(C&P) Regs
   21 CIS/2057/1998
   22 CIS/1721/1998; CIS/3749/1998; CSIS/
      256/1999; CIS/610/1998; CJSA/4066/
      1998; CIS/4354/1999; CIS/4490/1999;
      CIS/3994/1998

   23 CIS/5430/1999; CJSA/1136/1998
   24 R(SB) 17/83; R(IS) 5/91; CIS/812/1992
   25 R(P) 2/85
   26 Regs 6(11)-(30) and 19(6)-(7) SS(C&P)
      Regs; memo DMG vol 1 04/02
   27 Reg 8 TC(CN) Regs
   28 Reg 83(5) HB Regs; reg 64 HB(SPC)
      Regs; regs 64 and 69 CTB Regs; regs 48
      and 53 HB(SPC) Regs
   29 Reg 69 CTB Regs; reg 53 CTB(SPC) Regs
   30 CS/371/1949; para A2.23 and Part A2
      Annex A GM
   31 Reg 28 SS&CS(DA) Regs; reg 10
      HB&CTB(DA) Regs
   32 Reg 32(1) SS(C&P) Regs; reg 88 HB
      Regs; reg 69 HB(SPC) Regs; reg 74 CTB
      Regs; reg 59 CTB(SPC) Regs

3. **Payments**
   33 Regs 9, 13 and 14 TC(PB) Regs
   34 Reg 25 SS(C&P) Regs; s124(5) and (6)
      and reg 73 IS Regs
   35 Regs 22-26A SS(C&P) Regs
   36 Sch 9 SS(C&P) Regs
   37 Reg 34 SS(C&P) Regs
   38 Reg 2 SS(PAOR) Regs
   39 Reg 91 HB Regs
   40 Regs 16, 17 and 19 SS&CS(DA) Regs;
      regs 11 and 13 HB&CTB(DA) Regs
   41 s71 SSAA 1992
   42 Reg 100 HB Regs; reg 81 HB(SPC) Regs;
      reg 83 CTB Regs; reg 68 CTB(SPC) Regs
   43 s28 TCA 2002
   44 CIS/2178/2001

4. **Challenging decisions**

45 s9 SSA 1998; reg 3(1) SS&CS(DA) Regs; Sch 7 para 3 CSPSSA 2000; reg 4 HB&CTB(DA) Regs

46 Reg 4 SS&CS(DA) Regs; reg 5 HB&CTB(DA) Regs

47 Reg 31 SS&CS(DA) Regs; reg 4(4) HB&CTB(DA) Regs

48 Regs 1(3) and 3(5)(a) SS&CS(DA) Regs; regs 1(2) and 4(2)(a) HB&CTB(DA) Regs

49 Reg 3(5)(b) SS&CS(DA) Regs; reg 4(2)(b) HB&CTB(DA) Regs

50 Reg 3(7) SS&CS(DA) Regs

51 Reg 3(9) SS&CS(DA) Regs; reg 4(10) HB&CTB(DA) Regs

52 Regs 4(8) and 7(7) HB&CTB(DA) Regs

53 s9(2) SSA 1998; Sch 7 para 3(s) CSPSSA 2000

54 Reg 31(2)(a) SS&CS(DA) Regs; reg 18(3)(b) HB&CTB(DA) Regs

55 s9(3) SSA 1998; Sch 7 para 3(3) CSPSSA 2000

56 Reg 25 TC(CN) Regs

57 Reg 6(2) SS&CS(DA) Regs; reg 7(2) HB&CTB(DA) Regs

58 Regs 4(8) and 7(7) HB&CTB(DA) Regs

59 s10(2) SSA 1998; Sch 7 para 4(3) CSPSSA 2000

60 Reg 6(5) SS&CS(DA) Regs; reg 7(6) HB&CTB(DA) Regs

61 *Wood v Secretary of State for Work and Pensions* [2003] EWCA Civ 53

62 s10(5) SSA 1998; Sch 7 para 4(5) CSPSSA 2000

63 Regs 7 and 8 SS&CS(DA) Regs; regs 8 and 9 HB&CTB(DA) Regs

64 Reg 7(2)(c) SS&CS(DA) Regs; reg 8(2) HB&CTB(DA) Regs

65 Reg 26 TC(C&N) Regs

66 s12 and Schs 2 and 3 SSA 1998; Sch 7 para 6 CSPSSA 2000; s38 TCA 2002

67 Sch 2 SSA 1998; reg 27 and Sch 2 SS&CS(DA) Regs; s38 TCA 2002; reg 16 and Sch HB&CTB(DA) Regs

68 Reg 31(1)(a) SS&CS(DA) Regs; reg 18(1) HB&CTB(DA) Regs

69 Reg 31(1)(b) SS&CS(DA) Regs

70 Reg 18(2) HB&CTB(DA) Regs

71 s39(1) TCA 2002

72 Regs 33 and 34 SS&CS(DA) Regs; regs 20 and 21 HB&CTB(DA) Regs; TC(NA) Regs; reg 8 TC(A)(No.2) Regs

73 Regs 33(10) and 40 SS&CS(DA) Regs; regs 20(9) and 23 HB&CTB(DA) Regs

74 Regs 46-48 SS&CS(DA) Regs; reg 23 HB&CTB(DA) Regs; regs 16-17 TC(A)(No.2) Regs

75 s9(6) SSA 1998; reg 30 SS&CS(DA) Regs; Sch 7 para 3(3) and (6) CSPSSA 2000; reg 17 HB&CTB(DA) Regs; reg 3 TC(A) Regs

76 s26 SSA 1998; Sch 7 para 17 CSPSSA 2000

77 ss6(2) and 7(2) SSA 1998

78 Reg 36(6) SS&CS(DA) Regs; reg 9(2) TC(A)(No.2) Regs

79 Reg 36(2) SS&CS(DA) Regs

80 Reg 36(3) SS&CS(DA) Regs; reg 22(1) HB&CTB(DA) Regs; reg 9(3) TC(A)(No.2) Regs

81 Reg 36(1) and (9) SS&CS(DA) Regs; reg 22(1)(b) HB&CTB(DA) Regs; reg 9(1) TC(A)(No.2) Regs

82 Reg 50 SS&CS(DA) Regs; reg 23 HB&CTB(DA) Regs; reg 19 TC(A)(No.2) Regs

83 Reg 51 SS&CS(DA) Regs; reg 23 HB&CTB(DA) Regs; reg 20 TC(A)(No.2) Regs

84 Reg 49 SS&CS(DA) Regs; reg 23 HB&CTB(DA) Regs; reg 18 TC(A)(No.2) Regs

85 s20(3) SSA 1998; reg 52 SS&CS(DA) Regs

86 s12(8)(a) SSA 1998; Sch 7 para 6(9)(a) CSPSSA 2000; s39(5) TCA 2002

87 s12(8)(b) SSA 1998; Sch 7 para 6(9)(b) CSPSSA 2000; reg 4 TC(A) Regs

88 Regs 53 and 54 SS&CS(DA) Regs; reg 23 HB&CTB(DA) Regs; regs 21 and 22 TC(A)(No.2) Regs

89 Reg 57 SS&CS(DA) Regs; reg 23 HB&CTB(DA) Regs; reg 25 TC(A)(No.2) Regs

5. **Common problems**

90 *Financial Redress for Maladministration Guide*

91 Regs 76, 77(1)(a) and 88(3) HB Regs; regs 66, 67(1)(a) and 77(3) CTB Regs; CH/2155/2003

Chapter 7

Which benefits and tax credits you can claim

This chapter covers:
1. Types and combinations of benefits and tax credits (p117)
2. Disability benefits (p120)
3. Other non-means-tested benefits (p130)
4. Means-tested benefits and tax credits (p147)
5. People in hospital (p189)
6. Increasing your entitlement – examples (p191)

The following benefits are covered:

Disability benefits:
- disability living allowance (p120);
- attendance allowance (p125);
- industrial injuries benefits (p127);
- war pensions and compensation scheme (p129);
- vaccine damage payments (p130).

Other non-means-tested benefits:
- carer's allowance (p130);
- Healthy Start food and vitamins (p133);
- state retirement pension (p133);
- bereavement benefits (p136);
- widows' benefits (p139);
- incapacity benefit (and statutory sick pay) (p139);
- contributory employment and support allowance (p142);
- severe disablement allowance (p145);
- contribution-based jobseeker's allowance (p146);
- maternity, paternity and adoption benefits (p146);
- health in pregnancy grant (p146);
- child benefit and guardian's allowance (p147).

Means-tested benefits and tax credits:
- income support (p147);
- income-related employment and support allowance (p156);
- income-based jobseeker's allowance (p158);
- pension credit (p158);
- housing benefit (p163);
- council tax benefit (p171);
- tax credits (child tax credit and working tax credit) (p175);
- social fund payments (p182).

This chapter outlines the rules of entitlement to the main benefits and tax credits which you may be able to claim if you, or a member of your family, are sick or disabled, or a carer. The rules are complex and only an overview of the main conditions can be set out here. If you need further details, consult CPAG's *Welfare Benefits and Tax Credits Handbook* (see Appendix 3). If you are unsure whether you are receiving your correct entitlement, or you are refused benefit, seek advice (see Appendix 2). Some typical examples of how claimants can maximise their income from benefits and tax credits are given on p191.

Note that:
- general information about the administration of benefits and tax credits, claims, payments, appeals and common problems you may encounter can be found in Chapter 6;
- the assessment of income and capital for means-tested benefits is covered in Chapter 8;
- health benefits, housing grants, transport concessions and special funds for sick and disabled people are covered in Chapter 5;
- the special rules that apply if you are resident in a care home are covered in Chapter 16;
- special rules apply to people in prison or affected by a trade dispute (see CPAG's *Welfare Benefits and Tax Credits Handbook* for details).

All the rates of benefits and tax credits given apply from **April 2009 to April 2010**.

1. **Types and combinations of benefits and tax credits**

Types of benefits and tax credits

There are two main types of benefits and tax credits, **means-tested** and **non-means-tested**.

Means-tested

Means-tested benefits and tax credits are payable to people whose financial resources are below set levels. The amount you are entitled to depends on your financial and other circumstances. The main means-tested benefits and tax credits are list on p117.

Non-means-tested

Non-means-tested benefits are payable to people who are sick, disabled, unemployed, pregnant or bereaved, or who are carers, pensioners, or have dependent children. They are generally paid regardless of your financial circumstances but some benefits are affected by earnings and occupational pensions.

The main non-means-tested benefits are listed below in terms of whether they are contributory or non-contributory. **Contributory benefits** are only payable if you have made sufficient national insurance (NI) contributions. **Non-contributory benefits** are paid regardless of your NI contribution record. Maternity, paternity and adoption benefits are paid on the basis of employment (see p146).

Contributory benefits	*Non-contributory benefits*
state retirement pension	attendance allowance
bereavement and widows' benefits	disability living allowance
incapacity benefit (unless paid 'in youth' – see p142)	carer's allowance
contribution-based jobseeker's allowance	industrial injuries benefit
contributory employment and support allowance	child benefit
(unless paid 'in youth')	guardian's allowance

Combinations of benefits

You can generally claim any combination of benefits and tax credits to which you are entitled but you should note the following points.
- If you are entitled to more than one of the following **non-means-tested 'earnings replacement benefits'**, you can only be paid the highest amount for which you qualify:[1]
  - retirement pension;
  - bereavement allowance or widow's pension;
  - widowed parent's allowance or widowed mother's allowance;
  - incapacity benefit (IB);
  - severe disablement allowance (SDA);
  - employment and support allowance (ESA);
  - carer's allowance (CA);
  - maternity allowance;

– contribution-based JSA.

- **Other non-means-tested benefits** can be paid in addition to any other benefits and tax credits you are entitled to attendance allowance (AA), which is paid to people aged 65 and over and disability living allowance (DLA), which is paid to people who claim before they are 65, are particularly valuable benefits because they do not count as income when calculating your entitlement to means-tested benefits and tax credits (see below). They can also entitle you to additional amounts of means-tested benefits and tax credits.

- **Means-tested benefits and tax credits** can also be paid with any other benefits you are entitled to, but the amount you get depends on your assessed income, including income from some other benefits and tax credits. Most non-means-tested benefits count as income (but not AA or DLA) but some act as qualifying benefits to additional amounts of means-tested benefits and tax credits. IS, income-related ESA and PC are commonly paid to 'top-up' earnings replacement benefits such as CA, contributory ESA and retirement pension. If you are entitled to IS, income-based JSA, income-related ESA or the guarantee credit of PC, you are automatically eligible to maximum HB and CTB as well as social fund payments and health benefits (see Chapter 5), although you will still have to make separate claims for them. CTC is payable to most families with children, in addition to child benefit. WTC is paid to some lower-paid workers whether they have children or not.

The following table shows some typical combinations of benefits commonly claimed by the claimant groups listed in the first column. Child benefit and CTC are payable if you have dependent children. HB and CTB are payable if you are liable to pay rent and council tax.

Claimant group	Disability benefits	Other non-means-tested benefits	Means-tested benefits	Benefits for children
Disabled pensioner	attendance allowance	retirement pension	pension credit, housing benefit, council tax benefit	child benefit, child tax credit
Younger disabled person	disability living allowance	incapacity benefit or employment and support allowance (can still be payable if doing 'permitted work')	income support or income-related employment and support allowance, housing benefit, council tax benefit, working tax credit if working	child benefit, child tax credit

Disabled worker	disability living allowance		working tax credit, housing benefit, council tax benefit	child benefit, child tax credit
Carer		carer's allowance	income support, housing benefit, council tax benefit	child benefit, child tax credit

2. Disability benefits

Disability living allowance

Disability living allowance (DLA) is a weekly allowance paid to people who need help with personal care or who have difficulty getting around. Claimants must be under the age of 65 when they claim DLA, but once an award is in payment it can continue after the age of 65. There are no national insurance (NI) contribution conditions and DLA is not taxable. DLA is a particularly valuable benefit because it can be paid in addition to any other benefit, does not count as income for means-tested benefits and tax credits, and can entitle a claimant to extra amounts of means-tested benefits and tax credits.

Who can claim

You qualify for DLA if you:[2]
- are under the age of 65 when you first claim (if you have been awarded DLA you can continue to receive it after the age of 65); *and*
- are present and ordinarily resident in Great Britain and have been present for at least 26 weeks in the past year (disregarding temporary absences of up to 26 weeks); *and*
- are not subject to immigration control (see p121); *and*
- satisfy one of the care and/or mobility conditions (see pp121 and 122), have done so throughout the three months prior to your claim and are likely to continue to do so for at least another six months (unless you are 'terminally ill' – see p124).

DLA consists of a 'care component' paid at three different rates and a 'mobility component' paid at two different rates. You can qualify for one or both components but only for one rate of each component. You can be given an award for a fixed or indefinite period.[3] If your needs change and you have satisfied the conditions for a higher rate or another component for at least three months, you should request a supersession (see p106). If you are terminally ill, see p124.

Subject to immigration control

You are subject to immigration control if you do not have leave to enter or remain in the UK, or if your leave is subject to the condition that you do not have recourse to public funds, or is subject to a formal sponsorship undertaking. You are not subject to immigration control for benefit purposes if you are a British citizen, a national of a country which is part of the European Economic Area (EEA – see p150), a refugee, or a person with leave to remain in the UK outside the normal rules (exceptional, discretionary or humanitarian leave).

There are also other exceptions and the rules are complex. For further information, see CPAG's *Welfare Benefits and Tax Credits Handbook*. Always seek advice before claiming benefit, as this can sometimes affect your right to remain in the UK.

The care component[4]

- Higher rate care component – you qualify for the higher rate care component if you are so severely physically or mentally disabled that you require:
  - frequent attention throughout the day in connection with your bodily functions, or continual supervision throughout the day to avoid substantial danger to yourself or others; *and*
  - prolonged or repeated attention at night in connection with your bodily functions, or another person to be awake at night for a prolonged period or at frequent intervals to watch over you.

  If you are terminally ill (see p124), you are treated as satisfying the above conditions.
- Middle rate care component – you qualify for the middle rate care component if you satisfy either the 'day' or 'night' condition described above. You may also qualify automatically if you undergo regular renal dialysis.
- Lower rate care component – you qualify for the lower rate care component if you are:
  - aged 16 or over and so severely physically or mentally disabled that you cannot prepare a cooked main meal for yourself if you have the ingredients; *or*
  - so severely physically or mentally disabled that you require attention in connection with your bodily functions for a significant portion of the day, whether during a single period or a number of periods.

Additional rule for children

Children under 16 only qualify for the care component if they have attention or supervision requirements which are 'substantially in excess' of the normal requirements of children of the same age, or which children of the same age in normal health do not have.[5]

Meaning of terms

'**Attention**' means service of a close and intimate nature from another person, involving personal contact.[6] Attention is not confined to physical help but it must involve the physical presence of another person.[7]

'**Frequent attention throughout the day**' means help which is needed several times (not once or twice) at intervals spread throughout the day (not, for example, just in the early morning or evening).[8]

'**A significant portion of the day**' normally means about an hour.[9]

'**Prolonged**' attention at night means about 20 minutes.

'**Repeated**' simply means more than once.[10] You may, therefore, qualify if you need help to go to the toilet once in the night, which takes 20 minutes, or twice which only takes five minutes.

'**Bodily functions**' include breathing, hearing, seeing, communicating, eating, drinking, walking, sitting, sleeping, getting in and out of bed, dressing, undressing, washing, bathing, using the toilet and moving around. They do not generally include domestic tasks such as cooking, shopping, cleaning or laundry.[11]

'**Supervision**' and '**watching over**' involves keeping an eye on somebody to prevent substantial danger. It can be precautionary, without resulting in actual intervention.[12]

'**Continual supervision**' means frequent or regular, rather than continuous, supervision.[13]

'**Prolonged**' watching over at night normally means about 20 minutes.

'**Requires**' means 'reasonably requires' and not 'medically requires'.[14] Attention which you need in order to live as normal a life as possible (including having a social life) should count.[15] The test is whether you *need* attention or supervision, rather than whether you actually *receive* it. If you can only manage to carry out a 'bodily function' with great difficulty, you can argue that you 'reasonably require' attention in connection with it.

The '**cooking test**' for the lower rate is an abstract test of whether your disabilities would prevent you from preparing a labour-intensive main meal for one, freshly cooked on a traditional cooker (it is irrelevant whether you actually cook or know how to cook).[16] You should qualify if you are unable to peel and chop vegetables, or cope with hot pans, or turn taps, or read labels and instructions, or tell whether food is clean or cooked, or if you lack the motivation, concentration or mental ability to plan and cook a main meal.

The mobility component

There are two rates of the mobility component. Note that you cannot qualify for either rate if it is impossible for you to go out or be taken out (eg, you are in a coma or cannot be moved).[17] If you are awarded the higher rate mobility component, you are also entitled to certain transport concessions (see p87).

Higher rate mobility component

You qualify for the higher rate mobility component if you:[18]

- are unable to walk or 'virtually unable to walk' (see p123) because of a physical disability; *or*

- are unable to walk out of doors without help because you are both blind and deaf; *or*
- have no feet; *or*
- are severely mentally impaired, have severe behavioural problems and qualify for the higher rate care component.

You are only treated as being **'virtually unable to walk'** if:[19]
- your ability to walk out of doors is so limited, as regards the distance, speed, length of time, or manner in which you can walk without severe discomfort, that you are virtually unable to walk; *or*
- the exertion required to walk would constitute a danger to your life or would be likely to lead to a serious deterioration in your health.

Note that you must be unable or virtually unable to walk for a physical, rather than a purely psychological reason, although many behavioural and mental problems have an organic or physical cause. You do not have to have a recognised medical condition to qualify.[20] The test is applied as if you were using any artificial aid (eg, a stick) which would be suitable for you (unless you have no feet).[21] The test is whether you can walk out of doors, taking into account uneven surfaces and other obstacles and weather conditions.[22] There is no specific distance below which you qualify as 'virtually unable to walk'. Your stamina, speed, manner of walking and recovery time should be taken into account. Any walking you can only do with 'severe discomfort' must be ignored.[23] Severe discomfort can include pain, breathlessness and tiredness.[24]

Lower rate mobility component
You qualify for the lower rate mobility component if you are able to walk but are unable to take advantage of your walking ability outdoors, apart from on familiar routes, without guidance or supervision from another person for most of the time.

Any walking you can do on familiar routes is ignored. **'Guidance'** can include being physically led or directed, being helped to avoid obstacles and being persuaded or reassured. **'Supervision'** can include being monitored and encouraged. You may qualify for the lower rate if you have learning disabilities or are blind or deaf, or suffer from panic attacks, agoraphobia or epilepsy.[25]

You cannot qualify, however, on the basis of fear or anxiety, unless they are symptoms of a mental disability and are severe enough to prevent you from going out to unfamiliar places without guidance or supervision.[26]

Additional rules for children
Children can qualify for the higher rate mobility component from the age of 3 and the lower rate from the age of 5. The three months before the relevant birthday can count towards the three-month qualifying period.[27]

Children under 16 can only qualify for the lower rate mobility component if they need substantially more guidance or supervision than children of the same age in normal health, or guidance or supervision which such other children would not need.[28]

Terminal illness

You are regarded as **'terminally ill'** if you are suffering from a progressive disease and can reasonably be expected to die within six months as a result of that disease.[29] Claims for DLA on the basis of terminal illness are dealt with under special rules. If you are terminally ill, you automatically qualify for the higher rate care component without having to satisfy the three-month qualifying period, and you do not have to satisfy the three- and six-month qualifying conditions in respect of the mobility component either (see p120).[30] You also do not have to have been in Great Britain for 26 weeks in the last year to qualify for DLA.[31] You do not have to complete the sections of the claim form relating to care needs but you do need to submit a special form called a DS1500, which has to be completed by your doctor, giving details of your medical condition. You should still complete the section on mobility as that is not awarded automatically. Somebody can claim DLA for you without your knowledge or authority if you are terminally ill.[32]

DLA and other benefits

DLA is a particularly valuable benefit because it can be paid on top of any other benefit and does not count as income for means-tested benefits and tax credits. It can also entitle you to extra amounts of means-tested benefits and tax credits (in the form of disability and severe disability additions) and access to the Independent Living (2006) Fund, see p73.

If you get the higher rate mobility component, you can also qualify for parking concessions under the blue badge scheme, exemption from road tax and help from the Motability scheme to lease or buy a car (see p87).

Amount[33]

	£pw
Higher rate care component	70.35
Middle rate care component	47.10
Lower rate care component	18.65
Higher rate mobility component	49.10
Lower rate mobility component	18.65

How to claim

You can only claim DLA in respect of your own care and mobility needs. If your partner also qualifies, s/he should make a separate claim. A claim for a child under

16 must be made by an appointee (normally a parent). A claim can be made on your behalf by an appointee if you are unable to manage your own affairs (see p92). You can also claim online or download a claim form at www.dwp.gov.uk.

Claims are initially dealt with by a regional Department of Work and Pensions (DWP) Disability Benefits Centre, or in some areas a central New Claims Unit. A claim must be made on form DLA1. There is one claim pack for adults and one for children under 16. You can get a claim pack by contacting your local Jobcentre Plus Office, by using the tear-off slip on leaflet DS704, by ringing 0800 882 200 (textphone 0800 243 355), or by downloading a form from www.dwp.gov.uk. The pack should be date stamped and you can be awarded benefit from the date on the form, provided the Disability Benefits Centre or New Claims Unit receives your completed application within six weeks.[34] This may be reduced to two weeks in the near future. Once your award is in payment, your claim is dealt with by the Disability Contact and Processing Unit in Blackpool.

The forms are quite long and can seem difficult to complete. The quality and quantity of relevant information that you give will largely decide the outcome of the application so give as much information as possible about your difficulties. Seek advice if you are unsure about how to complete the forms.

The questions on the forms are designed to test whether you satisfy the legal criteria for the care and mobility components. When answering the questions about your care needs, bear in mind that the test concerns the help you **need**, not the help you actually **get**, and you can legitimately say you need help regardless of whether you actually receive it. Concentrate on the personal care tasks such as washing, dressing, eating, bathing, toileting etc and not on domestic tasks such as shopping, cleaning, gardening etc. You can also qualify for DLA if you have mental health problems and you need someone to motivate you, check on you, support you in everyday tasks etc. If you have sensory difficulties (sight and hearing), mention the help you need with ordinary social activities and day to day living.

When answering the questions about your mobility problems, remember to state how far you can walk *without severe discomfort* (see p122).

You may be required to undergo a medical examination by a visiting doctor on behalf of the DWP if further information is needed to decide your claim.[35] It can be several weeks before you receive a decision but claims on the basis of terminal illness (see p124) should be dealt with more quickly (normally within 10 days).

Attendance allowance

Attendance allowance (AA) is paid to people aged 65 or over who need help with personal care (whether or not they have a carer). There are no NI contribution conditions and AA is not taxable. AA is a particularly valuable benefit to claim because it can be paid in addition to any other benefit, does not count as income for means-tested benefits and can entitle a claimant to disability additions paid with means-tested benefits (see p151).

Who can claim

You qualify for AA if you:[36]

- are aged 65 or over; *and*
- are present and ordinarily resident in Great Britain and have been present for at least 26 weeks in the past year (disregarding temporary absences of up to 26 weeks); *and*
- are not subject to immigration control (see p121); *and*
- satisfy one of the care conditions (see below) and have done so throughout the six months prior to your claim, or you are terminally ill (see below).

The care conditions

You can qualify for either a higher or lower rate of AA. The conditions for the higher rate of AA are the same as those for the higher rate care component of DLA (see p121). The conditions for the lower rate of AA are the same as those for the middle rate care component of DLA (see p121).[37] There is no equivalent in AA of the lower rate of care component of DLA, or the mobility component. If you are receiving the lower rate of AA and your care needs increase, you can request a supersession (see p106) after you have satisfied the conditions for the higher rate for six months.

Terminal illness

You are regarded as terminally ill for AA as for DLA (see p124). If you are terminally ill, you automatically qualify for the higher rate of AA without having to satisfy the six-month qualifying period.[38] You also do not have to have been in Great Britain for 26 weeks in the past year.[39] The same rules relating to claims apply to AA as for DLA (see p124).

Amount[40]

	£pw
Higher rate	70.35
Lower rate	47.10

How to claim

You can only claim AA in respect of your own care needs. If your partner also qualifies, s/he should make a separate claim. A claim can be made on your behalf if you are unable to manage your own affairs (see p92) or if you are terminally ill (see p124).

Claims for AA are dealt with initially by a regional DWP Disability Benefits Centre, or in some areas a New Claims Unit. A claim must be made on form AA1. You can get a claim pack by ringing 0800 882 200 (textphone 0800 243 355), by using the tear-off slip on leaflet DS702, or by downloading a form from www.dwp.gov.uk. You may also be able to claim at a local 'designated' or 'alternative' office (see p95). The pack should be date-stamped and benefit is payable from the date stamped, provided the Disability Benefits Centre receives your completed application within six weeks.[41] This may reduce to two weeks in the near future.

The forms are difficult to complete and the quality and quantity of relevant information you give will largely decide the outcome of the application. The same principles apply to AA as to DLA care (see p121).

You may be required to undergo a medical examination by a visiting doctor on behalf of the DWP if further information is needed to decide your claim.[42] It can be several weeks before you receive a decision but claims on the basis of terminal illness should be dealt with more quickly (normally within 10 days).

Industrial injuries benefits

Industrial injuries benefits are paid to people who are disabled as a result of an accident at work or a prescribed industrial disease. There are no NI contribution conditions and industrial injuries benefits are not taxable. There are three industrial injury benefits. The main benefit is called **industrial injuries disablement benefit**, which pays a weekly allowance depending on the extent of your disablement. You can claim it even if you are still working. The other two benefits, **reduced earnings allowance** and **retirement allowance**, are meant to compensate for loss of earnings. They are gradually being phased out, however, as they are only paid to people who became disabled prior to 1 October 1990.

Who can claim

You qualify for industrial injuries benefits if:[43]
- you suffer a 'personal injury' caused by an 'accident' which arose 'out of and in the course of' your employment as an 'employed earner'; *or*
- you are suffering from a 'prescribed disease' as a result of working in a 'prescribed occupation' (see p128); *and*
- as a result, you have suffered a 'loss of faculty' which has caused 'disablement' (see p128).

In addition, you must satisfy the following rules to qualify for the different types of industrial injury benefit.
- To qualify for **industrial injuries disablement benefit**, your disablement must normally be assessed as at least 14 per cent (see p128) and 90 days (excluding Sundays) must normally have elapsed since the accident or onset of the disease.[44]
- To qualify for **reduced earnings allowance**, you must have had an accident or contracted a prescribed disease before 1 October 1990 and be assessed as at least 1 per cent disabled. You must also be incapable of following your regular or equivalent employment because of the accident or disease.[45]

• To qualify for **retirement allowance,** you must be over pensionable age (see p133) and getting reduced earnings allowance when you gave up regular employment.[46]

Meaning of terms

'**Personal injury**' encompasses both physical and psychological damage.[47]

An '**accident**' is an 'unlooked for occurrence' or 'mishap'.[48] There can be difficulties if you become injured over a long period. The DWP may decide this is a 'process' rather than an 'accident'. Seek advice if this happens.

The accident must arise '**out of and in the course of**' your employment. This means it must have had some connection with your work and happened at a time and place you could reasonably be expected to be working.[49] You should be covered during normal breaks on your employer's property.[50] You are not generally covered while you are travelling to and from work, unless this can be seen as part of your job.[51]

'**Employed earner**' covers most employees but excludes most self-employed people (although agency workers, office cleaners and taxi drivers should be covered).[52]

A '**prescribed disease**' means a disease listed in regulations, which is known to have a link with a particular '**prescribed occupation**', which is also so listed. You must show that you are suffering from the disease as a result of working in a relevant prescribed occupation.[53]

A '**loss of faculty**' means damage or impairment to the body or mind.

'**Disablement**' is any resulting inability to carry out a function.[54] The extent of your disablement is expressed in terms of a percentage figure. Some disabilities have prescribed percentages set out in regulations but others are left to the discretion of a DWP decision maker. Decision makers are not doctors but their decisions are usually based on a medical report following a DWP medical examination.[55] If your disablement is only partly due to an accident or prescribed disease there may be an 'offset' or addition to your percentage disablement. The rules on this and if you have suffered two or more accidents or diseases are complex and you should seek advice if this applies to you.[56] The decision maker also decides the period of your assessment, which can be fixed or for life.[57] If your condition deteriorates, you should request a re-assessment.

Amount

Disablement benefit

The amount you get depends on the extent of your disablement.[58]

% disablement	£pw
Between 14-20	28.72
Up to 30	43.08
Up to 40	57.44
Up to 50	71.80
Up to 60	86.16

Up to 70	100.52
Up to 80	114.88
Up to 90	129.24
Up to 100	143.60

Note: the amounts payable are less if you are under the age of 18.

You may also qualify for two increases of disablement benefit:

- **constant attendance allowance** of up to £115 a week is payable if you are assessed as 100 per cent disabled and need constant attendance;[59]
- **exceptionally severe disablement allowance** of £57.50 a week is payable if you are entitled to at least £57.50 constant attendance allowance and are likely to permanently require constant attendance.[60]

Reduced earnings allowance

You are entitled to the difference between the earnings you would have received in your previous regular occupation and the earnings you currently receive, or could receive in a job you could do. The calculation is complex and open to argument so seek advice if you are unhappy with your assessment. The maximum you can receive, however, is £57.44 a week and the total amount of your disablement benefit and reduced earnings allowance cannot exceed 140 per cent of the standard rate of industrial injuries disablement benefit.[61]

Retirement allowance

You are entitled to £14.36 a week, or 25 per cent of the reduced earnings allowance you were getting, whichever is the lower.[62]

How to claim

You should ask for the appropriate claim form by contacting your local Jobcentre Plus office. Leaflet NI6 has details about claiming disablement benefit. You can apply for a declaration that you have had an accident on form BI95, in readiness for a subsequent claim for disablement benefit. You are normally asked to attend a medical examination in connection with your claim (see p124).

War pensions and compensation scheme

Various levels of war pensions or compensation are payable to forces personnel disabled by war service, civilians disabled by war injury and war widows. For further details, contact the Service Personnel and Veterans Agency, Norcross, Thornton-Cleveleys FY5 3WP, telephone 0800 169 2277, or visit www.veterans-uk.info. War pensions and compensation are not taxable.

Vaccine damage payments

A tax-free lump sum payment of £120,000 is payable to anyone who is severely disabled as a result of specified vaccinations. If you received a lower payment in the past, you may be entitled to a top-up payment. For claim forms and further details contact the Vaccine Damage Payments Unit, Palatine House, Lancaster Road, Preston PR1 1HB, telephone 01772 899 944 or visit www.direct.gov.uk.

3. Other non-means-tested benefits

Carer's allowance

Carer's allowance (CA) is paid to people who are caring for a severely disabled person. There are no national insurance (NI) contribution conditions but CA is taxable (apart from increases for children).

Who can claim

You qualify for CA if:[63]

- you are 'regularly and substantially' caring for a 'severely disabled person' (see below); *and*
- you are present and ordinarily resident in Great Britain and have been present for at least 26 weeks in the past year (disregarding temporary absences of up to four weeks, or longer if you have gone abroad with the disabled person to look after her/him); *and*
- you are not subject to immigration control (p121); *and*
- you satisfy the rules about your age (see p131); *and*
- your net earnings from any employment do not exceed £95 a week; *and*
- you are not attending a course of education for more than 20 hours a week, excluding time spent on 'unsupervised study' (note that private study involving coursework may still count as 'supervised'[64]).

Regularly and substantially caring for a severely disabled person

To qualify for CA for any week, you must spend at least 35 hours in that week caring for a person who is receiving AA or the middle or higher rate care component of DLA (see pp121 and 125).[65] Care is not restricted to help with bodily functions and could include providing assistance (of any sort), supervision and even just company, as well as time spent preparing and clearing up after meals. You can have temporary breaks from caring without losing your CA, as long as they do not add up to more than four weeks in any six months (or 12 weeks if you or the disabled person has spent at least eight of those weeks in hospital).[66] Entitlement to CA also continues for up to eight weeks following the death of the person you are caring for.[67] Note the following rules.

- You cannot qualify for CA during any week in which you are caring for somebody for less than 35 hours a week (subject to the above rules about temporary breaks), even if you spend more than 35 hours on average looking after her/him.[68]
- You cannot satisfy the 35-hour rule by adding together the hours you spend looking after more than one disabled person.[69]
- If you are looking after two or more people for more than 35 hours a week each, you can only qualify for one award of CA. If you and another person each spend more than 35 hours a week looking after the same person, only one of you can receive CA (this rule may contravene the Human Rights Act but you will need specialist legal advice to challenge it).[70] If you both claim, the DWP will decide whom to pay. One of you may be better off claiming CA than another (see below).

Rules about your age

You must be aged 16 or over to claim CA.[71] There is no upper age limit.

If you were aged 65 or over and getting CA before 28 October 2002, you can continue to get it even if you are no longer caring for a disabled person or you are earning more than £95 a week.[72]

Net earnings from employment[73]

Your net earnings are your gross earnings from paid work, less tax, NI contributions and half of any contributions you make towards a pension scheme. If you have to pay someone, other than a close relative, to look after the person you are caring for while you are working, the amount you pay can be deducted from your earnings up to a maximum of 50 per cent of your net earnings. 'Close relative' means a parent, son, daughter, brother, sister, or partner of yours or of the person you are caring for. Certain childcare costs can also be deducted from your earnings.

Carer's allowance and other benefits

The relationship between CA and other benefits can be complex and claiming CA is not always in the best interests of yourself and others. If you are unsure whether you should claim CA, seek further advice (see Appendix 2).

- CA counts as income for means-tested benefits (see p213) but can entitle you to a carer premium with your income support (IS), income-based jobseeker's allowance (JSA), income-related employment and support allowance (ESA) or a carer's addition with your pension credit (PC).
- CA cannot be paid at the same time as another 'earnings replacement benefit' (see p118). It can still be worth claiming, however, because you are entitled to a carer premium/addition with your IS, income-related ESA or income-based JSA, PC, housing benefit (HB) and council tax benefit (CTB) if you are entitled to CA, even though you are not actually receiving it because you are getting

another 'earnings replacement benefit' (see p118). This is called 'underlying entitlement'. The carer premium/addition may also reduce your liability for home care charges by increasing the amount of the income you must be left with after paying charges (see Chapter 4).

- If you are receiving CA, the person you are caring for is not entitled to a severe disability premium/addition with her/his IS, income-based JSA, income-related ESA, HB, CTB or PC (see p151). In some circumstances, it may be better for the disabled person to get the severe disability premium/addition rather than you getting CA. Where, for example, you are receiving a means-tested benefit, your CA is fully taken into account as income and you only gain financially from the carer premium/addition, which may be worth considerably less to you than the severe disability premium/addition that the disabled person gets. If, however, you have claimed CA but are not receiving it because you are getting another 'earnings replacement benefit' (see p118), the person you are caring for remains entitled to the severe disability premium/addition and you can also get the carer premium/addition (see pp153 and 160). Backdated payments of CA do not affect payments of severe disability premium/addition which have already been made, so if, for example, you delay claiming CA and can get your claim backdated for three months, the person you are caring for can keep the severe disability premium/addition for that three months, whereas s/he would have lost it straight away had you claimed earlier.

- If you and somebody else are looking after the same person and are both eligible for CA, the above considerations may mean that it is financially better for one of you to claim it rather than the other.

- If you give up or fail to claim your entitlement to CA in order to qualify for, or get more, means-tested benefit, the DWP can treat you as if you were receiving it and deduct it from your means-tested benefit entitlement. This rule should not apply, however, if you give up CA so that the person you are caring for can get a severe disability premium/addition, as long as s/he is not a member of your family for benefit purposes.

Amount[74]

Basic allowance

The basic allowance is £53.10 a week.

Adult dependant addition

You are entitled to an additional weekly increase of £31.70 for your spouse or a registered civil partner, or an adult who is looking after your child, if s/he is residing with you. You still count as residing with her/him during the temporary absences or while either of you is in hospital. You are not entitled to an increase, however, if s/he is getting another 'earnings replacement benefit' (see p118), or has weekly net earnings and/or a private or occupational pension exceeding

£31.70. For details of how earnings are calculated for this purpose (including childcare allowances), see CPAG's *Welfare Benefits and Tax Credits Handbook*. Note that the earnings rules are different to those described in Chapter 8 for means-tested benefits.

How to claim

You should claim in writing on form DS700 (unless you get retirement pension, in which case you can use a shorter form – DS700(SP)). If you are 60 or over, you may also be able to claim at a local 'designated' or 'alternative' office in some areas (see p95). You can also claim online or download a claim form at www.direct.gov.uk/carers. You must make a separate claim for a dependant's addition as it is not paid automatically.

If the person you are caring for is in the process of claiming DLA or AA, you should claim CA anytime within three months of the date the cared for person receives her/his DLA/AA decision letter. Your CA will then be backdated to the date of s/he was awarded DLA/AA. In any other circumstances CA can only be backdated for three months.

Healthy Start food and vitamins

The Healthy Start scheme provides vouchers for free vitamins and food, which can be used to buy milk and fresh fruit and vegetables. The scheme is for pregnant women and those who have children under 4. You have to be in receipt of, or in a family where someone is in receipt of, IS, income-based JSA, income-related ESA, or CTC (but not with WTC) and have a gross annual income that does not exceed £16,040.

Asylum seekers in receipt of asylum support who are pregnant or have a child under three should receive an additional payment to help them buy healthy food.

Children under the age of 5 are also entitled to free milk for each day they are in daycare, provided they are there for two hours or more each day.

State retirement pension

State retirement pension is paid to people over pensionable age, which is currently 60 for women and 65 for men, although this increases for women from April 2010.[75] For most types of pensions, eligibility and the amount payable are dependent on your NI contribution record (see p135). State retirement pension is taxable (apart from increases for children).

Who can claim

There are three main categories of the basic state retirement pension (A, B and D). There is also an additional state pension scheme. Despite the name 'retirement pension', you do not actually have to retire to claim a pension (but you must be over pensionable age) and if you continue to work your earnings will not reduce your pension.

Category A pension
You qualify for a Category A pension if:[76]
- you satisfy the NI contribution conditions (see p135); *and*
- you are over pensionable age (see p133).

Category B pension
You qualify for a Category B pension if: [77]
- your spouse or registered civil partner satisfies the NI contribution conditions (see p135) and is entitled to a Category A pension (see above); *and*
- you are both over pensionable age (see p133).

You qualify for a Category B pension if you are a widow and:[78]
- your husband satisfied the NI contribution conditions (see p135) or died from an industrial injury or disease (see p127); *and*
- you were aged 60 or over when he died or you are aged 60 or over and entitled to a widow's pension; *or*
- your husband died on or after 9 April 2001 and you were entitled to bereavement allowance before you were 60, or widowed parent's allowance after you were 45.

You qualify for a Category B pension if you are a widower and:[79]
- your wife satisfied the NI contribution conditions (see p135); *and*
- you turned 65 after 5 April 1979; *and*
- your wife died when you were both over pensionable age; *or*
- your wife died on or after 9 April 2001 and you were entitled to bereavement allowance before you were 65, or widowed parent's allowance after you were 45.

Category D pension
You qualify for a Category D pension if:[80]
- you are aged 80 or over; *and*
- you have been resident in Great Britain for at least 10 of the 20 years which include the day before your 80th birthday; *and*
- you are not entitled to a higher category pension.

Additional state pension
You may be entitled to additional state pension under the State Earnings-Related Pension Scheme (SERPS), depending on your earnings and NI contributions as an employee from 1978 to 2002.[81] SERPS was replaced by the state second pension in April 2002 (SERPS entitlement already earned is protected).[82] You can accrue entitlement under this scheme through your earnings as an employee. If you are receiving CA, or long-term IB, or you are caring for a disabled adult or child, you may also be able to build up entitlement to state second pension while you are

not working (if you are a carer but are not receiving CA, you may need to inform the Revenue on form CF411, which you can get by calling 0845 302 1479).

National insurance contribution conditions[83]

NI contributions are payable on earnings above a certain limit. You can also be credited with contributions during periods of unemployment, incapacity for work or while you are receiving CA (see p132).

To qualify for a full Category A or B retirement pension, sufficient contributions must have been paid or credited for all the years of your 'working life' (less an allowance of up to five years). This reduces to 30 years from April 2010 for people who reach pension age after that point. A minimum number of contributions must have been paid during at least one tax year. Your **'working life'** normally runs from the age of 16 up to pensionable age or the year of death (if earlier) but does not include years spent out of the labour market while bringing up a child or caring for a disabled person (note that if you are not getting CA, you should notify the Revenue that you are a carer – see above). If you meet the NI conditions for a proportion of your working life, a reduced-rate pension may be payable. It may be possible to enhance your contribution record by paying Class 3 voluntary contributions at a later date (get advice before doing this). Widows, widowers and divorcees may be able to use the contribution record of their late or former spouse or registered civil partner to help them qualify for a Category A pension.

Amount

Full basic pension[84]

	£pw
Category A/Category B (widow/widower)	95.25
Category B other/Category D	57.05

Adult dependants[85]

You are entitled to a weekly increase of Category A retirement pension of up to £57.05 for a spouse or registered civil partner if s/he is 'residing with' you, or you are contributing to her/his maintenance at a weekly rate of at least the amount of the increase. You still count as 'residing with' her/him during temporary absences or while either of you is in hospital. You are only entitled to an increase for your husband if you were previously getting an increase in IB for him (see p138). You are not entitled to an increase for a spouse or civil partner, however, if s/he is receiving another 'earnings replacement benefit' (see p117), or if s/he has weekly net earnings and/or a private or occupational pension exceeding £64.30 (or exceeding the amount of the increase if s/he is not residing with you). For full details of how earnings are calculated for this purpose (including childcare allowances), see CPAG's *Welfare Benefits and Tax Credits Handbook*. Note that the earnings rules are different to those described in Chapter 8 for means-tested benefits.[86]

If you are not receiving an increase for a spouse or civil partner, you can claim an increase for another adult who is looking after a child for whom you are responsible. The rules are the same as for a spouse but you can also qualify for an increase for an adult you are employing (in which case the 'earnings rule' only applies if s/he is living with you, and the amount you are paying her/him is ignored).

Other additions and lump sums

- You may be entitled to additional pension under SERPS or the state second pension scheme (see p134).
- You may be entitled to graduated retirement benefit based on your NI contributions from 1961 to 1975.
- You can qualify for extra weekly pension or a lump sum by not claiming (deferring) your entitlement for a period of time.[87] You are entitled to a 1 per cent increase in your weekly pension for every five weeks you defer claiming it. Alternatively, you can get the pension you deferred in a lump sum, plus interest of 2 per cent above the Bank of England basic rate if you have deferred taking your pension for at least 12 months. You cannot accrue extra pension, however, if you are getting CA or severe disablement allowance. Seek advice about whether it is in your best interests to defer taking your pension before doing so (see Appendix 2). You should note, in particular, that any weekly pension you have deferred counts as notional income when calculating your PC, HB and CTB.

How to claim

The Pension Service should send you form BR1 about four months before you reach pensionable age. You can either complete and submit the claim form, or give your details over the telephone on 0800 731 7898 or 0800 731 7936 (Welsh language). Textphone is available on 0800 731 7339 and 0800 731 7013 (Welsh language). You must make a separate claim for increases for any dependants as they are not paid automatically. You can get a pension forecast of your likely entitlement by completing form BR19 or by phoning the Future Pension Centre on 0845 300 0168. You should claim a Category D pension on form BR2488. You can also get the claim forms and a pension forecast online at www.thepensionservice.gov.uk or in some areas, claim at a local 'designated' or 'alternative' office (see p95).

Bereavement benefits

Bereavement benefits, are payable to widows, widowers and, since 5 December 2005, bereaved civil partners (see p93). You can claim bereavement benefits in respect of a spouse or registered civil partner who died on or after 9 April

2001 (you can also claim widowed parent's allowance in respect of a wife who died before 9 April 2001, if you satisfied the qualifying conditions on 9 April 2001).

If your husband died before 9 April 2001, you are eligible for widows' benefits instead of bereavement benefits (see p139).

Who can claim

There are three types of bereavement benefits. You can get a bereavement payment and either widowed parent's allowance or bereavement allowance. Entitlement is not affected by any earnings or savings you have. Bereavement payment is not taxable. Bereavement allowance and widowed parent's allowance are taxable (apart from any increases for children).

To claim bereavement benefits as a widow or widower, you must generally have been legally married to your late spouse, or in a registered civil partnership with your late civil partner, when s/he died. The law is complex, however, and you should seek advice if:

- you lived with your late partner as 'husband and wife' for a long time but were never married; *or*
- your marriage was polygamous; *or*
- the DWP decides your marriage was not valid under UK law or does not accept that your spouse is dead.

You are not entitled to bereavement benefits if you remarry, or while you are living with another person as if you are 'husband and wife' or 'civil partners' (see p93).[88]

Bereavement payment

You qualify for a one-off lump sum bereavement payment of £2,000 if:[89]

- your spouse (or registered civil partner from 5 December 2005) died on or after 9 April 2001; *and*
- s/he paid a minimum number of NI contributions in any one tax year, or died from an industrial injury or disease (see p127); *and*
- when s/he died, you were either under pensionable age (see p133), or s/he was not entitled to a Category A retirement pension (see p134).

Widowed parent's allowance

You qualify for a weekly widowed parent's allowance if:[90]

- you are under pensionable age (see p133); *and*
- your spouse (or registered 'civil partner' from 5 December 2005 – see p93) died on or after 9 April 2001, or your wife died before 9 April 2001 and you were under 65 on that date and have not remarried; *and*
- s/he satisfied the NI contribution conditions (the conditions are as for retirement pensions – see p134) or died from an industrial injury or disease (see p127); *and*

- you are pregnant by your late husband (or by artificial means if you were residing with your husband when he died), or you are entitled to child benefit for a 'qualifying child' (ie, a child of yours and your late spouse, or a child for whom you, your late spouse or registered 'civil partner' were getting child benefit when your spouse died).

Bereavement allowance

You qualify for a weekly bereavement allowance for up to 52 weeks if:[91]
- you are under pensionable age (see p133); *and*
- your spouse (or registered civil partner from December 2005 – see p93) died on or after 9 April 2001; *and*
- s/he satisfied the NI contribution conditions (the conditions are as for retirement pensions, see p133) or died from an industrial injury or disease (see p127); *and*
- when s/he died you were aged over 45 but under pensionable age.

If you are entitled to widowed parent's allowance, you cannot qualify for bereavement allowance until your entitlement to widowed parent's allowance ceases.

Amount[92]

Basic amounts

Bereavement payment	£2,000 (lump sum)
Widowed parent's allowance	£95.25
Bereavement allowance	£95.25

Additional amounts

You may be entitled to additional widowed parent's allowance based on the earnings and NI contributions of your late spouse or registered 'civil partner' (see p93) under SERPS or the state second pension (see p135).

Reductions

Your widowed parent's allowance or bereavement allowance may be paid at a reduced rate if the NI record of your late spouse or registered 'civil partner' (see p93) was incomplete (see p135 – but note that you may be able to increase your entitlement by paying Class 3 contributions).

Your bereavement allowance is reduced by 7 per cent for each year or part year by which you were under 55 when your spouse or registered civil partner died.[93]

How to claim

Claim on form BB1 which you can get from your local Jobcentre Plus office or by telephoning a contact centre. If you are aged 60 or over, you may be able to claim at a local 'designated' or 'alternative' office (see p95). You must claim a bereavement payment within 12 months of your spouse's death, and your claim for widowed parent's allowance or a bereavement allowance can only be backdated for up to three months.[94] The time limits may be increased if you were unaware of your husband's death – seek advice if this applies to you.[95]

Widows' benefits[96]

Widows' benefits were replaced by bereavement benefits on 9 April 2001 and are only available to widows whose husbands died before that date.

Who can claim[97]

- **Widow's payment** is a lump sum payment of £1,000. The rules are the same as for bereavement payment (see p137), except that for 'spouse' read 'husband'. You can only now qualify for a widow's payment if you have only recently become aware of your husband's death.
- **Widowed mother's allowance** is a weekly benefit for widows with dependent children. The rules are the same as for widowed parent's allowance (see p137), except that for 'spouse' read 'husband' and there is no upper age limit.
- **Widow's pension** is payable under the same rules as bereavement allowance (see p138), except that for 'spouse' read 'husband'. In addition, widow's pension is payable for an indefinite period up to the age of 65.

Amount[98]

The amounts payable (basic amounts, additional amounts and reductions) are the same as for the equivalent bereavement benefits (see p138) except that the widow's payment is £1,000 and SERPS additions (see p138) are payable with widow's pension.

How to claim[99]

Claim forms BW1 are available from your local Jobcentre Plus office. The time limits are the same as for bereavement benefits (see p136).

Incapacity benefit

Incapacity benefit (IB) was abolished for new claims on 27 October 2008. This means you are only still entitled to it if you were eligible on that date unless you can be linked back to a previous claim (see below for linking rules).

You can only be entitled to IB now if you:[100]

- are already entitled to it (and continue to meet the qualifying conditions below); or
- were previously entitled to IB, your new (repeat) claim for IB can be linked to that previous award under the linking rules and you meet the qualifying conditions below; or

- are entitled to IS on grounds of 'disability', claim IB now and meet the qualifying conditions below.

For full details, see CPAG's *Welfare Benefits and Tax Credits Handbook*.

The qualifying conditions

You qualify for IB if:

- you are already entitled, can establish entitlement under the linking rules, or are getting IS on grounds of 'disability'; *and*
- you are assessed as, or treated as, incapable of work; *and*
- you are within a 'period of incapacity for work'; *and*
- for short-term IB you are not more than five years above pension age and, for long-term IB, you are not over pension age; *and*
- you are not entitled to statutory sick pay (SSP); *and either*
- you have paid (or been credited with) sufficient NI contributions; *or*
- you qualify as someone who became incapable of work in youth; *or*
- you are no more than five years over pension age (60 for a woman, 65 for a man), your period of incapacity for work began before you reached pension age, and you would qualify for a Category B retirement pension as a widow, widower or surviving civil partner, or a Category A retirement pension had you not deferred claiming it or 'de-retired'. (Note: this provision only allows you to qualify for short-term IB); *or*
- your spouse died before 9 April 2001 and you qualify as a widow or widower.

Linking rules

A new claim for IB can be linked to a previous IB claim if:[101]

- there has been a break in your incapacity for work and the start of your current period of incapacity for work falls no more than eight weeks after your previous period of incapacity for work ended; *or*
- you are a 'welfare to work beneficiary'.

This means that, in these circumstances, as long as you meet the normal IB entitlement conditions including, for the time being, the tests for incapacity for work, you can still qualify for IB. If you qualify for IB under these linking rules but you claim ESA, your claim for ESA is treated as a claim for IB.[102]

Amount

Basic amount

There are three rates of IB.[103]

- The lower rate of short-term IB is £67.75 a week. It is paid for the first 28 weeks of entitlement.
- The higher rate of short-term IB is £80.15 a week. It is paid after you have been receiving the lower rate of IB or SSP (see p142) for 28 weeks.

- The long-term rate of IB is £89.80 a week. It is paid after you have been receiving the higher rate of short-term IB for 28 weeks (ie, after a year of incapacity).

If you are terminally ill or entitled to the highest rate care component of DLA, you are entitled to the long-term rate of IB after six months, rather than a year, of incapacity.[104] Previous periods of incapacity may link to your current period to entitle you to a higher rate of IB (see p142).

Additional amounts
- If you are over pensionable age (see p133), short-term IB is paid at an enhanced rate of £86.20 (lower rate) or £89.80 (higher rate). You only qualify if you are less than five years over pensionable age, your period of incapacity began before you reached pensionable age and you have deferred entitlement to a Category A or B retirement pension (see p134).[105] You do not need to have satisfied the normal NI conditions for IB but you need to have satisfied the conditions for a Category A or B retirement pension (see p134).
- You are entitled to a weekly age addition of £15.65 with long-term IB if you were under 35, or £6.55 if you were under 45, when your period of incapacity began.[106]
- You may qualify for an extra £41.35 a week short-term IB (£51.10 if you are over pensionable age), or £53.10 long-term IB, for a spouse or registered civil partner (see p93) aged 60 or over, or for an adult who is looking after your child. The rules are the same as for Category A retirement pension (see p134) except that your spouse or registered civil partner must be aged 60 or over, or you must be residing with her/him and responsible for a child, and the earnings/private or occupational pension limit is £41.35 a week for short-term IB (£51.10 if you are over pensionable age) and £64.30 a week for long-term IB (£53.10 if you are maintaining an adult dependant who does not live with you).[107]
- If you were receiving invalidity benefit on 12 April 1995 and have remained incapable of work, you may be entitled to 'transitionally protected' higher amounts of IB.[108]

Reductions for private and occupational pensions
If your entitlement to IB began on or after 6 April 2001, your IB is reduced by 50 per cent of the weekly amount above £85 of any personal and occupational pensions you are receiving.[109] This does not apply, however, if you are getting the highest rate care component of DLA.[110]

How to claim
If you are still eligible to claim IB (ie, via the linking rules) claim on form SC1 from you local Jobcentre Plus office or by phoning 0800 055 6688.

Contributory employment and support allowance

Employment and support allowance (ESA) was introduced on 27 October 2008. It is a benefit for people who have 'limited capability for work' (ie, it is unreasonable to require them to work because of illness or disability), and who are not entitled to statutory sick pay (SSP). ESA replaced IB and IS on grounds of 'disability' for most *new* claimants (see the exceptions below). This means that *new claimants usually need to claim ESA instead of IB or instead of IS on disability grounds.*

There are two types of ESA. **Contributory** ESA is paid if you satisfy the NI conditions or your limited capacity began before you reached 20 (or 25 in some circumstances) – ESA in youth. There is no means test.

Income-related ESA is paid if you pass the means test. You do not have to satisfy the NI conditions. It is possible to receive contributory ESA (including ESA in youth) topped up with income-related ESA.

Who can claim

You qualify for contributory ESA if you:
- have 'limited capability for work' (see p143); *and*
- are not in work (with some exceptions – see below); *and*
- are aged 16 or over but under pension age; *and*
- are in Great Britain; *and*
- are not entitled in your own right to IS or jobseeker's allowance (JSA); *and*
- are not entitled to SSP; *and*
- satisfy the NI contribution conditions or the rules for ESA in youth.

National insurance contribution conditions

There are two contribution conditions. First, you must have paid a minimum number of NI contributions in one of the three tax years before the start of the calendar year in which you claim (if you were entitled to IB or CA in the tax year before you claim, the contributions can have been paid in *any* tax year).[111] Second, you must have paid or been credited with a minimum number of contributions during each of the last two tax years before the start of the calendar year in which your period of incapacity for work began.[112] Tax years run from April to April.

ESA in youth

You can qualify for ESA without satisfying the NI contribution conditions if you are:[113]
- aged 16 or over; *and*
- aged under 20 (or in some circumstances aged under 25) when the 'period of limited capability for work' began; *and*
- not under 19 and attending a course of education for 21 hours or more a week, excluding special tuition for people with disabilities; *and*
- present and ordinarily resident in the UK and have been here for at least 26 weeks in the last year; *and*

- not subject to immigration control; *and*
- you have had limited capability for work for a continuous period of 28 weeks before the first day your entitlement can begin and you still have limited capability for work.

If you previously qualified for ESA on the basis of your age, you may be able to re-qualify even if you are now over 20 (or 25). Seek advice if this may apply to you.

You should also note the following points.

- If you are an employee aged under 65, and your gross earnings are at least £95 a week, you will normally be entitled to SSP of £79.15 a week from your employer for up to 28 weeks while you are off sick. For full details of the SSP rules, see CPAG's *Welfare Benefits and Tax Credits Handbook*. You may also be entitled to sick pay under your contract of employment. You cannot be paid ESA while you are entitled to SSP.
- Although you need a medical certificate from your doctor to start an ESA claim, you will normally also undergo a work capability assessment (WCA) organised by Jobcentre Plus. This process may mean you are classed as not having a limited capacity for work – ie, you are fit to work. See below and CPAG's *Welfare Benefits and Tax Credits Handbook* for more information about the WCA.
- You must be incapable of work for at least four consecutive days to qualify for ESA. Periods of incapacity which are separated by 12 weeks or less are treated as a single period. In some circumstances, the linking period can be extended to up to two years if you have been working or training. The linking rules mean you may be able to automatically re-qualify for ESA. The rules are complex, however, and you should seek advice if you think using them may assist you. ESA is not payable for the first three days of a period of incapacity (**'waiting days'**) but you do not have to wait a further three days if you become sick again in the same 'period of incapacity'.
- You will have to attend a series of 'work-focused interviews' while you are claiming ESA and complete an 'action plan' aiming to get you back to work.
- Existing IB claimants will be transferred to ESA in the next few years.

Limited capacity for work

The **work capability assessment** (WCA) measures your ability to perform a range of physical and mental activities which are laid down in regulations.[114] Each descriptor is allocated a fixed number of points. To be incapable of work for benefit purposes, you must score at least 15 points. For a full list of the descriptors and details of their application, see CPAG's *Welfare Benefits and Tax Credits Handbook*.

You are generally not entitled to ESA in any week in which you work. However, some work is allowed. Its is called **'permitted work'** and includes:[115]

- voluntary work;

- domestic work in your home or caring for a relative;
- work for an unlimited period for which you earn up to £20 a week;
- work paying up to £92 a week, which is part of a hospital treatment programme, or supervised by someone employed by a public or local authority, or voluntary organisation to find work for people with disabilities (this could include work done in a sheltered workshop);
- work of less than 16 hours a week paying up to £92 a week for a maximum of 52 weeks. If you are treated as having limited capability for work related activity and are in the support group, you can do this work for an unlimited period. Otherwise, you can start a new period of work once you have been off benefit for at least eight weeks, or after 52 weeks have elapsed since you last worked.

Your earnings for the purposes of the above rules are your net earnings, after tax, NI contributions and, in certain circumstances, childcare costs. For more details, see CPAG's *Welfare Benefits and Tax Credits Handbook*. If you do 'permitted' work within the earnings limits above this will not affect either you contributory or income-related ESA. However, also note, that the earnings rules are different to those described in Chapter 8 for other means-tested benefits. For example, a person on ESA and HB may think s/he can earn £92 before her/his benefits are affected. In fact, earnings of that level could reduce the HB, as that benefit only has a £20 earnings disregard.

You can appeal against any decision that you are capable of work (see p107)

Amount

The assessment phase

ESA claimants will normally go through an assessment phase that lasts for 13 weeks. During this period rates are:

Contributory ESA

Single claimant aged 25 or over	£64.30
Single claimant under 25	£50.95

The main phase

Once the assessment phase is over, a number of changes are made. Firstly, under 25s become entitled to the same rate as those aged 25 and over. Secondly, you become entitled to either a work-related activity component or a support component. These are added to the basic allowance.

Work-related activity and support components

As part of the WCA two decision are made: firstly whether or not you have limited capability for work and therefore continue to be entitled to ESA; secondly, whether you also have limited capability for work-related activity. If you satisfy this you are placed in the support group. If not, you are placed in the work-related activity group.

The amounts for each component are:

Work-related activity component	£25.50
Support component	£30.85

There is no couple rate of either component and you can only receive one of the components.

If you are placed in the work-related activity group you are required to attend a work-focused health related assessment and WFIs. Failure to attend these, without a good reason, may lead to reductions in your benefit.

Reductions for private and occupational pensions

Your ESA is reduced by 50 per cent of the weekly amount above £85 of any personal and occupational pensions you are receiving. This does not apply, however, if you are getting the highest rate care component of DLA.

How to claim

Claim by phoning the Jobcentre Plus contact centre on 0800 055 6688.

You can also notify your wish to make a claim online, by submitting a short electronic form at www.dwp.gov.uk/eservice. Someone from the DWP should then telephone you. But submitting the electronic form is not the same as actually making a claim, so if you do not get a quick reply, seek advice.

Appeals

You can appeal decisions about whether you have failed the limited capability for work test, if you have been subjected to sanctions, or if you think you should have been placed in the support group. While your appeal is pending you are treated as if you are still in the assessment phase and are paid the basic allowance.

Severe disablement allowance[116]

Severe disablement allowance (SDA) was abolished for new claimants from 6 April 2001. This means that you can only qualify for SDA if you were already entitled to it before that date and remain incapable of work. You may be able to re-qualify for SDA in certain circumstances if your entitlement has stopped. The rules are complex so seek advice about this.

SDA is paid to severely disabled people over the age of 20 who have been incapable of work (see p143) for at least 28 weeks but cannot qualify for IB because they have not made sufficient NI contributions.

The basic rate of SDA is £57.45 a week. Age and dependants' additions are also payable.

Contribution-based jobseeker's allowance

Contribution-based jobseeker's allowance (JSA) is paid for up to six months to people who are not in full-time work or subject to immigration control (see p121). You must have made sufficient NI contributions to qualify and must be capable of work, available for work and actively seeking work (the 'labour market conditions'). If you do not satisfy the NI conditions, you may qualify for income-based JSA (see p158). If you do not satisfy the labour market conditions, you may qualify for IS (see p147). Weekly payments of contribution-based JSA are £64.30 or £50.95 if you are under 25. For more details, see CPAG's *Welfare Benefits and Tax Credits Handbook*.

Maternity, paternity and adoption benefits

There are two types of maternity benefits (plus the 'Sure Start maternity grant' and health in pregnancy grant – see pp183 and below).
* **Statutory maternity pay**[117] (SMP) is paid by employers to women who have ceased work because of pregnancy. You must have been working for an employer for at least 26 weeks and earning an average of more than £95 a week to qualify. SMP is paid for up to 39 weeks, at the rate of 90 per cent of your average weekly earnings for six weeks and £123.06 a week for a further 33 weeks (or 90 per cent of your average earnings if this is less).
* **Maternity allowance**[118] is paid by the DWP to pregnant women who are not entitled to SMP. You must have been working as an employee or self-employed person for at least 26 of the 66 weeks before you have your baby. It is paid for 39 weeks at the rate of £123.06 a week (or 90 per cent of your average weekly earnings if this is less).

Alternatively you can qualify for:[119]
* **statutory adoption pay** (SAP), if you have adopted a child (the rules are similar to SMP and the amount payable is the lesser of £123.06 a week or 90 per cent of your average weekly earnings);
* **statutory paternity pay**, if you are the partner of a new mother or adoptive parent and are taking leave from work to look after her/him or the new child (the rules are similar to SMP but it is only paid for up to two weeks). The amount is the same as for SAP.

Health in pregnancy grant

From April 2009 pregnant women can claim a health in pregnancy grant of £190 from the 25th week of pregnancy. It does not matter how much income or savings you have but you must have received appropriate health advice from a health professional – eg, midwife. Claims forms should be available from your midwife or doctor or by phoning 0845 366 7885. See www.direct.gov.uk for more information.

Child benefit and guardian's allowance

Child benefit of £20 a week for the eldest or only child and £13.20 for other children, can be claimed by anyone who is responsible for a child who is under 16, or under 20 and in (or who recently left) full-time non-advanced education or approved training. Guardian's allowance of £14.10 a week per child can be claimed by anyone bringing up a child whose parents are dead (or one is dead and the other is missing, or in prison for at least two years or detained in hospital 'under section'). Neither benefit is taxable and there are no NI contribution conditions. Both benefits are administered and paid by the Revenue and you can get claim forms from Revenue and Jobcentre Plus offices, or from www.hmrc.gov.uk.

4. Means-tested benefits and tax credits

Income support

Income support (IS) is a tax-free weekly benefit paid to specified categories of people aged under 60 who are not required to be available for work and whose income and capital are below set levels. People on IS are eligible for maximum housing benefit (HB) and council tax benefit (CTB – see p163), social fund payments (see p182) and other sources of financial assistance (see Chapter 5). People who are not eligible for IS may be able to instead claim pension credit (PC) if they are aged 60 or over (see p158), or income-based jobseeker's allowance (JSA) if they are under pensionable age and available for and actively seeking work (see p158) or income-related employment and support allowance (ESA) if they have limited capability for work.

Who can claim

You qualify for IS if:[120]
- you are aged 16 or over and under 60; *and*
- you fall into one of the categories of people who are eligible to claim (see p149); *and*
- neither you nor your partner (see p93) are working 'full time' (see p149 for details and the exceptions to this rule); *and*
- you are not studying full time (but see p149 for exceptions); *and*
- you are present and habitually resident in the UK and not subject to immigration control (see p150); *and*
- you are not receiving income-based or contribution-based JSA or ESA and your partner is not receiving income-based JSA or ESA, or PC; *and*
- your (and your partner's) income is less than your applicable amount (see p151); *and*

• you (and your partner) do not have savings and other capital worth more than £16,000,[121]

If you are aged 16 or 17 and you are in full-time education, or you are a looked-after young person or care leaver who is being maintained by a local authority, you are only eligible for IS in specified circumstances.[122]

Couples

If you have a partner, you must claim IS for both of you and your capital and income is jointly assessed. For the meaning of 'partner', see p93.

If you separate permanently from your partner, you no longer count as members of the same household and you can only claim IS as a single claimant. If you are temporarily separated from your partner, you continue to count as members of the same household, unless you have no intention of living together again, or you are likely to be apart for more than 52 weeks (this period can be extended in exceptional circumstances – eg, if you or your partner are in hospital – provided the period of your separation is not likely to be 'substantially' longer than 52 weeks).[123]

If only one of you is eligible to claim IS (see p149), s/he must be the claimant for you both. If you are both eligible to claim, you can choose who is the claimant. You can also 'swap' claimants. It is sometimes advantageous for one partner to be the claimant rather than the other (eg, where this would entitle you to a disability premium – see p152). Where there is a choice of claiming IS or income-based JSA, you may be better off claiming IS, and you will not have to be 'available for work' and 'actively seeking work'. If one of you is aged 60 or over and the other is under 60, you can claim either IS or PC. It is normally better to claim PC because it has more generous income and capital rules (see Chapter 8).

Claimants with children

You only get IS for dependant children if you were already doing so on 6 April 2004 and have not been awarded child tax credit (CTC – see p175).[124] New claimants cannot get IS for children and should claim CTC instead. Claimants already receiving IS for children can continue to get it until they claim CTC (you may be better off claiming CTC – seek advice about this) or until they are 'migrated' onto CTC by the DWP.

If you live with your child(ren) but are separated or divorced from the other parent, you may have applied for child support maintenance via the Child Support Agency (being replaced by the Child Maintenance and Enforcement Commission).[125] Most maintenance payments made to you count as income for IS. See CPAG's *Child Support Handbook* for further information.

Categories of people eligible to claim IS

You are eligible to claim IS if:[126]

- before 27 October 2008, you were found to be 'incapable of work', or treated as incapable of work, under the same rules and assessment procedures that apply to incapacity benefit (IB – p139), or you are entitled to statutory sick pay (SSP). After that date, you have to claim income-related ESA instead; or
- you are appealing against a decision that you are capable of work in accordance with the 'own occupation test' or the personal capability assessment (see p143) (your IS personal allowance is reduced by 20 per cent while you are appealing against a personal capability assessment); or
- you are a 'disabled worker', or are working while living in a care home (see below); or
- you are registered blind; or
- you are a carer and you are receiving carer's allowance (CA – see p130), or you are looking after somebody who is receiving attendance allowance (AA – see p125) or the middle or higher rate care component of disability living allowance (DLA – see p121), or you are looking after somebody who has claimed these benefits in the last 26 weeks and is waiting for a decision (you can also continue to claim IS for eight weeks after these conditions cease to apply); or
- you are a lone parent who is responsible for a child under 12 (this will be reduced to 10 in October 2009 and 7 in October 2010). This change does not apply to foster carers or parents of disabled children; or
- you are looking after your partner or child because s/he is temporarily ill, or you are looking after a child whose parent is ill or temporarily away, or you are fostering a child and do not have a partner, or you are on unpaid parental leave and were previously entitled to tax credits or HB/CTB; or
- you are expecting a baby in the next 11 weeks, or had a baby in the last 15 weeks, or are incapable of work because of pregnancy.

There are other less common categories of eligible claimants. For a full list and details, see CPAG's *Welfare Benefits and Tax Credits Handbook*.

People working full time

You are not generally entitled to IS if you are working (for payment) for 16 hours or more a week, or if your partner is working 24 or more hours a week.[127] If both of you work less than this, you can claim IS but most of your earnings will be taken into account. Even if you or your partner are working more than the prescribed hours, you are not excluded from IS under the full-time work rule if you are:[128]

- a 'disabled worker' – ie, you are mentally or physically disabled and as a result your earnings or hours of work are 75 per cent or less of what a person without your disability would expect from the same or comparable employment; or
- a carer who is eligible to claim IS (see above); or

- working at home as a childminder, or you are being paid by social services or a health authority or voluntary organisation to foster a child or care for a person in your home; *or*
- living in a care home.

Studying full time

You are not generally entitled to IS if you are studying full time but there are exceptions. The rules are complex and for further details see CPAG's student handbooks (see Appendix 3). You are not excluded from IS under the full-time student rule if you are:[129]

- under 20, in non-advanced education and are estranged from your parents or an orphan (this age limit may be increased to 21 in April 2009); *or*
- a lone parent.

Residence and immigration conditions

You must be present in the UK to get IS (or PC – see p158) but entitlement can continue during temporary absences of up to four weeks (eight weeks if you are taking a child abroad for medical treatment).[130]

You are not entitled to IS, PC, income-based JSA, income-related ESA, HB or CTB unless you are **'habitually resident'** in the UK. This applies to all claimants including British citizens. Certain people are automatically treated as being habitually resident including refugees, people with exceptional or indefinite leave to remain in the UK and people classed as EEA 'workers' and their dependants (see below). There is no statutory definition of habitual residence but it involves establishing a settled intention to live in the UK and, in most cases, an actual period of residence in the UK. It is also necessary to have a 'right to reside' in the UK (this test is primarily aimed at excluding 'economically inactive' EEA nationals from benefit entitlement). For more details about the habitual residence test, see CPAG's *Migration and Social Security Handbook*. Seek advice if you are refused benefit because you are not habitually resident.

You are also generally excluded from IS (and other means-tested benefits) if you are **'subject to immigration control'**. You are 'subject to immigration control' if you do not have leave to enter or remain in the UK, or if your leave is subject to a formal sponsorship undertaking or a prohibition on claiming public funds. You remain entitled to benefit, however, if you are:

- an EEA national (ie, a national of one of the EU member states plus Switzerland, although special rules apply to A8 (Romanian) and A2 (Bulgarian) nationals);
- a sponsored immigrant who has been in the UK for five years or more, or whose sponsor has died;
- an asylum seeker who claimed asylum on entering the UK before 2 April 2000 or who has been receiving benefit since 5 February 1996 (IS is payable at a reduced 'urgent cases' rate).

For more details about the effects of immigration status on benefit entitlement, see CPAG's *Migration and Social Security Handbook*. Seek advice before claiming benefit (as this can sometimes affect your right to remain in the UK), or if you are refused benefit because of your immigration status.

Amount

IS is a means-tested benefit and the amount you are entitled to depends on your financial and family circumstances. There are three steps involved in working out your IS. An example is given on p153.

Step one: Calculate your applicable amount. This represents the minimum weekly income the government decides you need to live on. It is made up of fixed amounts, depending on your age, the size of your family and other circumstances. Details of how to calculate your applicable amount are set out below.

Step two: Calculate your weekly income. Details of how to calculate your income are set out in Chapter 8. Note that not all of your income counts when working out your IS. Any AA and DLA (see pp125 and 120) you receive, for example, is ignored but IB and CA (see pp156 and 130) count in full. Some of your earnings are disregarded. If you have capital over fixed limits, you are treated as having a 'tariff income' (see p216).

Step three: Deduct your income from your applicable amount. The resulting amount is your IS.[131] If your income exceeds your applicable amount, you are not entitled to IS.

Applicable amount

Your applicable amount is made up of three elements:

- personal allowances;
- premiums in specific circumstances;
- housing costs, primarily for mortgage interest payments (rent payments are covered by the HB scheme – see p163).

Personal allowances[132]

Single claimant: £64.30 if aged 25 or over; £50.95 if aged under 25.
Lone parent: £64.30 if aged 18 or over; £50.95 if aged under 18.
Couple: £100.95 if both aged 18 or over; up to £76.90 if both aged under 18 (see CPAG's *Welfare Benefits and Tax Credits Handbook* for the different rates payable for under 18s).
Dependant child: £56.11. Note: this is only payable if you were getting IS on 6 April 2004 and are not getting CTC (see p148).

Premiums

Premiums are weekly allowances intended to help with extra expenses associated with age, disability or children. You can qualify for one or more premiums but you can only receive the highest of the disability premium, the pensioner premium and the higher pensioner premium.[133] You also cannot get the enhanced disability premium with the pensioner or higher pensioner premium. You may be able to claim arrears of a premium if you are entitled to it for a past period.

You are entitled to a:

- disability premium of £27.50 (single rate) or £39.15 (couple rate) if:[134]
  - you are aged under 60 and are registered blind, or receiving a qualifying benefit – ie, DLA (see p120), SDA (see p145), long-term IB (see p156), or the disability/severe disability element of WTC (see p179), or have been incapable of work (see p156 and below) for a continuous period of 52 weeks (or 28 weeks if you are terminally ill); or
  - your partner is aged under 60 and is registered blind or receiving a qualifying benefit.

  The couple rate is paid if you have a partner and if either condition is satisfied. Note that only the claimant's (not partner's) incapacity for work can qualify a couple for the premium (this is particularly relevant where there is a choice of claimant – see p155). Note also that you can only satisfy the incapable of work condition if you have claimed IB (whether you are entitled to it or not) or if you are entitled to SSP (see p142). You may be able to establish that you have been incapable of work for a past period by submitting a backdated medical certificate from your GP;

- **enhanced disability premium** of £13.40 (single) or £19.30 (couple) if you or your partner are aged under 60 and receiving the highest rate care component of DLA (see p121);[135]

- **severe disability premium** of £52.85 (single) or £105.70 (couple) if:[136]
  - you are receiving AA (see p125) or the middle or higher rate care component of DLA (see p120); and
  - you have no non-dependant, aged 18 or over, normally residing with you (see below); and
  - no one is being paid CA for looking after you (see p130). Note that a person is not treated as receiving CA if s/he is not getting it because of the overlapping benefit rules and they only have underlying entitlement (see p118).

  If you have a partner you must both satisfy the above rules. If you do, the couple rate is paid. If your partner does not satisfy the first condition but is registered blind, or if only one of you has a carer receiving CA, you are entitled to the single person's rate.

A **'non-dependant'** is anybody aged 18 or over who normally lives with you (whether in her/his home or yours) and with whom you share accommodation, apart from a bathroom, toilet, or common access area, or a communal room in sheltered accommodation.[137] This could include your grown-up son or daughter, or your parent. It does not include anyone who is getting AA or the middle or higher rate care component of DLA. See p169 for who else does not count as a non-dependant.

If a non-dependant comes to live with you for the first time to care for you or your partner, you can keep your entitlement to the severe disability premium for 12 weeks. After that, you will lose the premium, and the carer should consider claiming CA. In other situations, however, be aware that if somebody is receiving CA for looking after you, you lose your entitlement to the severe disability premium and this may leave you considerably worse off (see p131);

- **carer premium** of £29.50 if you or your partner are getting CA (see p130), or would get it but for the overlapping benefit rules (see p118). You remain entitled to the premium for eight weeks after you stop getting CA, or the person you are looking after stops getting AA or the care component of DLA. If both you and your partner satisfy the conditions for a carer premium, you are entitled to double the normal rate;[138]
- **pensioner premium** of £97.50 applies to couples only where your partner is aged 60 or over;[139]
- **family premium** of £17.30 if your family includes a child under 16, or under 20 and in full-time non-advanced education or approved training. **Note:** this is only payable if you were getting it on 6 April 2004 and are not getting CTC (see above);[140]
- **disabled child premium** of £51.24 for each child who gets DLA or is registered blind (an additional £20.65 **enhanced disability premium** is paid if the child gets the highest rate care component of DLA). **Note:** these premiums are only payable if you were getting them on 6 April 2004 and are not getting CTC (see p148).[141]

Housing costs

The final element of your applicable amount is housing costs.[142] These are paid to home-owners to help meet the costs of:

- mortgage interest payments;
- interest payments on loans for specified home repairs and improvements (including adapting a dwelling for the special needs of a disabled person[143]);
- service charges, other than for specified repairs and improvements.

Housing costs for mortgage interest payments are usually paid directly to the lender.

The rules and conditions relating to IS housing costs are complex (see CPAG's *Welfare Benefits and Tax Credits Handbook* for more details). Note, particularly, the following restrictions.

- You may not be entitled to help with interest payments on a mortgage taken out while you were getting IS or income-based JSA but this rule does not apply if the loan was taken out to buy a more suitable home for the needs of a disabled person – ie, somebody who could satisfy the conditions for a disability, disabled child, pensioner or higher pensioner premium.
- Your housing costs may be restricted if excessive (but the needs of disabled members of your family must be considered). There is also a temporary ceiling of £200,000 on eligible loans at present. Normally, it is £100,000
- If you or your partner are aged 60 or over you are paid all your housing costs straight away. If you are under 60 you are not entitled to housing costs until you have been receiving IS for 13 weeks. If you have not been able to qualify for IS because the mortgage interest has not been added to your applicable amount, the waiting period still applies and a fresh IS claim can be made when it is completed.
- Deductions may be made from your housing costs if you have a non-dependant living with you (see p151). The amounts deducted are the same as apply to HB (see p169). Note that, as for HB, no deductions are made for non-dependants if you or your partner receive AA or DLA or are registered blind.
- You can only get help with interest payments on eligible loans (not capital repayments and insurance premiums), and a standard rate of interest is used to calculate your entitlement.

Housing costs are payable in respect of the dwelling you normally occupy as your home.[144] If you are temporarily away from home, you can normally continue to get housing costs for 13 weeks, as long as your absence is unlikely to exceed 13 weeks.[145] You can also continue to get housing costs on your normal home for up to 13 weeks if you are in a care home for a trial period.[146] If you are in a care home for short-term or respite care, you can continue to get housing costs on your normal home for up to 52 weeks.[147] The 52-week rule also applies if you are in hospital, or receiving medical treatment or convalescence, or providing medically approved care to another person. The 52-week period may, however, be extended if the reason for your temporary absence is that essential repairs are being carried out on your home.[148] In either case, once you return home, even if this is only for a weekend or even a day, you may be able to claim housing costs for a new 13- or 52-week period of temporary absence.[149]

You may be paid housing costs for two homes for up to four weeks in certain circumstances (the rules are the same as for HB – see p163).[150] You may also be paid housing costs for up to four weeks before you move into a new home if your move is delayed because it is being adapted for a disabled person or because you are waiting for a social fund payment, and you are entitled to a disability or pensioner premium.[151]

You can continue to get housing costs for the first four weeks you or your partner are in full-time work if you have been receiving IS or income-based JSA for the previous 26 weeks.[152]

Example of an IS calculation

Mr and Mrs Earnshaw, both aged 35, have two children aged 8 and 12. They live in rented accommodation. Mr Earnshaw has been unable to work due to ill-health for three years and Mrs Earnshaw spends a lot of time looking after and supervising him. Mr Earnshaw receives the highest rate care component of DLA but hasn't got an NI record that would have enabled him to claim IB. Mrs Earnshaw receives CA, CTC and child benefit. The family have no other income and no savings. Mrs Earnshaw claims IS as a carer.

Step one: Applicable amount

Personal allowance for a couple	£100.95
Disability premium	£39.15
Enhanced disability premium	£19.30
Carer premium	£29.50
Total applicable amount	£188.90

Step two: Income (Note: DLA, CTC and child benefit are ignored as income)

CA (including increase for Mr Earnshaw)	£84.80
Total income	£84.80

Step three: Deduct income from applicable amount

Applicable amount	£188.90
less income	£ 84.80
= IS	£104.10

Mrs Earnshaw is entitled to IS of £104.10 a week

How to claim

In most cases you will need to start your claim by telephoning the Jobcentre Plus contact centre, which will establish the details of your claim and, where appropriate, arrange for you to attend a local office for a 'work-focused interview' (see p95).

You must fully complete the claim form or provide the details required by the contact centre and supply any documentation required (eg, proof of savings and payslips) for your claim to be valid. If you have a mortgage you should ask your lender to complete form MI12, which comes with the claim pack.

Claims can only normally be backdated for up to three months in special circumstances (see p98 – but note the special rule on p99 if you are claiming a qualifying benefit).

Income-related employment and support allowance

Income–related ESA is paid to people who have a limited capability for work and who have not made sufficient NI contributions to get contributory ESA or who qualify for a top up of income-related ESA in addition to their contributory ESA.

You qualify for income-related ESA if you:[153]

- have 'limited capability for work' (see p143); *and*
- are aged 16 or over but under pension age; *and*
- are in Great Britain; *and*
- are not subject to immigration control and satisfy the habitual residence test; *and*
- are not entitled to IS, JSA, or PC (and if you have a partner s/he is not entitled to income-related ESA, income-based JSA, IS or PC in his/her own right); *and*
- are not working (and if you have a partner, s/he is not working 24 hours or more a week); *and*
- are not in full time education, unless you are a disabled students who is getting DLA; *and*
- are not entitled to SSP; *and*
- satisfy the income and capital rules which are similar to those for IS.

Although you need a medical certificate from your doctor to start an ESA claim, you will normally also undergo a **work capability assessment** (WCA) organised by Jobcentre Plus.

The same conditionality that applies to contributory ESA also applies to income-related ESA. For more information about limited capability for work, work focused health-related assessments and WCAs, see pp143–145.

Generally, you are not allowed to work and claim ESA. However, some 'permitted work' is allowed (see p143). Note that the earnings rules for 'permitted work' if you are on ESA are different to those described in this chapter for other means-tested benefits. This is often a major source of confusion and mis-advice. For example, a person on income-related ESA can earn £92 before her/his ESA is affected, while a person on IS only has a £20 earnings disregard.

Amount

Income-related ESA is calculated in a similar way to IS. It has an applicable amount made up of allowances for single people and couples, premiums and eligible housing costs. There is an assessment phase for the first 13 weeks of the claim and a main phase – for more information, see p144.

Assessment phase (first 13 weeks)

Single claimant aged 25 or over	£64.30
Single claimant under 25	£50.95
Couple both aged 18 or over	£100.95

(See CPAG's *Welfare Benefits and Tax Credits Handbook* for lone parents under 25 and other couple rates.)

Income-related ESA can also include the enhanced disability, severe disability, carer and pensioner premiums. The rules are similar to IS (see p151). Note: that the disability premium is not payable with ESA.

The main phase

Once the assessment phase is over, a number of changes are made. Firstly, under 25s become entitled to the same rate as those aged 25 and over. Secondly, you become entitled to either a work-related activity component or a support component (see p151). These are added to the basic allowance and any premiums or housing costs.

Work-related activity and support components

The amounts for each component are:

Work-related activity component	£25.50
Support component	£30.85

Note that if you are allocated to the support group you will automatically become entitled to the enhanced disability premium of £13.40 (£19.30 for couples).

Reductions for private and occupational pensions

Your income-related ESA is reduced by the weekly amount of any personal and occupational pensions you receive. This is different to how it is treated for contributory ESA purposes.

How to claim

Claim by phoning the Jobcentre Plus contact centre on 0800 055 6688. Claim forms are also available at www.dwp.gov.uk.

How to appeal

You can appeal decisions about whether you have failed the limited capability for work test, if you have been subjected to sanctions, or if you think you should have been placed in the support group. While your appeal is pending you will be treated as if you are still in the assessment phase and will only be paid the basis allowance.

Income-based jobseeker's allowance[154]

Income-based jobseeker's allowance (JSA) is paid to people under pensionable age (65 for men, 60 for women) whose income and capital are below set limits.

Who can claim

The rules are the same as for IS (see p147), except that you do not have to be in one of the categories of people eligible to claim IS but you do have to be available for work and actively seeking work (the 'labour market conditions'). You must normally be willing and able to take up work of at least 40 hours a week but you may be permitted to restrict your availability if you have a disability or caring responsibilities. For full details, see CPAG's *Welfare Benefits and Tax Credits Handbook*. Special rules apply if you are aged 16 or 17. The rules about claiming for children and liability to maintain are as for IS (see p148).

People who have paid sufficient NI contributions may be able to claim contribution-based JSA (see p146) instead of, or in addition to, income-based JSA. Some people may be eligible to claim IS (eg, carers or some lone parents) or PC (men aged 60-65) instead of income-based JSA and are generally better off doing so, as they do not have to satisfy the labour market conditions and the PC income and capital rules are more generous.

Amount

Income-based JSA is calculated in the same way as IS, taking into account the applicable amount and income and capital of you and your partner (see p151). Note, however, that the pensioner or higher pensioner premium is payable if either you or your partner satisfy the conditions (see p153).

How to claim

You are usually required to start your claim by telephoning the Jobcentre Plus contact centre. You are then required to attend an interview at your local Jobcentre Plus office to discuss your work prospects and to sign a jobseeker's agreement setting out the steps you have agreed to take to obtain employment.

If you have a partner but no children, you are required to make a joint claim and both you and your partner have to satisfy the labour market conditions. You have to regularly 'sign on' at the Jobcentre Plus and attend further interviews during your claim to establish that you continue to satisfy the conditions.

Pension credit

Pension credit (PC) is a tax-free weekly benefit paid to people aged 60 or over, whose income is below set levels (people under 60 can claim IS or income-based

JSA instead). Unlike IS, there is no capital limit for claiming PC (although an assumed 'tariff income' from capital will be taken into account – see p216), no full-time work rule (although earnings from work are taken into account) and certain increases in income are ignored for a fixed period (see p204).

PC consists of two different elements:

- **guarantee credit**, which is designed to bring your income up to a minimum level; *and*
- **savings credit**, which is designed to reward you if you have made some provision for your retirement over and above the basic state retirement pension.

You can qualify for either or both credits. If you get the guarantee credit, you are eligible for maximum HB (see p165) and CTB (see p173), social fund payments (see p182) and other sources of financial assistance (see Chapter 5). PC does not include any amounts for children – claim CTC if you are responsible for a child (see p175).

Who can claim

You qualify for PC if:[155]

- you are aged 60 or over, and in the case of savings credit, you or your partner are aged 65 or over; *and*
- you are present and habitually resident in the UK and not subject to immigration control (the rules are similar to those that apply to IS – see p150); *and*
- your income is below set levels (see p199).

If you are a member of a couple, you must claim PC for both you and your partner and your joint income is assessed.[156] For the meaning of partner, see p93.

Amount

PC is a means-tested benefit and the amount you are entitled to depends on your income and whether you have a partner, disabilities, caring responsibilities and eligible housing costs. Examples of calculations are given on p161.

Guarantee credit

There are three steps involved in calculating your entitlement to guarantee credit.[157]

Step one: Calculate your appropriate minimum guarantee. This represents the minimum weekly income the government decides you need to live on. It is made up of fixed amounts, depending on your personal circumstances. Details of how to calculate your appropriate minimum guarantee are set out on p160.

Step two: Calculate your weekly income. This is the amount you have coming in each week from your pension and other sources. Not all your income counts (eg, AA and DLA are ignored) and some income is subject to disregards. If you have capital of more than £6,000 (£10,000 if you live in a care home), you are treated as having income of £1 for every £500 of capital over that amount. Some capital, however, is disregarded. Full details of how to calculate your income and capital are set out in Chapter 8.

Step three: Deduct your income from your appropriate minimum guarantee. The resulting amount is your guarantee credit. If your income exceeds your appropriate minimum guarantee, you are not entitled to guarantee credit.

Appropriate minimum guarantee

Your appropriate minimum guarantee is made up of the following elements:[158]

- the 'standard minimum guarantee' of £130 if you are a single claimant, or £198.45 if you have a partner;
- a severe disability addition of £52.85, if you satisfy the conditions that apply for the IS severe disability premium (see p152). If you have a partner you must both satisfy the conditions. If you do, you are entitled to an addition of £105.70. Otherwise you can get the single person's addition under the same rules as apply to IS;
- a carer's addition of £29.50, if you satisfy the same conditions that apply for the IS carer premium, including having 'underlying entitlement' to CA that isn't paid because your retirement pension is higher. If you and your partner both satisfy the conditions, you are entitled to two additions;
- eligible housing costs if you are a homeowner, in respect of mortgage interest payments, interest payments on loans for specified home repairs and improvements, and certain service charges. The rules are very similar to those that apply to IS housing costs (see p153).

Savings credit

The maximum amount of savings credit you are entitled to is £20.40 a week if you are a single claimant and £27.03 a week if you have a partner. You or your partner must be aged 65 or over to qualify for savings credit.

There are three steps involved in calculating your entitlement to savings credit.[159]

Step one: Compare your 'qualifying income' with the savings credit threshold. Your 'qualifying income' is your total weekly income as calculated for guarantee credit (see p159) less any maintenance payments you are getting for yourself from your spouse or former spouse, and less the following benefits: working tax credit, IB, ESA, SDA, contribution-based JSA and maternity allowance. The 'savings credit threshold' is £96 if you are a single claimant and £153.40 if you have a partner. If your qualifying income is below the threshold, you do not qualify for any savings credit. If it is above the threshold, proceed to step two.

Step two: Calculate 60 per cent of your qualifying income above the savings credit threshold. In other words, subtract £96 if you are a single claimant, or

£153.40 if you have a partner, from your qualifying income and multiply the result by 60 per cent. The result is the maximum savings credit you can get, subject to a cap of £20.40 if you are single and £27.03 if you have a partner. This is the amount of savings credit you will get if you are entitled to guarantee credit (see above). If you are not entitled to guarantee credit, because your income is too high, proceed to step three.

Step three: Calculate 40 per cent of your total weekly income above your appropriate minimum guarantee and deduct it from the amount of savings credit calculated in step two. The result is your savings credit. If you cannot deduct it because it is more than the savings credit calculated in step two, you are not entitled to any savings credit.

Examples of PC calculations

Mrs Andrews is aged 70 and lives alone in a house she owns, on which there is no mortgage. Her weekly income is £95.25 state retirement pension and £47.10 AA.

Her guarantee credit is calculated as follows:

Step one: Her appropriate minimum guarantee is £130 standard minimum guarantee *plus* £52.85 severe disability addition = £182.85.

Step two: Her total weekly income is £95.25 (her AA is ignored as income).

Step three: Guarantee credit is £182.85 (appropriate minimum guarantee) *less* £95.25 (income) = £87.60

She is not entitled to savings credit because:

Step one: Her qualifying income of £95.25 is less than the savings credit threshold of £96.

If Mrs Andrews also had a weekly occupational pension of £30, her guarantee credit would be calculated as follows:

Step one: Her appropriate minimum guarantee is £182.85.

Step two: Her total weekly income is £125.25 (state pension and occupational pension).

Step three: Guarantee credit is £182.85 *less* £125.25 = £57.60.

Her savings credit would be calculated as follows:

Step one: Her qualifying income of £125.25 is more than the savings credit threshold of £96, so she is eligible for savings credit.

Step two: £125.25 qualifying income less £96 savings credit threshold = £29.25 x 60% = £17.55 . As this is less than the cap (£20.40) and Mrs Andrews is entitled to guarantee credit (see above), £17.55 is the amount of savings credit payable.

If Mrs Andrews also had savings of £38,000, her guarantee credit would be calculated as follows:

Step one: Her appropriate minimum guarantee is £182.85.

Step two: Her total weekly income is £125.25 (state pension and occupational pension) *plus* £64 deemed income from savings (£1 for every £500 in excess of £6,000) = £189.25.

Step three: As her income of £189.25 exceeds her appropriate minimum guarantee of £182.85, she is not entitled to guarantee credit.

Her savings credit would be calculated as follows:

Step one: Her qualifying income of £189.25 is more than the savings credit threshold of £96, so she is eligible for savings credit.

Step two: £189.25 qualifying income *less* £96 savings credit threshold = £93.25 x 60% = £55.95. As this is more than the cap (£20.40), the maximum savings credit payable is £20.40. Mrs Andrews is not entitled to guarantee credit (see above), so step three of the calculation applies.

Step three: Total income (£189.25) *less* appropriate minimum guarantee (£182.85) = £6.40 x 40% = £2.56. Savings credit = £20.40 *less* £2.56 = £17.84.

Changes of circumstances

You are generally under a duty to notify the DWP of any changes of circumstances, including increases in your income, which may affect the amount of PC you are entitled to. If, however, you or your partner are aged 65 or over and neither of you is under 60, you may be given an 'assessed income period' during which time any increases in the following types of income do not have to be notified:

- retirement pensions other than the state retirement pension (eg, private and occupational pensions);
- income from annuities;
- income from capital.

During the assessed income period, which may be for life, any increases in income from your retirement pensions and annuities are automatically taken into account in accordance with the terms of your pension/annuity (normally annually), or (if the terms do not specify the date and amount of the increases) in line with the social security uprating of the state second pension. Any **increases** in your income from capital are ignored until the end of the assessed income period (this means that any capital you acquire during an assessed income period is ignored until the end of the period).

You can and should, however, report any **decreases** in your income from the above sources during the assessed income period as your PC can be increased immediately to take account of this.

Your assessed income period will end if:

- you start or cease to live with a partner; *or*
- you or your partner become 65; *or*
- you are single and enter a care home permanently; *or*
- payment of any of your pensions or annuities stops temporarily or is less than the amount due.[160]

How to claim[161]

You can claim PC by telephoning the PC claims line on 0800 99 1234 (textphone 0800 169 0133), in which case an application form can be sent to you, or completed over the phone and sent to you for checking and signing. In some areas, you can visit your local 'designated' or 'alternative' office (see p95). You can also download a form from www.thepensionservice.gov.uk.

Claims can be backdated for up to 13 weeks (see p98 – but note the special rule on p99 if you are claiming a qualifying benefit).

Housing benefit

Housing benefit (HB) is a tax free, means-tested weekly benefit paid to people who are liable to pay rent. It can be claimed if you are working, unemployed or retired. HB is paid and administered by local authorities (councils).

Who can claim

You qualify for HB if:[162]

- you or your partner (see p163) are liable to pay rent on the dwelling you occupy as your home (see below); *and*
- you do not fall within any of the categories of excluded people listed on p164; *and*
- your (and your partner's) income is low enough to qualify (see p165); *and*
- you and your partner do not have savings and other capital worth more than £16,000 (see Chapter 8 for how your capital is calculated), unless you or your partner are getting the guarantee credit of PC (see p159), in which case your capital is not taken into account.

Claiming for others

You must claim HB for yourself and your family. Your family means your partner (see p93) and any dependant children aged under 16, or under 20 in full-time non-advanced education or approved training, who you normally live with. Note that unlike IS and PC, amounts for children are still included in the HB calculation. The amount of HB you receive depends on the circumstances of your family.[163]

Liability to pay rent for your home

'Rent' includes any payments you make for the use and occupation of premises, including certain service charges and payments for hostel, bed and breakfast and other types of accommodation.[164] Some payments, however, including some types of service charges, are not eligible for HB (see p166).

To qualify for HB, you or your partner must be liable to pay rent under a legally enforceable agreement, although the agreement does not have to be in writing.[165] If you are not legally liable to pay rent but have to do so to keep your home because the liable person has stopped paying, you can be treated as liable.[166] Some people are excluded from HB, however, even though they are liable to pay rent (see p166). If you live with a partner (see p164), only one of you can claim HB.[167] If you are jointly liable to pay rent with other people who are not members of your family (see p164), you can claim HB for your proportion of the rent.[168]

HB is only usually payable in respect of your normal home. If you are temporarily absent from your home, you can get HB for up to 13 weeks or 52 weeks. The rules are the same as for IS housing costs (see p153).[169]

If you move into a new home, you can get up to four weeks' HB on your:
- old home for the period after you move in, if you cannot reasonably avoid having to continue to pay rent on your old home;[170]
- new home for the period before you moved in, if your move was delayed because the home was being adapted for disability needs, or because you were in hospital or a care home, or because you were waiting for a social fund payment connected to the move (see p185) and you are aged 60 or over or qualify for one of the disability or pensioner premiums (see p152).[171] You may be able to get HB for longer than four weeks if you moved your furniture and belongings into your new home but were unable to move in yourself – eg, because you were in hospital.[172]

Note, however, that you cannot get HB on your new *and* old homes for the same period, unless you satisfy the rules below.

You can only get HB for two homes for the same period if:
- you have temporarily left your home because of fear of violence (HB can be paid for up to 52 weeks on your old and new homes);[173] *or*
- you have moved into a new home and cannot reasonably avoid having to continue to pay rent on your old home (HB can be paid for up to four weeks on your old and new homes).[174] DWP guidance[175] suggests that this only applies if you have moved permanently but the regulations do not specify this, so you could argue you are entitled to HB for two homes for up to four weeks, if you have moved into temporary accommodation – eg, supported housing for rehabilitation purposes following a community care assessment; *or*
- your move to a new home was delayed while it was being adapted for disability needs (HB can be paid on your old and new homes for the four weeks prior to the date you moved).[176]

People excluded from housing benefit
You are excluded from HB if you fall into any of the following categories.
- You are not habitually resident in the UK or you are subject to immigration control (see p121).[177]
- You are a full-time student. Some full-time students are eligible for HB, however, including those who qualify for IS or income-based JSA/income-related ESA, anyone over pensionable age (see p133), some lone parents, people who have been incapable of work for 28 weeks and those who qualify for the disability or severe disability premiums (see p151), or a disabled student's allowance because of deafness.[178]
- You are permanently resident in one of most types of care home.[179] See Chapter 9 for details of how you can get help with your home fees.

- You own your home, or have a lease of more than 21 years, or are receiving IS, JSA or ESA housing costs for your accommodation.[180]
- Your rental agreement is not 'commercial' – taking into account, in particular, whether the terms are legally enforceable.[181] The fact that you are paying less than the market rent, or that you are renting from a friend, relative or carer, does not necessarily mean that your agreement is not commercial.[182]
- You pay rent to a 'close relative' of yours or your partner's who shares your accommodation.[183] **'Close relative'** means parent, parent-in-law, son, son-in-law, daughter, daughter-in-law, step-parent, step-son, step-daughter, brother, sister or partner of any of the above.[184] You do not count as sharing accommodation if you only share a bathroom, toilet or common access area, or communal rooms in sheltered accommodation, and the rule may not apply if you have exclusive occupation of one or more rooms.[185]
- You are renting a home from your ex-partner, or partner's ex-partner, which you formerly shared with them.[186]
- A child of the person you are renting from is living as part of your family.[187]
- Within the last five years, you or your partner previously owned the accommodation you are renting, unless you can show that you had to relinquish ownership to keep your home – eg, because of mortgage arrears.[188]
- You were previously a non-dependant (see p169) of someone living in your accommodation, or you pay rent to a company or trust with which you, or your partner, or a resident close relative (see above), have some connection, unless in either case you can show that your rental agreement was not created to enable you to claim HB.[189]
- None of the above apply, but the local authority decides that your agreement to pay rent was 'contrived' – ie, solely or mainly created to enable you to claim HB.[190] Seek advice if this rule is applied to you.

Amount

The amount you are entitled to depends on your 'applicable amount', your 'income' and your 'eligible rent'.

If you are receiving IS, income-based JSA, income-related ESA or the guarantee credit of PC, you are entitled to maximum HB, which is your weekly eligible rent less any non-dependant deductions (see p169).[191] If you have been receiving IS or income-based JSA or income related ESA for 26 continuous weeks, you can continue to get maximum HB for the first four weeks you or your partner take up full-time employment, as long as you notify the local authority within that period.[192]

If you are not receiving IS, income-based JSA, income-related ESA or the guarantee credit of PC, you are entitled to maximum HB (see above) less 65 per cent of the difference between your income and applicable amount (see p166). If your income is less than your applicable amount, you are entitled to maximum HB.[193]

Examples of HB calculations are given on p170.

Applicable amount

Your applicable amount is worked out as for IS[194] (see p151) except that:

*   if you are aged 60 or over and you are not claiming IS or income-based JSA, your personal allowance is £130 if you are a single claimant (£150.40 if you are aged 65 or over), or £198.45 if you have a partner (£225.50 if either of you is aged 65 or over), but you cannot qualify for a pensioner, higher pensioner, disability or enhanced disability premium (see p152);
*   you are entitled to a personal allowance of £56.11 for each child aged under 16, or under 20 in full-time non-advanced education or approved training, with whom you are normally living;
*   you are entitled to a family premium of £17.30 if you have a dependant child (£27.80 if you have a child under 1 year old);
*   for the purposes of the severe disability premium, any joint tenant or owner, or a landlord or tenant of yours who lives with you, counts as a non-dependant if s/he falls into one of the categories of people who are excluded from HB (see p164);[195]
*   IS or PC housing costs are not included in your applicable amount (you are not entitled to HB if you are receiving them – see p164).

Income

Details of how to calculate your income are set out in Chapter 8. Not all your income counts when working out your HB and there are different rules if you or your partner are aged 60 or over. Any AA and DLA (see pp125 and 120) you receive is ignored, but IB, contributory ESA and CA (see pp156, 000 and 131) count in full. From October 2009, child benefit will no longer count as income. Some of your earnings are disregarded, as is any maintenance that you receive. If you have capital over fixed amounts, you are treated as having a 'tariff income' (see p216).[196]

Eligible rent and local housing allowance

Your 'eligible rent' is the amount of rent which is taken into account when calculating your HB. It can include any service charges you have to pay, apart from those excluded under the rules set out below. 'Eligible service charges' include those for management and maintenance costs, lifts, entry phones, gardens, furniture and household equipment and rubbish removal.

Your eligible rent may be significantly less than the rent you actually pay because of the deductions and restrictions described below. This means that HB may not cover the whole of your rent payments even if you are entitled to maximum HB (see p151). You may be able to claim a discretionary housing payment if you need extra help to pay your rent (see p170).

Service charges for which housing benefit is not paid

The following charges are not eligible for HB and are deducted from the rent you pay, when calculating your HB.

- **Fuel charges.**[197] If your rent includes a specified amount for fuel, that amount is deducted when calculating your eligible rent. If your rent includes an unspecified amount for fuel, the following fixed weekly amounts are deducted:
  - £21.55 for heating;
  - £2.50 for hot water;
  - £1.75 for lighting;
  - £2.50 for cooking.

  If you (and your family) occupy only one room, only £9.25 is deducted for heating, or heating plus hot water and/or lighting. Fuel charges for common access areas and for communal rooms in sheltered accommodation are eligible for HB, as are specified charges for the maintenance of a heating system.[198]

- **Water charges.**[199] Any water charges which are included in your rent are not covered by HB.

- **Charges for meals.**[200] If you pay for meals, the following fixed weekly deductions are made when calculating your eligible rent, regardless of the charge you actually pay:
  - £22.95 for each member of your family aged 16 or over and £11.60 for each child who receives at least three meals a day;
  - £2.80 for each member of your family who receives breakfast only;
  - £15.25 for each member of your family aged 16 or over and £7.65 for each child in other cases – ie, half board.

- Certain other service charges.[201]Charges for the following items are also ineligible for HB:
  - personal laundry (but charges for the provision of a laundry room or machines are eligible);
  - cleaning rooms and windows, other than those in communal areas and the exterior of windows, where you and other members of your household are unable to clean yourselves;
  - transport and leisure items such as sports facilities or TV costs (other than relay for terrestrial channels);
  - emergency alarm systems;
  - medical expenses and personal and nursing care;
  - counselling and support services;
  - any other services not connected with the provision of adequate accommodation.

If you are jointly liable for rent which includes ineligible service charges, proportionate deductions are made from your share of the rent.[202] If you live in supported accommodation (see Chapter 3), HB no longer covers service charges for counselling and support, cleaning and emergency alarms. Local authorities can instead fund providers of supported accommodation to arrange for the provision of support and care services to their residents through the Supporting People scheme (see p52).

Local housing allowance

If you are a private tenant, the local council will use a local housing allowance (LHA) figure in its HB calculation instead of the eligible rent. This LHA is based on your family size and the number of bedrooms that you require (up to a maximum of five bedrooms). It is established by the local rent officer each month for each Broad Market Rental Area (BMRA – ie, the town or part of the city or county that you live in).

If you are entitled to maximum HB then you are paid the LHA relevant to your family size and BMRA. However, if your rent is more than £15 below the LHA, your HB is capped at your rent plus £15. If your rent is above the LHA, you may be able to ask for a discretionary housing payment to meet the shortfall, even if just temporarily (see p170).

Once your rent has been calculated using the LHA, it is normally fixed for one year.

Private tenants who are aged under 25 will often find that their LHA is limited to the level of rent paid for shared accommodation, as opposed to self-contained accommodation. This restriction should not apply in some cases however – eg, if you are a parent or severely disabled or a care-leaver. See CPAG's *Welfare Benefits and Tax Credits Handbook* for further details about the procedure.

Rent restrictions

If you are a tenant who doesn't get the LHA, your eligible rent may still be restricted to an amount determined by the local rent officer. This will not apply to you if you:[203]
- live in local authority or registered housing association accommodation; *or*
- live in accommodation provided by a housing association, registered charity or voluntary organisation where care, support or supervision is provided, or in accommodation funded by the Resettlement Agency; *or*
- have been receiving HB for the same accommodation since 1 January 1996.

If you fall into one of the above categories, the local authority can still restrict your eligible rent if it decides your home is unreasonably large or expensive. Seek advice if this happens.

If you do not fall into one of the above categories, the local authority will refer your HB claim to a local rent officer who will use set criteria to determine whether your eligible rent should be restricted because your home is too large or expensive, or because you are under 25.[204] See CPAG's *Welfare Benefits and Tax Credits Handbook* for further details about the procedure.

The local authority is bound by the rent officer's determinations.[205] In practice, this means that in most cases, your eligible rent cannot exceed the average local rent for the size of accommodation you need. Seek advice if you wish to challenge a rent restriction. If you are considering renting private accommodation, ask the local authority for a 'pre-tenancy determination' to find out whether HB will cover your full rent.

Non-dependant deductions

If other people normally live with you in your home who are not part of your family, set deductions are made from your HB on the assumption that s/he is making a contribution towards your rent (whether s/he is or not). Examples of non-dependants are adult sons and daughters, or elderly relatives who share your home.

A non-dependant is anyone who normally resides with you, does not have a normal home elsewhere, and shares accommodation with you apart from a bathroom, toilet or common access area, or a communal room in sheltered accommodation.[206] The following people, however, do not count as non-dependants:[207]

- anyone who is separately liable to pay rent or other housing costs;
- a member of your family for benefit purposes (see p163);
- a person employed by a charitable or voluntary organisation as a resident carer for you or your partner;
- anyone who pays you or your partner, or to whom you pay, rent on a commercial basis;
- anyone who jointly occupies your home and is either a co-owner or joint tenant.

Anyone falling into the last two categories, however, will count as a non-dependant if s/he is excluded from HB under the rules set out on p164 (apart from students and persons subject to immigration control or who are not habitually resident in the UK).

No non-dependant deductions are made if:

- you or your partner receive AA (see p125) or DLA care component (see p121), or are registered blind; *or*
- a non-dependant is aged under 18, or is aged under 25 and receiving IS or income-based JSA, or is getting PC, or has been in hospital for more than 52 weeks, or is a full-time student.

The amount deducted depends on the income of the non-dependant.[208] If the non-dependant is not working more than 16 hours a week, there is a standard deduction of £7.40 a week. If the non-dependant is working for more than 16 hours a week, the deductions are as follows:

Weekly gross income	Weekly deduction
£382 or more	£47.75
£306-£381.99	£43.50
£231-£305.99	£38.20
£178-£230.99	£23.35
£120-£177.99	£17.00
Less than £120.00	£7.40

If you or your partner are aged 65 or over and claiming HB and a non-dependant comes to live with you, a deduction will not be made for the first 26 weeks (any increase in deductions because of a rise in the income of a non-dependant is also delayed for 26 weeks).

A deduction is made for each non-dependant but only one deduction is made for a non-dependant couple.

Discretionary housing payments[209]

You can be paid a discretionary housing payment (DHP) by the local authority in addition to your HB if you need further help to pay your rent – eg, because of a rent restriction or a non-dependant deduction.

The amount and period of payment is up to the local authority but you cannot get a DHP:

- if you are not entitled to HB, or your HB has been suspended;
- which exceeds your rent (less service charges which are not eligible for HB – see p167);
- for any such ineligible service charges (see p167).

You must make a separate claim for a DHP to the local authority. There is no legal right to a payment and no right of appeal to the First-tier Tribunal. You can, however, request a review of any decision relating to a DHP.

Examples of HB calculations

Mr and Mrs Khan are both aged 53 and get income-based JSA. They live with their son, aged 28, who has learning difficulties and receives IS and DLA. Their rent is £120 a week, including all their fuel costs. No restrictions are imposed by the rent officer.

They are entitled to maximum HB because they are receiving income-based JSA.

1. Their eligible rent = £120 *less* £21.55 deduction for fuel charges (see p167) = £98.45.
2. HB = £98.45 eligible rent *less* £7.40 non-dependant deduction (see p169) = £91.05

If Mr Khan starts working and is no longer entitled to JSA, and his earnings (after disregards) are assessed for HB purposes as £200 a week, the maximum HB of £91.05 would be reduced by 65 per cent of the difference between their income and their applicable amount.

1. Their applicable amount is £100.95 (personal allowance for a couple).
2. Their income (£200) *less* their applicable amount (£100.95) = £99.05 x 65% = £64.38.
3. HB = £91.05 *less* £64.38= £26.67

Note that if Mr and Mrs Khan were both aged 60, rather than 53, and were getting the guarantee credit of PC instead of JSA, their HB would still have been £91.05. When Mr Khan started working, however, their HB applicable amount for the purposes of the above calculation would have been £198.45 and their HB would only have been reduced to £90.05 (£200 income *less* £198.45 applicable amount = £1.55 x 65% = £1.00; £91.05 *less* £1.00 = £90.05).

How to claim

Claim forms are available from your local authority or the DWP and should be returned to the HB section of the authority. If you are claiming IS, income-based JSA or income-related ESA, you should claim HB on the standard claim form HCTB1 which should be given to you when you want to claim. If you claim PC over the phone, you can apply for HB at the same time. Claims can be backdated for up to 13 or 26 weeks (see p99 – but note the special rule if you are claiming a qualifying benefit).

You claim HB for yourself and your family (see p163). Either you or your partner can be the claimant and, as with IS, you can sometimes be better off if one of you claims rather the other (see p155). This may particularly be the case for couples where one or both are getting ESA. If you are a local authority tenant, your HB is paid by reducing your rent (rent rebate). If you are a private tenant, your HB is usually paid to you (rent allowance) but in specified circumstances (eg, if you are vulnerable), it can be paid directly to your landlord.[210]

Council tax benefit

Council tax benefit (CTB) is a tax free, means-tested weekly benefit paid to people who are liable to pay council tax. It can be claimed by people who are working, unemployed or retired. CTB is paid and administered by local authorities (councils).

Who can claim

You qualify for CTB if:[211]

* you are liable to pay council tax (see p172); *and*
* your income is low enough (see p173); *and*
* you and your partner do not have savings and other capital worth more than £16,000 (see Chapter 8 for details of how your capital is calculated), unless you or your partner are getting the guarantee credit of PC (see p159), in which case your capital is not taken into account; *and*

- you are not a full-time student (there are exceptions, however, as for HB, see p164); *and*
- you are habitually resident in the UK and you are not subject to immigration control (see p121).

As with HB, you claim CTB for yourself and your family, including your partner and dependent children (see p163), and the amount you receive depends on your financial and other circumstances.[212]

In certain circumstances, you can qualify for CTB in the form of a 'second adult rebate' regardless of your income or capital, if you have a non-dependant living with you who has a low income and who is not disregarded for council tax discount purposes (see p173).[213] For more details, see CPAG's *Welfare Benefits and Tax Credits Handbook*.

Liability to pay council tax

Council tax is payable on most residential dwellings, unless they are exempt (see below). There are eight different 'bands' (or levels) of council tax (labelled A to H), depending on the valuation of the dwelling. You are liable to pay council tax in respect of your 'sole or main residence'[214] even if you are temporarily absent from it. You should remain eligible for CTB as long as you remain liable to pay council tax, including while you are away from home in the circumstances during which IS housing costs remain payable (see p153).[215] Only one council tax bill is payable in respect of each dwelling. A 'hierarchy of liability' determines which resident is liable to pay the bill. In general, owner-occupiers are primarily liable, then tenants, then licensees, then other residents. Partners, joint owners and joint tenants are normally jointly liable. Owners of care homes (and some hostels) and houses in multiple occupation are usually liable rather than the residents.

Exemptions from liability

Some dwellings are exempt from council tax, including:[216]

- dwellings which are unoccupied because the former resident has recently died, or is permanently in hospital, a care home, a hostel where care is provided, or anywhere else (including someone else's home) where s/he is receiving *or providing* personal care relating to old age, disablement, illness, mental disorder or drug/alcohol dependence;
- dwellings wholly occupied by people who are 'severely mentally impaired' – ie, have a permanent severe impairment of intelligence and social functioning (whatever the cause) and are entitled to AA, DLA middle or higher rate care component, IB, ESA, SDA or IS including a disability premium (or would be entitled if they were under pension age);
- dwellings with a self-contained unit occupied by a dependent relative of the occupier of the main part of the dwelling, where that dependent relative is aged over 65 (eg, a 'granny flat'), or 'substantially and permanently disabled'

(see below), or 'severely mentally impaired' (see p172). This exemption only applies in England and Wales and only the self-contained unit is exempt from the tax.

The disability reduction scheme

Your council tax is reduced by one valuation band (or by one-sixth if your property is in band A) under the disability reduction scheme if your dwelling is occupied by somebody (of any age) who is 'substantially and permanently disabled' (whether mentally or physically) and the property has been made suitable for her/his needs. For example, there must also be an additional bathroom or kitchen to meet her/his needs, or another room is being used predominantly for her/his needs, or adaptations or alterations have been done to make enough space for her/him to use a wheelchair. Your council should have a form you can use to apply for a reduction and you can appeal against the refusal of a reduction.[217]

The discount scheme

The discount scheme[218] reduces your bill by 25 per cent if there is only one adult resident in the dwelling, or 50 per cent if there are no adult residents. Some people are disregarded as residents, including anyone who is:

- under the age of 18 or a student; *or*
- solely or mainly resident in a care home, hospital or hostels providing personal care; *or*
- 'severely mentally impaired' (see p172); *or*
- a carer who provides:
  - at least 35 hours care a week for a person living in the same dwelling who is not her/his partner or child aged under 18 and who receives the highest rate of AA or DLA care component; *or*
  - care and/or support for at least 24 hours a week, and is employed by the person being looked after and was introduced to that person by, or provides the care or support on behalf of, a local authority, government department or charity and is on low pay.

Amount

CTB is a means-tested benefit and the amount you are entitled to depends on your circumstances. CTB is paid in the form of a rebate – ie, a reduction in your bill.

If you are receiving IS (see p147), income-based JSA (see p158), income-related ESA (see p156) or the guarantee credit of PC (see p158), your council tax is fully rebated apart from any non-dependant deductions which you have to pay (see p174). If you have been receiving IS, income-based JSA or income-related ESA for at least 26 continuous weeks, your council tax remains fully rebated for the first four weeks you or your partner take up full-time employment, as long as you notify the local authority within that period.[219]

If you are not receiving IS, income-based JSA, income-related ESA or the guarantee credit of PC, your weekly council tax liability is reduced to 20 per cent of the difference between your income and your applicable amount (see below), plus any non-dependant deductions which you have to pay (see p174). If this figure exceeds your council tax liability you are not entitled to any CTB. If your income is less than your applicable amount your council tax is fully rebated.[220]

Your income is calculated in the same way as for HB (see Chapter 8). Your applicable amount is also worked out in the same way as for HB (see p166), except that the categories of people who do not count as non-dependants for the purposes of the severe disability premium (see p151) are slightly different.

Examples of CTB calculations are given on p175.

Note the following points.

- If you are jointly liable for council tax with someone other than your partner, your CTB is calculated on your proportionate share of the bill.[221]
- If you qualify for a second adult rebate (see p171), your council tax is rebated by up to 25 per cent, depending on the income of your non-dependant.[222]
- You can request a discretionary housing payment in addition to CTB to help meet your liability for council tax (see p175).

Non-dependant deductions

If you have a non-dependant living with you, a deduction is made from your CTB and will not form part of your rebate, on the assumption that s/he is making a contribution towards your council tax (whether s/he is or not). The rules about non-dependant deductions are the same as for HB (see p169), apart from the following differences.

- The last two categories on p169 of people who do not count as non-dependants for HB do not apply to CTB. For CTB, a joint occupier who is jointly liable for council tax, or a person other than a close relative (see p400) who is liable to pay you rent on a commercial basis, does not count as a non-dependant unless her/his liability was created to take advantage of the CTB scheme.[223]
- No non-dependant deduction is made for anyone who is receiving IS or income-based JSA, income-related ESA or PC (not just those under 25 as for HB), or anyone who is disregarded for council tax discount purposes, apart from students (see p171).[224]
- The standard deduction for a non-dependant who is not working more than 16 hours a week is £2.30.[225]
- The deduction for a non-dependant who is getting PC and who is working more than 16 hours a week is £2.30, regardless of her/his income.

- If the non-dependant is working more than 16 hours a week, the amount of deduction is as follows:[226]

Weekly gross income	Weekly deduction
£382 or over	£6.95
£306-£381.99	£5.80
£178-£305.99	£4.60
Less than £178	£2.30

Discretionary housing payments[227]

You can be paid a DHP by the local authority in addition to your CTB if you need further help to pay your council tax. The amount and period of payment is up to the local authority but you cannot get a DHP:

- if you are not entitled to CTB, or your CTB has been suspended, or you are only entitled to a 'second adult rebate' (see p172);
- which exceeds your weekly council tax liability.

You must make a separate claim for a DHP to the local authority. There is no legal right to a payment and no right of appeal to the First-tier Tribunal. You can, however, request a review of any decision relating to a DHP.

Examples of CTB calculations

Mr and Mrs Khan, whose circumstances are set out on p170, live in a band C property. While they are getting income-based JSA or the guarantee credit of PC, they are entitled to a full rebate of their council tax (there is no non-dependant deduction for their son because he is in receipt of IS).

When Mr Khan starts work, their weekly council tax is affected as follows: income (after disregards) (£200) *less* their applicable amount (£100.95) = £99.05 x 20% = £19.81. If this is more than their weekly liability, they do not qualify for CTB. If it is less, they get the balance as CTB.

How to claim

The procedure is the same as for HB (see p171). Application forms are available from your local authority, or you can claim on form HCTB1 if you also claiming IS, or income-based JSA or income-related ESA. CTB is paid by reducing your council tax liability.

Tax credits

Tax credits are tax-free, means-tested benefits paid to people who are responsible for children or in low paid work. Although they are called tax credits and are paid and administered by HM Revenue and Customs (the Revenue), they are similar in character to other social security benefits and should not be confused with income tax allowances. There are two tax credits:

- **child tax credit (CTC)** is paid to families with children;
- **working tax credit (WTC)** is paid to people in low paid work.

You can qualify for either or both tax credits.

Who can claim

To qualify for either tax credit you must be:[228]

- aged 16 or over; *and*
- present and ordinarily resident in the UK (you are treated as present during a temporary absence of up to eight weeks, or up to 12 weeks if the absence is in connection with the treatment of illness or disability of you, your partner, your child or another relative or the death of your partner, your child or another relative). **Note:** to get CTC you must also have the 'right to reside in the UK' – see p150); *and*
- not subject to immigration control (see p121). The rules are complex and there are exceptions. See CPAG's *Welfare Benefits and Tax Credits Handbook* for details. Note that if you have a partner (see below) and only one of you is subject to immigration control or has the right to reside in the UK, your entitlement to tax credits is not affected; *and*
- assessed as having a low enough income (see below).

If you have a partner, you must make a joint claim for tax credits unless you are permanently separated, and your income and entitlement is jointly assessed. For the meaning of partner, see p93.

To qualify for CTC you or your partner must be responsible for:[229]

- a child under 16; *or*
- a young person under 20 in full-time non-advanced education or approved training.

You can claim CTC whether or not you are working. You are **'responsible'** for a child or young person if s/he is 'normally living with' you. Only one person can get CTC for a child (the **'main carer'**). You cannot get CTC for a child being maintained or accommodated by a local authority (unless the child has been accommodated under the Children Act because of a disability).

You can continue to get CTC:

- for eight weeks after a child or young person dies;
- until the September after the 16th birthday of a child who leaves school at 16;
- for 20 weeks after a young person under 18 leaves education, if s/he registers with the careers or Connexions service.

To qualify for WTC you or your partner must be:[230]

- working at least 16 hours a week and responsible for a child or young person (the rules about when you are responsible are the same as for CTC – see p176); *or*
- aged 25 or over and working at least 30 hours a week; *or*
- aged 50 or over, working at least 16 hours a week and were getting IS, JSA, ESA, IB, SDA or retirement pension plus PC, or a training allowance for six months before you claim WTC (note that if you, or your partner, were getting CA, BA or WPA immediately before making a successful claim for any of these benefits, this will count towards the six month's qualifying period); *or*
- working at least 16 hours a week; *and*
  - have one of the disabilities (specified functional difficulties) listed in the claims pack which puts you at a disadvantage of getting a job; *and*
  - satisfy the benefit condition below.

You satisfy the **benefit condition** if you:[231]
- are getting AA or DLA when you claim WTC; *or*
- were getting, for at least one day in the 28 weeks before your claim for WTC, the long-term or higher rate short-term IB (see p156), SDA, a disability or higher pensioner premium of IS, JSA, HB or CTB (see p151), or ESA, where you have been entitled to ESA (or a combination of ESA and SSP) for at least 28 weeks; *or*
- were incapable of work and as a result you were getting SSP or sick pay (see p143), lower rate short-term IB (see p156), ESA, IS, or NI contributions (see p135) for at least 20 weeks ending in the eight weeks before you claim WTC, and you have a disability which is likely to last for at least six months and your earnings are at least 20 per cent less than they were before your disability began; *or*
- have undertaken government 'training for work' for at least one day in the 56 days immediately before the claim and have been getting higher rate short term IB, long term IB, SDA or contributory ESA (where you have been entitled to that, or a combination of that and SSP, for at least 28 weeks), within the 56 days before the training started.

To get WTC, you must be working, or due to start work within seven days, when you claim. The work must be for payment (other than expenses) and be expected to last for at least four weeks. When calculating whether you work for at least 16 or 30 hours a week, the hours you 'normally work' are assessed, ignoring unpaid meal breaks and paid holidays. You can be treated as working for at least 16 or 30 hours a week for up to 26 weeks, if you were doing so immediately before you were sick, or on maternity, paternity or adoption leave.

Amount
Tax credits are means-tested and the amount you are entitled to depends on your income and other circumstances. Note that there is no capital limit for claiming

tax credits but your income from capital is taken into account. Examples of calculations are given on p180.

There are three steps involved in calculating your entitlement to tax credits.[232]

Step one: Calculate your maximum entitlement (see below). This is the total of all the elements of CTC and WTC to which you are entitled.

Step two: Compare your income (see p179) with the relevant threshold (see p179). If your income is below the threshold, you are entitled to maximum tax credits, as calculated in step one. You are automatically entitled to the maximum if you are getting IS, income-based JSA, income-related ESA or PC. If your income is above the threshold, proceed to step three.

Step three: Reduce maximum entitlement by 39 per cent of the amount by which your income exceeds the relevant threshold. The elements of WTC (other than the childcare element) are reduced first, followed by the childcare element and then the child elements of CTC. Entitlement to the family element of CTC is retained unless your income exceeds £50,000 a year, in which case it is reduced by 6.67 per cent of the amount by which your income exceeds that figure.

Note that:

- if you have a partner, the calculation is based on your joint income;
- entitlement to both tax credits is calculated together;
- entitlement is calculated using annual figures for your income (see p179) and maximum entitlement for the tax year (April to April) in which you claim (but you are actually paid tax credits weekly or four-weekly);
- if you claim part-way through the tax year, or your maximum entitlement changes during the tax year (eg, because you have a baby, or start or stop working), the calculation must be repeated for each relevant period by pro rating the figures for maximum entitlement, income and thresholds according to the number of days in the period.

Maximum entitlement[233]

Add up the following amounts which are applicable to you:

If you qualify for CTC:

Family element (one per family)	£545 (£1,090 if you have a baby under 1)
Child element (per child)	£2,235
Disabled child element (for each child who gets DLA or is registered blind)	£2,670
Severely disabled child element (for each child who gets the highest rate care component of DLA)	£1,075

If you qualify for WTC:

Basic element	£1,890
Second adult or lone parent element (if you have a partner or are a lone parent)	£1,860
30-hour element (if you or your partner work at least 30 hours a week – couples with a child can add their hours together)	£775
Disabled worker element (if you or your partner work at least 16 hours a week and satisfy the disability and benefit conditions set out on p177)	£2,530
Severe disability element (if you or your partner get the highest rate care component of DLA)	£1,075
50 plus element (if you qualify for WTC on the basis of being aged 50 or over – see p177)	
Working 16-29 hours	£1,300
Working 30+ hours	£1,935
Childcare element (if you are a lone parent, or you and your partner are both working, or one of you is working and the other is incapacitated)	80% of relevant childcare costs (see below)

Childcare must be 'relevant childcare' such as registered childminders and before/after school clubs – see Revenue leaflet WTC5 for what counts as relevant childcare where you live. The maximum payable for one child is £140 (80 per cent of £175) a week and for two or more children is £240 (80 per cent of £300) a week.[234]

Income

Your income for tax credit purposes is explained in Chapter 8. It is calculated on an annual basis. If you claim tax credits in 2009/10, your entitlement will be initially calculated using your income during the tax year 2008/9.[235] If your income goes down after you claim, or increases by more than £25,000, inform the Revenue and your award will be re-assessed.[236] Alternatively, you can wait until you receive a final decision at the end of the tax year (see p180) and your award will be re-adjusted. Rises of £25,000 over the previous year are ignored. Any underpayment will be refunded to you. Any overpayment will be recoverable from you (usually by reducing your following year's award).

Thresholds

The relevant threshold if you are eligible for CTC only is £16,040. The relevant threshold if you are entitled to WTC (with or without CTC) is £6,420.[237]

Examples of tax credit calculations

Mr and Mrs Jones have one child, aged 9, who is severely disabled and gets the highest rate care component of DLA. If they are claiming IS or income-based JSA, their entitlement to CTC is calculated as follows:

Step one: Their maximum entitlement is:

CTC family element	£545
CTC child element	£2,235
CTC disabled child element	£2,670
CTC severely disabled child element	£1,075
maximum CTC	£6,525

Step two: They are entitled to maximum CTC because they are getting IS.

If Mr Jones was working 25 hours a week and earning £15,000 a year, their tax credit entitlement would be calculated as follows:

Step one: Their maximum entitlement is:

CTC (see above)	£6,525
WTC basic element	£1,890
WTC second adult element	£1,860
maximum tax credit entitlement	£10,275

Step two: Their income of £15,000 exceeds the relevant threshold of £6,420 by £8,580

Step three: Their maximum entitlement of £10,275 is reduced by £3,346.20 (39% of £8,580) to give actual entitlement of £6,928.80. This is all be paid as CTC (because it is less than the maximum CTC payable).

How to claim

Claim on form TC600, which you can get from the Revenue or DWP offices or by telephoning 0845 300 3900 (textphone 0845 300 3909). Both tax credits are claimed together on one form.

Tax credits are paid directly into bank accounts. If you make a joint claim, any CTC and the childcare element of WTC is paid to whoever is the main carer. WTC is paid to the worker's bank account and if you are a member of a couple, where both are working at least 16 hours a week, you can decide who should receive it.[238]

Change of circumstances

When you first make your claim, you receive an 'initial award' for the rest of the tax year, based on your circumstances when you claim and your previous year's income. If your circumstances change during the year, your award can be re-assessed if you notify the Revenue. Otherwise, you will receive a notice at the end of the tax year asking you to confirm whether the information used to assess your award was correct and to notify any changes there have been during the year. You will then receive a final decision, which will confirm your entitlement for the previous year. If you received more than your entitlement, the Revenue will seek to recover the overpayment (see below). If you received less than your entitlement, you will be paid the amount owing to you. The end of year notice is treated as an automatic claim for the following year if you are still entitled to tax credits.[239]

You must notify the Revenue of the following changes within one month:[240]

- you start or stop living with a partner;
- your childcare costs stop or reduce by £10 a week or more for four consecutive weeks;[241]
- you or your partner leave the UK for more than eight weeks (12 weeks on grounds of illness or death);
- you or your partner stop working at least 16 or 30 hours a week;
- for couples with children, you and your partner stop normally working a combined total of 30 hours a week;
- you or your partner are no longer responsible for a child or the child no longer counts for tax credits purposes.

If you fail to notify these changes within one month you can be fined up to £300 and become liable for overpayments. In some of the above circumstances your claim will have ceased and you will need to make a new claim. See CPAG's *Welfare Benefits and Tax Credits Handbook* for further details.

If your maximum entitlement increases during the year, notify the Revenue within three months, as only three months of arrears can be paid as a result of such changes.[242] If your income changes, you can inform the Revenue straight away or wait until the end of the tax year.

Overpayments

You may be overpaid tax credits if you do not inform the Revenue about a change of circumstances which reduces your entitlement, or you make a mistake about your information, or the Revenue makes an error about your entitlement. Overpayments can arise during the course of the year ('in year overpayments') or at the end of the tax year after your award has been finalised ('end of year overpayments'). The Revenue may recover all or part of the overpayment, but does not have to. Recovery may be by deductions from an ongoing award (at set levels) or directly to the Revenue. There is no right of appeal against the decision to recover an overpayment but you can dispute the recovery if there has been official error (ie, the Revenue fails to meet its responsibilities) or you are suffering hardship. You may also be able to get additional payments or negotiate longer repayment periods. For more information see the Revenue's COP 26 Code of Guidance (available at www.hmrc.gov.uk) or CPAG's *Welfare Benefits and Tax Credits Handbook*.

Social fund payments

The social fund is a government fund which makes payments to people on low incomes to meet specified needs. The fund is administered by the DWP. There are two types of payments available from the social fund:

- **funeral grants, maternity grants and winter payments** – you are legally entitled to these payments if you satisfy the rules;
- **community care grants, budgeting loans and crisis loans** – you are eligible for these payments if you satisfy the rules, but awards are discretionary and budget limited.

You are not entitled to a social fund payment (apart from a crisis loan following a disaster) if you are 'subject to immigration control' (see p121).

Note that references to 'partner' in the following information, have the same meaning as for IS (see p93).

Funeral grants

Funeral grants are paid to help with the cost of a funeral of a close relative or friend.

Who can claim

You qualify for a funeral grant if:[243]

- you or your partner have been awarded IS, income-based JSA, income-related ESA, PC, HB, CTB, CTC (at a rate which exceeds the family element – see p178) or WTC (which includes the disability or severe disability element – see p178) when you claim a funeral grant, or you receive a backdated award of one of these benefits which covers the date of your claim; *and*
- you or your partner are in one of the categories of people who are eligible to claim (see below); *and*
- you or your partner have accepted responsibility for paying the cost of a funeral (ie, you are liable to pay the cost because, for example, the funeral director's bill is in your name); *and*
- the deceased was ordinarily resident in the UK when s/he died and the funeral takes place in the UK (or, in certain circumstances, in an EEA country – see p150).

You are eligible to claim a funeral grant if you, or your partner, fall into one of the following categories.[244]

- You were the partner of the deceased when s/he died.
- The deceased was a child for whom you were responsible (you may be excluded if the child had an absent parent who was not getting one of the qualifying benefits listed above).
- You were a 'close relative' or close friend of the deceased and it is reasonable for you to accept responsibility for the funeral costs, given the nature and

extent of your contact with the deceased.[245] **'Close relative'** means parent, son, daughter, brother, sister (actual, 'in-laws', or 'step'). You are excluded from getting a grant as a close relative or close friend, however, if the deceased has a partner, parent or adult son or daughter (unless the parent, son or daughter is receiving one of the qualifying benefits listed above, or was estranged from the deceased when s/he died, or is a student, prisoner, asylum seeker receiving asylum support or not resident in the UK).[246] You are also excluded if there is a close relative of the deceased who was in closer contact with her/him than you were, or equally close contact if the close relative (or partner) is not getting a qualifying benefit.[247]

Amount

The following amounts can be paid, subject to the deductions below:[248]
- the costs of burial or cremation (including documentation); *plus*
- specified transport costs; *plus*
- up to £700 for other costs – eg, funeral directors' fees, flowers, religious costs.

The following amounts are deducted from an award of a funeral grant:
- any of the deceased's assets available to you without probate or letters of administration[249] (note that the DWP can recover a funeral grant from the deceased's estate);[250]
- any payment made on the death of the deceased from an insurance policy, occupational pension scheme, pre-paid funeral plan, burial club, charity or relative of yours.[251]

How to claim

Claim on form SF200, which you can get from your local Jobcentre Plus office, or by telephoning a regional Jobcentre Plus contact centre. You must claim within three months of the date of the funeral.[252]

Sure Start maternity grants

Sure Start maternity grants are one-off payments to help with the cost of maternity expenses.

Who can claim

You qualify for a Sure Start maternity grant if:[253]
- you or your partner have been awarded IS, income-based JSA, income-related ESA, PC, CTC (at a rate which exceeds the family element – see p178) or WTC (which includes the disability or severe disability element – see p178) when you claim a maternity grant, or you receive a backdated award of one of these benefits which covers the date of your claim; *and*
- you or a member of your family (as defined for IS – see p163) are pregnant, or have given birth in the last three months (including stillbirth after 24 weeks of

pregnancy), or have adopted a baby under 12 months old, or have a parental order for a surrogate child.

Amount

The maternity grant is £500 for each qualifying child.[254]

How to claim

Claim on form SF100 available from your local Jobcentre Plus or DWP office. You must claim in the 11 weeks before the expected week of birth or in the three months after the birth, adoption or parental order. Your claim form must be signed by a health professional to confirm that you have received health and welfare advice.

Winter fuel payments

Winter fuel payments are made to help with the cost of fuel bills.

Who can claim

There are two types of winter payments.

- **Cold weather payments** are paid between November and March if the average temperature in your area falls below zero degrees Celsius for at least seven consecutive days. You qualify for a payment if you are receiving IS, income-based JSA, income-related ESA and either you have a child under 5, or you are receiving a pensioner, higher pensioner, disability, enhanced disability, severe disability or disabled child premium (see p151), or you are receiving PC. You cannot get a payment, however, if you are living in a care home.[255]
- **Winter fuel payments** are paid to people who are aged 60 or over in the week beginning on the third Monday in September. You cannot get a payment, however, if at that time you have been in hospital for more than 52 weeks, or you are receiving IS, income-based JSA, income-related ESA or PC and are in a care home and have been throughout the previous 12 weeks.[256] If you are in a care home and are not getting IS, JSA, ESA or PC, you can get 50 per cent of the payment.

Amount

Cold weather payments are normally £8.50 for each qualifying week but for Winter 2009 they are £25. Winter fuel payments are one-off grants of £250 a household or £400 if you or your partner are aged 80 or over.

How to claim

There is no need to make a claim for a cold weather payment. You should be paid automatically if you qualify. Anyone who received a winter fuel payment last year or who is getting a retirement pension or other benefit (apart from HB and CTB) in the qualifying week should automatically receive a winter fuel payment.

Others should make a claim. You can get a claim form by ringing a special local rate helpline on 08459 15 15 15 (textphone 08456 015 613).

Community care grants

Community care grants (CCGs) are paid to help people on IS, income-based JSA, income-related ESA or PC to live independently in the community.

Who can claim

You are eligible for a CCG if:

- you are receiving IS, income-based JSA, income-related ESA or PC when you claim a CCG, or you are due to leave institutional or residential care within six weeks of claiming a CCG and are likely to get one of those benefits when you leave;[257] *and*
- you do not have too much capital (see p186); *and*
- the CCG is not for an 'excluded item' (see p186); *and*
- you need the CCG to:
  - help you or a member of your family, or someone for whom you or a member of your family will be providing care, to become established in the community following a stay in institutional or residential care, or to remain in the community rather than enter such care; *or*
  - ease exceptional pressures on you and your family; *or*
  - help you set up home as part of a planned resettlement programme; *or*
  - help you care for a prisoner or young offender on temporary release; *or*
  - help you with travel expenses to visit someone who is ill, attend a relative's funeral, ease a domestic crisis or move to more suitable accommodation.[258]

There is no legal entitlement to a CCG. Payments are discretionary and each DWP district office is given a fixed annual budget for CCGs. Guidance is issued by the DWP (the *Social Fund Guide*) and by each district on the circumstances in which a CCG should be awarded. The guidance is not legally binding, however, and decisions must take into account all the circumstances of each application, including the nature, extent and urgency of the need.[259] The guidance suggests that priority should be given where there is mental or physical disability, illness, general frailty, abuse or neglect, unstable family circumstances, an unsettled way of life and drug or alcohol misuse.

The following points should be noted.

- You must specify the items for which you need the CCG. You can ask for a CCG for any items which are not excluded (see p186). If, however, you have been awarded or refused a CCG for a particular item, you cannot get a CCG for the same item for four weeks from the date of your application.[260]
- CCGs are most often awarded to help people move out of, or stay out of, institutional or residential care. This could include hospital, care homes, group homes, supported lodgings, sheltered housing, hostels and any other

accommodation which provides residents with substantial care or supervision. If you are moving out of care you need to show that a CCG will help you establish yourself in the community – eg, by helping you set up home. If you live in your own home, you need to show that a CCG will lessen the risk of you going into hospital or residential care – eg, by improving your ability to cope at home and to stay healthy. The type of items you could claim for include furniture and household equipment, moving expenses, clothing, footwear and non-medical items needed because of sickness and disability, including wheelchairs and special beds, mattresses, chairs and equipment to help with everyday living.

- You can also claim a CCG to ease exceptional pressures on you and your family. 'Family' is not defined in the law and could encompass couples (married or not, of any sex), children and adult sons and daughters and other relatives living together. People living on their own, however, are excluded under this provision.[261] 'Exceptional pressures' are not defined in the law and could include disability, sickness, depression, bereavement, family breakdown, poor living conditions and child behavioural problems.

Excluded items

You cannot get a CCG for any of the following items:[262]

- the cost of domestic assistance (including home care) or respite care;
- a medical, surgical, optical, aural or dental item. A medical item, however, should not include an everyday item needed because of a medical condition – eg, non-allergic bedding, a special bed or mattress, special shoes, equipment for everyday living and a wheelchair;
- most housing costs including repairs and improvements (other than minor ones), rent, deposits, mortgage payments, residential accommodation charges and council tax and water charges;
- telephone and fuel charges, educational or training needs, work-related expenses, debts to government departments, court fines and fees, needs which a local authority has a statutory duty to meet and most daily living expenses;
- a need which occurs outside the UK.

There are other exclusions. For a full list, see CPAG's *Welfare Benefits and Tax Credits Handbook*.

Amount

You must specify the actual or estimated amount of CCG you need on your application form. There is no legal maximum but the minimum you can be awarded is £30 (unless the CCG is for travel expenses).[263] The amount you request should be allowed unless it is unreasonable. The DWP often refers to catalogue prices as a guide to what is reasonable.

Any CCG you are awarded is reduced by the amount of capital you and your partner have in excess of £500 (£1,000 if either of you is aged 60 or over).[264]

How to claim

Apply for a CCG by telephoning a Regional Social Fund office or on form SF300 obtainable from your local Jobcentre Plus office. You should explain why you need the items, with reference to the purposes for which a CCG can be awarded (see p188), and why your application should be given high priority. A supporting letter from your doctor, social worker or other professional involved in your care may help your case.

Budgeting loans

Budgeting loans (BLs) are interest-free loans paid to help people on IS, income-based JSA, income-related ESA or PC with one-off expenses.

Who can claim

You are eligible for a BL if:[265]

- you are in receipt of IS, income-based JSA, income-related ESA or PC when you claim a BL and you and/or your partner have been receiving one of those benefits throughout the 26 weeks before your claim is determined, apart from any breaks of up to 28 days; *and*
- you do not have too much capital (see p188); *and*
- the BL is for one or more of the following items:
  - furniture or household equipment;
  - clothing and footwear;
  - rent in advance and/or removal expenses on moving;
  - improvement, maintenance and security of the home;
  - travelling expenses;
  - expenses related to seeking or re-entering work;
  - hire purchase and other debts for any of the above.

As with CCGs (see p185), there is no legal entitlement to a payment and each DWP district office is given a fixed annual budget for loans. Unlike CCGs, however, applications are decided in accordance with set criteria, rather than on a discretionary basis.

Repayment of BLs can cause hardship so apply for a CCG rather than a BL if you are eligible (see p185).

Amount

You can request a BL of between £100 and £1,500.[266] Whether you are actually offered a BL and the amount you are offered depends on a number of factors including:[267]

- the length of time you have been receiving benefit;

- the size of your family;
- the amount of any outstanding BLs you have;
- your ability to repay a BL within 104 weeks.

If you are offered a loan, you are given up to three options for repaying the loan, but you cannot be asked to pay a rate of more than 20 per cent of your IS/income-related ESA/income-based JSA applicable amount/PC appropriate minimum guarantee (excluding housing costs).

Any award, however, is reduced by the amount of any capital you or your partner have in excess of £500 (£1,000 if either of you is aged 60 or over).[268]

BLs are normally recovered by direct deductions from your weekly benefit.

How to claim

Apply for a BL by phoning a Regional Social Fund office or on form SF500 available from your local Jobcentre Plus office. If you are offered a loan, you are given 14 days to return your acceptance.

Crisis loans

Crisis loans (CLs) are paid to people who have no money because of a crisis. Unlike budgeting loans, they are not restricted to people on benefit.

Who can claim

You are eligible for a CL if:[269]

- you are aged 16 or over; *and*
- you have insufficient resources to meet the immediate needs of yourself and/or your family; *and*
- you need a CL to prevent serious damage or serious risk to your (or a member of your family's) health and safety following an emergency or disaster; *or*
- you need a CL for rent in advance to secure private accommodation following a stay in care (you must also have been awarded a CCG – see p185); *and*
- you are not in hospital or a care home (unless your discharge is planned within the next two weeks); *and*
- the CL is not for an excluded item. Items excluded are the same as for CCGs (see p186) except that living expenses and fuel costs are not excluded but telephone, TV and vehicle costs, mobility needs, and holidays are; *and*
- you are likely to be able to repay the loan.

As with CCGs (see p185), there is no legal entitlement to a CL. Payments are discretionary and must take into account the circumstances of each case (including the urgency of the need) and guidance is set out in the *Social Fund Guide*. The *Guide* gives examples of when a CL may be appropriate, including where you have lost money, you are waiting for a benefit claim to be processed, or you have had an emergency or disaster such as a fire or flood. You can, however, claim in any situation where you have no money.

Amount

You can request a lump sum CL of up to £1,500.[270] You will not usually be offered more than you can repay in 104 weeks and you will be given details of the weekly repayment rate.

How to claim

You can still claim a CL on form SF400 or SF401 from your local Jobcentre Plus office although most claims are now made over the phone to a Regional Social Fund office. Jobcentre Plus staff sometimes advise potential applicants that they shouldn't bother applying as they will not qualify. Always insist on formally completing an application and being given a written decision. You are normally interviewed about your application (in person or over the phone).

Challenging a social fund decision

If you are refused a CCG, BL or CL you can request a review of the decision in writing within 28 days of the date the decision was issued to you. If you are still unhappy with the decision, request a further review by writing to the social fund inspectors within 28 days of the date of the review decision.

5. **People in hospital**

Your benefit may be affected after you or your dependants have been receiving free NHS funded treatment as an inpatient in a hospital or similar institution for the periods specified below.[271] A **'similar institution'** to a hospital could include some care homes, hospices and rehabilitation units which provide medical or nursing care, but only if your maintenance and treatment are being directly funded by a health authority and your placement was not arranged by a local authority (even if the NHS is contributing to the cost of your nursing care – see p239).[272]

Separate spells as an inpatient which are separated by 28 days or less are linked together when calculating the periods specified below. For most benefits, you do not count as an inpatient on the day you enter hospital, but you do on the day you are discharged.[273] For attendance allowance (AA) and disability living allowance (DLA), however, you do not count as an inpatient on both the days you enter and leave hospital.[274]

Inform the benefit authorities promptly if you think that your benefit may be affected by the rules set out below, to avoid being overpaid or underpaid benefit. If you need to claim benefit on the basis of incapacity for work, the hospital can issue medical certificates. You can arrange for someone to collect your benefit while you are in hospital and if you are unable to manage your affairs, another person can act as your appointee (see p92).

See p79 if you need help with fares if you have to attend a hospital for treatment. You may be eligible for a community care grant to cover fares to visit someone in hospital (see p185).

After four weeks

- Any **AA or DLA** you are getting stops after you have been an inpatient for 28 days (but note the special rule below about the mobility component of DLA and that any DLA you are getting for a child continues to be paid until s/he has been an inpatient for 12 weeks).[275] If you are re-admitted as an inpatient within 28 days of a previous stay, your AA or DLA will stop sooner or immediately, because of the linking rule (see p189). Also, if you are not entitled to AA or DLA care component because you are living in a care home (see p346), you will not be entitled to either of them when you become an inpatient, because periods spent in both types of accommodation link, unless they are separated by more than 28 days (this rule does not apply to DLA mobility component).[276] Your AA and DLA should be paid as normal when you are discharged – you should not have to make a fresh claim but should inform the DWP as soon as you are discharged. **Note:** if you first become entitled to AA or DLA while you are an inpatient, you cannot receive any benefit until you are discharged.[277]

- You can continue to receive the **mobility component of DLA** while you are an inpatient if you had a Motability agreement (see p87) when you entered hospital (benefit normally continues until the agreement ends).[278] If you are terminally ill, you can continue to receive AA or DLA while you are in a non-NHS hospice.[279]

- Your entitlement to the **severe disability premium** paid with income support (IS) or income-related employment and support allowance (ESA), housing benefit (HB) and council tax benefit (CTB) and the **severe disability addition** paid with pension credit (PC) stops once you are no longer entitled to AA or DLA. If, however, you are a member of a couple and one or both of you are an inpatient, you can qualify for the premium/addition at the single person's rate. Your entitlement to the disability, enhanced disability, higher pensioner or disabled child premiums (see p151) paid with IS, is not affected by the withdrawal of AA or DLA.[280] If your IS or PC stops because of the loss of the severe disability premium/addition, your HB and CTB will also stop and you will need to submit a new claim.

- Your entitlement to **carer's allowance** (CA) stops when the person you are caring for loses entitlement to AA or DLA care component. The **carer premium/addition** paid with IS, income-related ESA, HB, CTB and PC can continue to be paid for eight weeks after CA, or AA/DLA care component stops.

After 12 weeks

- **DLA paid for a child** under 16 stops after s/he has been an inpatient for 12 weeks.[281]
- **You remain entitled to CA for up to 12 weeks** in any period of 26 weeks while you, or the person you are caring for, are an inpatient.[282] If, however, the person you are caring for is no longer entitled to AA or DLA because s/he is an inpatient, your CA will stop at that point. If your CA stops because you are an inpatient, the person you usually care for may become entitled to the severe disability premium/addition with her/his IS/income-related ESA or PC.
- Child-related premiums remain payable, including the disabled child premium (even after the cessation of DLA), as long as the child still counts as a member of your family.[283] **Child benefit** stops after the child has been an inpatient for 12 weeks, unless you continue to regularly incur expenditure in respect of her/him.[284] This may affect whether you can get any personal allowances and premiums/additional amounts for your child. Child tax credit is not affected.

After 52 weeks

- **HB** and **CTB** may be paid at a reduced rate if you (or if you are a member of a couple, both you and your partner) have been an inpatient for more than 52 weeks. The enhanced disability premium is not included in your applicable amount.[285]
- **Non-dependant deductions** from HB, CTB and housing costs paid with IS, income-based JSA, income-related ESA and PC are no longer made in respect of a non-dependant who has been an inpatient for more than 52 weeks.[286]
- Any disability premium, enhanced disability premium, higher pension premium or housing costs paid with you **IS** or **income-related ESA** may stop. Any disabled child premium and enhanced disability premium included in the applicable amount for you child will stop.

---

6. **Increasing your entitlement to benefit – examples**

Many people do not claim all the benefits to which they are entitled. The following examples illustrate how claimants in different circumstances can significantly enhance their income by claiming extra benefits. They particularly show how claiming one benefit can increase entitlement to other benefits.

Examples

The abbreviations used in the examples refer to the following benefits. For more details about each benefit, go to the relevant page indicated below:

Attendance allowance (AA – see p125)
Carer's allowance (CA – see p130)
Council tax benefit (CTB – see p171)
Disability living allowance (DLA – see p120)
Employment and support allowance (ESA – see p156)
Housing benefit (HB – see p163)
Incapacity benefit (IB – see p156)
Income support (IS – see p147)
Pension credit (PC – see p158)

Example 1 – single pensioner living alone

Monica is aged 66 and lives alone in a house she owns (she has paid off the mortgage). She receives a state retirement pension of £100 a week, from which she pays £10 a week council tax. She has no savings.

As her income of £100 is less than her PC appropriate minimum guarantee of £130 (see p160), she should be advised to claim PC. She will be entitled to £30 PC guarantee credit (the difference between the appropriate minimum guarantee and her income). She will also qualify for £2.40 savings credit (see p160). She will also be entitled to maximum CTB so that she will not have to pay any of her £10 a week council tax. By claiming both PC and CTB she will be £42.40 a week better off. She may also be able to backdate her claims to get up to 13 weeks arrears of PC and CTB (see p99).

By claiming PC, she is also eligible for social fund payments (see also Chapter 5 for other sources of financial assistance which may now be available to her).

If Monica's health deteriorated to the extent that she qualified for the lower rate of AA (see p126), this would be worth an additional £47.10 a week. The award of AA would, in turn, mean that she would qualify for the severe disability addition of PC guarantee credit (see p159), worth an additional £52.85 a week. Altogether, her income would have gone up from £100 a week, to £232.35 a week, with no council tax to pay.

Example 2 – pensioner couple with disabilities

Margaret and Steve are a married couple who live together in their own home (without a mortgage). They are both aged 79. Their combined income from their state retirement pension and occupational pensions is £200 a week, out of which they pay £20 a week council tax. They have no savings. Their health has been deteriorating recently and they are now receiving community care services for several hours a day to assist them with their personal care needs.

As their income of £200 is higher than their PC appropriate minimum guarantee of £198.45 they are not entitled to PC guarantee credit (see p159). They would, however, qualify for PC savings credit of £26.41 a week (see p160). They would also be entitled to a council tax rebate of £19.82 (see p173). They should, therefore, be advised to claim PC and CTB. They may also be able to backdate their claims to get up to 13 weeks arrears (see p99). By claiming PC, they are also eligible for social fund payments (see also Chapter 5 for other sources of financial assistance which may now be available to them).

In view of their deteriorating health and the extent of their personal care needs, they should also both be advised to claim AA. If they are both awarded AA for their care needs during the day, this will be worth an extra £94.20 a week (£47.10 x 2). This, in turn, would mean that are now entitled to PC guarantee credit of £104.15 (because they qualify for a severe disability addition of £105.70, increasing their appropriate minimum guarantee from £198.45 to £304.15, which is £104.15 more than their income of £200). They would also qualify for the maximum savings credit of £27.03. Their total income would, therefore, have more than doubled from £200 to £425.38 a week and they would also not have to pay the £20 a week council tax. Note also that if Margaret and Steve are spending more than 35 hours a week looking after each other, they could both claim CA, which would entitle them to an extra £59 PC guarantee credit (the carer's addition – see p160).

Example 3 – couple (disabled person and carer)

Brian and Sheila are a married couple aged 58 and 55 who live together in rented accommodation. Brian has physical disabilities and depends on Sheila to help with his personal care needs throughout the day and night. Sheila has also been incapable of work for some time. Their weekly rent is £150 and council tax £20. They have £5,000 savings. They each receive an award of long-term IB of £89.80 a week (totalling £179.60). They also get HB and CTB which means they only have to pay £33.57 a week towards their rent and council tax. Their income for IS purposes of £179.60 is higher than their IS applicable amount of £140.10 (£100.950 personal allowance plus £39.15disability premium) so they are not currently entitled to IS.

Because of his extensive personal care needs, Brian should be advised to claim DLA. He should qualify for the highest rate care component of £70.35 a week. Sheila should be advised to claim CA. Although she will not actually receive any payment of CA because she is receiving a higher 'earnings replacement benefit' (IB – see p156), claiming CA will enable her to qualify for an IS carer premium (see p153). Brian will qualify for an enhanced disability premium because of his DLA and this, plus the carer premium will mean that they will be entitled to IS of £9.30 a week because their applicable amount of £188.90 (£100.95 personal allowance, plus £39.15 disability premium, plus £19.30 enhanced disability premium, plus £29.50 carer premium) exceeds their income of £179.60 by £9.30 a week. They would also then be entitled to maximum HB and CTB, worth another £33.57 a week. Altogether, they would be £113.22 a week better off by claiming DLA, CA and IS.

They will now be eligible for social fund payments (see also Chapter 5, for other sources of financial assistance which may now be available to them).

Example 4 – single disabled person and carer

Liz is aged 56 and severely disabled. She lives alone in rented accommodation. She receives IS of £91.80 a week (£64.30 personal allowance plus £27.50 disability premium). She also gets maximum HB and CTB and the mobility and middle rate care components of DLA. Her son Ernie, who lives on his own nearby, is aged 26. He spends a lot of time caring for his mother and gets CA of £53.10 a week. He was working part-time but recently gave up his job because of stress and illness. He has no savings or other income.

Ernie should be advised to claim ESA, which will include a carer premium of £29.50 a week. Although he will no longer get CA if he is entitled to ESA (because ESA is an 'earnings replacement benefit' that is paid at a higher rate than CA), he will still qualify for the carer premium (see p153). As he is no longer actually receiving CA, however, his mother will become entitled to the severe disability premium with her IS (see p84), worth an extra £52.85 a week.

Notes

1. Types and combinations of benefits and tax credits
1 Reg 4 SS(OB) Regs

2. Disability benefits
2 ss71-73 and 75 SSCBA 1992; reg 2 SS(DLA) Regs
3 s71(3) SSCBA 1992
4 s72 SSCBA 1992
5 s72(6) SSCBA 1992
6 *R v NI Commissioner ex parte Secretary of State for Social Services* [1981] reported as an appendix to R(A) 2/80; *Mallinson v Secretary of State for Social Security* [1994] reported as an appendix to R(A) 3/94
7 Reg 8BA SS(AA) Regs; reg 10C SS(DLA) Regs
8 *R v NI Commissioner ex parte Secretary of State for Social Services* [1981] reported as an appendix to R(A) 2/80; CA/281/1989
9 CDLA/58/1993
10 *R v NI Commissioner ex parte Secretary of State for Social Services* [1981] reported as an appendix to R(A) 2/80
11 *R v NI Commissioner ex parte Secretary of State for Social Services* [1981] reported as an appendix to R(A) 2/80; *Woodling (HL) (1984)* reported as an appendix to R(A) 2/80
12 *Moran v Secretary of State for Social Services*, reported as an appendix to R(A) 1/88
13 R(A) 2/75

14 R(A) 3/86; *Mallinson v Secretary of State for Social Services* [1994]
15 *Secretary of State for Social Security v Fairey (aka Halliday)* (HL), 21 May 1997
16 R(DLA) 2/95
17 s73(8) SSCBA 1992
18 s73(1) and (2) SSCBA 1992; reg 12 SS(DLA) Regs
19 Reg 12(1)(a) SS(DLA) Regs
20 CM/98/1989; CDLA/1742/2004
21 Reg 12(4) SS(DLA) Regs
22 CM/208/1989
23 R(M) 1/81; CM/267/93
24 R(M) 1/83; R(M) 1/91
25 CDLA/42/1994; CDLA/14307/1996
26 Reg 12(7) and (8) SS(DLA) Regs
27 s73(1) SSCBA 1992
28 s73(4) SSCBA 1992
29 s66(2)(a) SSCBA 1992
30 ss72(5) and 73(12) SSCBA 1992
31 Reg 2(4) SS(DLA) Regs
32 s1(3) SSAA 1992
33 Reg 4 SS(DLA) Regs
34 Reg 6(8) SS(C&P) Regs
35 s19 SSA 1998
36 ss64-66 SSCBA 1992; reg 2 SS(AA) Regs
37 s64 SSCBA 1992
38 s66 SSCBA 1992
39 Reg 2(3) SS(AA) Regs
40 s65(3) and Sch 4 SSCBA 1992
41 Reg 6(8) SS(C&P) Regs
42 s19 SSA 1998
43 ss94, 108 and 109 SSCBA 1992
44 ss103 and 108 SSCBA 1992
45 Sch 7 paras 11 and 12 SSCBA 1992

46 Sch 7 para 13 SSCBA 1992
47 R(I) 22/59; CI/257/1949; CI/159/1950
48 *Fenton v Thorley* [1903] AC 443 (HC)
49 *Moore v Manchester Liners Ltd* [1910] AC 498 (HL)
50 *R v Industrial injuries Commissioner ex parte AEU* [1966] reported as an appendix to R(I) 4/66
51 s99 SSCBA 1992; R(I) 1/88; R(I) 12/75; R(I) 4/70; R(I) 7/85
52 s2(1) SSCBA 1992
53 ss108 and 109 SSCBA 1992; Sch 1 SS(IIPD) Regs
54 *Jones v Secretary of State for Social Services* [1972] reported as an appendix to R(I) 3/69
55 Reg 11(8) and Sch 2 SS(GB) Regs
56 Reg 11 SS(GB) Regs
57 Sch 6 SSCBA 1992
58 Sch 4 SSCBA 1992
59 s104 and Sch 4 SSCBA 1992; reg 19 SS(GB) Regs
60 s105 SSCBA 1992
61 Sch 7 para 11(10) SSCBA 1992
62 Sch 7 para 13 SSCBA 1992

3. Other non-means-tested benefits
63 s70 SSCBA 1992; regs 5, 8 and 9 SS(CA) Regs; regs 10 and 13 SS(CE) Regs
64 *Flemming v SoS for Work and Pensions* [2002] EWCA Civ 641, May 10 2002
65 Reg 4 SS(CA) Regs
66 Reg 4(2) SS(CA) Regs
67 RR(CA)O
68 R(G) 3/91
69 Reg 4(1A) SS(CA) Regs
70 s70(7) SSCBA 1992
71 s70(3) and (5) SSCBA 1992
72 s70(6) SSCBA 1992; reg 11 SS(CA) Regs; RR(CA)O
73 Regs 9, 10 and 13 and Sch 3 SS(CE) Regs
74 s90 and Sch 4 SSCBA 1992; SSB(Dep) Regs
75 s122(1) SSCBA 1992
76 s44(1) SSCBA 1992
77 s48A SSCBA 1992
78 ss48B and 48BB SSCBA 1992
79 ss48B and 51 SSCBA 1992
80 s78(3) SSCBA 1992; reg 10 SS(WB&RP) Regs
81 ss45, 46, 48A-C 48B SSCBA 1992
82 Sch 4A para 2 SSCBA 1992
83 Sch 3 para 5 SSCBA 1992
84 s44 and Sch 4 SSCBA 1992
85 ss82-85, 86A and 90 SSCBA 1992; SSB(Dep) Regs; SSB(PRT) Regs
86 SS(CE) Regs
87 s297 and Sch 11 PA 2004

88 ss36(2), 39A(4), 39A(5)(b), 39B(4) and 39B(5)(b) SSCBA 1992
89 s36 SSCBA 1992
90 s39A SSCBA 1992
91 ss39B and 60(2) and (3) SSCBA 1992
92 ss39C, 44-45A, 46 and 80(5), Schs 4 and 4A SSCBA 1992
93 s39C(5) SSCBA 1992
94 Reg 19(2) SS(C&P) Regs
95 s3 SSAA 1992
96 ss36A-39 SSCBA 1992
97 ss36A-39 SSCBA 1992
98 ss36A-39 SSCBA 1992
99 ss36A-39 SSCBA 1992
100 Reg 2 ESA(TP) Regs
101 Reg 2(2)(a) and (b) ESA(TP) Regs
102 Sch 4 para 11 WRA 2007; reg 3(2) ESA(TP) Regs
103 ss30A and 30B and Sch 4 SSCBA 1992
104 s30B(4) SSCBA 1992
105 ss30A and 30B SSCBA 1992
106 s30B(7) SSCBA 1992; reg 10 SS(IB) Regs
107 s86A and Sch 4 SSCBA 1992; SS(IB-ID) Regs
108 SS(IB)T Regs
109 s30DD SSCBA 1992
110 Reg 26 SS(IB) Regs
111 Reg 8 ESA Regs
112 s21 and Sch 3 SSCBA 1992
113 Sch 1 para 4 WRA 2007
114 Sch 2 ESA Regs
115 Reg 45 ESA Regs
116 s65 WRPA 1999; WRPA(No.9)O Regs
117 s164 SSCBA 1992; SMP Regs
118 s35A SSCBA 1992; SS(MA) Regs
119 s171ZA, B and L SSCBA 1992; SPP&SAP Regs

4. Means-tested benefits and tax credits
120 s124 SSCBA 1992
121 para 5.45 'Building a Fairer Society' (Budget Report 2005)
122 Reg 13 IS Regs; C(LC)SSB Regs
123 Regs 14-16 and Sch 7 para 9 IS Regs
124 SS(CTCWTC)(CA) Regs, as amended
125 ss78(6)–(9) and 105(3) SSAA 1992
126 Reg 4ZA and Sch 1B IS Regs
127 Reg 5 IS Regs
128 Reg 6 IS Regs
129 Regs 4ZA(3), 13(2)(b) and Sch 1B paras 10 and 12 IS Regs
130 Reg 4 IS Regs; reg 3 SPC Regs
131 s124(4) SSCBA 1992
132 Part 1, Sch 2 IS Regs
133 para 5 Sch 2 IS Regs
134 Sch 2 paras 11, 12 and 15 IS Regs
135 Sch 2 para 13A IS Regs

136 Regs 2(1) and 3 and Sch 2 paras 13 and
     15 IS Regs
137 Reg 3(1), (4) and (5) IS Regs
138 Sch 2 paras 14ZA and 15 IS Regs
139 Sch 2 paras 9, 9A, 10, 12 and 15 IS Regs
140 Part II, Sch 2 IS Regs
141 Sch 2 paras 14 and 15 IS Regs
142 Sch 3 IS Regs
143 Sch 3 para 16(2)(k) IS Regs
144 Sch 3 para 3(1) IS Regs
145 Sch 3 para 3(10) IS Regs
146 Sch 3 para 3(8) and (9) IS Regs
147 Sch 3 para 3(11) IS Regs
148 Sch 3 para 3(5) IS Regs; CIS/719/1994
149 *R v Penwith DC ex parte Burt* [1988] 22
     HLR 292, QBD
150 Sch 3 para 3(6) IS Regs
151 Sch 3 para 3(7) IS Regs
152 Reg 6(5)-(8) IS Regs
153 Sch 1 para 6 WRA 2007
154 JSA 1995; JSA Regs
155 ss1-4 SPCA 2002; regs 2-4 SPC Regs
156 Reg 5 SPC Regs
157 s2(2) SPCA 2002
158 s2(3) SPCA 2002; reg 6 and Schs 1 and 2
     SPC Regs
159 s3 SPCA 2002; regs 7 and 9 SPC Regs
160 s6-10 SPCA 2002; regs 10-12 SPC Regs
161 Regs 4D-4F SS(C&P) Regs
162 s130 SSCBA 1992; HB Regs; HB(SPC)
     Regs
163 s137 SSCBA 1992; regs 19-21 HB Regs;
     regs 19-21 HB(SPC) Regs
164 Reg 12 HB Regs; reg 12 HB(SPC) Regs
165 *R v Rugby BC HBRB ex parte Harrison*
     [1994] 28 HLR; *R v Poole BC ex parte Ross*
     [1995] 28 HLR; *R v Warrington BC ex*
     parte Williams [1997]
166 Reg 8 HB Regs; reg 8 HB(SPC) Regs
167 s134(2) SSCBA 1992; reg 9 HB Regs; reg
     9 HB(SPC) Regs
168 Reg 12 HB Regs; reg 12 HB(SPC) Regs
169 s130(1) SSCBA 1992; reg 7 HB Regs; reg
     7 HB(SPC) Regs
170 Reg 7(7) HB Regs; reg 7(7) HB(SPC)
     Regs
171 Reg 7(8) HB Regs; reg 7(8) HB(SPC)
     Regs
172 CH/2957/2004
173 Reg 7(6)(a) HB Regs; reg 7(6)(a)
     HB(SPC) Regs
174 Reg 7(6)(d) HB Regs; reg 7(6)(d)
     HB(SPC) Regs
175 HB GM para 3.55.4
176 Reg 7(6)(e) HB Regs; reg 7(6)(e)
     HB(SPC) Regs
177 Reg 10 HB Regs; reg 10 HB(SPC) Regs
178 Reg 56 HB Regs

179 Reg 9(1)(k) HB Regs; reg 9(1)(k)
     HB(SPC) Regs
180 Reg 11(2) HB Regs
181 Reg 9(1)(a) and (2) HB Regs; reg 9(1)(a)
     and (2) HB(SPC) Regs
182 CH/1976/2002; CH/296/2004; CH/
     1097/2004; *R v Poole BC ex parte Ross*
     [1995]
183 Reg 9(1)(b) HB Regs; reg 9(1)(b)
     HB(SPC) Regs
184 Reg 2(1) HB Regs; reg 2(1) HB(SPC)
     Regs
185 Regs 3(4) and 9(1)(b) HB Regs; regs 3(4)
     and 9(1)(b) HB(SPC) Regs
186 Reg 9(1)(c) HB Regs; reg 9(1)(c)
     HB(SPC) Regs
187 Reg 9(1)(d) HB Regs; reg 9(1)(d)
     HB(SPC) Regs
188 Reg 9(1)(h) HB Regs; reg 9(1)(h)
     HB(SPC) Regs
189 Reg 9(1) (e)-(g) HB Regs; reg 9(1)(e)-(g)
     HB(SPC) Regs
190 Reg 9(1)(l) HB Regs; reg 9(1)(l) HB(SPC)
     Regs
191 s130(3)(a) SSCBA 1992; reg 70 HB Regs;
     reg 50 HB(SPC) Regs
192 Sch 5 HB Regs
193 s130(3)(b) SSCBA 1992; reg 70 HB
     Regs; reg 50 HB(SPC) Regs
194 Reg 22 and Sch 3 HB Regs; reg 22 and
     Sch 3 HB(SPC) Regs
195 Reg 3(3) HB Regs; reg 3(3) HB(SPC)
     Regs
196 Part 6 HB Regs; Part 6 HB(SPC) Regs
197 Sch 1 Part 2 HB Regs; Sch 1 Part 2
     HB(SPC) Regs
198 Sch 1 paras 5 and 8 HB Regs; Sch 1 paras
     5 and 8 HB(SPC) Regs
199 Reg 12B(2)(a) HB Regs; reg 12B(2)
     HB(SPC) Regs
200 Sch 1 para 2 HB Regs; Sch 1 para 2
     HB(SPC) Regs
201 Sch 1 para 1 HB Regs; Sch 1 para 1
     HB(SPC) Regs
202 Reg 12B HB Regs; reg 12B HB(SPC) Regs
203 Reg 14 and Sch 2 HB Regs; reg 14 and
     Sch 2HB(SPC) Regs
204 Reg 14 HB Regs; reg 14 HB(SPC) Regs
205 Reg 13 HB Regs; reg 13 HB(SPC) Regs
206 Reg 3 HB Regs; reg 3 HB(SPC) Regs
207 Regs 3 and 74 HB Regs; regs 6 and 55
     HB(SPC) Regs; reg 55 HB(SPC) Regs
208 Reg 87 HB Regs; reg 68 HB(SPC) Regs
209 s69 CSPSSA 2000; reg 2(1) DFA Regs
210 Regs 95 and 96 HB Regs; regs76 and 77
     HB(SPC) Regs
211 s131 SSCBA 1992

212 s137 SSCBA 1992; regs 9-11 CTB Regs; regs 9-11 CTB(SPC) Regs
213 s131(6) SSCBA 1992
214 ss6(5) and 99(1) LGFA 1992
215 s131(3) SSCBA 1992; reg 8 CTB Regs; reg 8 CTB(SPC) Regs
216 CT(ED)O
217 ss13 and 80 LGFA 1992; CT(RD)O
218 ss11 and 79 LGFA 1992
219 Sch 6 CTB Regs
220 s131 SSCBA 1992
221 Reg 57(3) CTB Regs; reg 40(3) CTB(SPC) Regs
222 Reg 62 and Sch 2 CTB Regs; reg 46 and Sch 6 CTB(SPC) Regs
223 Reg 3 CTB Regs; reg 3 CTB(SPC) Regs
224 Reg 58(6)-(8) CTB Regs; reg 42 CTB(SPC) Regs
225 Reg 58 CTB Regs; reg 42 CTB(SPC) Regs
226 Reg 58 CTB Regs; reg 42 CTB(SPC) Regs
227 s69 CSPSSA 2000; DFA Regs
228 ss3 and 42 TCA 2002; TC(R) Regs; TC(I) Regs
229 Regs 3-5 CTC Regs
230 Regs 4 and 9 WTC(EMR) Regs
231 Reg 9 WTC(EMR) Regs
232 TC(ITDR) Regs
233 Regs 7-8 CTC Regs; WTC(EMR) Regs
234 Regs 13-16 WTC(EMR) Regs
235 TC(C)(TP)(A) Regs
236 s7(3) TCA 2002; reg 5 TC(ITDR) Regs
237 Reg 3 TC(ITDR) Regs
238 ss224(6) and 25 TCA 2002; TC(PB) Regs; TC(PE) Regs
239 ss14-17 TCA 2002
240 s32 TCA 2002
241 Reg 21 TC(CN) Regs
242 Reg 25 TC(CN) Regs
243 Reg 7 SFM&FE Regs
244 Reg 7(1)(e) SFM&FE Regs
245 Reg 7(5) SFM&FE Regs
246 Reg 7(1), (3) and (4) SFM&FE Regs
247 Reg 7(6) SFM&FE Regs
248 Reg 7A SFM&FE Regs
249 Reg 8(1)(a) SFM&FE Regs
250 s78(4) SSAA 1992
251 Reg 8(1) SFM&FE Regs
252 Sch 4 para 9 SS(C&P) Regs
253 Reg 5(1) SFM&FE Regs
254 Reg 5(2) SFM&FE Regs
255 Regs 1A and 2 SFCWP Regs
256 SFWFP Regs
257 SF Dir 25
258 SF Dir 4
259 s140 SSCBA 1992
260 s140(4)(a) SSCBA 1992: SF Dir 7
261 *R v Secretary of State ex parte Healey*, 22 April 1991, *The Times*

262 SF Dirs 23 and 29
263 SF Dir 28
264 SF Dir 27
265 SF Dirs 2, 8 and 9
266 SF Dir 10
267 SF Dirs 50-53
268 SF Dir 9
269 SF Dirs 3, 14-16, 22 and 23
270 SF Dirs 18, 20 and 21

5. People in hospital

271 Reg 2(2) SS(HIP) Regs
272 *White v CAO, The Times*, 2 August 1993; *Botchett v CAO*, 8 May 1996, *The Times*; *R v North & East Devon HA ex parte Coughlan*, (CCLR), September 1999; paras 18059, 24321 and 24363 DMG; CIS/3325/2000
273 Reg 2(2A) SS(HIP) Regs
274 Reg 6(2A) SS(AA) Regs; regs 8(2A) and 12A(2A) SS(DLA) Regs
275 Regs 6 and 8(1) SS(AA) Regs; regs 8, 10(1), 12A and 12B(1) SS(DLA) Regs
276 Reg 8(2) SS(AA) Regs; reg 10(5) SS(DLA) Regs
277 Reg 8(3) SS(AA) Regs; regs 10(3) and 12B(2) SS(DLA) Regs
278 Regs 12B(7) and (8) SS(DLA) Regs
279 Reg 8(4) SS(AA) Regs; regs 10(6) and 12B(9A) SS(DLA) Regs
280 Sch 2 paras 12(1)(c)(ii), 13A(1) and 14(3) IS Regs
281 Regs 10(2) and 12B(b) SS(DLA) Regs
282 Reg 4(2) SS(ICA) Regs
283 Sch 2 para 14(6) IS Regs
284 Reg 13 SS(HIP) Regs; reg 4 CB Regs
285 Sch 3 para 15(2) HB Regs; Sch 3 para 15(2) CTB Regs
286 Sch 3 para 18(7)(g) IS Regs; Sch 2 para 14(7)(e) SPC Regs; Sch 6 para 19(7)(g) ESA Regs; Sch 2 para 17(7)(g) JSA Regs; reg 74(7)(f) HB Regs; reg 42(7)(d) HB(SPC) Regs; reg 58(7)(d) CTB Regs; reg 42(7)(d) CTB(SPC) Regs

Chapter 8

• •

Capital and income for means-tested benefits and tax credits

This chapter covers:
1. The capital limits (p199)
2. What capital counts (p200)
3. Disregarded capital (p206)
4. How capital is valued (p210)
5. General rules about income (p212)
6. Income other than earnings (p213)
7. Earnings from employment and self-employment (p225)

Your entitlement to means-tested benefits and tax credits depends on the amount of capital and income you have. This chapter explains how your capital and income are assessed. The rules are complex and only an outline can be given here, focussing on the main rules most likely to affect you if you or a member of your family have a disability or are a carer. More details about the capital and income rules can be found in CPAG's *Welfare Benefits and Tax Credits Handbook* (see Appendix 3). If you are unsure whether, or how, a particular type of capital or income affects your entitlement, seek advice (see Appendix 2).

Different capital rules apply to social fund community care grants and budgeting loans (see pp185 and 187), the low-income scheme for health benefits (see p79), the Independent Living (2006) Fund (see p73) and housing grants (see p82).

The rules in this chapter do not apply to non-means-tested benefits (see p118), which are not affected by capital and most forms of income. Some non-means-tested benefits are, however, affected by earnings and occupational pensions, which are assessed under different rules. Chapter 7 indicates when and how this applies. For details of the special rules that apply if you are living in a care home, see Chapter 16. Note that many of the rules used to assess your capital and income when calculating your care home charges if your placement is being funded by social services are similar to those outlined in this chapter. There are also significant differences, however, which are highlighted in Chapters 11 and 12.

1. **The capital limits**

Most means-tested benefits are not payable if you have capital over an upper limit. There is also generally a lower limit, at and below which capital is ignored. Capital between the lower and upper limits is deemed to produce a 'tariff income' (see p216). The amount of the upper and lower limits depends on your age, which benefit you are claiming, and whether you are permanently living in a care home. The capital limit is the same for a couple as it is for a single person.

There is no upper capital limit for pension credit (PC) (see p158) but capital above the lower limit is deemed to produce a tariff income (see p216). In rare cases, actual income from some types of capital are taken into account for PC and housing benefit (HB)/council tax benefit (CTB) if you or your partner are aged 60 or over (see p216).

There are no capital limits at all for tax credits but actual income from your investments and savings is taken into account (see p215).

Your capital is ignored for HB/CTB purposes if you are receiving income support (IS), income-based jobseeker's allowance (JSA), income-related employment and support allowance (ESA) or the guarantee credit of PC and you are automatically entitled to maximum HB and CTB without any need to calculate your capital again.

If you (and your partner) are aged under 60[1]

The upper limit above which benefit is not payable is:
- £16,000 for IS, income-based JSA and income-related ESA, HB and CTB.

The lower limit at and below which capital is ignored is:
- £6,000 for IS, income-based JSA and income-related ESA, HB and CTB.

Note: see below if you are permanently living in a care home.

If you (or your partner) are aged 60 or over[2]

The upper limit above which benefit is not payable is:
- £16,000 for HB and CTB, unless you are getting the guarantee credit of PC, in which case there is no upper limit and all your capital is ignored.

The lower limit at and below which capital is ignored is:
- £6,000 for HB and CTB, unless you are getting the guarantee credit of PC, in which case there is no lower limit and all your capital is ignored.

Note:
- There is no upper limit for PC.

- You cannot claim IS if you are aged 60 or over, or JSA if you over pensionable age, but your partner may be able to claim these benefits if s/he is under the age limits.

If you are living in a care home

The capital limits are higher if you are permanently living in a care home (see p337).
- The upper limit for IS, income-based JSA and income-related ESA and HB is £16,000.
- The lower limit for IS, income-based JSA and income-related ESA, PC and HB is £10,000.

2. What capital counts

The term 'capital' is not defined in social security legislation. In general, it means lump sum or one-off payments rather than a series of payments.[3] It includes savings, property and redundancy payments. Capital payments can normally be distinguished from income because they are not payable in respect of any specified period or periods, and they do not form nor are intended to form part of a regular series of payments[4] (although capital can be paid by instalments). However, some capital is treated as income (see p217), and some income is treated as capital (see p203).

Any unspent income becomes capital as soon as the period for which the income can be said to have been paid has lapsed[5] – eg, a weekly retirement pension payment becomes capital a week after it is paid and a monthly occupational pension becomes capital after a month.

Some of your capital is partially or wholly disregarded (see p206). In certain circumstances, however, you can be treated as possessing capital that you no longer have (see p203).

If you are getting PC and have been given an 'assessed income period', any additional capital you obtain during the period is ignored until the period ends (see p162).

If you are getting IS, income-based JSA, income-related ESA or the guarantee credit of PC, you are automatically entitled to maximum HB and CTB and there is no need to calculate your capital again (all your capital is ignored). For tax credits, none of your capital counts but actual income from some capital is taken into account (see p215).

Whose capital counts

Capital belonging to you and your partner (see p93) is taken into account when calculating your entitlement to means-tested benefits and tax credits.[6] It does not matter whether the capital is held jointly or separately. Once you no longer count as a couple, however (eg, because one of you is permanently in a care home), your capital is no longer jointly assessed.

Capital belonging to a dependent child does not count[7] (you cannot, however, get IS or income-based JSA for a child who has more than £3,000 capital[8]).

Savings

Your savings (eg, cash you have at home or in a bank or building society, premium bonds, stocks and shares and unit trusts) generally count as capital.

Your savings from past earnings can only be treated as capital when all relevant debts, including tax liabilities, have been deducted.[9] Savings from other past income (including benefits) is also treated as capital after the period for which the income was paid has passed (although payments of arrears of certain benefits may be disregarded for certain periods). There is no provision for disregarding money put aside to pay bills.[10] If you have savings close to the capital limit it may be best to pay bills (eg, gas, electricity, telephone) as soon as possible or by monthly direct debit, to prevent your capital going over the limit.

Fixed term investments

Capital held in fixed term investments counts. However, if it is presently unobtainable it may have little or no value (but see p211 for jointly held capital). If you can sell your interest, or raise a loan through a reputable bank using the asset as security, or otherwise convert the investment into a realisable form, its value counts. If it takes time to produce evidence about the nature and value of the investment, you may be able to get an interim payment of benefit (see p103) or a social fund crisis loan (see p182).

Property and land

Any property or land which you own counts as capital, although many types of property are disregarded (see p206), including your normal home.

Loans

A loan usually counts as money you possess. You should not, however, be treated as having any capital from:
- a loan granted on condition that you only use the interest but do not touch the capital because the capital element has never been at your disposal;[11]
- money paid to you to be used for a particular purpose on condition that the money must be returned if not used in that way;[12]
- a property you have bought on behalf of someone else who is paying the mortgage;[13]
- money you are holding in a bank account on behalf of someone else and which has to be returned to them at a future date.[14]

Trusts

A trust is a legal arrangement whereby a 'trustee' owns and manages assets for the benefit of a 'beneficiary'. In theory, the asset is split into two notional parts: the legal title owned by the trustee, and the beneficial interest owned by the beneficiary. A trustee can never have use of the asset, only the responsibility of looking after it. An adult beneficiary, on the other hand, can ask for the asset at any time. Anything can be held on trust – eg, money, houses or shares. The rules on trusts for social security and other purposes are extremely complex and you should always seek legal advice before setting up a trust and if you think that the benefit authorities are wrongly valuing a trust.

Beneficiaries of trusts

If you are aged under 60 and a beneficiary of a:
* non-discretionary trust, you can obtain the asset from the trustee at any time and therefore effectively own it, so it counts as your capital (if you are under 18, you will have no right to payment until you are 18 but the trust can still have a capital value);[15]
* discretionary trust, the asset itself does not normally count as your capital because you cannot demand payments (of either income or capital) which are only made at the discretion of the trustee within the terms of the trust;
* trust which gives you the right to receive payments in the future (eg, on reaching the age of 25), this right has a present capital value, unless it is disregarded (see p206);
* **life interest** only (or, in Scotland, a life rent) in an asset (ie, you have the right to enjoy the asset in your lifetime but the asset will pass on to someone else when you die), the value of your interest is disregarded,[16] but not the income itself if you get any.

If you or your partner are aged 60 or over, money or property held in a trust for your benefit is ignored for the purposes of calculating your tariff income (see p216).[17] Actual payments from the trust, however, may be taken into account as income (if made regularly) or capital (if made irregularly).

Trustees

If you hold an asset as a trustee, it is not part of your capital. You are only a trustee if someone gives you an asset on the expressed condition that you hold it for someone else (or use it for their benefit), or if you have expressed the clearest intention that your own asset is for someone else's benefit, and you have renounced its use for yourself[18] (assets other than money may need to be transferred in a particular way to the trust). If money or another asset is given to you to be used for a special purpose, it may be possible to argue that it should not count as your capital. This is called a purpose trust.[19]

Trust funds from personal injury compensation

The value of any trust fund is ignored if it has been set up out of money paid because of a personal injury to you (or to your partner for PC, HB and CTB only, if you or your partner are aged 60 or over).[20] It is not necessary for the trust to be set up by a formal deed so long as the beneficiary has no direct access to the funds.

Personal injuries compensation (including compensation to minors for the death of a parent) held in a special fund administered by a court (eg, the Court of Protection because the injured person is incapable of managing her/his own affairs) is also ignored.[21]

'Personal injury' includes not only accidental and criminal injuries, but also any disease and injury resulting from a disease.

Any payments made to you from trust funds or court funds may count in full as income or capital, depending on the nature of the payment.[22] They are ignored completely, however, for PC and HB/CTB if you or your partner are aged 60 or over, as are all payments for personal injury, whether or not they are placed in a trust.[23] Also, trustees may have a discretion to use the funds to purchase items that would normally be disregarded as capital (eg, personal possessions such as a wheelchair, car or new furniture), or to make payments that would normally be disregarded as income (eg, ineligible housing costs), or to clear debts or pay for holidays, leisure items or educational or medical needs.

Note that the notional income and capital rules (see pp222 and below) do not apply to personal injury compensation paid into trusts (or court funds) even if some time has passed before they are paid in. Personal injury payments are disregarded for 52 weeks to give you time to spend some or all of the payment, or put it into a trust, before your benefit is affected. However, in other cases if there is no trust, or until one can be set up, the whole of a compensation payment counts as capital, even if the money is held by your solicitor.[24] This does not apply, however, to PC and HB/CTB if you or your partner are aged 60 or over (the payment is ignored completely as capital).[25]

Income treated as capital

In certain circumstances, some payments which appear to be income are nevertheless treated as capital. These include income from capital (eg, interest from a bank account), rental income (but rent from disregarded property – see p206 – counts as income), irregular, one-off charitable payments, most payments from trust funds administered by a court and PAYE income tax refunds.[26] These rules do not apply, however, to tax credits, or, if you or your partner are aged 60 or over, PC or HB/CTB.

Notional capital

In certain circumstances you are treated as having capital which you do not in fact possess. This is called notional capital.[27] There is a similar rule for notional income (see p222).

You can be treated as having notional capital if:

- you deliberately deprive yourself of capital in order to claim or increase benefit (see below); *or*
- you fail to apply for capital which is available to you (see p205); *or*
- someone else makes a payment of capital to a third party on your behalf (see p206); *or*
- you receive a payment of capital on behalf of a third party and, instead of handing it on, you use or keep it (see p206).

Note: if you or your partner are aged 60 or over only the first situation above (deprivation of capital) applies to PC and HB/CTB and it does not apply if you pay off or reduce a debt which you owe, or you pay for goods and services and this is reasonable in your circumstances. The rules do not apply to tax credits.

Notional capital counts in the same way as capital you actually possess (and is normally subject to the same disregards – see p206), except that in cases of deprivation of capital, a diminishing notional capital rule may be applied so that the value of the notional capital you are treated as having will be considered to reduce over time (see p205).

Deprivation of capital in order to claim or increase benefit

If you deliberately dispose of capital in order to qualify for benefit or more benefit, you are treated as still possessing it. Seek advice if you think this rule may be, or is, applied to you. Bear in mind the following points.

- The rule can only apply if one of your motives (not necessarily the only or predominant motive) for disposing of capital was to retain, gain, or increase your entitlement to benefit (eg, you buy an expensive item because you want it and because using some of your savings will qualify you for benefit).[28] Note that in the case of PC and HB/CTB if you or your partner are aged 60 or over, the rules do not apply if your purchase of goods and services is reasonable in the circumstances of your case.
- What you know about the capital rules, or could reasonably be expected to know from your dealings with the benefit system, is an important factor.[29]
- The longer the period that has elapsed since the disposal of the capital, the less likely it is that it was for the purpose of obtaining benefit,[30] but there is no set 'safe period' after which benefit can be claimed.[31]
- If you pay off a debt which you are required by law to repay immediately, the deprivation rule should not apply.[32] Even if you pay off a debt which you do not have to repay immediately, it must still be shown that you did so with the intention of gaining benefit.[33] Note that for PC and HB/CTB if you or your partner are aged 60 or over, the deprivation rule does not apply if you are paying off or reducing any debt which you owe.
- For IS and income-based JSA, the rule does not apply if you have placed compensation derived from a personal injury in a trust fund.

- In practice, arguing successfully that you have not deprived yourself of capital to gain benefit may boil down to whether you can show that you would have spent the money in the way you did regardless of the effect on your benefit entitlement. Where this is unclear, the burden of proof lies with the decision maker.
- For IS, income-based JSA or income-related ESA, you can only be affected by this rule if the capital in question is actual capital.[34] So if you are counted as owning half a bank account under the rule about jointly held capital (see p211), but your real share is only a quarter, you cannot be affected by any deprivation of the other quarter. It is even arguable that the deprivation rule should not apply to the quarter which you actually own.[35] There is no equivalent rule for HB/CTB, but you should argue that the same principle applies.
- If a person acting as your attorney has misspent your money for her/his own benefit, the amount spent cannot be notional capital (because the disposal will have been unlawful) or actual capital (because you no longer have it), but your right to recover the money may still have an actual capital value.[36]
- Deprivation for the purposes of claiming one benefit (eg, IS) cannot be held to be deprivation for the purposes of claiming another (eg, HB) and each decision maker must reach her/his own decision on each benefit. Even deprivation decisions for HB must be made independently of decisions for CTB.[37] This may result in different conclusions being drawn on any disposal for each benefit, and even where intent is found in two different benefits, there may be different views about the amount of capital that has been deliberately disposed of.[38] Similarly, social services must apply their deprivation rule (see p223), independently of any benefit decision.

The diminishing notional capital rule

There are complicated rules for working out how notional capital under the above deprivation rule should be treated as spent, so that its value is deemed to diminish over time. Broadly, the rules aim to provide for your notional capital to be gradually reduced by the weekly amount of any means-tested benefit you would have been entitled to but for the notional capital rule. For details, see CPAG's *Welfare Benefits and Tax Credits Handbook.*

Failing to apply for capital[39]

Under this rule you are treated as having capital you could get if you applied for it. This does not apply if you fail to apply for capital from a:

- discretionary trust; *or*
- trust (or court fund) from money paid as a result of a personal injury; *or*
- personal pension scheme or retirement annuity contract; *or*
- loan which you could only get if you gave your home or other disregarded capital as security.

Capital payments made to a third party on your behalf

If someone else pays an amount to a third party (eg, an utility company) for you or a member of your family, this may count as your capital if the payment is for food, household fuel, council tax, ordinary clothing or footwear, rent for which HB is payable (less non-dependant deductions), water charges or (for IS, income-based JSA or income-related ESA only) housing costs met by IS, income-based JSA or income-related ESA.[40]

Payments for other kinds of expenses (eg, care home charges, or mortgage capital repayments) are disregarded as are any payments from the Independent Living (2006) Fund, the Macfarlane Trusts, the Fund, the Skipton Fund and the Eileen Trust.

Payments from an occupational or personal pension (and payments of certain war pensions for IS, income-based JSA and income-related ESA only) to a third party count as belonging to you.[41]

Capital payments paid to you for a third party

If you (or a member of your family) get a payment for someone not in your family (eg, a relative who does not have a bank account) it only counts as yours if it is kept or used by you.

3. Disregarded capital

Some or all of your capital can be disregarded under the rules below. For most benefits, this means that it will not count for the purposes of deciding whether you are over the upper limit (for eligibility) or lower limit (for the calculation of tariff income – see p216). There are no capital limits for tax credits, so none of the rules below apply to them. There is no upper capital limit for pension credit (PC), which means that the rules below are only relevant for deciding how much of your capital counts for the purpose of the tariff income rules (see p216).

Your home

If you own the home you normally live in, its value is ignored.[42] This also applies if you are living away from your home temporarily (see p337) – eg, because you are in a care home.

Your home includes any garage, garden, outbuildings and land, together with any premises that you do not occupy as your home but which it is impractical or unreasonable to sell separately – eg, croft land. If you own more than one property only the value of the one normally occupied is disregarded under this rule.

Even if you do not live in it, the value of property can be disregarded during temporary absences and in the following circumstances.[43]

* **If you have left your former home following a marriage or relationship breakdown,** the value of the property is ignored for six months from the date

you left, or longer if any of the steps below are taken. If the property is occupied by your former partner who is a lone parent, its value is ignored as long as s/he lives there.

- **If you have sought legal advice or have started legal proceedings in order to occupy property as your home**, the value of the property is ignored for six months from the date you first took either of these steps, or longer if it is reasonable.

- **If you are taking reasonable steps to dispose of any property**, the value of the property is ignored for six months from the date you *first* took such steps, or longer if it is reasonable. This may include a period before you claimed benefit.[44] 'Property' here may include land on its own, even if there are no buildings on it.[45] The test for what constitutes 'reasonable steps' is an objective one. Putting the property in the hands of an estate agent or getting in touch with a prospective purchaser should count,[46] but any period when the house is advertised at an unrealistic sale price would not.[47]

- **If you are carrying out essential repairs or alterations** which are needed so that you can occupy a property as your home, the value of the property is ignored for six months from the date you first take steps to carry out the repairs. 'Steps' may include applying for planning permission or a grant or a loan to make the property habitable, employing an architect or finding someone to do the work.[48] If you cannot move into the property within that period because the work is not finished, its value can be disregarded for as long as is necessary to allow the work to be carried out.

- **If you have acquired a house or flat for occupation** as your home but have not yet moved in, the value of the property is ignored if you intend to live there within six months. The value can be ignored for longer if it is reasonable.

- **If you sell your home** and intend to use the money from the sale to buy another home, the capital is ignored for six months from the date of sale, or longer if it is reasonable. This also applies even if you do not actually own the home but, for a price, you surrender your tenancy rights to a landlord.[49] You do not need to have decided within the six months to buy a *particular* property. It is sufficient if you intend to use the proceeds to buy *some* other home, although your intention must involve more than a mere hope or aspiration. There must be an element of certainty which may be shown by evidence of a practical commitment to another purchase, although this need not involve any binding obligation.[50] If you intend to use only part of the proceeds of the sale to buy another home, only that part is disregarded even if, for example, you have put the rest of the money aside to renovate your new home.[51]

- **If your home is damaged or you lose it altogether**, any payment, including compensation, which you intend to use for its repair, or for acquiring another home, is ignored for six months or longer if it is reasonable.

- **If you have taken out a loan or been given money for the express purpose of essential repairs and improvements** to your home, the value of the loan is ignored for six months, or longer if it is reasonable. If it is a condition of the loan that it must be returned if the improvements are not carried out, argue that it should be ignored altogether.

- **If you have deposited money with a housing association as a condition of occupying your home**, the value of the money is ignored indefinitely. If money deposited for this purpose is to be used to buy another home, this is ignored for six months, or longer if reasonable, in order to allow you to complete the purchase.
- **Grants made to local authority tenants to buy a home or carry out repairs/ alterations to it** can also be ignored for six months, or longer if reasonable, to allow completion of the purchase or the repairs/alterations.

Note: the last four disregards do not apply to PC or housing benefit (HB)/council tax benefit (CTB) if you or your partner are aged 60 or over. The following disregards apply instead.

- Any amounts paid to you for the sole purpose of buying a home for you to live in, or carrying out essential repairs or alterations to your actual or intended home, are ignored for up to a year, or for PC only until the end of any 'assessed income period', if this is longer.
- Any compensation paid under an insurance policy because of loss or damage to your home, is ignored for up to a year or for PC only until the end of any 'assessed income period', if this is longer.

When considering whether to increase the period of any of the above disregards past six months, all the circumstances should be considered, especially your (and your family's) personal circumstances, any efforts made by you to use or dispose of the home[52] (if relevant) and the general state of the market (if relevant). In practice, periods of around 18 months are not considered unusual.

It is possible for property to be ignored under more than one of the above disregards in succession.[53]

Some income generated from property which is disregarded is ignored (see p217).

For the treatment of jointly owned property, see p211. For the different rules on the treatment of unoccupied property (which may not be disregarded in financial assessments) by social services, see Chapter 12.

The home of a partner, former partner or relative

The value of a home is also ignored if it is occupied wholly or partly as a home by your:[54]

- partner, or a relative (see p209) of yours, or any member of your family, provided that (in either case) s/he is aged 60 or over or is incapacitated ('incapacitated' is not defined but it should include anyone who could qualify for an incapacity or disability benefit[55]); *or*

- former partner from whom you are not estranged or divorced or out of a civil partnership; *or*
- former partner from whom you are estranged, or divorced, or out of a civil partnership, if s/he is a lone parent.

'Relative' includes a parent; son; daughter; step-parent/son/daughter or parent/son/daughter-in-law; brother or sister; or a partner of any of these people; or a grandparent or grandchild, uncle, aunt, nephew or niece. It also includes half-brothers and sisters and adopted children.

Although the rules themselves do not say so, it has been held that this disregard only applies to a property which you previously occupied yourself.[56]

For the treatment of jointly owned property, see p211. For the similar (but sometimes more generous) rules on the treatment of occupied properties in financial assessments by social services, see Chapter 12.

Other disregards[57]

- A **future interest** (ie, one which will only revert to you or become yours after a future event) in most types of property (but not in a property let by you to tenants) and the right to receive future payments from a variety of sources is ignored, as, in most cases, is the **value of the right to receive a future payment** (eg, from a future pension or life interest).
- **Arrears of certain social security benefits** (including attendance allowance, disability living allowance, tax credits, income support (IS), income-based jobseeker's allowance or income-related employment and support allowance (ESA), PC, HB/CTB) are ignored for up to 52 weeks (or in certain circumstances until the end of your benefit award) after they have been paid. For full details of which benefit arrears are disregarded as capital for which benefits, see CPAG's *Welfare Benefits and Tax Credits Handbook*.
- All **personal possessions**, including items such as jewellery, furniture or a car, are ignored, unless you have bought them in order to be able to claim or get more IS, income-based JSA, income-related ESA and HB/CTB if you and your partner, if you have one, are aged under 60.
- If you are self-employed, your **business assets** are ignored for as long as you continue to work in that business. If you stop working in the business, you are allowed a reasonable time to sell the assets without their value affecting your benefit.
- The value of a fund held under a **personal pension scheme or retirement annuity contract** is ignored (unless you are claiming PC, or HB/CTB and you or your partner are aged 60 or over).
- The surrender value of any **life assurance** or **endowment policy or annuity** is ignored. This applies even if the life assurance aspect of a policy is not the sole or even the main aspect (although the other features of any policy may still be considered under the actual or notional income and capital rules – see pp222

and 203). Any payments under the annuity count as income (but see p221 for when these are ignored).

- Payments to you from **the Supporting People scheme** (see p52) or the **social fund** (see p182) are ignored indefinitely, or for 52 weeks (for PC and HB/CTB if you or your partner are aged 60 or over). Community care 'direct payments' (see p220) are ignored indefinitely.
- **Payments by social services for children in need and young people who were previously in care** are ignored.
- **Charitable payments** in kind are ignored (unless you are claiming PC, or HB/CTB and you or your partner are aged 60 or over), as are all payments from the Macfarlane Trust, the Fund, the Eileen Trust, the Skipton Fund and Independent Living Fund (see p73), as are certain payments from money which originally came from them (the rules are the same as for income – see p218).
- Certain payments **to assist disabled people with employment** (including blind homeworkers) are disregarded indefinitely. Special rules apply to the treatment of payments under the New Deal and other employment programmes (see CPAG's *Welfare Benefits and Tax Credits Handbook* for details).
- **Some World War Two compensation payments** to victims and former Japanese prisoners of war are disregarded.
- Payments from trusts to people who have contracted variant **Creutzfeld-Jakob disease** and to their families are ignored for varying periods (see CPAG's *Welfare Benefits and Tax Credits Handbook*).
- The value of **a funeral plan contract** is ignored for PC and HB/CTB if you or your partner are aged 60 or over.
- Capital treated as income (see p217) does not count as capital.

For further details of the above disregards and a full list of other disregards, see CPAG's *Welfare Benefits and Tax Credits Handbook*.

4. **How capital is valued**

Capital is generally valued at its current market or surrender value (ie, the price that would be paid by a willing buyer), less the value of any debts secured on it, and a deduction of 10 per cent of its value if there would be expenses involved in selling it. If an asset is difficult or impossible to sell, its market value should be heavily discounted, or even nil.[58]

It is not uncommon for an unrealistic assessment to be made of the value of your capital. If you disagree with any decision you can request a revision or appeal (see Chapter 6).

For the valuation of jointly owned property, see p211.

Detailed rules apply for the valuation of national savings certificates, shares, unit trusts and overseas assets. See CPAG's *Welfare Benefits and Tax Credit Handbook* for details.

Jointly owned capital

If you jointly own any capital asset in the UK or abroad under a 'joint tenancy' you are treated as owning an equal share of the asset with all other owners – eg, if there are two co-owners, you are each deemed to have a 50 per cent share.[59] This rule does not apply, however, if you jointly own the asset as 'tenants in common'.[60] The key difference between a joint tenancy and a tenancy in common is that with the former each person owns the whole asset (and his/her interest would automatically pass to the other owner(s) if s/he died), whereas with the latter, each person owns a discrete share in the asset (which would be passed on death to whoever is willed to receive it).

In the case of a tenancy in common, your actual share of the asset has to be valued.

In the case of a joint tenancy, only the value of your deemed share counts. This will usually be considerably less than the same proportion of the value of the whole asset. If the asset is a house worth £100,000, for example, the value of a deemed 50 per cent share is likely to be worth considerably less than £50,000 and may be very small or even worthless, particularly if the house is occupied and the other owner is unwilling to sell her/his share. Whether a sale can be forced[61] will depend on individual circumstances,[62] and valuations should take into account legal costs and the length of time it could take to gain possession. Valuations often fail to take into account official guidance on a range of factors relevant to the assessment of jointly owned properties,[63] and have been criticised for this,[64] and you may need to challenge any decision based on an inadequate valuation. If you are unsure whether the DWP has correctly valued your share of a jointly owned property, seek advice (see Appendix 2) and if necessary appeal (see Chapter 6).

Treatment of assets when partners separate

When partners separate, assets such as their former home or a bank account may be in joint names and the above rules about jointly owned capital apply. For example, if a bank account is in joint names, both partners are treated as having a 50 per cent share each. If there is clear evidence, however, that part or all of the money belongs to one party alone, and the joint account has merely been used for convenience, that money should count as if it is in her/his sole ownership.[65] Many couples use joint accounts only for convenience, and it is often only on separation (eg, because one partner needs care in a care home) that they will take steps to separate how much belongs to each. If your former partner is claiming sole ownership of the account (and, for example, puts a stop on the account), you could argue that your interest in the account should be disregarded until the issue of ownership is resolved.

A former partner may also have a right to some or all of an asset that is in your sole name – eg, s/he may have deposited most of the money in a building society account in your name. If this is established, then you may be able to argue that some or all of the asset should not be treated as yours because you are only holding it on trust for your former partner.[66] In that event, the rule about jointly owned capital may have the effect of treating you as owning half of the amount in the account.

5. General rules about income

What counts as income

The term 'income' is not defined for the purposes of income support (IS), income-based jobseeker's allowance (JSA), income-related employment and support allowance (ESA), or housing benefit (HB)/council tax benefit (CTB) if you and your partner (if you have one) are aged under 60. Payments of income are normally made in respect of a specified period or periods and form, or are intended to form, part of a regular series of payments.[67] In this way, payments of income can usually be distinguished from payments of capital (see p200). However, some income is treated as capital (see p203), and some capital is treated as income (see p210). In addition, income will only count if it is paid to you for your own use, and may not count if you cannot prevent it being paid to a third party instead – eg, under an attachment of earnings order.[68]

For pension credit (PC), HB/CTB if you or your partner are aged 60 or over, and tax credits, only income listed in the legislation counts.[69] If you are getting PC and are given an 'assessed income period', see p162 for how increases in your retirement provision are calculated.

For tax credits, most taxable income counts and most non-taxable income is ignored. Income is calculated on an annual basis and increases of less than £25,000 are ignored (see p179).

Not all your income counts. Some of your income is partially or wholly disregarded. In certain circumstances, however, you can be treated as possessing income that you no longer have (see p222).

If you are getting IS, income-based JSA, income-related ESA, or the guarantee credit of PC, you are automatically entitled to maximum HB/CTB and there is no need to calculate your income again (all of your income is ignored). If you only get the savings credit of PC (see p158), your income for HB/CTB is that used by the DWP to work out your PC (plus the amount of savings credit).

Whose income counts

If you have a partner (see p93), her/his income is added to yours and calculated in the same way as if it were yours.[70] It does not matter whether the income is received jointly or separately. Once you no longer count as a couple, however (eg, because one of you is permanently in a care home), your income is no longer jointly assessed.

The income of a dependant child does not count as yours (unless in certain circumstances and subject to disregards, you are still getting IS or income-based JSA for her/him – see CPAG's *Welfare Benefits and Tax Credits Handbook* for details).

Converting income into a weekly amount

IS, income-based JSA, income-related ESA, PC, HB and CTB are all calculated on a weekly basis, so your income has to be converted into a weekly amount to determine your entitlement to benefit. Complex rules determine how this is done for each benefit and different types of income and earnings. For HB and CTB, your average weekly income is estimated with reference to an appropriate past period. For IS, income-based JSA, income-related ESA, and PC, there are detailed rules for converting your income into a weekly amount, including special rules if your income fluctuates (eg, because you do not work every week), or if it is paid for a part week. For full details of all the rules, see CPAG's *Welfare Benefits and Tax Credits Handbook*.

The period covered by income

For HB/CTB, your average weekly income (see above) is used to calculate your weekly entitlement.

For IS/income-based JSA and income-related ESA there are special rules for deciding from when, and for how long, payments of income count.[71] Income is usually taken into account from the day it is due to be paid, for a period equal to that in respect of which it was paid (eg, a month's wages is taken into account for a month from the date it is paid). For further details, see CPAG's *Welfare Benefits and Tax Credits Handbook*.

For tax credits, your income is assessed on an annual basis and any increase in your income of less than £25,000 compared with the previous year is ignored.

6. Income other than earnings

Most forms of income are taken into account when assessing your entitlement to means-tested benefits and tax credits but some income is partly or wholly disregarded and there are different rules for different benefits.

For tax credits, your gross income (before the deduction of tax) is taken into account. For other benefits, income is taken into account after the deduction of any tax due on it.

Income from other benefits and tax credits

When calculating your entitlement to means-tested benefits, other benefits and tax credits paid to you (or your partner) are either counted in full, or fully or partially ignored. The main categories are listed below. For a complete list, see CPAG's *Welfare Benefits and Tax Credits Handbook*.

Benefits and tax credits which count in full
- contribution-based jobseeker's allowance (JSA);
- contributory employment and support allowance (ESA);
- incapacity benefit (IB – but the short-term lower rate is ignored for tax credits);
- severe disablement allowance (SDA – but this is ignored for tax credits);
- carer's allowance;
- retirement pensions (note that for tax credits, up to £300 a year is disregarded from your income from pensions and investments – see p215);
- bereavement and widow's allowances (bereavement payments are ignored) (note for tax credits, widow's pension, widowed mother's and widowed parent's allowance are treated as pension income);
- industrial injuries benefits (but these are ignored for tax credits);
- child benefit counts as income for income support (IS)/income-based JSA if you are still getting benefit for a child);
- child benefit currently counts in full for housing benefit (HB)/council tax benefit (CTB) but the Government has announced that from October 2009 it will no longer count;
- child tax credit counts in full for HB/CTB;
- working tax credit;
- statutory sick pay and statutory maternity/paternity/adoption pay, less any tax, Class 1 national insurance contributions, half of any pension contributions and for pension credit (PC) and HB/CTB only, any relevant earnings disregards (see p227) (note for tax credits there is a £100 disregard for SMP, SPP and SAP);
- maternity allowance (MA – but this is ignored for tax credits).

Note also that the above benefits should only be taken into account if you are actually receiving them. If you are entitled to a benefit but it is not being paid because of the overlapping benefit rules (see p118) or because of delays in payment (or where payment has been suspended), it should not be taken into account as income. If you are due to receive a contributory benefit but it is being reduced (eg, to repay an overpayment), the full amount is assumed to be in payment if you claim a means-tested top-up.

Benefits which are ignored completely
- attendance allowance (AA), disability living allowance (DLA), constant attendance allowance, exceptionally severe disablement allowance and mobility supplement;
- HB and CTB (including discretionary housing payments);
- IS, income-based JSA and income-related ESA are ignored for HB, CTB and tax credits;
- child benefit and CTC (but see above for when these count as income);
- guardian's allowance;
- Christmas bonus;
- social fund payments;
- certain special war widows' or widowers' payments;
- bereavement payments;
- for tax credits only, PC, MA, SDA, industrial injuries benefit and short-term lower rate of IB are ignored.

Benefits which are partially ignored
- the first £15 (for HB/CTB), or £10 (for IS, income-based JSA or PC), of any award of widowed mother's allowance and widowed parent's allowance;
- the first £10 of most war pensions (only one disregard of £10 is generally allowed, even if you are receiving more than one pension, but local authorities have some discretion to increase the disregard for HB/CTB purposes). **Note:** this disregard does not apply to tax credits.

Income from capital

Actual income from capital

Tax credits

For tax credits, your actual taxable investment income from capital counts – eg, interest and dividends from investments. Certain types of investment income are ignored, however, including:[72]
- interest, dividend or bonus from an ISA;
- income from savings certificates and the first £70 of interest from National Savings and Investments deposits;
- winnings from lotteries, pools and betting;
- interest on personal injury damages;
- annuity payments under a Criminal Injuries Compensation Scheme award and interest on payments of life annuities.

Also, up to £300 a year is disregarded from your total income from investments, property, pensions (including state retirement pension), and any notional income (see p222).[73]

Other benefits

For most benefits, actual income generated from capital (eg, interest on savings) is ignored as income but counts as capital from the date you are due to receive it.

Income derived from certain categories of disregarded capital, however, (including your home, your former home, property you intend to occupy, property occupied by a partner or relative, property up for sale and personal injury trusts not administered by a court – see p206) is treated as income. In most cases, the income is ignored up to the amount of the total mortgage repayments, council tax and water rates paid in respect of the property for the same period over which the income is received. This might apply, for example, to any rent you receive from letting your home while you are in a care home (but see p217 for the treatment of rent from other properties).

The above rules do not apply to PC or HB/CTB if you or your partner are aged 60 or over. Actual income from disregarded capital (see p206) is ignored for these benefits. In rare cases, actual income from certain types of other capital can be taken into account (eg, income from some types of property held in trust), if it is not disregarded under other rules.[74]

Tariff income from capital[75]

For benefits other than tax credits, any capital (other than disregarded capital) you have between the 'lower' and 'upper' capital limits (see p199) is treated as producing an assumed income called a 'tariff income'. There are two rates of tariff income.

- For IS, income-based JSA, income-related ESA and HB/CTB if you and your partner (if you have one) are aged under 60, the tariff income is £1 for every £250 (or part of £250) you have in excess of £6,000 or £10,000 if you are permanently resident in a care home. The upper limit for IS, income-based JSA and income-related ESA is £16,000. The upper limit for HB/CTB is also £16,000, but if you are getting IS, income-based JSA or income-related ESA, all your capital is ignored.
- For PC and HB/CTB if you or your partner are aged 60 or over, the tariff income is £1 for every £500 capital (or part of £500) you have in excess of £6,000 (£10,000 if you are permanently resident in a care home). There is no upper limit for PC. The upper limit for HB/CTB is £16,000 but if you are getting the guarantee element of PC, all your capital is ignored.

Report any increases or decreases in any capital over the lower capital limit as soon as possible to avoid any overpayments or underpayments of benefit (but note the special rules if you are getting PC and are given an 'assessed income period – see p162).

Note that different capital limits apply to financial assessments undertaken by social services (see Chapter 12).

Capital which counts as income

In certain circumstances, payments of capital count as income (this rule does not apply, however, to tax credits, PC, or HB/CTB if you or your partner are aged 60 or over). They include:

- instalments of capital outstanding either when you first claim benefit, or when your benefit is reviewed, if they would bring you over the relevant capital limit (any balance over the capital limit counts as income and is spread over the number of weeks between each instalment);
- any payment from an annuity[76] (but see p162 for when this is disregarded), including 'structured income settlements' from personal injury compensation awards;[77]
- most arrears of maintenance payments from liable relatives (see p219).

Capital which is counted as income cannot also be treated as producing a tariff income.

For HB/CTB, withdrawals from a capital sum (eg, loans to cover extra expenses for respite care) are sometimes treated as income.[78] However, argue that unless it is paid in instalments it should be treated as capital. Any payments of capital, or any irregular withdrawals from a capital sum which are clearly for one-off items and not regular living expenses, should be treated as capital.

Income from tenants and lodgers

Lettings in your own home

- For IS, income-based JSA, income-related ESA and HB/CTB if you and your partner (if you have one) are aged under 60, £20 of your weekly income from tenants or licensees under a formal contractual arrangement is ignored, or the actual amount where the payment is less than £20.[79] If someone shares your home under an informal arrangement, any payment made by her/him to you for her/his living and accommodation costs is ignored,[80] but a non-dependant deduction may be made from HB/CTB or housing costs paid with IS/income-based JSA.
- For PC and HB/CTB if you or your partner are aged 60 or over, £20 of the weekly rent you receive is ignored as income.[81]
- If you have boarders to whom you provide a room and meals on a commercial basis and who are not your close relatives, the first £20 of the weekly charge for each boarder is ignored and half of any balance remaining is then taken into account as your income.
  Note: if income left after applying any of the above disregards is intended to be used to meet any housing costs of your own which are not met by IS, income-based JSA, income-related ESA or HB (if you and your partner are under 60), it can also be disregarded for the purposes of those benefits.[82]
- For tax credits, all the taxable income you receive from lettings counts as income unless it is exempt from tax under the 'Rent a Room Scheme'. This

allows you to rent furnished accommodation in your own home earning up to £4,250 a year tax-free. Note: up to £300 a year is disregarded from your total income from property, investments and pensions.[83]

Lettings in other properties

If you let property other than your own home, the rent you receive:
- is normally treated as capital for IS, income-based JSA, income-related ESA and HB/CTB if you and your partner (if you have one) are aged under 60;[84]
- is ignored for PC and HB/CTB if you or your partner are aged 60 or over (but the value of the property is treated as producing a 'tariff income' (see p216);[85]
- counts as income for tax credits, to the extent that it is taxable, (but up to £300 a year is disregarded from your income from property, investments and pensions).[86]

Charitable, voluntary and personal injury payments

Payments from the Macfarlane and similar trusts

Any payments, including payments in kind, from the Macfarlane Trusts, the Fund, the Eileen Trust, the Skipton Fund, the variant CJD Fund, or the Independent Living (2006) Fund (see p73) are disregarded in full.

Other payments

IS, income-based JSA/income-related ESA and HB/CTB (if aged under 60)

For the purposes of these benefits, **charitable, voluntary or personal injury payments** (see below for definitions) which are made *irregularly* and are intended to be made irregularly are treated as capital and are unlikely to affect your claim unless they take your capital above the lower or upper capital limits (see p199).

Charitable, voluntary or personal injury payments made, or due to be made, *regularly* are completely ignored if they are intended, and used, for anything *except* food, ordinary clothing or footwear, household fuel, council tax, water rates and rent (less any non-dependant deductions) for which HB is payable. For IS, income-based JSA, income-related ESA only, they are also ignored if they are for housing costs not met by IS, income-based JSA and income-related ESA.

All charitable, voluntary and personal injury payments have been disregarded for HB and CTB.

For the treatment of payments for care home costs, see p220.

If not ignored altogether, charitable, voluntary or personal injury payments have a £20 a week disregard (although that may overlap with other disregards for certain war pensions – see p215).

'Charitable' and 'voluntary' payments are not defined in the regulations but a charitable payment is likely to be one made under a charitable trust while a voluntary payment is one where the giver receives nothing in return. Any voluntary payments from a former partner or the parent of your child are treated as maintenance payments (see below). 'Personal injury payments' are payments from a trust or annuity set up from money paid because of a personal injury to you, or payments received under an agreement or court order because of a personal injury to you.[87]

PC and HB/CTB (if aged 60 or over)

For PC and HB/CTB if you or your partner are aged 60, most charitable, voluntary and personal injury payments do not count as income. Any payments from a discretionary trust are ignored, unless they are used for food, ordinary clothing and footwear, household fuel, rent, council tax, water charges, housing costs for which PC is payable, or fees payable by you or your partner to a care home, in which case there is a disregard of £20 a week. Payments received under an agreement or court order because of a personal injury to you or your partner (or your child for HB/CTB) are also ignored.

Tax credits

Any payments which are not taxable are normally disregarded for tax credits.[88] This includes most charitable, voluntary and personal injury payments.

Maintenance payments

If you have separated from your partner, you may be entitled to maintenance payments for yourself and your children. Payments can be made voluntarily, under a court order, or in the case of child maintenance, via the child support scheme, administered by the Child Support Agency. (The CSA is being wound-down and its functions are being taken over by a new Child Maintenance and Enforcement Commission – CMEC.) In some cases, your husband or wife is legally liable to maintain you if you are claiming IS, income-based JSA or PC and this liability can be enforced by the DWP. For more details, see CPAG's *Child Support Handbook*.

Some of the maintenance you receive counts as income for your means-tested benefits but not for tax credits (see p220). Seek advice before negotiating maintenance agreements and if the application of the rules causes you hardship. If you are paying maintenance to a former partner, the payments are not disregarded when calculating your income for means-tested benefits.[89] The Government has announced its intention to introduce a full child maintenance disregard in all income-related benefits from April 2010.

Pension credit

Any maintenance you receive from your spouse or former spouse is taken into account in full as income but does not count as 'qualifying income' when calculating savings credit (see p160). Any maintenance you receive from her/him for a child, however, is ignored.[90]

Tax credits

Any maintenance payments you receive from your former partner, or the parent of your child is ignored.[91]

Income support, income-based jobseeker's allowance and income-related employment and support allowance

If you are getting maintenance for yourself from your spouse (eg, because you are separated following your admission into a care home) or former spouse (eg, because you are divorced), most of your regular payments will count as income. Arrears of maintenance payments also normally count as income and special rules apply for attributing the payment to a past or future period. The rules are complex, however, so seek advice if you receive a lump sum payment of maintenance. Certain types of payments are not treated as maintenance and count as income or capital (and may be disregarded) under the rules set out in the rest of this chapter. These include payments arising from a property settlement on separation or divorce, payments made after the death of your spouse or former spouse and payments made to someone else for your benefit (eg, mortgage capital payments) which it is unreasonable to take account of, and payments you have already used before the DWP makes a decision about it.[92]

If you are getting child support maintenance, £20 a week is disregarded as income[93] and this amount is expected to rise to a full disregard from April 2010. For further details, see CPAG's *Child Support Handbook*.

Housing benefit and council tax benefit

Child maintenance payments are ignored in full for HB/CTB.

Payments for care home costs

The following rules apply to IS, income-related ESA and income-based JSA only.
- Payments made by social services to a care home for a placement they have arranged for you do not count as your income.[94]
- If your placement in a care home has been arranged by social services and you have chosen to enter a home which is more expensive than the local authority would normally fund for a person with your needs, any charitable or voluntary payment (see Chapter 14) to meet the shortfall in fees is ignored as income (this also applies to PC and HB/CTB).[95]
- If your placement in a care home was not arranged by social services, any payment towards your costs in the home is ignored as your income, up to the amount of the difference between your applicable amount (see p151) and the weekly charge for the accommodation.[96]

Community care payments

Most community care payments are not taken into account as income for PC, tax credits and HB/CTB (if you or your partner are aged 60 or over).[97]

There are also specific disregards relating to tax credits, IS, income-based JSA, income-related ESA and HB/CTB if you and your partner (if you have one) are aged under 60, including:

- community care 'direct payments' (see p69);[98]
- payments made under the Supporting People programme (see p52);[99]
- payments you receive for looking after a person temporarily in your care are ignored if paid under community care arrangements by a local authority, health authority, voluntary organisation, or the person being care for.[100]

Payments for certain housing costs

- For IS, income-based JSA and income-related ESA only, payments you receive under a mortgage protection policy which you use to pay housing costs which are not included in your applicable amount (see p151) are ignored. If, however, the amount you receive exceeds the interest and capital payments on a qualifying loan and the premiums on the mortgage protection policy and any buildings insurance policy, the excess counts as your income.
- For IS, income-based JSA and income-related ESA only, as long as you have not already used insurance payments for the same purpose, any money you receive which is used to make:
  - capital and interest payments which are not included in your applicable amount;
  - payments of premiums on a building insurance policy or on an insurance policy which you took out against the risk of not being able to make the payments on a loan secured on your home;
  - any rent that is not covered by HB,
  are ignored.[101]
- For tax credits and HB/CTB if you and your partner (if you have one) are aged under 60, payments you receive under an insurance policy to insure against the risk of being unable to maintain payments on a loan secured on your home are ignored (if you actually use them to maintain your payments). If, however, the amount you receive exceeds the premiums on the policy and any policy to insure against loss or damage to your home, the excess counts as your income.

Private pensions and annuities

- Occupational and private pensions and retirement annuity contracts count as income.[102]
- Payments from other annuities generally count as income but payments from 'home income schemes' equal to the net interest (after tax) payable on the loan with which the annuity was bought, are ignored for IS, income-based JSA, income-related ESA, HB and CTB (but see below), as long as at least 90 per cent of the loan was used to buy the annuity, the loan is secured on your home and was taken out when you (and your partner) were aged 65 or over, and the annuity will end when you and your partner die.[103] For PC and HB/CTB if you

or your partner are aged 60 or over, the above disregard applies to any annuity, if the conditions set out above are satisfied.[104]

Student grants and loans

The rules are complex and are set out in full in CPAG's *Welfare Benefits and Tax Credits Handbook, Student Support and Benefits Handbook: England, Wales and Northern Ireland,* and *Benefits for Students in Scotland Handbook.* However, note the following points.

- Most student loans and grants are ignored as income for tax credits, and, if you are aged 60 or over, PC and HB/CTB.
- If you are under 60 most income from grants, loans and certain other forms of financial support are taken into account for means tested benefits and you can be treated as receiving a student loan, even if you have not applied for one.
- Education maintenance allowances (paid to some young people staying on at school or college after the age of 16) are ignored as income.
- For HB and CTB, some or all of any parental contributions you make to a student's grant or living expenses can be disregarded from your income.

Other income which is disregarded

Brief details of some other types of income which is wholly or partly disregarded is given below. For further details and a complete list, see CPAG's *Welfare Benefits and Tax Credits Handbook.*

- Most payments from social services to assist children in need and young people who have left care are ignored.
- Certain payments under the New Deal and other government training and employment programmes are disregarded as income (other than training allowances).
- Any payments to cover expenses if you are working as a volunteer are ignored.
- Payments in kind which may include food, fuel, clothing, holidays, gifts, accommodation or transport are ignored.
- Fares to hospital are ignored.
- Most payments from discretionary trusts are wholly or partially ignored for PC and HB/CTB if you or your partner are aged 60 or over.

Notional income

In the circumstances set out below, you can be treated as having income you do not have. This is called notional income. There is a similar rule for notional capital (see p203).

Deprivation of income in order to claim or increase benefit[105]

If you deliberately dispose of income in order to claim or increase your benefit or tax credits, you are treated as though you are still in receipt of the income. The issues involved are the same as those that apply to the deliberate deprivation of capital (see p204).

Note that the rule can only apply if the purpose of the deprivation is to gain benefit for yourself (or your family). It should not, therefore, apply if you stop claiming carer's allowance (CA) so that another person (who is not a member of your family) can become or remain entitled to the severe disability premium/addition (see p151).[106] However, if you do not claim a benefit which would clearly be paid if you did, it may be argued that you have failed to apply for income (see below).

A deliberate decision to 'de-retire' and give up your retirement pension (in the expectation of achieving an overall increase in benefit in the future) can come within this deprivation rule.[107]

Failing to apply for income

IS, income-based JSA, income-related ESA, tax credits and HB/CTB (aged under 60)

If you fail to apply for income to which you are entitled without having to fulfil further conditions, you are deemed to have received it from the date you could have obtained it. This rule does not apply, however, to income from:[108]

- a discretionary trust, a trust set up from money paid as a result of a personal injury, or funds administered by a court as a result of a personal injury or the death of a parent of someone under 18;
- a personal pension scheme or retirement annuity if you are under 60 (it does apply in certain circumstances if you are aged 60 or over);
- a rehabilitation allowance made under the Employment and Training Act 1973;
- tax credits.

The rule can only apply if is certain that the relevant income would be paid to you upon application. It may be difficult for the benefit authorities to show that this applies in a case where you do not claim CA because of the effect it would have on another person's severe disability premium/addition (see p151).

PC and HB/CTB (aged under 60)

For PC and HB/CTB if you or your partner are aged 60 or over, you can only be treated as receiving the following income for which you fail to apply:

- the amount of any retirement pension to which you are entitled;
- income from an occupational pension you elect to defer;
- income from a retirement annuity in certain circumstances.[109]

Income due to you which has not been paid[110]

For IS, income-based JSA, income-related ESA only, you may be treated as possessing any income owing to you (provided that the income is due to you, or your family, and would be for your own benefit). Examples of when the rule could apply are where you are owed wages (unless you have been made redundant) or an occupational pension (unless there are insufficient funds in the pension scheme to pay you) which are legally due to you. The rule does not apply to payments from a discretionary trust or a trust set up with funds from personal injury money. It should also not apply if any social security benefit, training allowance or similar payment is delayed.

Income paid to a third party on your behalf[111]

If money is paid to a third party on your behalf (eg, the landlord for your rent) it can count as notional income. For most benefits, the rule applies in the same way as it does for notional capital (see p205) with the same exceptions. It does not apply, however, to tax credits, and in the case of PC and HB/CTB if you or your partner are aged 60 or over, any money paid to a third party on your behalf counts as your income.

Income payments paid to you for a third party[112]

If you or a member of your family get a payment for somebody not in your family (eg, for a relative living with you), it counts as your income if you keep any of it yourself or spend it on yourself or your family. This does not apply if it is a payment from the Macfarlane Trust, the Fund, the Eileen Trust or the Independent Living (2006) Fund, or a grant for participating in a government training or employment scheme. This rule does not apply to tax credits or PC and HB/CTB if you or your partner are aged 60 or over.

Cheap or unpaid labour

If you are helping another person or an organisation by doing work of a kind which would normally command a wage, or a higher wage, you are deemed to receive a wage similar to that normally paid for that kind of job in that area. This rule does not apply if you:
- can show that the person cannot, in fact, afford to pay, or pay more; *or*
- work for a charitable or voluntary organisation, or as a volunteer and it is reasonable for you to give your services free of charge; *or*
- are on most types of government work or training schemes and are not getting a training allowance.

The rule also does not apply for PC and HB/CTB if you or your partner are aged 60 or over.

Even if you are caring for a sick or disabled relative or another person, it may be considered reasonable for her/him to pay you from her/his benefits, unless you

Chapter 8: Capital and income for means-tested benefits and tax credits
7. Earnings from employment and self-employment

8

can bring yourself within the above exceptions.[113] You should be able to argue, however, that it is reasonable for you to provide services without charge to a close relative out of a sense of family duty, particularly if charging would compromise the relationship. Whether it is reasonable to provide care free of charge depends on the basis on which the arrangement is made, the expectations of the family members concerned, the housing arrangements and the reasons (if appropriate) why a carer gave up any paid work. The risk of a carer losing entitlement to CA if a charge were made should also be considered as should the likelihood that a relative being looked after would no longer be able to contribute to the household expenses. If there is no realistic alternative to the carer providing services free to a relative who simply will not pay, this would also make it reasonable not to charge.[114]

If you are receiving direct payments from the local authority to employ a carer, the money you receive doesn't count as income for means-tested benefit purposes. However, when it is passed on by you to the carer, it becomes her/his income and could effect any benefits that s/he receives. If you are using your direct payment to 'employ' your spouse, as can sometimes happen with local authority consent, her/his 'wage' will count as income for means-tested benefit purposes. S/he may be able to claim working tax credit however.

Sometimes it may be reasonable to do a job for free out of a sense of community duty, particularly if the job would otherwise have remained undone, and there would be no financial profit to an employer.[115]

7. Earnings from employment and self-employment

This section gives a brief outline of the main rules for assessing how your earnings are taken into account for means-tested benefits. The rules are complex so seek advice if you are unsure how your earnings affect your benefits. Further details of the rules can be found in CPAG's *Welfare Benefits and Tax Credits Handbook*.

Earnings from employment

Note: the following rules do not apply to tax credits (see p229).

Calculating your earnings

If you are working for an employer, your gross and net earnings need to be calculated. '**Gross earnings**' means the amount received from your employer less deductions for expenses 'wholly, necessarily and exclusively' incurred by you in order to carry out the duties of your employment (eg, for tools, work equipment, special clothing or uniforms, or the costs of running a car).[116] '**Net earnings**' means your gross earnings less deductions for income tax, Class 1 national

8

Chapter 8: Capital and income for means-tested benefits and tax credits
7. Earnings from employment and self-employment

insurance (NI) contributions and half of contributions made to a personal or occupational pension scheme.[117]

What counts as earnings

Earnings means 'any remuneration or profit derived from . . . employment'. As well as wages, this includes:[118]

- bonus or commission (including tips);
- holiday pay;
- payments made by your employer for expenses which are *not* 'wholly, exclusively and necessarily' incurred in carrying out your job (including travel expenses to and from work and payments to you for looking after members of your family);
- a retainer fee or a guarantee payment;
- for means tested benefits any statutory sick pay, contractual sick pay or maternity/paternity/adoption pay;
- non-cash vouchers (except to the extent that they are exempt from liability for NI contributions);
- certain compensation payments in respect of your employment – eg, pay in lieu of notice and certain employment tribunal awards.

The following are examples of **payments not counted as earnings**:[119]

- payments in kind (other than non-cash vouchers – see above) – but see p222 for the rules on notional income;
- the value of any accommodation provided as part of your job is ignored for IS and income-based JSA;
- an advance of earnings or a loan from your employer (which counts instead as capital);
- payments towards expenses which are 'wholly, exclusively and necessarily' incurred – eg, travelling expenses in the course of your work;
- occupational pensions (which count in full as income other than earnings).

Amount of and period covered by earnings

Complex rules apply to determine the average weekly amount of your earnings and the period which earnings cover (see p225). There are also special rules on how payments you receive at the end of a job (eg, pay in lieu of notice, holiday pay and compensation payments) are treated. See CPAG's *Welfare Benefits and Tax Credits Handbook* for full details.

Earnings from self-employment

Note: the following rules do not apply to tax credits (see p229).

Your net profit over the period before you claim must be worked out. Net profit consists of all your earnings from self-employment minus:[120]

Chapter 8: Capital and income for means-tested benefits and tax credits
7. Earnings from employment and self-employment

8

- any reasonable expenses (see below); *and*
- income tax and national insurance contributions; *and*
- half of any premium paid in respect of a personal pension scheme or a retirement annuity contract which is eligible for tax relief.

Payments for fostering a child or providing temporary respite care under community care arrangements do not count as earnings but as other income which may be ignored.

Expenses which may be offset from earnings from self-employment must be reasonable and 'wholly, necessarily and exclusively' incurred for the purposes of your business. They include repayments of capital on loans for replacing equipment and machinery or repairing business assets and interest on loans taken out for the business, but do not include any money for setting up or expanding a business, capital expenditure and capital repayments on business loans, most depreciation costs and entertainment expenses.

Childminders are treated as self-employed but their net profit is deemed to be one-third of their earnings less income tax, NI contributions and half of certain pension contributions; the rest of their earnings are completely ignored.[121]

Your weekly earnings from self-employment are determined by looking at an 'appropriate period' (normally your last year's trading accounts).

Disregarded earnings[122]

Note: the following rules do not apply to tax credits (see p229).

Some of your net earnings from employment or self-employment are disregarded and do not affect your benefit. The amount of the disregard depends on your circumstances. There are three levels of earnings disregard and the highest one which applies to your circumstances will be allowed. Certain childcare costs may also be offset from earnings (see p229).

£25 disregard

Lone parents claiming HB or CTB have £25 of their earnings ignored. This does not apply to anyone claiming IS, income-based JSA, income-related ESA or PC.

£20 disregard

£20 of your earnings is disregarded if:
- for IS, income-based JSA, income-related ESA and PC, you are a lone parent; *or*
- you, or your partner, qualify for a carer's premium/addition (see pp151 and 160); *or*
- you or your partner qualify for the disability premium (see p151) (or, for IS/income-based JSA only, you would do if you were not in hospital or a care home); *or*

- you have a partner, one of you is under 60, and your benefit would include a disability premium but for the fact that one of you qualifies for the higher pensioner premium (see p151) (or, for IS/income-based JSA only, you would do if you were not in hospital or a care home); *or*
- you or your partner are aged 60 or over and qualify for the higher pensioner premium (or, for IS/income-based JSA only, you would if you were not in hospital or a care home) and immediately before you became 60;
  - you were entitled to the £20 disregard because you qualified for the disability premium (see above) (or, for HB and CTB, would have done but for the fact that the higher pensioner premium was payable instead); *and*
  - you were in employment (part-time for IS and income-based JSA) and have remained in employment (ignoring breaks of up to eight weeks).

Note: the last three bullet points do not apply to PC and HB/CTB if you or your partner are aged 60 or over and are not claiming IS or income-based JSA. Instead, you qualify for the £20 disregard if:

- you or your partner are getting long-term incapacity benefit (IB), severe disablement allowance (SDA), attendance allowance, disability living allowance, mobility supplement, or the disability or severe disability element of working tax credit (WTC); *or*
- you or your partner are registered blind; *or*
- for HB and CTB only, you or your partner have been assessed as incapable of work (see p143) for a continuous period of 364 days (196 days if you are terminally ill); *or*
- you or your partner previously qualified for a £20 disregard in a previous award of IS, income-based JSA, HB or CTB not more than eight weeks before (for PC) you first became entitled to PC, or (for HB or CTB) you reached the age of 60 and the employment you were in is continuing (ignoring breaks of up to eight weeks for HB/CTB); *or*
- for PC only, you or your partner qualified for a £20 disregard immediately before you reached pensionable age because you were getting long-term IB or SDA and there is no break of more than eight weeks in your claim for PC.

If you qualify under more than one of the above categories, only £20 of your earnings is ignored.

Basic £10 or £5 disregard

If you do not qualify for a £25 or £20 disregard, £5 of your earnings is disregarded if you are single, or £10 if you have a partner (whether or not you are both working).

Chapter 8: Capital and income for means-tested benefits and tax credits
7. Earnings from employment and self-employment

8

Additional full-time work disregard for housing benefit and council tax benefit

For HB and CTB, there is an additional disregard of £16.85 if:

- you or your partner receive the 30-hour element of WTC; *or*
- you or your partner or are aged 25 or over and are working at least 30 hours a week; *or*
- you or your partner work at least 16 hours a week and your HB/CTB includes a family premium, or the person who is working is disabled (ie, qualifies for a disability or higher pensioner premium, or, if you or your partner are aged 60 or over, a disability or incapacity benefit); *or*
- you are a lone parent and are working at least 16 hours a week; *or*
- you or your partner get a 50-plus element in WTC, or would qualify for one if you applied for WTC.

Childcare costs disregard for housing benefit and council tax benefit

For HB and CTB, certain childcare costs (for registered or other approved childcare) of up to £175 a week in respect of one child or £300 in respect of two or more children can be deducted from your earnings if you are a lone parent working at least 16 hours a week, or a couple and both of you are working at least 16 hours a week, or one of you is working at least 16 hours a week and the other is incapacitated. For further details, see CPAG's *Welfare Benefits and Tax Credits Handbook*.

Calculating your earnings for tax credits

Earnings from employment

Your gross earnings from employment (before tax and other deductions) are taken into account, including taxable expenses and vouchers, statutory sick pay, and any payment of statutory maternity, paternity or adoption pay which exceeds £100 a week.[123]

Deductions allowed include payments of expenses 'wholly, exclusively and necessarily' incurred in the performance of the duties of the claimant's employment', contributions to approved personal or occupational pensions, childcare vouchers and certain travelling and car parking expenses.[124] If you are a volunteer with a charity or voluntary organisation, all your expenses are ignored.[125]

Earnings are assessed along with your other income, on an annual basis.

Earnings from self-employment

Your taxable profits from self-employment, including any trade, profession or vocation (or your share in a partnership's profits) are taken into account and assessed on an annual basis.[126] Expenses 'wholly, necessarily and exclusively' incurred for the purposes of your business can be deducted when calculating taxable profits, plus any contributions you make to an approved personal pension or retirement annuity.

Notes

1. The capital limits

1 Regs 45 and 53(1) IS Regs; regs 107(a) and 116(1) JSA Regs; regs 43 and 52 HB Regs; regs 33 and 42 CTB Regs
2 Regs 25 and 26 HB(SPC) Regs; regs 15 and 16 CTB Regs; reg 15(6) SPC Regs
3 para C2.21 GM; para 29020 DMG
4 *R v SBC ex parte Singer* [1973] 1 WLR 713
5 R(IS) 3/93, para 22
6 s136 SSCBA 1992; s13(2) JSA 1995; s5 SPCA 2002; s7 TCA 2002
7 Reg 47 IS Regs; reg 109 JSA Regs; reg 25(3) HB Regs; reg 23(3) HB(SPC) Regs; reg 15(3) CTB Regs; reg 13(3) CTB(SPC) Regs
8 Reg 17(1)(b) IS Regs; reg 83(b) JSA Regs
9 R(SB) 2/83; R(SB) 35/83; R(IS) 3/93
10 CIS/654/1991
11 R(SB) 12/86
12 R(SB) 53/83; R(SB) 1/85
13 R(SB) 49/83
14 R(SB) 23/85
15 *Peters v CAO* reported as an appendix to R(SB) 3/89
16 Sch 10 para 13 IS Regs; Sch 8 para 18 JSA Regs; Sch 6 para 15 HB Regs; Sch 6 para 11 HB(SPC) Regs; Sch 5 para 15 CTB Regs; Sch 4 para 27 CTB(SPC) Regs
17 Sch 5 para 28 SPC Regs; Sch 6 HB(SPC) Regs; Sch 4 CTB(SPC) Regs
18 R(IS) 1/90
19 *Barclays Bank v Quistclose Investments Ltd* [1970] AC 567; R(SB) 49/83; CFC/21/1989
20 Sch 10 para 12A IS Regs; Sch 8 para 17A JSA Regs; Sch 6 para 14A HB Regs; Sch Sch 5 para 14A CTB Regs
21 Sch 10 paras 44 and 45 IS Regs; Sch 8 paras 42 and 43 JSA Regs; Sch 9 ESA Regs; Sch 6 paras 46 and 47 HB Regs; Sch 6 HB(SPC) Regs; Sch 5 paras 46 and 47 CTB Regs; Sch 4 CTB(SPC); Sch 5 para 16(2) SPC Regs
22 Regs 40 and 46 IS Regs; regs 103 and 108 JSA Regs; regs 39 and 44 HB; regs 36 and 42 HB(SPC) Regs; regs 30 and 34 CTB Regs; regs 28 and 32 CTB(SPC) Regs; CIS/559/1991
23 Sch 5 para 16(1) SPC Regs; Sch 6 para 17(1) HB(SPC) Regs; Sch 4 para 17(1) CTB(SPC)
24 *Thomas v CAO* (appendix to R(SB) 17/87)
25 Sch 5 para 16(1) SPC Regs; Sch 6 para 17(1) HB(SPC) Regs; Sch 4 para 17(1) CTB(SPC)
26 Reg 48 IS Regs; reg 110 JSA Regs; reg 46 HB Regs; reg 39 HB(SPC) Regs; reg 36 CTB Regs; reg 39 CTB(SPC) Regs
27 Reg 51 IS Regs; reg 113 JSA Regs; reg 49 HB Regs; reg 42 HB(SPC) Regs; reg 41 CTB Regs; reg 47 CTB(SPC) regs; reg 21 SPC Regs
28 R(SB) 38/85
29 CIS/124/1990; CSB/1198/1989; R(SB)9/91
30 CIS/264/1989
31 R(IS) 7/98
32 R(SB) 12/91; *Verna Jones v Sec of State for Work and Pensions* [2003] EWCA Civ 964, 10 July 2003
33 CIS/2627/1995; *Verna Jones* (see above)
34 Reg 51(7) IS Regs; reg 113(7) JSA Regs
35 CIS/240/1992
36 CIS/12403/1996
37 para C2.69 GM
38 para C2.97 GM
39 Reg 51(2) IS Regs; reg 113(2) JSA Regs; reg 50 HB Regs; reg 48 HB(SPC) Regs; reg 39 CTB Regs; reg 37 CTB(SPC) Regs; CIS/368/1994

40 Reg 51(3)(a)(ii) and (8) IS Regs; reg 113(3)(a)(ii) JSA Regs; reg 115(3)(c) ESA Regs; reg 49 HB Regs; reg 42 HB(SPC) Regs; reg 39 CTB Regs; reg 37 CTB(SPC) Regs

41 Reg 51(3)(a) IS Regs; reg 113(a) JSA Regs; reg 115(3)(b) ESA Regs; reg 49(3)(a) HB Regs; reg 42 HB(SPC) Regs; reg 39(3)(a) CTB Regs; reg 37 CTB(SPC) Regs

3. Disregarded capital

42 Sch 10 para 1 IS Regs; Sch 8 para 1 JSA Regs; SCh 9 para 1 ESA Regs; Sch 6 para 1 HB Regs; Sch 6 para 26 HB(SPC) Regs; Sch 5 para 1 CTB Regs; Sch 4 para 26 CTB(SPC) Regs; Sch 5 para 1A SPC Regs

43 Sch 10 IS Regs; Sch 8 JSA Regs; Sch 9 ESA Regs; Sch 6 HB Regs; Sch 6 HB(SPC) Regs; Sch 5 CTB Regs; Sch 4 CTB(SPC) Regs; Sch 5 SPC Regs

44 CIS/562/1992

45 CIS/7319/1995

46 R(SB) 32/83

47 CIS/7319/1995, para 22

48 *R v London Borough of Tower Hamlets Housing Benefit Review Board ex parte Kapur*, 12 June 2000

49 R(IS) 6/95

50 CIS/685/1992; CIS/8475/1995; CIS/15984/1996

51 R(SB) 14/85

52 para 29578 DMG

53 CIS/6908/1995

54 Sch 10 para 4 IS Regs; Sch 8 para 4 JSA Regs; Sch 9 para 4 ESA Regs; Sch 6 paras 4 HB Regs; Sch 6 para 4 HB(SPC) Regs; Sch 5 paras 4 CTB Regs; Sch 4 para 4 CTB(SPC) Regs; Sch 5 para 4 SPC Regs

55 Para 29432 DMG; para C2 Annexe A, A2.00 GM

56 R(IS) 3/96

57 Sch 10 IS Regs; Sch 8 JSA Regs; Sch 9 ESA Regs; Sch 6 HB Regs; Sch 4 Regs; Sch 5 PC Regs

58 R(SB) 18/83

59 Reg 52 IS Regs; reg 115 JSA Regs; reg 117 ESA Regs; reg 51 HB Regs; reg 49 HB(SPC) Regs; reg 41 CTB Regs; reg 39 CTB(SPC) Regs; reg 23 SPC Regs

60 *Secretary of State for Work and Pensions v Hourigan* [2000] EWCA Civ. 1890, 19 December 2002

61 Under s30 Law of Property Act 1925 or, since 1 January 1997, ss14-15 Trusts of Land and Appointment of Trustees Act 1996

62 Contrast R(IS) 3/96 and *Wilkinson v CAO*, CA, 24 March 2000

63 Memo AOG JSA/IS 35, October 1998

64 CJSA/1114/2000

65 CIS/7097/1995; CIS/15936/1996; CIS/263/1997; CIS/3283/1997 (joint decision – common appendix para 17)

66 R(IS) 2/93

5. General rules about income

67 *R v SBC ex parte Singer* [1973] 1 WLR 713

68 R(IS)4/01

69 Reg 15 SPC Regs

70 s136(1) SSCBA 1992; s13(2) JSA 1995; s5 SPCA 2002; s7 TCA 2002

71 Reg 29 IS Regs; reg 94 JSA Regs

72 Reg 10 TC(DCI) Regs

73 Reg 10 TC(DCI) Regs

74 s51(1)(i) SPCA 2002; reg 17(6) and Sch 5 Part II SPC Regs; reg 33HB Regs; Sch 6 HB(SPC) Regs; Sch 4 CTB(SPC) reg 23 CTB Regs

75 Reg 53 IS Regs; reg 116 JSA Regs; reg 118 ESA Regs; reg 52 HB Regs; reg 42 CTB Regs; reg 15(6) SPC Regs

76 Reg 41(2) IS Regs; reg 104(2) JSA Regs; reg 105(2) ESA Regs; reg 41(2) HB Regs; reg 31(2) CTB Regs

77 *Beattie v Secretary of State for Social Security*, [2001]EWCA Civ.498, 9 April 2001 (following R(IS) 10/01)

78 *R v SBC ex parte Singer* [1973] 1 All ER 931; *R v Oxford County Council ex parte Jack* [1984] 17 HLR 419; *R v West Dorset DC ex parte Poupard* [1988] 20 HLR 295; para C3.118 GM

79 Sch 9 para 19 IS Regs; Sch 7 para 20 JSA Regs; Sch 8 para 20 ESA Regs; Sch 5 para 22 HB Regs; Sch 4 para 22 CTB Regs

80 Sch 9 para 18 IS Regs; Sch 7 para 19 JSA Regs; Sch 8 para 19 ESA Regs; Sch 5 para 21 HB Regs; Sch 4 para 21 CTB Regs

81 Sch 4 para 9 SPC Regs; Sch 5 para 10 HB(SPC) Regs; Sch 3 para 10 CTB(SPC) Regs

82 CIS/13059/1996

83 Regs 10 and 11 TC(DCI) Regs

84 *CAO v Palfrey and Others, The Times,* 17 February 1995; reg 48(4) IS Regs; reg 110(4) JSA Regs; reg 112(4) ESA Regs; reg 46(4) HB Regs; reg 36(4) CTB Regs

85 s15(1)(i) SPCA 2002; reg 29(1)(i) HB(SPC) Regs; reg 19(1)(i) CTB(SPC) Regs

86 Regs 10 and 11 TC(DCI) Regs

87 *R v Doncaster Borough Council, ex parte Boulton, The Times* December 31 1992

88 TC(DCI) Regs

89 CIS/683/1993
90 Regs 9 and 15(5)(d) SPC Regs
91 Reg 19, para 10, Table 6 TC(DCI) Regs
92 Regs 54-60 IS Regs; regs 117-124 JSA Regs; CSB/1160/1986; R(SB) 1/89
93 Regs 60A–60E IS Regs; regs 125-129 JSA Regs; Sch 9 para 73 IS Regs; paras 7 and 70 JSA Regs
94 Sch 9 para 66 IS Regs; Sch 7 para 64 JSA Regs; Sch 8 para 56 ESA Regs
95 Sch 9 paras 15A and 30 IS Regs; Sch 7 para 16 JSA Regs; Sch 8 para 34 ESA Regs
96 Sch 9 para 30A IS Regs; Sch 7 para 32 JSA Regs; Sch 8 para 34 ESA Regs
97 s15 SPCA 2002; TC(DCI) Regs; regs 8, 17 and 21 HB&CTB(SPC) Regs
98 Sch 9 para 58 IS Regs; Sch 7 para 56 JSA Regs; Sch 5 para 57 HB Regs; Sch 4 para 57 CTB Regs; reg 19 Table 6 para 14 TC(DCI) Regs; Sch 8 para 53 ESA Regs
99 Sch 9 para 76 IS Regs; Sch 7 para 72 JSA Regs; Sch 5 para 63 HB Regs; Sch 4 para 63 CTB Regs; Reg 19 Table 6 para 14A TC(DCI) Regs; Sch 8 para 63 ESA Regs
100 Sch 9 para 27 IS Regs; Sch 7 para 28 JSA Regs; Sch 5 para 27 HB Regs; Sch 4 para 28 CTB Regs; reg 19, Table 8 para 3 TC(DCI) Regs; Sch 8 para 29 ESA Regs
101 Sch 9 para 30 IS Regs; Sch 7 para 31 JSA Regs; Sch 8 para 32 ESA Regs
102 Regs 2(1) and 40(4) IS Regs; regs 2(1) 103(6) and 98(2) JSA Regs; regs 2(1) and 40(10) HB regs; Reg 2(1) and 30(11) CTB Regs; reg 16 SPC Regs; reg 5(1) TC(DCI) Regs; regs 2(1) and 104(8) ESA Regs
103 Reg 41(2) and Sch 9 para 17 IS Regs; reg 104(2) and Sch 7 para 18 JSA Regs; reg 41(2)HB Regs; reg 31(2) CTB Regs
104 Sch 4 para 10 SPC Regs; Sch 5 para 11 HB(SPC) Regs; Sch 3 para 11 CTB(SPC) Regs
105 Reg 42(1) IS Regs; reg 105(1) JSA Regs; reg 42(1) HB Regs; regs 32(1) CTB Regs; reg 41(8) CTB(SPC) Regs; reg 31(8) CTB(SPC) Regs; reg 18(6) SPC Regs; reg 15 TC(DCI) Regs
106 paras 28608-616 DMG; CIS/15052/1996
107 CSIS/57/1992
108 Reg 42(2) IS Regs; reg 106(1) ESA Regs; reg 105(2) JSA Regs; reg 42(2) HB Regs; reg 32(2) CTB Regs; reg 16 TC(DCI) Regs
109 Reg 18(1)-(5) SPC Regs; regs 41(1)–(7) HB(SPC) Regs; reg 31(1)–(7) CTB(SPC) Regs

110 Reg 42(3) and (5) IS Regs; reg 105(6) and (10) JSA Regs; reg 107(1) ESA Regs
111 Reg 42 IS Regs; reg 105 JSA Regs; reg 42 HB Regs; reg 32 CTB Regs; reg 24 SPC Regs; regs 47 HB(SPC) Regs; reg 30 CTB(SPC) Regs; reg 106 ESA Regs
112 Reg 42(4)(b) IS Regs; reg 107(4) ESA Regs; reg 105(10)(b) JSA Regs; reg 43(6) HB Regs; reg 32(6) CTB Regs
113 *Sharrock v CAO* (CA), 26 March 1991; CIS/93/1991
114 CIS/93/1991; CIS/422/1992; CIS/701/1994
115 CIS/147/1993

7. **Earnings from employment and self-employment**

116 *Parsons v Hogg* [1985] 2 All ER 897, CA, appendix to R(FIS) 4/85; R(FC) 1/90
117 Reg 36(3) IS Regs; reg 99(1) and (4) JSA Regs; reg 96(3) ESA Regs; reg 36(3) HB Regs; reg 36(2) and (4) HB(SPC) Regs; regs 26(3) CTB Regs; reg 17(4)(b) and (c) CTB(SPC) Regs; regs 17 and 17A SPC Regs
118 Regs 35(1) IS Regs; regs 98(1) JSA Regs; reg 95(1) ESA Regs; reg 35(1) HB Regs; reg 35(1) HB(SPC) Regs; regs 25(1) CTB Regs; reg 25(1) CTB(SPC) Regs; reg 17A(2) SPC Regs
119 Regs 35 and Sch 9 IS Regs; reg 98 and Sch 7 JSA Regs; reg 95 and Sch 8 ESA Regs; reg 35 and Sch 5 HB Regs; reg 35(SPC) Regs; reg 25 and Sch CTB Regs; reg 25 CTB(SPC) Regs; reg 17A SPC Regs
120 Reg 38(3) IS Regs; reg 101(4) JSA Regs; reg 98(3) ESA Regs; regs 38(3) HB Regs; Reg 39 HB(SPC) Regs; regs 28(3) CTB Regs; reg 29 CTB(SPC) Regs; reg 17B SPC Regs
121 Reg 38(9) IS Regs; reg 101(10) JSA Regs; reg 98(9) ESA Regs; reg 39(9) HB Regs; reg 39(8) HB(SPC) Regs; reg 28(9) CTB Regs; reg 29(8) CTB(SPC) Regs; reg 17B SPC Regs
122 Sch 8 IS Regs; Sch 6 JSA Regs; Sch 7 ESA Regs; Sch 4 HB Regs; Sch 4 HB(SPC) Regs; Sch 3 CTB Regs; Sch 2 CTB(SPC) Regs; Sch 6 SPC Regs
123 Reg 4 TC (DCI) Regs
124 Regs 3(7)(c) and 4 Table 1 TC(DCI) Regs
125 Reg 19 Table 7 para 1 TC(DCI) Regs
126 Reg 6 TC(DCI) Regs

Part 3

People living in a care home

Chapter 9

Accommodation in a care home

This chapter covers:
1. Deciding to move into a care home (below)
2. Choosing a home (p236)
3. Fees which are fully paid by the state (p239)
4. Help with fees from adult social care services (p243)
5. NHS-funded nursing care (England and Wales) (p252)
6. Paying the full fees yourself (p245)
7. Dealing with your money in a care home (p257)

1. Deciding to move into a care home

The decision to move into a care home is one of the most important decisions that you can have to make. It may mean giving up your home and sometimes moving to a different area, and is often seen as giving up your independence. But it can be an opportunity to make new, or renew old, friendships and be free of the worries of looking after yourself and doing day-to-day chores. It is, however, expensive so it is very important to be sure that you actually need this type of care, and to establish whether you can get any help with the fees. This chapter explains who can get their fees fully covered by the state (see p239), who can get some help from adult social care services (see p243), who gets help from the NHS for nursing costs (see p252), and who has to pay their fees in full (see p254). It is possible to move from one category to another, so you could start by paying for all of the fees yourself but at a later stage ask for help from adult social care services when your capital reduces to a certain level, or at any stage become eligible for NHS-funded care if your health needs meet the criteria.

Chapter 16 explains the way your benefits are affected by the type of home, and by whether you are being funded by adult social care services or the NHS.

In this chapter we use the term **'care home'** to cover all types of home which are registered as care homes. Some homes provide nursing care as well as personal care, and where necessary we will make it clear when we are referring only to such homes. The term 'care home' reflects the terminology used in the registration of homes, which are no longer referred to as residential care homes or nursing homes.

Getting an assessment

Before adult social care services can assist with funding the cost of a care home, they have to assess you to establish that you need this type of care (see p34). Even if you can afford to pay the fees of the care home, it is advisable to have your needs assessed by adult social care services. If you are likely to need help with funding in the near future, it is important to be sure that adult social care services have agreed that you need the level of care provided in a care home.

Assessments are explained in detail in Chapter 2. The assessment should look at all the options, such as help at home, sheltered accommodation, extra care housing, and aids and equipment that could help you. You may decide after the assessment, or a period of intermediate care in a care home, that there are ways for you to manage at home. If you do need to enter a care home, the assessment should identify which type of home would be suitable for your needs.

If your needs are primarily for health or medical care, then you should be assessed to see whether you are eligible for continuing NHS health care services, including fully funded care in a care home (see p240) which can have considerable financial benefits. In England and Wales the NHS is also responsible for meeting the cost of care provided by registered nurses in care homes.

Adult social care services have been told that they cannot refuse to assess the needs of anyone on the grounds that s/he has financial resources over the capital limit (see p291), and that they should give the person advice about the type of care s/he requires and what services are available.[1] Following a House of Lords ruling,[2] local authorities in Scotland have been advised that they must make the arrangements for anyone assessed as needing residential care 'regardless of their ability to pay'.[3] See p305 for more details about this judgment.

2. Choosing a home

Although there are many different types of homes, the registration standards mean that all homes should be fit for their purpose, and provide the required standard of care set down by the national regulatory bodies. Some charities provide factsheets or booklets giving information about what you should look for when choosing a home. In England, Counsel and Care has published a *Care Home Handbook* supported by the Department of Health

Each home should have a statement of purpose and a service users' guide. You should be given a copy of the most recent inspection report as part of the service users' guide. Alternatively you can request a copy of the recent inspection report directly from the regulatory body.

Regulatory and inspection bodies
Care Quality Commission (CQC) – England
Care and Social Services Inspectorate Wales (CSSIW) – Wales
Scottish Commission for the Regulation of Care (known as the Care Commission) – Scotland
See Appendix 1 for contact details.

CQC has set up a quality rating system for care homes in England, similar to those used for hotels. A care home that has been awarded zero stars will have been awarded a poor quality rating, while three stars indicate that CQC has judged that the quality of care is excellent. However, the service user guide would also be important to give you an idea of the way the home is run on a day-to-day basis. For example, some homes allow you to take pets or your own furniture for your room, or they have a kitchen area where you can make yourself a light meal. Make sure the home will take notice of your likes and dislikes.

Try to go to several homes before you make a decision. What may sound ideal in a brochure might not be so. A visit will help you get a feel for whether you would be comfortable there and get on with the staff and other residents. If you cannot go yourself, make sure someone goes who knows your tastes. Many homes will send staff to visit prospective residents if they cannot go themselves. You should be offered the chance to visit or to have a trial period in the home before making up your mind.

Try to resist being hurried into making a decision and going into the first home you see. This may be difficult if you are in hospital and your bed is needed, but remember it is vital that you are comfortable in the home you live in.

If you are making your own arrangements with the home it is also important to establish exactly what is covered by the fees quoted and whether there are any extra costs that you might have to meet (see p251). You should be given a written contract stating which room you will be occupying, the overall care and services covered in the fee, what the fee is, additional services to be paid for over and above the fee, rights and obligations of the service user and the provider, and the terms and conditions of occupancy.[4] If you are being funded by adult social care services or the NHS, they should arrange what is covered in their contract but you should still get a statement of terms and conditions.

The Office of Fair Trading (OFT) has produced guidance on potentially unfair terms and conditions in contracts made between care homes and residents.[5] The OFT also has a shorter leaflet giving an overview of the guidance.[6]

In June 2005, the OFT published a report on the care homes market. It raised concerns about the apparent lack of clear and accurate information provided by care homes about the fees being charged and the services the fees covered. The report also raised concerns about the lack of transparency in care home contracts and the lack of protection for residents against unreasonable price increases. The

Government responded to the OFT's report with the Care Standards Act 2000 (Establishments and Agencies) (Miscellaneous Amendments) Regulations 2006 with the intention of increasing price transparency for care home residents.

In October 2007, the Commission for Social Care Inspection (now CQC) published *A Fair Contract with Older People?* This report highlighted that although there had been some improvements in the system, there were still some areas of concern for people who are self-funding their care home placement.

If your care is being arranged by adult social care services, you are allowed your choice of accommodation provided it is suitable for your needs and with certain other restrictions. Your right to choose your accommodation is described in detail on p246. If the NHS is fully funding your care you do not have the same right to choose the home you are in, but you should complain if you think the NHS body arranging your care is being unreasonably restrictive (see p40).

If you are unhappy with the home you are in

Even if you are initially happy with the home you choose, you may find that problems later arise. The home might change hands and the new management have different ideas. Or there may be some aspect which you did not consider when you moved in. It is usually best to sort out problems informally as far as possible. If you cannot, then use the home's complaints procedure. All care homes must have a complaints procedure which is clear and accessible. Complaints must be responded to within a maximum of 28 days. If this does not resolve the problem, then:

- if your complaint is about the standard of care you are receiving, you should be informed about how you can take your complaint to the regulatory body (see p237);
- if you are in a local authority home or adult social care services have arranged your care, you can also use their complaints procedure if you have a complaint against the home they have provided or arranged (see p40). In Scotland, if your complaint is about the standard of nursing in a home providing nursing and adult social care services have arranged your care, they have the responsibility of ensuring that the care is delivered properly.[7] In England and Wales, nursing care is arranged by the NHS so if you have a complaint about the standard of nursing you should complain to the NHS, although you can still complain to adult social care services if other aspects of your care are unsatisfactory. If the NHS has arranged your care in a home providing nursing care then you can use the NHS complaints procedures (see p40).

The different types of accommodation

English court cases have established that adult social care services can arrange your accommodation in ordinary housing,[8] but in the vast majority of cases care is provided in either local authority homes or independent care homes which are registered and regulated by the appropriate national body (see p237). Some of the independent homes provide nursing care in addition to personal care. Independent homes can be provided by private individuals, private companies or voluntary or not-for-profit organisations. Some adult social care services are either closing their homes or transferring them to the independent sector. As long as there are sufficient independent homes in the area, local authorities do not have to provide them directly.[9] Compare the costs of local authority homes with those of independent sector homes, as local authority homes can be more expensive.

All care homes are required to be registered and inspected by CQC, CSSIW or the Care Commission depending on where you live. The regulation of care homes in England and Wales, is governed by the Care Standards Act (CSA) 2000, which sets national minimum standards which must be adhered to.

Homes which provide nursing care can be run by NHS bodies, or privately by individuals or organisations. Some homes providing nursing are run by not-for-profit organisations. NHS bodies can arrange your accommodation in homes which provide nursing care or hospices. It is a registration requirement that there must be a suitably qualified registered nurse on the premises at all times.

3. **Fees which are fully paid by the state**

The amount of public funding you can receive towards your care home costs is based on a number of variables, and some people receive different amounts of help at different times. The main forms of state help are when your fees are paid by the NHS (which is free and not based on your income or capital); when you get help towards paying your fees through the local authority (which is based on your income and capital); and when a part of your fees in a home providing registered nurse care are met by the NHS. The system in Scotland is different in that although your accommodation and living costs are means-tested, there are set levels of payment towards your personal and nursing care costs if you are 65 or over, and for your nursing care alone if you are under 65. You may still qualify for fully funded care paid for by the NHS if your condition means you remain the responsibility of the NHS.

At the time of writing, the Government is consulting on a forthcoming Green Paper on long-term care and support for older people, with a focus on how long-term care can be funded.

This section looks at who can get full help with their fees in a care home from the state. Although not many people are able to get their fees paid in full by the state, for the individuals concerned this is very important. There are four groups who can get their accommodation and care free of charge in a care home:
- people in a home providing nursing arranged and funded in full by the NHS;
- people receiving intermediate care in a care home (see p242);

- people receiving aftercare in a care home who have previously been detained for treatment in hospital for their psychiatric condition (see p242);
- war pensioners who need skilled nursing care because of disability (see p129).

The responsibility of the NHS to fully fund care in a home providing nursing care

If you want the NHS to fund in full your place in a home providing nursing care you will need to show that you come within the eligibility criteria for continuing NHS health care, rehabilitation or palliative care. Guidance suggests that such options should always be considered[10] but low numbers of places in homes providing nursing are arranged and funded by the NHS.

If your assessment (see p34) shows that you need continuing NHS health care (called continuing inpatient care in Scotland) which can either be in hospital or in a home providing nursing, then your local NHS body should arrange it.[11] It is free like any stay in hospital. You are still considered to be a hospital inpatient and so have limited choice about which home you can go to. Likewise, you will be treated as a hospital inpatient for social security purposes, so your benefits may be reduced (see p189). It may also be appropriate to receive NHS fully funded care in your own home.[12]

In 2007, a national framework and accompanying directions were implemented providing a national criteria for every Strategic Health Authority (SHA) or local Primary Care Trust (PCT) in England to use to define who is eligible for NHS continuing healthcare. Previously, each SHA had its own eligibility criteria. This national framework should be a common process, with national tools to support decision-making.

In England, eligibility for NHS continuing healthcare depends on whether your primary need is a health need. You may demonstrate a 'primary health need' if you:

- require frequent supervision by a member of the NHS multi-disciplinary team;
- require routine use of specialist healthcare equipment under supervision of NHS staff;
- have a rapidly deteriorating or unstable medical, physical or mental health condition and requires regular supervision by a member of the NHS multi-disciplinary team;
- are in the final stages of a terminal illness.[13]

It is not just the severity or diagnosis of your condition that should be taken into consideration, but the type of care required to meet the needs resulting from your health condition.

Even if you do not come under the criteria for fully funded care, the NHS still has the responsibility for providing care that you need over and above what the care home can provide (eg, physiotherapy, occupational therapy and specialist equipment) in the same way as if you were in any other setting.[14]

In Wales and Scotland you meet the national eligibility criteria for fully funded care in a home providing nursing care if you:

- have a complex medical, nursing or other clinical need, or need frequent but not easily predictable interventions under the supervision of a consultant or specialist nurse or other NHS team member; *or*
- need routine specialist health care equipment or treatments which need specialist staff; *or*
- have a rapidly degenerating or unstable condition; *or*
- have a prognosis which suggests you are likely to die in the very near future.[15]

Directions in England require the NHS to assess whether hospital inpatients qualify for continuing NHS health care services before involving adult social care services in the discharge procedure. The outcome should be recorded on your notes and you should be notified of the decision and of your right to request a review of it (see p42).[16] Further directions require PCTs to take reasonable steps to provide assessments to individuals currently in settings other than acute hospital beds.[17]

If you think the NHS should be responsible for your care in a care home, it is useful to have a copy of the eligibility criteria – get a copy from your local NHS body, adult social care services or hospital.

If you are about to be discharged from hospital

A stay in hospital often precedes the need to go into a care home. It is important to know what should happen before you are discharged, including assessments to establish whether you are eligible for any assistance from the NHS or adult social care services.

The NHS must carry out an assessment of your eligibility for continuing NHS health care services before notifying adult social care services that you may need community care services.[18] Once adult social care services have been notified that you are ready to be discharged, they assess you and arrange suitable services for you within strict time limits and are fined if these are not met. The DH also publishes guidance on good practice in hospital discharges called *Discharge from hospital: pathway process and practice*.[19] Guidance on hospital discharge has also been issued in Wales and Scotland.[20] In all three countries the guidance emphasises the need for the different agencies involved in the discharge process to work together. You, your family and carers should be given information about the process and be actively involved in it.

Although you do not have the right to stay in hospital indefinitely, if it has been decided that you no longer need hospital care you do have the right to refuse to be discharged into a care home. A small number of people under mental health legislation do not have this right. Other options should be explored but, if you reject these, it may be necessary to implement your discharge home with a package of health and social care. You can also ask for a review of the decision not to provide you with continuing NHS health care services. You will probably be charged for your social care in England and Wales, and in Scotland if you are under 65. You might have to pay for any assistance (eg, shopping or housework) in Scotland which does not come under the definition of personal care (see p244).

See p42 for details of your rights for a review or appeal if you disagree with the decision to discharge you. In addition, you can use the health and social services complaints procedures (p40).

Part funding by the NHS

A number of NHS bodies offer other arrangements, often via adult social care services, whereby the health body will meet some of the costs of a home providing nursing care. This is often referred to as 50/50 funding. This is different from the NHS payments made for nursing care described on p239.

If the NHS is prepared to pay some of your care home fees, it is worth checking whether you should in fact have all of your fees met, as it may be that you are borderline for fitting into the eligibility criteria for continuing NHS health care.

If your benefits are affected by such an arrangement it is important to appeal.

Ordinary residence

If you are taken ill and are in hospital, away from home or in a specialist unit in a different health area, the health body in which you are registered with your GP will normally be responsible for your care. In Wales, the Local Health Board where the care home is will pay any NHS costs. If you move to a care home outside the area of your current PCT you should register with a GP in the new area. The PCT for the new area then becomes responsible for meeting your primary care needs.[21] At the time of writing, the Scottish Government is consulting on proposed changes to ordinary residence regulations and guidance.[22]

Fully funded intermediate care: England and Wales

In England and Wales, if you need intermediate care (see p58) provided in a care home, you should not have to pay for it. In order to achieve this, local authorities should agree with their health service partners that the NHS should have underlying responsibility for intermediate care in care homes. Such care would typically last no longer than six weeks.[23] Adult social care services in England cannot charge for intermediate care services.[24]

The responsibility to fund aftercare: England and Wales

If you have been compulsorily detained in hospital for treatment under certain sections of the Mental Health Act 1983 (MHA)[25] and have left hospital, both health and adult social care services have a duty under s117 of that Act to provide aftercare services until such time as it is agreed by both that such services are no longer needed.[26] Local authorities have no power to charge for services provided under section 117 MHA so if you are placed in a care home under section 117 MHA, it will be free.[27] Aftercare services are not defined but can include residential services.[28]

The High Court[29] has addressed the question of how long aftercare services continue, especially if you still need care in a care home. It found that there may be cases where, in due course, there will be no need for aftercare services for the person's mental condition but services are still needed for other needs such as physical disability. Each case will have to be examined on the facts. Where the resident has dementia, the Court found it difficult to see how the mental condition could improve to the point where aftercare services would no longer be needed. Seek advice if your condition has not improved and you still need to remain in a care home, but the authorities have decided that you no longer need aftercare and start charging you. Settling in a care home does not in itself mean that you no longer need residential aftercare services.[30] An Ombudsman found maladministration where a local authority retrospectively decided aftercare had ended (in this case after the resident had died) from a certain date.[31]

Effects on benefits

In spite of the fact that you do not currently have to pay anything towards your fees in a care home, you can still receive the full rate of income support and other benefits, although it is likely that your attendance allowance (or disability living allowance care component) will not be paid (see p346).

The responsibility to fund aftercare: Scotland

In Scotland, if you are or have been suffering from a mental disorder it is the duty of the social work department to provide aftercare.[32] Accommodation provided as part of aftercare under s25 Mental Health (Care and Treatment) (Scotland) Act 2003 comes under the same charging procedures as are described in Chapter 10 so you are normally charged for your accommodation and living costs, but not your personal or nursing care.

---

4. Help with fees from adult social care services

If you are not able to get your care home fees fully funded in any of the ways described above, you may still be eligible for some help towards your fees. Adult social care services can act as gatekeepers to funding for care in care homes.

Adult social care services responsibilities: England and Wales

When adult social care services provides or arranges accommodation in a care home for either a temporary or permanent stay, it is nearly always under the

National Assistance Act 1948 but see p24 for services arranged under s117 Mental Health Act 1983. Adult social care services have a *duty*[33] to provide or arrange accommodation if:

- you are 18 or over;[34] *and*
- you need care and attention due to:
  - age;
  - illness;
  - disability; *or*
  - any other circumstance (which specifically includes mental disorder, and drug and alcohol dependency); *and*
- it is not otherwise available to you; *and*
- you normally live in that local authority area; *or*
- you do not but your need is urgent.

Adult social care services have a *power* to provide or arrange care in a care home if you:

- are pregnant or have recently had a baby (it does not matter if you are under 18); *or*
- ordinarily live in another authority's area, provided that authority agrees.[35]

Adult social care services also have the power to provide hostel accommodation for disabled people who work in workshops provided the local authority.[36]

Adult social care services have national rules for working out the amount you will have to contribute towards the cost of accommodation and social care that is provided. Care provided by a registered nurse is the responsibility of the NHS (see p252).

Social work responsibilities: Scotland

Social work departments have a *duty* to provide or arrange this kind of accommodation if you are:

- 18 or over;
- in need[37] of community care services due to needing care and attention because of infirmity or age;
- have an illness or mental disorder or are substantially handicapped by disability; *or*
- in need of care and attention because of drug or alcohol dependency or release from prison or other detention.

'Free' personal and nursing care in Scotland

The Community Care and Health (Scotland) Act 2002 prohibits local authorities from charging for social and personal care provided by them. See Appendix 4 for the definition of the personal and social care for which charges should not be made. This means that social work departments are responsible for certain costs of your care regardless of whether you have over £22,500 (the capital limit in Scotland) or an income large enough to meet your care home fees as long as you need such care. For people aged 65 and over, the social work department is responsible for paying £149 a week if you need personal care and £216 a week if you need both personal and nursing care. If you are under 65 then it is just responsible for paying £67. This amount is paid direct to the home.

If you have over £22,500, you should be able to choose the way the care is contracted. You can choose to contract for the accommodation and living costs yourself with the local authority contracting for the personal and/or nursing care, or the local authority can contract for the whole of the placement on your behalf and then charge you the full cost of the accommodation and living charges.

If you have less than £22,500, the national charging rules apply, but where after a financial assessment a local authority's contribution is less than £149 a week (or £216 if you require care in a home providing nursing), it should be increased to that amount.

Deciding if you need help from adult social care services

Before you can get any help with your fees, adult social care services will first assess whether you need care in a care home based on its eligibility criteria for such care. See Chapter 2 for details about assessment and eligibility criteria.

If adult social care services decide you need care in a home providing nursing care, they must obtain the consent of the appropriate local NHS body before arranging your accommodation. In an emergency, adult social care services can place you in a home without the consent of the NHS but this must be obtained as soon as possible.[38]

If your situation is very urgent adult social care services can place you in a care home without an assessment[39] and do one as soon as possible afterwards.

If you want help from adult social care services with funding your stay in a care home but are told you do not need such care, or that you only need a care home that does not provide nursing when you think you need nursing care, you can complain and ask for a reassessment. It is important to get a copy of your needs assessment to show why you need the particular care you think you do. Any medical evidence you can get to support you will be helpful.

Accommodation arranged by adult social care services

If adult social care services have agreed that you need care in a care home, the following points should be considered.

How quickly should accommodation be arranged?

Once adult social care services decide that you need a care home placement arranged for you, it should be done as soon as you have found a suitable place and

9

you are able to move in. There may be delays if there are no vacancies in the home of your choice and you might need to move into another home while you are waiting. Much will depend on your circumstances and whether you can arrange suitable care at home while you are waiting for a vacancy, or whether you can stay in hospital during this time.

Delays can occur if adult social care services do not have the resources to fund you and you may be placed on a waiting list. But adult social care services cannot use lack of resources as a reason for not making the arrangements once a decision has been made that you need the care.[40] They have a duty to provide the accommodation from the date the decision is made.[41] Adult social care services should make arrangements without 'undue delay' and if there is going to be a delay they should ensure that suitable arrangements are in place to meet your needs and those of your carer.[42] Guidance states that where individuals need to wait, their access to the most appropriate service should be prioritised according to their eligible needs solely, and councils should ensure that in the interim adequate alternative services are provided. Individuals who are waiting should not be asked to pay more than their assessed financial contribution to meet the costs of alternative residential care services arranged or suggested by the council.[43] An Ombudsman found maladministration where a local authority placed a person on a waiting list although there was a place available.[44]

Complain if you are waiting for funding from adult social care services and have been told that the delay is because of lack of resources.

The right to choose accommodation

Directions issued by government[45] give you the right to choose which home you live in as long as:

- it is suitable to your assessed needs;
- a bed is available;
- the person in charge is willing to provide the accommodation subject to the usual terms and conditions laid down by adult social care services;
- it would not cost adult social care services more than it would normally cost to meet your assessed needs.

You also have the right to go into accommodation that is more expensive than adult social care services would be prepared to pay for provided you have a third party to meet the difference in cost. In some cases you can use your own money to meet the difference. See Chapter 14 for how top-ups work.

If you are already in a home and want to move, you can do so on the same basis as anyone moving into a home for the first time.

If adult social care services decide not to arrange accommodation in the home of your choice, they must have a clear, justifiable reason which relates to the criteria of the direction.[46] Adult social care services should not try to restrict your choice just to suit local arrangements – eg, if there are vacancies in one of their own homes or they have a block booking with an independent home.

Having a number of homes to choose from

You should be able to exercise reasonable choice in where you live. Adult social care services must not set arbitrary ceilings on the amount they are willing to pay for care homes, and must not routinely expect third parties to make up the difference. They must be able to show that there are homes which could provide you with the services you need within the usual cost.[47] If you think that your choice has been limited because only a few homes are within the cost adult social care services will normally pay, seek advice.

Choosing a more expensive home

If you enter a home which costs more than the local authority would usually agree to contract for, guidance explains the circumstances under which the local authority should meet the extra cost. If you have to enter a more expensive home, because there are no homes at the local authority rate or because your assessed needs require a more expensive home, the local authority should agree to pay more than usual.[48] If suitable accommodation is available at the usual cost but you choose a more expensive home, the local authority can require a third party to make a top-up payment.

Something which is very important to you should be considered as part of your assessed needs – eg, it may be important to be in a home which respects your religious beliefs, or where there are staff who speak your language, or where you can remain in close contact with your friends. Adult social care services have to take into account your psychological and social needs when making their assessment. In some cases, a very strongly held preference could be considered to be a psychological or social need.

If fees increase by more than adult social care services will pay

Sometimes homes which have been within the adult social care services level of fees increase them to above the amount adult social care services will pay for your level of need. In such circumstances you could:

- ask for a reassessment to see if adult social care services agree that it is an integral part of your needs to remain in that home; *and/or*
- find a third party to meet the difference; *or*
- ask adult social care services to negotiate on your behalf for the home to only charge what adult social care services will pay; *or*
- move to another home with fees which adult social care services will pay.

If the home is meeting your needs and you are settled there, ask for an assessment about the level of risk involved in your having to move. This, along with your social and psychological needs, should be taken into account in your assessment.

If adult social care services agree that it is part of your assessed need to stay in that particular home, they should meet the full cost.

If they disagree, you will need a third party to top up the fee, usually a relative. Ask adult social care services to help you find a third party. Adult social care services will remain responsible for the full fees and will arrange with the third party for her/his contribution to be paid. Adult social care services cannot vary their usual cost based on length of residence in a home and so expect certain residents' relatives to pay larger top-ups according to how long the residents have been there.[49]

The home should not make its own arrangements with either you or your relatives outside of the adult social care services contract in order to have the increase in fees met. Adult social care services must be involved as they are responsible for the fees (see p250).

If you do not want to move it is important to seek help so that every avenue can be explored – eg, seeing if the home will only charge you what adult social care services will pay. You could complain to local councillors and your MP, if you think that adult social care services should pay the full cost. You may wish to seek advice about whether Articles 2 or 8 of the Convention on Human Rights may help you (see p46).

Moving into a home in another area

If you want to move into a home in another area, you should be allowed to exercise your choice to do so. However, the cost of homes varies around the country and you may have difficulties if the area you are moving to only has homes which are much more expensive than your adult social care services will normally pay. The direction tells adult social care services that where the need to be in another area is an integral part of your assessed needs (eg, being near relatives), they should agree to pay more than their usual amount if necessary.[50] A blanket policy of refusing to pay more than the usual amount could be challenged as it implies adult social care services is not prepared to look at your assessed needs.

Cross-border placements

It can be difficult if you wish to move into a care home in another part of the UK. At the time of writing, new protocols are being developed to deal with placements between England, Wales and Scotland to take into account the different arrangements for free registered nursing care in England and Wales and free personal and nursing care in Scotland and the regulatory provisions in all three countries. Seek advice if this applies to you.

Seeing if you like the home (trial periods)

Normally you are given a little time to see if you like the home you have moved into and there is a trial period before any permanent decision is made. You need to be clear whether adult social care services regards this trial period as a:

- temporary stay (ie, you might go home); *or*
- permanent stay (you need to live in a care home, even if you decide not to stay in the current one).

This is important as it will affect the way you are charged (see p264) and it could also affect your benefits (see p337). You also need to be sure that adult social care services and the DWP are treating you in the same way and that you agree with the basis for your trial period. The decision whether you are temporary or permanent should be with your agreement, and should be considered to be temporary where there is uncertainty that permanent admission is required.[51]

Guidance also states that a stay which is expected to be permanent might turn out to be temporary and equally a stay which is temporary might turn out to be permanent. In the former case, it suggests that it would be unreasonable to continue to apply the rules as if you were permanent, especially those about the way your own home is treated. If your stay is temporary but later becomes permanent, you should only be charged as a permanent resident from the date that decision is made.[52]

Moving to a different adult social care services area

Sometimes moving into a care home means moving to a different area of the country. In order to avoid disputes between different local authorities about who should be responsible for helping towards the cost of your care, there is guidance about 'ordinary residence'.[53] It is not defined and so does not follow the rules for habitual residence used by the DWP. If you have freely chosen to move into an area with the intention of settling there, you are 'ordinarily resident' in that area. However, if your care in a care home is provided by adult social care services, you are deemed as continuing to be ordinarily resident in that authority's area even if the home is in another area. But if you move to another authority's area and make your own arrangements with a care home, you are ordinarily resident in the area where that home is. If you later need any help with the funding, you should apply to adult social care services where the home is.

If you are told by adult social care services that you are the responsibility of another authority, you should not be left without help during the time it takes to sort out which authority is responsible for you. Seek advice if this happens. If you have no settled residence, have come from another local authority or from abroad,[54] adult social care services where you are now should provisionally accept responsibility and provide you with the services you need.[55] Some people from abroad come under provisions which debar certain individuals from being able to access care services including residential care. If you are refused care on these grounds, seek advice from a specialist agency dealing with nationality and immigration issues.

The Health and Social Care Act 2008 has implications for the resolution of disputes about ordinary residence. Where previously the councils involved had to make representations to the Secretary of State for Health and possibly then to the courts, the new Act modifies these arrangements making it clear that arrangements can be made to resolve disputes between English and Welsh authorities.[56]

Paying your share of the fees

Once adult social care services have made the arrangements for your care, they will work out how much you need to pay according to the rules which are described in the following chapters. Adult social care services are liable for the full fees (or in the case of their own homes, the cost of running them). The cost to adult social care services known as the 'standard charge'. If you have more than the capital limit (see p291) or a high income, you will have to pay the standard charge. If you cannot afford the standard charge, you will be assessed to decide how much you should pay.[57]

Usually adult social care services will pay the home the full cost and you pay your contribution direct to adult social care services. There may be advantages to this method of payment; the home does not have to know how much your contribution is and any third party payment has to be paid through the local authority.

You can pay your contribution direct to the home with adult social care services paying the remainder, sometimes known as 'net payment' (see p320). This can only be done if there is agreement to do so from all three parties – ie, you, the home and adult social care services.[58] If you would prefer to pay direct to adult social care services, you cannot be made to pay your contribution direct to the home.

Adult social care services remain liable for the whole amount of the fees. If you do not pay your share, they will pay the full amount but will take steps to recover your contribution from you. They will also be liable for any top-up payment should this not be paid. Adult social care services should make a contract with the home specifying what is covered by the contracted fees. You should receive a statement of the terms and conditions of the contract. It is useful to know what the home should provide within the contract and what is considered to be extra services.

NHS services to care homes

If you are getting help with fees from adult social care services and are in a care home, you should still receive NHS services free of charge. You should be able to receive community health services such as district nursing, incontinence supplies, chiropody and specialist equipment even if your care is purchased by the local authority. Your eligibility for these services should be assessed on the same basis as if you were in your own home, according to local criteria. Some residents find they have to pay out of their personal expenses allowance (PEA – see Chapter 13) for adequate supplies of incontinence pads or chiropody services. Guidance stresses that the PEA should not be spent on services that have been assessed as necessary to meet your needs by the council or the NHS, and further that any need for incontinence supplies (and in England the guidance also includes chiropody services) should be fully reflected in the care plan.[59] Age Concern Cymru have a campaign 'Little steps can make a big difference' for clearer eligibility criteria for chiropody, due to ever tightening eligibility criteria and different services in different parts of the country, and for free foot care for all older people in Wales.

If you receive help with fees from adult social care services, you should qualify for full help for those NHS services which incur a charge via health benefits (see p76).

Paying for extras

You may wish to pay for extra services supplied by the home which are not part of the basic care package contracted for by adult social care services. Extra services might include your choice of newspaper or magazine, or having a hairdresser visit the home. In England, the Department of Health's view is that as long as you have the legal capacity to do so, and you are not facing any pressure from either the home or adult social care services, then you can enter into an arrangement with the home owner to provide extra services outside the package to meet your assessed needs.[60] Before you enter into such a contract you should be clear that you know what will be provided under adult social care services' contract. Some local authority contracts specifically exclude owners of care homes entering into any contract in relation to you outside of the local authority's own contract. This is to avoid the possibility of owners entering into private contracts with residents or relatives to boost the amount of money they receive for looking after you.

Sometimes adult social care services arrange non-residential services even if you live in a care home – eg, daytime activities. If they have been negotiated as part of the care home package, they should be included in the standard charge. If it is a separate package, adult social care services can decide whether or not to charge you under its discretionary charging powers (see p76). However, as you only have a PEA and any disregarded income available, the charge, if any, should be minimal.[61]

Other help with the fees

There is nothing to stop you getting help from friends and relatives. In some cases, if you have not been assessed as needing care in a care home you may need to turn to them. Relatives may feel they should help with your fees if there is a waiting list for adult social care services funding, but you should be careful of allowing adult social care services to avoid their duties if they have assessed you as needing care in a care home (see p243).

5. NHS-funded nursing care (England and Wales)

'NHS-funded nursing care' is funding paid by the NHS to care homes registered to provide nursing care. The payment is made by the Primary Care Trust (PCT) in which the home is based.

In June 2007, the Department of Health (DH) published the *National Framework for NHS Continuing Healthcare and NHS-funded Nursing Care*. The National Framework applies in England only but most of the rules also apply in Wales, although there are some differences. The National Framework is supported by tools and checklists to help with decision-making – they can be found on the DH website.

The registered nurse assessment

The definition of what nursing care the NHS pays for is laid down in legislation,[62] and covers the care provided by a registered nurse and time spent monitoring, supervising or delegating care by the registered nurse. It does not cover the time spent by other care staff undertaking the care that has been delegated to them by a registered nurse.

Under the *National Framework for NHS Continuing Healthcare and NHS-funded Nursing Care* there is a single eligibility assessment. The first stage is usually to have your care needs screened against a standard checklist by a nurse, doctor, other healthcare professional or social worker. They will use the checklist to decide if you should be referred for a full assessment. If your initial screening shows that you should be referred, a multidisciplinary team of health and social care professionals will carry out a comprehensive assessment of all your care needs, using a 'decision support tool'. As well as your nursing care needs, they will assess your physical, mental, psychological and emotional needs.

If you're not referred for a full assessment after your initial screening, your case will be reviewed three months later.

Your need for registered nursing care should be reviewed three months after the first assessment and following this every 12 months. You can ask for a review or an assessment for continuing care funding at any time if your condition has worsened. To ask for a review or a new assessment, you need to contact the nursing home co-ordinator – the manager of your care home or your GP will be able to tell you where s/he is based.

Payments to care homes

In England, prior to the introduction of the National Framework, there were three nursing bands of low, medium and high, where care home residents received either £40, £87 or £139 a week from the NHS, depending on their level of need.

Now, those residents who were previously on the low or medium band have been moved onto a flat rate payment of £106.30 a week. Those on the high band will remain on this until they are reassessed, where depending on the outcome, may either receive fully funded NHS continuing healthcare if their needs have increased, receive the flat rate if their needs have reduced, or remain on the higher band if their needs fall between the two. The higher band has been increased to £146.30 a week.

In Wales, each local health board has been given the responsibility for setting its own amount for NHS-funded nursing care payment. This means that the amount may vary across the country, although most of the health boards have opted for a set rate of £117 a week.

Once you have been assessed, the PCT will make the payment to the care home. In England if you are funded by the local authority, it is likely that the local authority will still pay the fees but it is doing so on behalf of the NHS.

The care home should only charge you for the accommodation and personal care that you receive and your fees should reflect this. You should have a written contract which makes clear what is included in the fees. The fees should be broken down to show the fees payable for accommodation and food, nursing and personal care. If you fund your own care, the home should account for how the registered nurse care contribution has been used or make arrangements for the amount you pay to be reduced by that amount.

Hospital stays

If you are admitted to hospital from a care home, the PCT does not pay nursing care costs during your stay. PCTs are encouraged to pay a retainer to safeguard care home places while residents are in hospital.[63]

Incontinence supplies and other equipment

The NHS is responsible for providing incontinence products, such as pads, to those who meet local eligibility criteria, including care home residents. In England, the provision of incontinence supplies is in addition to the registered nursing contribution. In Wales, the weekly registered nursing care payment includes the cost of incontinence products. In Scotland, incontinence supplies are provided on prescription.

You should be able to receive the full range of equipment you are assessed as needing which is not supplied by the home as part of its regulatory requirements. The equipment you need should be specified in your care plan.

Effects on benefits and tax credits

There should be no effect on any benefit or tax credits you are paid if you are funding your own care. Regulations have been introduced to ensure that your entitlement to state benefits, including attendance allowance and disability living allowance care component, is not affected by the NHS paying your registered nursing care costs.[64] Local authority funding may affect your benefits (see Chapter 17).

6. **Paying the full fees yourself**

If you are not entitled to help from adult social care services or free care from the NHS, you have to pay the full fees yourself. This means either that you make your own contract with the home or that, in some circumstances, adult social care services will make the contract for you but charge you the full cost. Section 5 explains the help you get towards your registered nurse costs if you are in a home providing nursing.

When adult social care services charges you the full cost

If you have capital over the upper capital limit, you can choose to make your own arrangements. You are entitled to a needs assessment even if you can afford the fees yourself. Adult social care services must be satisfied that you are *able* to make your own arrangements with a care home, or have others who are *willing and able* to do so for you.[65] If you are not able and there is no one else who is willing and able, adult social care services must arrange your care in a care home.

In Scotland, authorities are required to make the arrangements for your care in a care home if you are assessed as needing such care, regardless of whether you have capital above the upper capital limit.[66]

If adult social care services arranges your care, they charge you the full cost until your capital is reduced to the capital limit for your country (see p291) – although the full cost does not include nursing care or, in Scotland, personal care if you are 65 or over.

If adult social care services have decided that you have deliberately deprived yourself of income or capital to get help with your fees, they may decide to charge you the full cost.

Temporary or interim help from adult social care services

If you have a property or capital which is not immediately available, you may be able to get help with your fees on a temporary or interim basis. You will normally contribute towards the cost of your care from your income during this period and then repay the balance of the cost to adult social care services once the capital is realised. See p272 for details about the deferred payments schemes that are available if you have a property. Remember that for the first 12 weeks of a permanent stay in a care home the local authority has to disregard the value of your property (see p292). If you own a property and have less than the upper capital limit in other savings, the local authority should make arrangements for you. You will not have to repay the authority for assistance provided during this period. At the end of the first 12 weeks you can either make your own arrangements or use the deferred payments scheme. It may be to your financial advantage to have the arrangements made by the local authority. Complain if adult social care services fail to inform you about the 12-week disregard.

Making your own arrangements with a care home

If you make your own arrangements with a care home, you will need to make your own contract with them. In addition to all the points everybody needs to consider when choosing a home (see p236), it is very important to be clear about, and have written information on, all the financial implications. These include:

- exactly what is included in the fees – eg, laundry, hairdressing, newspapers and chiropody (but ask if you can get chiropody from the local NHS body before you agree to pay for private chiropody in the fees) are sometimes included in the fees but sometimes the cost of services are not included. The costs of continence supplies should not be included in the fees as these are supplied by the NHS;
- whether a deposit is required, what it is for and when is it returnable;
- how often the fees are reviewed and what notice is given;
- the minimum period of notice you have to give to leave the home;
- whether you can have a trial period;
- what effect a period in hospital or away on holiday would have on your fees. In the case of a care home providing nursing care, you also need to know the extent of the NHS payment for registered nursing care while you are away.[67]

Although it is not always easy to ask, it is also important to be sure what payment the home would continue to expect if you die, and how soon your room would need to be cleared. It is important that relatives are aware of this to avoid any dispute after your death.

The Care Standards Act 2000 requires homes to provide written contracts including much of the information suggested above. Legislation in 2006 clarified the information to be provided by registered establishments in the service user guide about fees and related services. It also clarifies the information they should provide to current residents about fees and increases.[68] It also introduced requirements that registered providers establish a system for evaluating the quality of their service and that they provide a quality assurance assessment when required to do so. Providers also have to produce an improvement plan when requested to do so by the Care Quality Commission.

Remember a contract is an agreement and to some extent you can negotiate the terms and conditions. The Office of Fair Trading (OFT) investigated care home contracts and found that standard terms contained in some providers' contracts were unfair. A standard term may be unfair if it creates an imbalance in the rights and obligations of the parties to the contract. If so, the term is not enforceable. The OFT has produced a guide to contract terms for care home residents.[69] Seek advice if you are unsure about the terms of your contract.

You should still be able to get any NHS services which are supplied in the community, if they are not provided as part of the registration requirements of the home.

Guidance also provides a comprehensive list of the required standards for care homes.[70]

The level of the fees

Research has shown that people making their own arrangements may be charged more for exactly the same facilities as those residents who are funded by adult social care services.[71] Homes will sometimes negotiate fees, so it is useful to know what adult social care services would normally pay for someone with your needs to compare this to the fees of the homes you visit.

If you are likely to need help from adult social care services in the future, it is important to establish whether the home will drop its fees to the adult social care services level if it takes over the arrangements. Some homes are prepared to do this, but if not you may have to find a third party to meet the difference (see Chapter 14).

Getting help if you have been funding yourself

Even if you make your own arrangements with a care home you may later need to approach adult social care services to get help with funding once your capital approaches the capital limit. You will normally need to approach the local authority where you now live. Adult social care services will assess you to see if you need the type of care you are getting. This may take some time so it is worth approaching adult social care services a few months before your capital reaches the capital limit so they have time to assess your needs and undertake a financial assessment. Adult social care services have been told that when approached by a resident who's capital is approaching the capital limit, they should undertake the assessment as soon as reasonably practicable and if necessary take over the arrangements to ensure that the resident is not forced to use capital below the limit.[72] Guidance in England has reminded local authorities that once aware of a resident's circumstances any undue delay in assessment or funding would be in breach of statutory duties, therefore the local authority could be liable to reimburse the resident.[73]

If you are over 60, you may qualify for pension credit even if you cannot yet get help from adult social care services as there is no upper capital limit for this benefit (see p158).

Occasionally adult social care services will decide you do not need care in a care home and will neither make the arrangements nor help to fund you. If they do not think you need nursing care you may need to move to a care home which does not provide nursing. This does not happen very often. If it does, ask for a review of the assessment to make sure adult social care services have taken all your needs into account. You should also seek advice.

Couples

If you are one of a couple with a joint account of over £46,000 and you are funding yourself in a care home, it may be worth considering splitting your account. This is because you will not get help from adult social care services until your joint capital is down to £46,000 (when you are counted as each having £23,000). For example, if you have a joint account of £56,000 you will need to spend £10,000 on fees before you can get help. If you split your account so you each have £28,000, you will only need to spend £5,000 before you can get help. Different capital limits apply in Scotland and Wales (see p291).

Getting funding from the NHS

If your condition worsens while you are in a care home you may meet the National Framework eligibility criteria for NHS funding (see p240). If you spend time as a hospital inpatient you should be assessed under the hospital discharge rules (see p241).[74] You may continue to be nursed through your worsening condition in your current home without going to hospital. If so, ask your GP for an assessment to see whether you now come under the eligibility criteria for continuing NHS health care. If you do, then the NHS should take over the funding of your care, although it may not agree to do so at the home you are in.

---

7. Dealing with your money in a care home

If you are able to manage your financial affairs you should remain in control of them and pay the charges yourself, unless you decide to appoint an attorney to do this for you. In this way, you can be sure the correct charge is paid and that you keep your personal expenses allowance.

Benefits are usually paid into a bank, building society or post office account. Depending upon the type of account you have, you should be able to set up a standing order or direct debit to pay your fees. Alternatively, your benefits can be collected from the post office on your behalf.

If you cannot manage your financial affairs

If you are unable to give adult social care services the information needed to assess your charge because you lack the mental capacity, then they have to find out if anyone has power of attorney, or if anyone has been appointed as a deputy (a financial power of attorney, a financial intervenor, a withdrawer or appointeeship in Scotland). If no one has taken on any of these roles, adult social care services cannot properly financially assess you until someone has been duly authorised to act for you. In practice, many authorities will make the arrangements for your care and give an estimate of the likely costs to you. They are unlikely to refuse to make the arrangements just because you have no one to give them financial details.

If there is no one suitable to act for you, adult social care services may become your deputy (guardian in Scotland), depending on your financial circumstances, but this would only be as a last resort.

There are some very significant legal differences in Scotland regarding the management of another person's affairs, with a wide variety of different legal appointments possible under the Adults with Incapacity (Scotland) Act 2000. The court system is also very different from England and Wales and legal advice should be sought about these matters.

Appointeeship

The Secretary of State can authorise someone to act on your behalf in relation to benefits if you cannot claim for yourself or if you can no longer deal with your financial affairs.[75] Your appointee takes on all the rights and responsibilities of a claimant – eg, notifying a change of circumstances. Your appointee is responsible for making sure the benefits received are spent on your behalf. If you are in a care home this includes ensuring that the benefits are used to pay your assessed charge. The manager or owner of your care home can act as your appointee if no one else is available.[76]

Appointeeship only gives authority to deal with your benefits and any small amount of capital which has accumulated from those benefits. It *does not* give any authority to deal with your other income or capital. In England and Wales, if you have other income or capital, there would need to be an application to the Court of Protection through the Office of the Public Guardian. However, the Office of the Public Guardian has indicated that if you have savings from benefits of no more than one month's accommodation costs and about £500 as a cash float, no other authority is normally needed.

Authority to access funds (Scotland)

In Scotland, carers and other individuals (but not social work staff) can obtain authority to access your funds to meet day-to-day living expenses such as the regular bills if you live at home or payments for care in a care home. Under the Access to Funds scheme, an application is made to the Office of the Public Guardian (Scotland) (OPG), the authority responsible for managing and supervising access to accounts. The OPG authorises how much money may be transferred from your account to a designated account, and issues a certificate to the person who is allowed to open the designated account and access the funds. The OPG is able to request records. Authority to access funds in this way is usually set for three years at the first application, although this may be reduced or extended.[77]

Third party mandates

With a third party mandate, you can instruct your bank or building society to give another person authorised access to your money. You must still have mental capacity to make such a decision as you need to be very clear on the level of access they can have and be able to monitor what they do. It is therefore very important that you trust the person involved. The agreement can be terminated by you at any time. A third party mandate agreement becomes invalid if, after setting it, up you then lose mental capacity.

Ordinary Power of Attorney

An Ordinary Power of Attorney is a legal document authorizing one or more people you trust, such as a friend, neighbour or member of the family to act on your behalf to deal with your money, finances and property. It can be a temporary arrangement that can be set up if you are in hospital or on holiday, for example. You, the 'donor' can authorize the 'attorney' to have general powers to manage your finances (with no restrictions) or specified powers (eg, to pay your bills or sell your property). Depending on the powers you grant to the attorney, s/he can have access to your bank account, can make payments, withdraw money and sign cheques on your behalf.

In order to authorise Power of Attorney, you must have full mental capacity as you will need to make all the decisions about how the 'attorney' deals with your financial affairs. You will still need to be able to supervise her/his actions. You can revoke the attorney's powers if you think that they are not managing your money in your best interests.

You can buy an ordinary Power of Attorney document from a law stationer or instruct a solicitor to draw one up for you, for which there will be a charge.

Power of Attorney becomes invalid if you lose mental capacity and are unable to supervise the attorney's actions. If you want a person to be able to act as your attorney both now and in the future if you lose mental capacity, then you may wish to consider setting up a Lasting Power of Attorney (LPA), rather than an Ordinary Power of Attorney. Lasting Power of Attorney must be arranged while you still have capacity to make the decision, but you can set it up so the powers only become valid if you then lose capacity.

Lasting Power of Attorney

LPA was created with the full implementation of the Mental Capacity Act in October 2007. If you set up an LPA, you grant a legal power to someone else to make personal welfare decisions and/or financial decisions for a time when you lack capacity to make them for yourself. It replaces the role of Enduring Power of

Attorney (EPA). While EPA only covered financial decisions, a LPA can cover both financial and personal welfare decisions.

There are two types of LPA that can be set up: one for your finances and property and one for your personal welfare. The same person can be given authority to deal with both, but you have to apply on different forms to set each up.

While the LPA for finances and property can be used while you still have capacity, the LPA for personal welfare can only be used by the attorney once you have lost capacity to make such decisions yourself. Both types of LPA need to be registered with the Office of the Public Guardian before the documents can legally be used.

The LPA must have a good understanding of how you would like your affairs to be managed and the responsibilities of the role. While s/he is overseen by the Court of Protection, s/he can be given complete authority over your financial affairs and your personal welfare. This is why it is paramount that the LPA you choose should be someone you feel you can trust completely to make decisions that work in your best interests in the future when you are no longer able to make such decisions yourself. It is possible to set up a joint LPA, with one attorney for your finances and property and one for your personal welfare, so that responsibilities for managing your affairs are shared. You can also specify exactly what decisions can or cannot take on your behalf. You may also want to name a replacement attorney in the case that the current attorney is no longer able to carry out the responsibilities of the role.

Existing Enduring Power of Attorney

Since October 2007, you can no longer set up a new EPA. However, if you hold or someone else currently holds an EPA for you, this will continue to remain valid.

While an EPA will not automatically change to the status of an LPA, if you already have an EPA set up and want to replace it with an LPA, you can do this provided that you still have the capacity to make such a decision.

If you have already lost capacity

If you have lost capacity and have not already set up someone to be your LPA or EPA (before October 2007), a court-appointed deputy can make personal welfare or financial decisions on your behalf.

In order to set up a deputy, an application must be sent to the Court of Protection. The Court will appoint a deputy (usually a relative, but could be a professional such as a solicitor, or adult social care services) if lost capacity is established. For more details about the Court of Protection, contact the Office of the Public Guardian.

Deprivation of liberty safeguards[78]

New measures are due to come into force in April 2009 relating to people who lack mental capacity to make decisions on, or give consent to, the arrangements for their care and treatment and who are deprived of their liberty in a care home or hospital.

The new legislation aims to provide safeguards to ensure people are only deprived of their liberty where this is necessary for their own safety, and to provide the care and treatment they need, and where a lawful procedure has been followed to authorise this. It also provides people with access to a court to challenge their detention.

Power of attorney (Scotland)

In Scotland, there is a system of 'continuing attorneys' (sometimes referred to as the 'financial attorney') and 'welfare attorneys'. If you wish to have someone to look after your financial affairs if you lose capacity, you can stipulate this when granting a power of attorney. A welfare attorney can be granted to someone you want to make welfare decisions once you no longer have the capacity to do so yourself. The power of attorney must be written, and signed by the person granting it, stating clearly what powers are granted. It must also include a certificate signed by a solicitor, advocate or medical practitioner that s/he is satisfied that you understand what you are signing and are not acting under undue influence. The powers of a welfare attorney cannot be exercised until the person granting the attorney loses capacity in relation to these areas. The power of attorney must be registered with the Public Guardian and any changes must be notified to the Public Guardian.[79]

The implications of the Adults with Incapacity (Scotland) Act 2000 for powers of attorney granted prior to its implementation can be complicated. Seek legal advice if you are unsure about the status of a power that you have granted or that has been granted to you.

Financial guardians (Scotland)

In Scotland, a person known as a financial guardian can be appointed to manage your financial affairs. This replaced the previous system of appointing a *curator bonis*. Those already appointed as a *curator bonis* before April 2002 are subject to the same controls as guardians. An application may be made to the sheriff's court. Financial guardians are supervised by the Office of the Public Guardian. Applications from lay people are encouraged. However, where the management of your finances is likely to be complex then you may wish to employ an accountant to help. Solicitors may also be appointed as financial guardians. In some circumstances the local authority may petition the court to appoint a financial guardian. Local authorities are not allowed to petition to become financial guardians themselves. Individuals or local authorities can apply to the court for an **intervention order**. This is an application to make a 'one-off' decision which may be of a financial nature (eg, the sale of the house) or legal nature (eg, signing a care home agreement). Intervention orders can cover both financial and welfare matters.

For further information and application forms contact The Office of the Public Guardian (Scotland) (see Appendix 3) or visit www.publicguardian-scotland.gov.uk.

Part 4 of the Adults with Incapacity (Scotland) Act 2000 provides for the management, by care homes and independent hospitals, of the funds and property of the residents who are unable to carry out this function themselves. Authorisation, control and regulation of these arrangements are the responsibility of the Scottish Commission for the Regulation of Care.

Notes

1. Deciding to move into a care home
1 LAC (98)19; WOC 27/98; Scottish CRAG Annex G
2 *Robertson v Fife Council,* 5 CCLR 543
3 Annex D HLD (2003)7
4 Reg 5 Care Homes Regulations 2001 SI No. 3965
5 *Guidance on unfair terms in care home contracts,* Office of Fair Trading (available at www.oft.gov.uk)
6 *Fair terms for care,* Office of Fair Trading (available at www.oft.gov.uk)
7 LGOR 97/A/4002 Bexley
8 *R v Bristol City Council ex parte Penfold* (CCLR), June 1998; *R v Wigan MBC ex parte Tammadge* (CCLR), December 1998
9 *R v Wandsworth LBC ex parte Beckwith*

3. Fees which are fully paid by the state
10 *The National Framework for NHS Continuing Healthcare and NHS-funded Nursing Care,* DH, June2007
11 ss3(1) and 23 NHSA 1977; NHS(S)A 1978
12 see *Pointon Case,* Case no E.22/02/02-03 Funding for Long Term Care
13 *The National Framework for NHS Continuing Healthcare and NHS-funded Nursing Care,* DH, June 2007
14 *The National Framework for NHS Continuing Healthcare and NHS-funded Nursing Care,* DH, June 2007
15 *National Framework for Continuing NHS Health Care,* Welsh Assembly Government; CEL 6 (2008)

16 Delayed Discharges (Continuing Care) Directions 2007
17 Continuing Care (National Health Service Responsibilities) Directions 2007
18 The Delayed Discharges (Continuing Care) Directions 2007
19 *Discharge from hospital: pathway process and practice,* DH, March 2007
20 WHC (2005)035; CEL (2008)6
21 *Who pays? Establishing the responsible commissioner,* DH, September 2007
22 *Recovery of Expenditure for Provision of Social Care Consultation on Regulations and Revised Guidance Ordinary Residence,* October 2008
23 LAC (2001)1; NAFWC 43/02
24 Community Care (Delayed Discharges etc.) Act (Qualifying Services) (England) Regs 2003 SI No.1196
25 ss3, 37, 47 or 48 MHA 1983
26 s117 MHA 1983
27 *R v Manchester CC ex p Stennet (HoL)* 5 CCLR, December 2002
28 *Clunis v Camden and Islington Health Authority* (CCLR), March 1998
29 *R v LB Richmond ex parte Watson; R v Redcar and Cleveland ex parte Armstrong; R v Manchester ex parte Stennett; R v Harrow ex parte Cobham* (CCLR), December 1999
30 LGOR 97/0177 and 97/0755 Clywd and Conwy
31 LGOR 00/B/8307 Leicestershire CC
32 s8(1) MH(S)A 1984

4. **Help with fees from adult social care services**

33 ss21 and 24 NAA 1948; LAC (93)10; WOC 35/93

34 Those under 18 come under the CA 1989

35 LAC (93)10; WOC 35/93

36 s29 NAA 1948

37 s12 SW(S)A 1968

38 s26 NAA 1948

39 s47(5) NHSCCA 1990; s12A(5) SW(S)A 1968

40 *R v Sefton MBC ex parte Help the Aged and Blanchard (CA) (CCLR)*, December 1997

41 *R v Wigan MBC ex parte Tammadge (CCLR)*, December 1998

42 LAC (98)19; WOC 27/98; SWSG 2/99

43 LAC (2004)20; NAfW 14/02; CCD 3/2002

44 LGOR 00/B/599

45 LAC (2004)20; WOC 12/93; SWSG 5/93 *Choice of Accommodation Directions*

46 LAC (2004)20; WOC 12/93; SWSG 5/93 para 7

47 LAC (2004)20; WOC 12/93; SWSG 5/93 para 10

48 *R v Avon County Council ex parte M (CCLR)*, June 1999

49 LGOR 03/C/02451 Bolton Metropolitan Council

50 LAC (2004)20; WOC 12/93; SWSG 5/93 para 7.6

51 LAC (2006)12; NAfWC 14/02; CCD 3/2002

52 paras 3.004 and 3.004A CRAG; paras 3.004 and 3.004A Scottish CRAG

53 LAC (93)7; WOC 41/93; SWSG 1/96

54 See *R (London Borough of Greenwich) v Secretary of State for Health and another* [2006] EWHC 2576 (Admin) which is about asylum, ordinary residence and provision of services.

55 LAC (93)10; WOC 35/93; SWSG 1/96

56 s148 HSCA 2008

57 s22 NAA 1948; NA(AR) Regs

58 s26(3A) NAA 1948; para 1.023 CRAG; para 1.015 Scottish CRAG

5. **NHS-funded nursing care (England and Wales)**

59 LAC (2002)11; LAC (2003)8; NAfW 14/02; CCD 3/2002; HLD (2003)7

60 Letter from the DH to the Association of County Councils, November 1996

61 para 1.024A CRAG; para 1.017A Scottish CRAG

62 s49 HSCA 2001

63 *The National Framework for NHS Continuing Healthcare and NHS-funded Nursing Care,* DH, June 2007

64 SS(AA/DLA) Regs

6. **Paying the full fees yourself**

65 LAC (98)19; WOC 27/98; SWSG 2/99

66 HLD (2003)7 Annex D

67 LAC (2003)7; HSC 2003/6

68 Care Standards Act 2000 (Establishments and Agencies) (Miscellaneous Amendments) Regulations 2006;

69 *Guidance on unfair terms in care home contracts,* Office of Fair Trading (available at www.oft.gov.uk)

70 *The Care Homes for Older People, National Minimum Standards and the Care Home Regulations 2001,* DH, February 2003

71 *Disparities between market rates and state funding and residential care,* JRF Finding 678, June 1998

72 LAC 98/19; LAC (2001)25; WOC 27/98; SWSG 2/99

73 LAC (2001)25

74 Delayed Discharges (Continuing Care) Directions 2007

7. **Dealing with your money in a care home**

75 Reg 33 SS(C&P) Regs

76 Standard 35, *National minimum standards for care homes for older people.*

77 *Adults with Incapacity (Scotland) Act 2000 Code of Practice – Access to Funds,* Scottish Government, April 2008

78 *Mental Capacity Act 2005: Deprivation of liberty safeguards – Code of Practice to supplement the main Mental Capacity Act 2005 Code of Practice,* DH, August 2008

79 Part 2 Adults with Incapacity (Scotland) Act 2000; *Code of Practice for Continuing and Welfare Attorneys,* Scottish Executive, March 2001

10

Chapter 10

Financial assessments and charges in care homes

This chapter covers:
1. The financial assessment (below)
2. Reviews of your assessment (p269)
3. Complaints about your charge (p270)
4. Paying the full cost of your care home (including deferred payment agreements) (p271)
5. Types of stay in a care home (p275)
6. Temporary absences from care homes (p277)

All references to income support also apply to income-based jobseeker's allowance.

The Department of Health (DH) produces guidance, *Charging for Residential Accommodation Guide* (CRAG), which is regularly updated and is available on the DH website (www.dh.gov.uk).[1] Wales and Scotland have similar guidance.

1. The financial assessment

There are no set rules about the way the financial assessment is carried out. Guidance makes it clear that the financial assessment should be carried out after the decision on what sort of care you need (the needs assessment).[2] This means that you should not be asked questions about your finances until you have had a needs assessment and it has been agreed that care in a care home is appropriate. If you are asked about your capital early on in your needs assessment or told you will have to make your own arrangements, before a proper calculation of your income or capital is done, or if you are not told about when your property is disregarded, you should complain (see p270).

If it is determined that you need care in a care home, legislation allows adult social care services to calculate your resources (see Chapters 11 and 12) to establish whether you need to be provided with residential accommodation by the local authority or you can afford to make your own arrangements (see p236).[3] If you have capital of above the capital limit for your country (see p291) then in most circumstances adult social care services will decide they do not need to make the arrangements for you (see p271).

If this happens you will still be eligible for payments from the NHS towards any nursing care in a care home which provides nursing (the funded nursing care (FNC) contribution). These payments are made directly to the care home and the fee charged to you should be reduced accordingly by the amount of the FNC. You may be entitled to fully funded NHS continuing healthcare if your social care needs are ancillary and incidental to your healthcare needs (see p252). In Scotland, you can still receive payments towards both your nursing and personal care if you have above the capital limit and you are 65 or over. If you are under 65 you can receive payments towards your nursing care (see p244).

It is important to note that following the *Robertson v Fife* case[4] it has been made clear that the provision of services to a person who is assessed as being in need of them is not related to the ability of the person to meet the costs (see p305).

If you are placed in a care home by adult social care services, legislation requires that you repay them the cost of the accommodation if you are capable of doing so.[5] A 'standard rate' is fixed for the accommodation and if you have sufficient income or capital you will be required to pay the full cost – ie, the 'standard rate'.[6]

The 'standard rate' for local authority care homes is the full cost to adult social care services of your placement.[7] The 'standard rate' for independent care homes is the gross cost to adult social care services of providing or paying for your placement under the contract with the home.[8]

If you cannot meet the cost in full, and you provide the necessary financial information for an assessment to be carried out, adult social care services will only charge the amount determined by the assessment.[9] However, if you refuse to co-operate with the financial assessment adult social care services will charge the full standard rate.

If you help in the running of your care home and it is managed by the local authority, part of your charges may be waived in recognition of this.[10]

Legislation provides for the assessment of resources required by adult social care services to establish your contribution to the cost of your placement in a care home – ie, the charge (see Chapters 11 and 12).[11] After you have paid the assessed charge you should not normally be left with less than £21.90 or £22 in Wales a week for your personal expenses (see Chapter 13).

For the first eight weeks of any placement, adult social care services do not have to carry out a financial assessment (although some do). Instead they can charge what they consider to be reasonable.[12] If you disagree, you can ask for a full financial assessment. Temporary periods of accommodation for up to six weeks in order to receive intermediate care services are provided free of charge (see p242).

Calculation used by adult social care services in the financial assessment to determine your contribution to the cost

Total assessable income (including any tariff income from your capital, see Chapters 11 and 12)

minus

Outgoings (for a temporary resident who has outgoings for her/his home in the community, see Chapter 13)

minus

Personal expenses allowance (see Chapter 13)

equals

Contribution to accommodation and care costs (charge)

See Chapter 17 for example calculations.

Collecting financial information

The way local authorities collect financial information varies. In some areas a financial assessment officer will go through the assessment with you. In other authorities your care assessor/social worker/manager will help you fill in the form. In others you will be sent a form to complete yourself.

However, once the form is completed, it will normally go to the finance section in adult social care services which will calculate how much you will have to pay.

Adult social care services can undertake a financial assessment *before* you enter a care home if you are a prospective resident.[13] This means that the income they assess includes benefits that are applicable to you in the community. As explained in Chapter 16, in some situations some benefits will change when you enter the care home so the initial contribution calculated will not be the amount that you will actually be required to pay when you enter the care home. This can be confusing, although some adult social care services attempt to explain the situation in the letter they send you about your financial assessment.

If your benefits change as a result of entering the care home, tell adult social care services the new amounts so a retrospective reassessment can be completed which will advise you of the actual amount that you will be required to contribute.

Unlike for social security benefits, there is no standard form used throughout the country for the financial assessment. Each local authority has devised its own form. In some cases the same form will cover both domiciliary and residential charges. As these charges are based on different legislation, the form should make it clear which parts you need to fill in if you are going into a care home.

The forms should not require information about your partner's income and capital as it is only your resources which can be taken into account.[14] However, adult social care services can request the financial details of your partner in order to help ensure that they are leaving enough money for your partner to live on when calculating your charge.[15] They may also do this in order to find out whether your partner should be asked to contribute to the charge because s/he receives social security benefits paid in respect of both of you (see below). Some adult social care services have a separate form which your partner may be asked to complete, although they cannot insist on its completion or on your partner disclosing information about her/his resources.

One of a couple temporarily in a care home

If you are one of a couple[16] going temporarily into a care home and your partner is claiming income support (IS) or income-related employment and support allowance (ESA) or pension credit (PC) for both of you, guidance states that 'it would be reasonable to expect the partner receiving the IS/income-related ESA/PC to contribute to the charge for accommodation for the other partner a sum equivalent to the IS/income-related ESA/PC payable for that partner.'[17]

The issue that arises for adult social care services is what constitutes a reasonable amount. For couples in receipt of IS or income-related ESA the situation is straightforward, as, in most cases, the applicable amount in these circumstances is usually calculated using two single persons' applicable amounts added together (see p166), which can be apportioned easily to find out the amount paid in respect of the resident. However, for couples getting PC, the situation is complicated by the fact that PC is calculated using the couple appropriate minimum guarantee (see p160).

The same apportionment issue arises for adult social care services when deciding by how much to increase the personal expenses allowance to allow an amount for the partner in the community when it is the resident who is the claimant of IS/income-related ESA/PC for both members of the couple. The most common approaches by adult social care services to this issue are discussed in Chapter 13.

Liable relatives

There is currently provision for the local authority to approach a spouse (but not an unmarried or civil partner, as they do not have liability[18]) and inform her/him of her/his duty as a 'liable relative' under s42 NAA to maintain her/his spouse. However, the Health and Social Care Act 2008 removes this power by abolishing the liable relative rules.[19] The relevant section is due to be implemented from April 2009. Guidance states that in the interim the Department of Health strongly encourages local authorities to exercise their discretion not to apply the liable relatives rule.[20] In Scotland, the liable relatives legislation has been repealed.[21]

See p282 if you pay maintenance to someone else from your income.

Verifying the details you have given

Adult social care services have been told it is good practice to verify information – eg, to look at bank statements. They should also make use of information available to them from other departments within the authority (eg, housing benefit and council tax records) to verify details. They have been advised to check, with your permission, with other agencies such as the DWP, banks and pension firms. It is for authorities themselves to determine the extent to which, and circumstances in which, they will verify information.[22]

Claiming social security benefits

As some benefits are used to pay adult social care services charges, it is in their interests to ensure that you claim all the benefits to which you are entitled (see Chapter 16). Adult social care services have been advised to maintain good links with the DWP.[23] It should be made as smooth as possible for you to claim benefits and for details to be transferred from one department to another.

How much help you get from adult social care services in claiming benefits varies around the country. In some areas the person filling in the financial assessment form will also help you to complete the income-related ESA/IS (for people aged under 60) or PC (for people aged 60 or over) claim form at the same time, if this is appropriate, and send it to the DWP. In other areas you will be advised to make a claim and told how to get the claim form.

Assuming income support, income-related employment and support allowance or pension credit

If adult social care services undertakes a financial assessment *before* you enter a care home they may make an assumption about your entitlement to, and the amount of, IS, income-related ESA or PC that will become payable when you enter the care home. This can cause problems because it involves treating IS/income-related ESA/PC as notional income (see p286) and also because adult social care services financial assessors are not usually benefit specialists and may make an incorrect assumption. This is a problem particularly with regard to the severe disability premium/additional amount element of IS/income-related ESA/PC which is subject to complex rules.

If your benefit entitlement has been assumed, check that what you actually receive when your entitlement has been decided is the same amount as adult social care services has assumed. If it is not, challenge the adult social care services decision using the complaints procedure (see p270). Alternatively, the amount of your IS/income-related ESA/PC may be incorrect. In this situation, adult social care services may be able to help you challenge the DWP decision.

Paying your assessed charge

You can pay your assessed charge direct to adult social care services or, if you are in an independent sector care home, and all parties (you, the care home manager and adult social care services) agree, you can pay your assessed charge direct to the care home with adult social care services paying the remainder. However, this type of direct contractual relationship with the care home can sometimes lead to you being asked to pay a top-up without the knowledge of adult social care services. If this happens, advise adult social care services. Many adult social care services have a clause in their contracts with care homes that protects residents (and their relatives) from being asked for top-ups.

Information about how much you have to pay

Adult social care services should give you clear information about how much you should be expected to pay, and how this has been calculated. They should explain the normal weekly assessed charge and any reasons why the charge may change.[24] Changes in charges are most likely to occur during the first few weeks in a care home when your attendance allowance or disability living allowance care component is usually withdrawn or extra IS may become payable (see Chapter 16). Changes may also occur if there is any other increase or decrease in the amount of your income and/or capital (see below).

Adult social care services should also explain how you should pay. If you have agreed to pay your part of the charge directly to the home, you will need to arrange with the home how frequently you will pay. If you are going to be billed by adult social care services, you should be given some choice about the method of payment. Most adult social care services prefer direct debit, but if you want to choose to pay in another way you should explore the possibility with them. Complain if you think that adult social care services have limited the range of payment methods (see p270).

---

2. Reviews of your assessment

It has been left to each local authority to make its own arrangements about how frequently and when your charge will be reviewed and the policy to adopt if undercharging or overcharging occurs.[25]

Nearly all adult social care services review their charges annually at the time when your benefits are uprated. This is also the time when the home you are in is most likely to alter its fees.

However, your income or capital could change at any time – eg, you could inherit money, your occupational or private pension could go up, or your savings could go down because you have been using some of the money to supplement the personal expenses allowance (see p310). You should inform adult social care services when you have a change of circumstances, in the same way as you should inform the DWP.

If you have capital between the lower and upper capital limit you should inform adult social care services every time it goes up or down a £250 band (see p285). Unless you do this, when your capital has gone down you are likely to continue to be charged at a higher rate until the annual review of charges. Some adult social care services have computer systems to track the tariff income and will alter it automatically. Others do not and so it is safer to regularly inform them of changes. If they refuse to reassess you when you tell them about a change of circumstances, you should complain as you may be charged too much.

3. **Complaints about your charge**

If you have a concern about your charge, you have a right to complain about it using the local authority complaints procedure[26] (see p40). As the rules for charging are national, a complaint will normally be about resolving an error in the calculation or the interpretation of the rules. These are often dealt with in the initial stage by discussing them with the finance officer dealing with your case.

It is important to check the calculation very carefully to make sure that your income and capital used in the calculation are correct. You also need to check that any bills presented on the sale of your former home accurately reflect whether you were a temporary or permanent resident at the start of your stay. You should be clear about exactly what period is covered and that increases in fees are correctly recorded, along with what you may have already paid from your income.

Adult social care services have some discretion, which includes:
- the way jointly owned property is valued (see p294);
- whether your former home can be disregarded (see p297);
- whether you have deprived yourself of capital (see p302);
- whether your personal expenses allowance will be varied (see p310);
- whether you are required to have a third party to top up (see p314);
- whether you count as a temporary or permanent resident (see p275);
- how frequently reviews are carried out (see p269).

In these cases it is more likely that you will need to take your complaint through to the formal stage and maybe to a complaints panel. Some adult social care services have a separate procedure for appeals against charges. While this is a sensible approach to resolving charging complaints, it does not stop you from exercising your right to make a formal complaint under the complaints procedure either in addition to your appeal or instead of it. You should not have to go through any local charging appeal procedure before you are allowed to make a formal complaint. If you have concerns about your charges you can also use the other remedies outlined in Chapter 2. It is always wise to seek advice.

Chapter 10: Financial assessments and charges in care homes
4. Self-funding (including deferred payment agreements)

10

4. Self-funding (including deferred payment agreements)

If you have capital in excess of the capital limit for your country (see p291) you will be required to pay the full cost of your accommodation and care[27] – ie, you will be **self-funding**. However, this does not mean that you cannot receive help from adult social care services in terms of an assessment of your needs to establish what services you require, and help to find a suitable care home.[28] Contacting adult social care services for this type of help will benefit you if or when your capital reduces to the capital limit for your country (see p291), because at that point adult social care services will help fund your placement (as long as your assessable income after deducting the personal expenses allowance, is less than the care home fee), as they will have previously agreed that it meets your assessed needs.

Even if you are self-funding you could still benefit from adult social care services arranging your placement and contracting with the care home as fees are often higher for self-funding residents without an adult social care services contract. However, some adult social care services authorities will not contract with a care home if you are self-funding (sometimes called full cost) unless you or your representative are unable to arrange the placement (see p245).

Prior to 6 October 2003 complex rules existed about self-funding and eligibility for social security benefits. Now, if you are paying the full cost of your accommodation and care without any financial help from the local authority (ie, you are **self-funding**) or you only receive financial help on an interim basis (ie, you are **retrospectively self-funding** – see below and p351) you can keep any attendance allowance (AA) or disability living allowance care component (DLA care) that you are entitled to even if you are in receipt of a means-tested benefit and/or adult social care services have contracted with the care home for the provision of your accommodation and care at full cost to you.[29] In Scotland, if you are aged 65 or over you will not be entitled to AA or DLA care if you are receiving help from the local authority with the cost of your care under the 'free personal care' arrangements. If you are aged under 65, you will still be paid DLA care if the only help you get is for 'free nursing care'.

If you are required to meet the full cost of your accommodation and care because you are a permanent resident and your home in the community (after the 12-week disregard – see p292) is valued at more than the capital limit for your country (see p291), you may not actually be able to pay the full cost until your house is sold. In this situation, adult social care services can help meet the cost of your accommodation and care and claim the amount back from you when your property is sold. A 'deferred payment agreement' provides for these circumstances (see p272). For AA/DLA care purposes you are considered to be retrospectively self-funding (see p351).

Deferred payment agreements

Since October 2001 (2002 in Scotland; 2003 in Wales) legislation has provided for deferred payment agreements.[30] This should be an option that is offered to you if you satisfy the eligibility criteria (see below). The local government ombudsman held that there had been maladministration when a council had failed to introduce a deferred payment scheme.[31] More recently maladministration was found when a council did not offer a deferred payment to a resident who required funding while he was pursuing a claim for fully funded NHS continuing healthcare. As a consequence, the resident sold the house and realised less than if it had not been sold until after his death when the value would have increased. The council paid the family £20,000.[32]

A deferred payment agreement allows adult social care services to take a legal charge in their favour on your main or only home or, in Scotland, a grant to the local authority of a standard security over the home, instead of the full contribution towards the cost of your accommodation and care in a care home. This arrangement allows you to keep your home while you are in a care home for the duration of the deferred payment agreement.[33]

The provision of adult social care services being able to take a legal charge on your property is not a new power. A power already existed and continues to exist under another enactment if you fail to pay the assessed charge in circumstances where an outstanding debt is being pursued.[34] Guidance reminds adult social care services that the existing power provides for situations where residents are unwilling to pay their assessed contribution.[35] It appears from research by the Scottish Government, however, that this guidance has largely been disregarded.[36] Deferred payments are only a way of putting off making payment of the full cost to adult social care services for your accommodation and care in a care home. The full cost payment will have to be made at some point from the proceeds of the sale of your property whether it is sold in your lifetime or not. It is not a way of preserving the asset to pass on to your family or friends after your death.

Eligibility

Deferred payment agreements are available to you if you:
- do not have a current mandatory or discretionary property disregard applied to your property (see p298) (although you may enter a deferred payment agreement following the 12-week property disregard);
- do not have capital (apart from the value of your home) above the upper capital limit in England (£23,000) and Wales (£22,000) or the lower capital limit in Scotland (£13,750);
- cannot meet the full cost of the care home from your income;
- do not wish to sell your home or you are unable to sell your home quickly enough to pay for your fees. In Scotland, you must also be able to grant the authority a standard security against your home to secure a reasonable estimate of the total amount which will be covered.

Chapter 10: Financial assessments and charges in care homes
4. Self-funding (including deferred payment agreements)

10

Adult social care services have discretion over whether they agree to a deferred payment agreement with individual residents. However, in Wales directions place a duty on local authorities to draw attention to and offer deferred payment arrangements to all eligible or prospective residents.[37] The guidance advises that discretion should be exercised in cases such as where there is an outstanding mortgage or other debt on the property or the deferred payment is very high, as these circumstances may limit the ability to offer deferred payments to other residents.[38] When your home is eventually sold, it should be possible for you or your estate to pay back the deferred contribution including any top-up (see Chapter 14).[39] A lack of capacity does not prevent residents from deferred payments. Where residents lack capacity, deferred payments can still be signed by those who hold a registered Enduring Power of Attorney or more recently, a Lasting Power of Attorney, or where the residents' affairs are administered by the Court of Protection.[40] Any refusal by adult social care services to agree to a deferred payment agreement should be put in writing, giving reasons. Complain if you wish to challenge the decision. Further guidance on deferred payment agreements was issued in October 2002 (England)[41] as there had only been limited use of the power to allow deferred payments by a number of local authorities. In Scotland similar guidance was issued in December 2004 and March 2005.[42] In Wales the original guidance, which introduced deferred payment agreements in April 2003, also contains a model deferred payment agreement.[43] Such a draft is no longer available on the DH website.

It appears that recently some adult social care services are refusing deferred payment agreements on the basis that getting a loan against the property could enable you to pay the care home until your property is sold or alternatively, you could arrange to owe the care home until your property is sold. Both of these suggestions go against the Government intention of the deferred payment scheme and better advice in CRAG to clarify this has been sought from the DH.

Operating the deferred payment scheme

Adult social care services should carry out a financial assessment in the normal way to determine the amount that you should contribute towards the cost of your accommodation and care. The amount that is then deferred, and ultimately recovered from the value of the property, is the difference between the contribution and the full cost of the care home. In addition, you may be able to defer the amount of any top-up required for more expensive accommodation, if appropriate (see Chapter 14).[44]

Deferred payment agreements:
- must be made in writing and adult social care services should ensure that you understand what you are committing yourself to;
- last from the day you enter into the agreement until 56 days after your death or the date you (or your representative) terminates the agreement – eg, because

10

Chapter 10: Financial assessments and charges in care homes
4. Self-funding (including deferred payment agreements)

a property is sold or you have become eligible for local authority funding because the net value of your property is now below the capital limit;

- cannot be terminated by adult social care services although they can advise you to terminate it;
- can include a reasonable rate of interest but only from 56 days after your death or the day after the agreement is terminated;
- cannot include any legal expenses such as the cost of land registry searches although adult social care services may ask you to pay these expenses up front.

If you wish to enter into a deferred payment agreement adult social care services should advise you to seek independent financial advice and be aware of how it will affect your social security benefits (see below).[45] Guidance states that adult social care services should be prepared to put you in touch with persons who can offer independent advice on requesting and agreeing to a deferred payment agreement.[46]

Social security benefits and adult social care services charging issues

- If you choose not to sell your property you will not be able to claim IS/income-related ESA if the property is worth more than £16,000 (net value after allowable deductions). Your weekly contribution to the fees will therefore be less. This means that the amount that adult social care services will eventually recover will be higher. However, for PC purposes there is no upper capital limit. A tariff income is applied on capital above £10,000 (permanent residents). This means that where the value of the property subject to a deferred payment agreement is not disregarded for PC purposes (ie, it is not for sale), the deemed income (ie, the tariff income) from the value of the property is considered as qualifying income for the savings credit element of PC. You may also qualify for the guarantee credit part of PC in these circumstances if the value of your property is low enough for the tariff income, when added to your other income, not to exceed your appropriate minimum guarantee.
- If your property is for sale and therefore its value is disregarded for PC purposes, the guarantee credit is more likely to be payable. However, unless you have any qualifying income such as a private pension, the savings credit would not be payable as there cannot be any qualifying deemed income from disregarded capital.
  You may therefore be faced with a 'better off' assessment – would you be better off with your property up for sale or not? You will need to get a benefit check showing how much total PC you would get in each situation.
- If you have a deferred payment arrangement you are entitled to continue to receive your AA/DLA care, as you will be repaying adult social care services the full amount of the cost of your accommodation and care, and therefore you

are a 'retrospective self-funder'. Since October 2003 this applies even if you are also in receipt of IS, income-related ESA or PC.

However adult social care services will include AA/DLA care in your assessed contribution, thus lowering the amount left to recover from the value of the property when it is eventually sold. In Scotland if the local authority is paying your care costs, you will not get AA/DLA care even if you have to repay your accommodation costs.

- If you have ongoing expenses to maintain your property, adult social care services has discretion to allow a variation of your personal expenses allowance (see p310) to enable you to maintain your property. However, this will increase the amount recoverable by adult social care services from the value of the property when it is eventually sold.

- You may need to check the net value of your capital (including the property against which your payment is deferred) every so often as when it reduces to the capital limit for your country (see p291) you may be able to get non-repayable funding from adult social care services. Remember that the net value of your property reduces each week by the amount of the deferred payment, and may also be affected by changes in property prices in that area.

- If you are 60 or over you may also need to check the net value of your capital (including the property against which your payment is deferred) every so often in order to determine when you may be able to claim PC. As there is no upper capital limit for claims to PC you may become entitled to this benefit before any entitlement to adult social care services funding. You may be able to get advice from adult social care services in advance about the level at which your capital would need to be in your circumstances to claim PC.

5. **Types of stay in a care home**

There are three basic types of stay in a care home.

- **Permanent stay:** for financial assessment purposes a **'permanent resident'** is defined as a 'resident who is not a temporary resident'.[47] Guidance states that 'an admission is permanent if the agreed intention is for the resident to remain in residential care.'[48]

- **Temporary stay:** a **'temporary resident'** is defined as one whose stay is unlikely to exceed 52 weeks or, in exceptional circumstances, unlikely substantially to exceed that period.[49] (This is a similar definition to that for social security benefit purposes except that for benefit purposes it is a temporary absence from your normal home with additional conditions that have to be satisfied – see p337.) Guidance states that 'an admission is temporary either if it is intended to last for a limited time period, such as respite or intermediate care, or there is uncertainty that permanent admission is required.'[50]

A planned programme of temporary stays or a temporary stay in order to give your carer a break are often referred to as **respite care.** Adult social care services may apply a flat-rate charge without assessment if the stay is for less than eight weeks (see p265).

- **Trial period stay:** this is not defined in the charging legislation. However, it is defined in social security legislation (see p337), and the 13-week rule for trial period stays is referred to in the charging guidance as 'applying to people who enter residential accommodation initially on a temporary basis during which it is decided whether they need to stay in residential accommodation or can return home. Their stay in residential accommodation is generally a conditional one with a number of factors influencing whether or not they will return home or eventually stay permanently in residential accommodation'.[51] This indicates that a trial period stay should be treated as a temporary stay until a decision is made as to whether it is to become permanent.

More recent guidance introduces the scenario of where there is uncertainty that permanent admission is required and states that in these circumstances the stay is temporary.[52]

However, some adult social care services treat a trial period (sometimes called temporary with a view to permanent) as a permanent stay. This is likely to be due to the fact that adult social care services are advised that their statistical returns for the Department of Health should treat trial periods as permanent stays.[53] This can be challenged using the complaints procedure (see p270) if you are disadvantaged in the financial assessment by having your stay treated as permanent – eg, if the value of your home in the community is taken into account as capital from the 13th week after the beginning of your trial period instead of the 13th week after the beginning of when it is agreed that your stay is now permanent.

Some adult social care services departments only use the 'permanent' or 'temporary' definitions of types of stay, which can cause problems for social security benefits in terms of whether the 52-week temporary rule or the 13-week trial period rule should be applied. In these circumstances you will need to provide further information to housing authorities and/or the DWP.

It is recognised that a stay which was initially expected to be permanent may turn out to be temporary and vice versa. In these circumstances, adult social care services are advised to assess you according to your actual circumstances at the time (see p297).[54] Similarly, in the case of a trial period, if it is decided that you will either definitely return home at a future date (ie, you become temporary) or that you will not be returning home (ie, you become permanent) then the financial assessment should be revised accordingly.

6. **Temporary absences from care homes**

Payment of care home fees

There are no rules governing the payment of care home fees during a temporary absence (including going into hospital). If your placement is funded wholly or partly by adult social care services the arrangements will usually be covered in its contract or service agreement with the care home (including temporary absence due to admission to hospital).

Many adult social care services departments have adopted or adapted the pre-1993 temporary absence rules for preserved rights which no longer exist. This means that often adult social care services make an 80 per cent payment to the care home if you are absent (eg, in hospital). However, this will usually only be for a limited number of weeks until a review of your circumstances is undertaken.

Variation of your contribution to the local authority

If you are away from the care home and as a result the amount of your social security benefits has changed, tell adult social care services. They should then review your financial assessment to establish a level of contribution to care costs which reflects your new level of benefit. However, if you receive attendance allowance (AA) or disability living allowance care component (DLA care) for any period that you are in the community, adult social care services may vary the personal expenses allowance (PEA – see below) by at least the same amount so that in effect the AA or DLA care is ignored in the calculation of your contribution during your absence.

Variation of personal expenses allowance

If you are away from the care home because you are on holiday or visiting family or friends, adult social care services can use its discretion to vary your PEA to enable you to have more money (see p310).[55]

Notes

1 At the time of writing the latest final version which is CRAG amendment 26 is with LAC(2007)4. However, there is a draft CRAG April 2008 on the DH website but it is doubtful whether a April 2008 version will be available before the April 2009 regulations and guidance. References in the *Handbook* are appropriate to the April 2008 Draft CRAG.
The Scottish CRAG has been amended with CCD 2/2008 and is available at http://www.sehd.scot.nhs.uk/publications/CC2008_02.pdf
The Welsh CRAG has been amended with WAGC 11/2008 (http://new.wales.gov.uk/1546306/circulars/2008/wagc1108/wag1108.pdf?lang=en) and is available at http://new.wales.gov.uk/topics/health/publications/socialcare/guidance/2008/cragamendment24?lang=en

1. **The financial assessment**

2 *Community Care in the Next Decade and Beyond*, Policy Guidance 1990; para 3.31 *Assessment and Care Management* SW11/91
3 paras 1.007A and 1.008 CRAG
4 *Robertson v Fife* 25 July 2002 HL [2002] UKHL35
5 s22(1) NAA 1948 as amended by NHSCCA 1990; s87 SW(S)A 1968
6 s22(3) NAA 1948
7 s22(2) NAA 1948
8 s26(2) NAA 1948
9 s22(2) NAA 1948
10 s23(3) NAA 1948
11 NA(AR) Regs as amended
12 s22(5A) NAA 1948
13 NA(AR)(Amdt2) Regs: para 5 LAC (98)19; WOC 27/98; SWSG 2/99;
14 paras 4.001, 4.002 and 11.005 CRAG and para 18(c) Annex to LAC (2002)11; NAFWC 14/02; CCD 3/2002
15 para 4.003 CRAG
16 'couple' includes civil partnership couples and same-sex couples who are living together as if they were civil partners: section 4 CRAG
17 para 4.005 CRAG

18 para 11.001 CRAG
19 s147 HSCA 2008
20 para 11.002 CRAG; LAC(2006)12
21 s62 ASP(S)A 2007
22 para 10 LAC (98)8; WOC 12/98 para 10; SWSG 6/98 para 9
23 para 1.026 CRAG; para 1.024 Scottish CRAG; Joint IS/JSA Bulletin 10/00
24 para 1.015 CRAG; para 1.013 Scottish CRAG

2. **Reviews of your assessment**

25 LAC (94)1; WOC 4/94; SWSG 5/94 para 16

3. **If you have a complaint about your charge**

26 para 1.027 CRAG This reference has not been updated since the introduction of the Department of Health *Learning From Complaints Social Services Complaints Procedure for Adults*, 2006 and the Welsh Assembly, *Listening and Learning: A guide to handling complaints and representations in local authority social services in Wales*, 2006; para 1.025 Scottish CRAG

4. **Self-funding (including deferred payment agreements)**

27 In Scotland, the full cost means the cost of the accommodation only, for those 65 or over where personal care is funded by the local authority. For those in a nursing home aged under 65 in Scotland or any age in England and Wales, the full cost means the cost of accommodation and personal care only, where the nursing care costs are met by the registered nursing care contribution paid by the NHS.
28 para 8 LAC (98)19; WOC 27/98; SWSG 2/99
29 Reg 3 Social Security (Attendance Allowance and Disability Allowance (Amendment) Regulations 2003 No.2259)
30 LAC (2001) 25; NAFWC 21/2003; CCD 7/2002 superseded by CCD 13/2004
31 Manchester City Council 04/C/4804 31.03.05

32 This was a Greenwich LBC case that was settled during the investigation and therefore was not reported. However, it was referred to in the annual letter which the LGO sends to each council and which is available on the LGO website. It is also referred to at Annex A para 14.189 in the Health Service and Parliamentary Ombudsman, *Report on retrospective continuing care funding and redress,* 2007

33 s55 HSCA 2001; s6 CCH(S)A 2002

34 ss22 and 23 HASSASSAA 1983;

35 para 7.019 CRAG; para 16 of Annex to LAC (2001)25; para 12 Annex to NAFWC 21/2003; para 7 and 12 Annex to CCD 13/2004

36 *An Evaluation and Assessment of Deferred Payment Agreements* 2008 Scottish Government Social Research available at www.scotland.gov.uk/socialresearch

37 The National Assistance Deferred Payments Directions at Appendix 3 to NAFWC 21/2003

38 para 9 LAC(2001)2; para 5 NAFWC 21/2003

39 para 7 Appendix 1 LAC (2001)29

40 para 16 LAC (2002) 11

41 LAC (2002)15; NAFWC 21/2003

42 CCD13/2004 and CCD2/2005

43 Appendix 2 NAFWC 21/2003

44 NA(RA)(RC)(E) Regs 2001; NA(RA)(APRCAS)(W) Regs; section III LAC (2001) 25; section III NAFWC 21/2003; para 22 CCD 13/2004

45 para 13 Annex to LAC (2001)25; para 9 NAFWC 21/2003

46 para 15 Annex to LAC (2002)11

47 Reg 2 NA(AR)(amdt2) Regs

48 para 25 Annex to LAC(2002) 11; para 3.001A CRAG

49 Reg 2(1) NA(AR) Regs

50 para 25 Annex to LAC(2002) 11; para 3.001A CRAG

51 paras 3.002 and 8 CRAG; para 3.002 SWSG 8/96; LAC (95)7; WOC 22/95; para 9 SWSG 13/95(9)

52 para 25 Annex to LAC(2002) 11; para 3.001A CRAG

53 Form SRI Local Authority Supported Residents 2001/02 Guidance Notes 3-4

54 paras 3.004 and 3.004A CRAG

6. Temporary absences from care homes
55 para 8 LAC (97)5 [check]; para 15 SWSG 7/97

11

Chapter 11

Income – financial assessments

This chapter covers:
1. General (below)
2. Treatment of income (p281)
3. Income fully taken into account (p281)
4. Income partially disregarded (p282)
5. Income fully disregarded (p283)
6. The savings disregard (p284)
7. Capital treated as income (p284)
8. Tariff income (p285)
9. Trust income, personal injury payments and charitable and voluntary payments (p285)
10. Notional income (p286)
11. Deprivation (p287)
12. Less dependent residents (p288)

Legislation provides for the assessment by adult social care services of a resident's or prospective resident's income to establish her/his contribution to the cost of placement in a care home.[1] Income is treated in a similar way to that for income support purposes (see Chapter 8). This chapter concentrates on the key differences.

1. General

Whatever your income, you will be left with no less than £21.90 (£22.00 in Wales) a week personal expenses allowance[2] in addition to any income disregarded in the assessment[3] (see p283). The rest of your income will go towards meeting the standard rate (see p265) for your accommodation.

All of your income is included as assessable income in the adult social care services' financial assessment unless it is partially or fully disregarded.[4] Your income is calculated on a weekly basis and includes capital treated as income (see p284), tariff income (see p285) and notional income (see p286).[5] The most common forms of income for people going into a care home are:
- state retirement pension and other social security benefits such as income support/income-related employment and support allowance (ESA)/income-

based jobseeker's allowance (if you are under 60) or pension credit (if you are 60 or over), housing benefit, council tax benefit, incapacity benefit/ contributory ESA, severe disablement allowance, disability living allowance and attendance allowance;

- insurance policy income;
- occupational or personal pensions (see p221);
- investment bond income;
- assumed tariff income from capital (see p285);
- trust income (see p285);
- personal injury payments (see p285)

If you have a partner (see p93), her/his income will not be included in the assessment even if you are only a temporary resident. Unlike the DWP, adult social care services do not have any powers to assess couples jointly.

2. Treatment of income

The treatment of income for financial assessment purposes is very similar to the treatment of income for the calculation of income support (see Chapter 8).[6]

Temporary residents' (including respite and trial period residents – see p275) and permanent residents' income is treated the same except that for temporary residents a disregard can be allowed to meet financial commitments for your usual home in the community. These are often called outgoings (see p312).[7] There are also differences in the way disability living allowance care component and attendance allowance are treated for temporary and permanent residents (see p283).

3. Income fully taken into account

Most income that is fully taken into account for income support (IS) purposes (see Chapter 8) is also fully taken into account for adult social care services' financial assessment purposes, with the important additions of:

- third party payments (see Chapter 14) are considered to be notional income (see p286);[8]
- IS/income-related employment and support allowance/income-based jobseeker's allowance (if you are under 60) minus any amount for housing costs (see p153);[9]
- pension credit (PC) if you are 60 or over, but see p284 for how a savings disregard is applied to the savings credit element of PC;
- attendance allowance (AA)/disability living allowance care component (DLA care) (including constant attendance allowance and exceptionally severe

disablement allowance payable with industrial injury disablement benefit or war disablement benefit – see pp127 and 129) where it is paid to **permanent** residents.[10] For temporary residents it is fully disregarded (see p283).
Note: AA/DLA care is not usually payable after 28 days (or less) of being in a care home (see p349);
- housing benefit (HB), if you are living permanently in an unregistered establishment and HB is being paid to meet the accommodation charge (see less dependent resident section, p288).[11] **Note:** this is only likely to apply to adult placement schemes now as all other establishments providing accommodation and personal care are required to register under the legislation.

Where a social security benefit is subject to a reduction (other than a reduction because of voluntary unemployment) – eg, because of an earlier overpayment – the amount taken into account is the gross amount of benefit before reduction.[12]

There is specific guidance regarding income from an insurance policy.[13] This type of income will be taken into account in full, unless it is income from a mortgage protection policy when it is fully disregarded.[14]

4. **Income partially disregarded**

Most income which is partially disregarded for income support purposes (see Chapter 8) is also partially disregarded for adult social care services' financial assessment purposes, with the important addition of:
- 50 per cent of an occupational pension, personal pension or payment from a retirement annuity if you pass at least this amount to your spouse/civil partner, as long as s/he is not living with you in the care home. If you pass nothing or less than 50 per cent then there is no disregard.[15] If you are an unmarried partner rather than a spouse or civil partner, adult social care services can use their discretionary powers to vary the personal expenses allowance to achieve a similar effect (see p310).[16] There is a proposal to the Department of Health for consultation on extending this disregard to include any state additional pension.[17]

If you are one of a married couple/civil partnership, you should be given advice by adult social care services about the 50 per cent disregard, including the fact that you can decide whether to pass 50 per cent of your pension to your spouse/civil partner or not, and whether s/he would be better off after taking account of the effect of the pension on benefits.[18]

If you are in a care home and you are contributing to the maintenance of someone, there is no specific provision to allow a disregard of the amount that you pay from the assessment of your income, unless it is the payment of at least

50 per cent of an occupational pension (as p283). There is also a provision not to treat any part of an occupational pension, personal pension or retirement annuity that your spouse is legally entitled to receive (eg, by means of a court order) as income belonging to you, and therefore it would not form part of your income for financial assessment purposes. If in addition you pass at least 50 per cent of the part of the occupational pension, personal pension or retirement annuity belonging to you to your spouse, the 50 per cent disregard will still apply.[19]

If you pay maintenance from income other than an occupational pension, personal pension or retirement annuity you may need to seek advice about whether the change in your circumstances (ie, becoming a resident in a care home) will affect your liability.

If you remain liable to make maintenance payments, adult social care services may, in special circumstances, be able to use their discretion to increase your personal expenses allowance in order to enable you to continue to meet the commitment.[20]

5. **Income fully disregarded**

Most income that is fully disregarded for income support (IS) purposes (see Chapter 8) is also fully disregarded for adult social care services' financial assessment purposes with the *important exception of:*

- attendance allowance (AA)/disability living allowance care component (DLA care), including constant attendance allowance and exceptionally severe disablement allowance payable with industrial injury disablement benefit or war disablement benefit (see pp127 and 129), where it is paid to **permanent** residents.[21] It is only fully disregarded for **temporary** residents (see p281);

and with the important addition of:

- housing costs (eg, mortgage interest) paid as part of IS/income-related employment and support allowance/income-based jobseeker's allowance (see p153) for your home in the community.[22]

As for IS, DLA mobility component, war widow's special pension, Supporting People payments (see p52), child benefit (see p147) and child support maintenance payments (unless the child is living with you), child tax credit, guardian's allowance, housing benefit and council tax benefit paid for your home in the community are also disregarded.[23] In April 2003, contributory benefits dependants' additions were abolished, although claims already in payment at the time continue to be protected and will continue to be disregarded as long as they are paid to the people for whom they are intended.

6. **The savings disregard**

Since the introduction of pension credit (PC), the Department of Health has applied a savings disregard for residents aged 65 or over.[24] The savings disregard applies in the following ways (2009/10 rates).

- If you are a resident in receipt of the savings credit element of PC with pre-PC qualifying income of between £96 (the pension savings credit threshold) and £130 (standard minimum guarantee) a week (or between £153.40 and £198.45 for couples), you will have a disregard of an amount equal to the savings credit award or £5.65 a week (£8.45 for couples) – whichever is less.
- If you are a resident in receipt of the savings credit element of PC with pre-PC qualifying income in excess of £130 a week (£198.45 for couples), you will have a disregard of £5.65 a week (£8.45 for couples).
- If you are a resident who is not in receipt of the savings credit element of PC because, although you have qualifying income, your total income is in excess of £181 a week (£266.03 for couples), you will have a disregard of £5.65 a week (£8.45 for couples).

7. **Capital treated as income**

Most capital treated as income for income support purposes (see p217) is also treated as income for adult social care services' financial assessment purposes. In addition, any capital payments from a third party are treated as income where adult social care services agrees to place you in a higher cost care home if there is a third party willing to contribute towards the higher costs (see Chapter 14).

A lump-sum payment made by the third party will be divided by the number of weeks for which the payment is made and taken fully into account as part of your income.[25] However, any third party payments made to you to help clear arrears of charges for your care home are treated as capital, not income.[26]

If such payments are made directly to adult social care services they are not treated as belonging to you.[27]

There is specific guidance regarding income from investment bonds.[28] In general actual payments of capital by periodic instalments, with or without life insurance, are treated as income provided that the outstanding instalment and any other capital sum not disregarded exceed £16,000. However, adult social care services should seek advice from their legal services department because of the complexity of the products available.

Chapter 11: Income – financial assessments
9. Trust income, personal injury payments and charitable and voluntary payments

11

8. Tariff income

As for income support (IS) (see p217), a tariff income amount of £1 for every £250 or part thereof is added to your weekly assessable income for financial assessment purposes where your capital is between the lower and upper capital limits for your country (see p291).[29] For example, in England for £16,500 capital you would be assessed as having a tariff income of £10 a week. For financial assessment purposes, these capital limits apply to both temporary and permanent residents.

Many adult social care services only review financial assessments annually and therefore, if your capital of more than the lower capital limit for your country (see p291) has reduced before the annual review, and as a result your tariff income reduces, you should make sure you inform adult social care services so that the correct tariff income can be applied from the correct date. If you are in receipt of IS/income-related employment and support allowance/income-based jobseeker's allowance or pension credit, you will also need to inform the DWP.

9. Trust income, personal injury payments and charitable and voluntary payments

As for income support (IS) (see p202), where you are the beneficiary of income only produced by a life interest trust but you are not absolutely entitled to the trust fund as a whole, the income is normally taken fully into account for financial assessment purposes.[30] The value of the right to receive income is a capital asset, but it is fully disregarded for financial assessment purposes (see p300).[31]

If you are the beneficiary of a discretionary trust fund where payments are made wholly at the discretion of the trustees and there is no absolute entitlement to either income or capital, the trust fund itself will not be treated as a capital asset.[32]

Income or payments from a discretionary trust (and some payments from fixed trusts where the trustees have a discretion within the terms of the trust) are treated as voluntary payments (as the trustees are under no obligation to make them)[33] and they are treated in the same way as for IS (see p218). If the payments are regular they are treated as income (see below), and if the payments are irregular they are treated as capital.[34]

Official guidance explains in some detail the different types of trust funds and how they should be treated for financial assessment purposes.[35]

In April 2008, the rules regarding personal injury payments were amended to reflect changes made to the IS rules (currently in England only but due to be amended in Wales and Scotland).[36] They aligned the way in which income from personal injury awards is treated when held in or out of court. It is now treated as income in both circumstances and fully disregarded. See p300 for how lump

11

Chapter 11: Income – financial assessments
9. Trust income, personal injury payments and charitable and voluntary payments

sum personal injury payments are treated. Changes were also made to the treatment of income from voluntary and charitable sources so that it is fully disregarded. The DH is due to update CRAG to reflect these changes in April 2009.

---

10. **Notional income**

As for income support (IS), in certain circumstances you are treated as having income which you do not actually have.[37] There are five types of income which are treated as notional income for financial assessment purposes:

- income paid to adult social care services by a third party to contribute towards the fees of a home where they are higher than the normal amounts that adult social care services will pay (see Chapter 14).[38] However, payments made by a third person directly to adult social care services in respect of a resident's arrears of charges for accommodation and care in a care home should not be treated as the resident's notional income;[39]
- income paid to a third party in respect of you or a member of your family for any item which was taken into account when the standard rate (see p265) was fixed for accommodation provided;[40]
- income which would be available on application[41] (see below);
- income which is due but has not yet been paid;[42]
- income you have deprived yourself of in order to avoid a charge or to reduce the charge payable (see below).[43]

Income available on application

For income which you have not yet acquired to be taken into account, adult social care services must be satisfied that it would in fact be available to you if you made an application. As for IS, some types of income cannot be taken into account as notional income. These include income which may be paid under a discretionary trust, working tax credit, severe disablement allowance and employment service rehabilitation allowance. In addition, any income which would be fully disregarded (eg, housing benefit) will not be included as notional income.[44]

If an income that would be available if you applied is taken into account as notional income (eg, occupational pension not claimed), adult social care services will assume that the application was made on the date that they first became aware of the possible income.[45]

Some adult social care services departments may assume an amount of IS/income-related employment and support allowance or pension credit as part of your income in the financial assessment, even if you are not receiving it or not have been advised to make a claim. If you are not aware that a source of income would be available to you upon application, it will be difficult for adult social care services to argue that it can be treated as notional income. If this has happened to you, seek further advice (see Appendix 2).

11. **Deprivation**

The rules on deprivation of income for financial assessment purposes are similar to the rules for income support (IS) (see p223). Any income which you have disposed of or deprived yourself of in order to avoid a charge or to reduce the charge payable, is considered by adult social care services to be notional income and will be treated as actual income taken into account in the financial assessment in addition to any other assessable income.[46] The avoidance test is subjective, therefore your evidence on the reasons for any deprivation are very important (see p223).[47]

You will be considered to have deprived yourself of a resource if adult social care services are aware that, as a result of your own act, you ceased to possess that resource[48] and you would have continued to benefit from it had you not relinquished or transferred it.[49] The onus is on you to prove that you no longer have an income, otherwise adult social care services will treat you as still possessing the actual income.[50]

Adult social care services should only consider the question of deprivation where the income concerned would have been taken into account in the financial assessment. Therefore, income such as a charitable payment, which is ignored in the financial assessment, would not be considered as deprivation.

Guidance to adult social care services on questions for consideration in deciding whether the deprivation was in order to *avoid* or *reduce* the charge, makes it clear that the specific purpose of the deprivation should be examined.[51] If there is more than one reason why you deprived yourself of an income and one of the reasons was to avoid or reduce the charge, it does not matter whether it was the main reason or not, as long as it was a significant reason.[52] The guidance also states that the timing of the deprivation should be considered,[53] although under the regulations[54] deprivation can be considered for resources disposed of at any time, as it is only in some circumstances[55] that the six-month restriction applies (see p326).

If you have sold the right to receive an income resource for the purposes of avoiding or reducing the charge, then your income has been converted into a capital asset and adult social care services can take account of either the former income resource or, where applicable, the difference between the former income resource and the tariff income or the increase in tariff income.[56]

It is important to note that, following the Scottish *Robertson v Fife* case (see p305), it has been made clear that the provision of services to a person who is assessed as being in need of them is not related to the ability of the person to meet the costs. Despite the differences in Scottish and English legislation, it is arguable that this ruling applies equally in England (see p305).

See pp302 and 348 for more information on issues of deprivation.

12. **Less dependent residents**

You are a 'less dependent resident' in England and Wales if you are a prospective resident or a resident for whom accommodation is provided in 'premises which are not an establishment which is carried on or managed by a person who is registered under Part 2 of the Care Standards Act 2000.' In Scotland, a less dependent resident is described as a person who lives in private or voluntary sector accommodation which is not registered as a care home or in local authority accommodation that does not provide board.

In these circumstances, adult social care services have complete discretion to ignore the whole of the charging assessment if it is 'reasonable in the circumstances.' This is because it has been recognised that to live as independently as possible, you will need to be left with more than the personal expenses allowance (PEA).[57]

However, since April 2002, under the Care Standards Act 2000 (or in Scotland, the Regulation of Care (Scotland) Act 2001), all care homes, even those not providing board, are required to register.[58] The same effect – allowing more than the normal amount of PEA in order to live as independently as possible – can be achieved by a variation of the PEA (see p310). The 'less dependent resident' provision may still be used where ordinary housing is provided for you by adult social care services under s21 National Assistance Act 1948, as you would have the cost of necessities such as food, fuel and clothing to provide and therefore it would not be appropriate to apply the charging rules as if you were in a care home. It may also be used where accommodation is provided under an adult placement scheme (see p55).

Notes

1 Part II NA(AR) Regs

1. General
2 NA(SPR)(E) Regs
3 s22(4) NAA 1948
4 Sch 2 (earnings) and Sch 3 (income other than earnings) NA(AR) Regs

5 Reg 9 NA(AR) Regs

2. Treatment of income
6 IS Regs
7 Sch 3 para 27 NA(AR) Regs

3. Income fully taken into account
8 Reg 17(4) NA(AR) Regs
9 Reg 15(1) and Sch 3 para 26 NA(AR) Regs; para 8.006 CRAG; para 8.006 Scottish CRAG
10 Reg 15(1) NA(AR) Regs and para 8.006 CRAG; para 8.006 Scottish CRAG
11 Reg 15(1) NA(AR) Regs and para 8.006 CRAG; para 8.006 SWSG 8/96
12 Reg 15(3) NA(AR) Regs and para 8.007 CRAG; WOC 29/27; para 8.007 Scottish CRAG
13 para 8.016 CRAG
14 para 8.033 CRAG

4. Income partially disregarded
15 Reg 10A NA(AR) Regs
16 para 5.005 CRAG; para 5.005 Scottish CRAG
17 Proposal submitted to the DH in October 2008 by the CRAG Stakeholders Group
18 para 4 LAC (97)5; para 4 SWSG 7/97
19 para 8.024C CRAG (England, Scotland and Wales)
20 s22(4) NAA 1948; para 5.005 CRAG (England, Scotland and Wales)

5. Income fully disregarded
21 Sch 3 para 6 NA(AR) Regs; para 8.006 CRAG
22 Sch 3 para 26 NA(AR) Regs; paras 8.039 & 8.040 CRAG
23 Sch 3 NA(AR) Regs; para 8.038 CRAG

6. The savings disregard
24 NA(AR)(A)(No.2)(E) Regs 2003

7. Capital treated as income
25 Reg 16(4) NA(AR) Regs
26 Reg 22(8) NA(AR) Regs; para 6.045A CRAG; para 6.044A Scottish CRAG
27 para 8.062A CRAG; para 8.062A Scottish CRAG
28 para 8.014A, 8.014B and 6.002C CRAG

8. Tariff income
29 Reg 28 NA(AR) Regs

9. Trust income
30 para 10.017 CRAG; para 10.017 Scottish CRAG
31 Sch 4 para 11 NA(AR) Regs; para 10.015 CRAG; para 10.015 Scottish CRAG
32 para 10.020 CRAG; para 10.020 Scottish CRAG
33 para 10.021 CRAG; para 10.021 Scottish CRAG

34 Reg 22(7) NA(AR) Regs; para 8.052 CRAG
35 s10 CRAG; s10 Scottish CRAG
36 Regs 5(1)(a) and (2) SI No.593/2008

10. Notional income
37 Reg 17 NA(AR) Regs
38 Reg 17(4) NA(AR) Regs
39 Reg 17(5) NA(AR) Regs
40 Reg 17(3) NA(AR) Regs
41 Reg 17(2) NA(AR) Regs
42 Reg 17(2) NA(AR) Regs
43 Reg 17(1) NA(AR) Regs
44 para 8.065 CRAG; para 8.065 Scottish CRAG
45 para 8.069 CRAG; para 8.069 Scottish CRAG

11. Deprivation
46 Reg 17(1) NA(AR) Regs
47 *The Queen (on the application of the Personal Representatives of Christopher Beeson) and Dorset County Council and the Secretary of State for Health* [2001] EWHC Admin 986, 30 November 2001, [2002] EWCA Civ 1812, 18 December 2002
48 para 8.072 CRAG; para 8.072 Scottish CRAG
49 para 8.075 CRAG; para 8.075 Scottish CRAG
50 para 8.076 CRAG; para 8.076 Scottish CRAG
51 paras 8.073-8.080 CRAG; paras 8.073-8.080 Scottish CRAG
52 para 8.077 CRAG; para 8.077 Scottish CRAG
53 para 8.078 CRAG; para 8.072 Scottish CRAG
54 Reg 17(1) NA(AR) Regs
55 s21 HASSASSAA 1983
56 para 8.080 CRAG; para 8.080 Scottish CRAG

12. Less dependent residents
57 Reg 5 NA(AR)Regs 1992; para 2.007 CRAG; para 2.005 Scottish CRAG
58 Section 2 of CRAG has not been updated to reflect the changes in Social Care legislation

Chapter 12

Capital and property – financial assessments

This chapter covers:
1. General (below)
2. Treatment of capital (p291)
3. If your home is up for sale (p296)
4. Capital disregarded indefinitely (p297)
5. Capital disregarded for 26 weeks or longer (p299)
6. Capital disregarded for 52 weeks (p299)
7. Income treated as capital (p300)
8. Trust funds and personal injury payments (p300)
9. Notional capital (p301)
10. Deprivation (p302)
11. Diminishing notional capital (p305)

Legislation provides for the assessment of a resident's or prospective resident's capital (including property) by adult social care services to establish the contribution to the cost of the placement in a care home.[1]

Capital and property are treated in a similar way to that for income support purposes (see Chapter 8). This chapter concentrates on the key differences.

1. General

Capital includes all assets, in or outside the UK, unless disregarded.[2] It also includes income treated as capital (see p300) and notional capital (see p301).[3] Some of the most common forms of capital are:

- property (buildings and land);
- savings;
- savings certificates from National Savings & Investments;
- premium bonds;
- stocks and shares or any other type of investment;
- personal injury payments;

- trust funds.

If you have a partner, her/his capital will not be included in the assessment even if you are only a temporary resident. Unlike the DWP, adult social care services do not have any powers to assess couples jointly.

2. **Treatment of capital**

The value of your capital, after the appropriate disregards (p297) have been applied, is assessed by adult social care services and may affect the amount of your contribution to the cost of your placement.

The capital limits are reviewed every year.[4] The capital limits from April 2009 are:

	Lower	Upper
	2009	2009
England	£14,000	£23,000
Wales	£20,750	£22,000
Scotland	£13,750	£22,500

Adult social care services will not assume any tariff income (see p285) on capital up to the lower limit for your country (see above).[5] If you have between the lower and upper capital limits for your country, adult social care services will assume a tariff income of £1 a week for every £250 or part thereof above the lower capital limit, thus increasing your assessable income (see p285).[6]

Unlike the capital limits for income support (IS), the capital limits for financial assessments apply to both temporary (including respite and trial period – see p275 for definitions) and permanent residents.

If you have capital of more than the upper capital limit for your country, you are expected to meet the whole cost[7] of your accommodation and care yourself until your capital drops to the upper capital limit or less.[8] This means that you will be 'self-funding', and it could affect some social security benefits payable to you (see p350).

Adult social care services must provide care in a care home for you if you are assessed as needing it, unless it is 'otherwise available' to you.[9] The Health and Social Care Act 2001 and its subsequent regulations reaffirm that adult social care services cannot say that accommodation is 'otherwise available' because of your capital if you have less than the upper capital limit. Comparable provision for Scotland is in the Community Care and Health (Scotland) Act 2002 (see Appendix 1).

It is also important to note that following the Scottish *Robertson v Fife* House of Lords case,[10] it has been made clear that the provision of services to a person who is assessed as needing them is not related to the ability of the person to meet the costs (see p305). Despite the differences in Scottish and English legislation, it is arguable that this ruling applies equally in England (see p305).

The treatment of capital for financial assessment purposes is very similar to the treatment of capital for the calculation of IS (see Chapter 8).[11] Temporary residents' (including respite and trial period residents – see p275 for definitions) and permanent residents' capital is treated in the same way except that for temporary residents the value of your home in the community is disregarded indefinitely (see below).

The value of your home in the community

Temporary residents

If you are a temporary resident (including respite and trial period residents – see p275 for definitions), the value of your home in the community is disregarded as long as:
- you intend to return to your home and it is still available to you; *or*
- you are selling your home in order to buy another more suitable home to return to.[12]

Permanent residents

First 12 weeks

If you are a permanent resident and the value of your home in the community is not disregarded indefinitely (see p297), then the 12-week property disregard will be applied.[13]

As the definition of 'resident' in the regulations[14] only applies to a person provided with accommodation under Part III of the National Assistance Act, if you were already in a care home as a self-funder you do not count as a resident within the definition until you are placed by adult social care services. Therefore, your 12-week property disregard (if you still have a property at this point) begins from the day adult social care services contracts with the care home. This is a recent interpretation of the law by the Department of Health (DH) in answer to an enquiry made by the Ombudsman during a case that was ultimately settled before a decision was issued. It is a departure from the original policy intention[15] where the purpose of the 12-week property disregard is stated as being to offer 'a breathing space between entering a care home on a permanent basis and deciding how best to fund the move'. This has been consistent with the practice of adult social care services and is unlikely to change until the revised guidance is issued.[16] This may result in adult social care services taking on the responsibility of arranging for accommodation and care when you still have liquid capital above the upper capital limit so that the 12-week property disregard will have expired before you need to access the capital in your property. There may also be a question raised by adult social care services about whether you would satisfy the condition that you would 'usually occupy' the property as your 'only or main home' if you have been a permanent resident in a care home for some time. The longer the period that you have spent in the care home (especially if it has been more than 52 weeks), the more likely it is that this question will arise. Seek advice if your adult social care services do not apply the disregard in these circumstances.

If you are a temporary resident and you subsequently become permanent, the 12-week property disregard will apply from the date on which you become a permanent resident.

If you are a permanent resident but you leave the care home before the end of the 12 weeks and then re-enter a care home again on a permanent basis within 52 weeks, you will be entitled to the balance of the 12-week disregard. If you re-enter a care home again on a permanent basis more than 52 weeks later, you will qualify for the 12-week disregard again.[17]

After 12 weeks

The value of your home in the community will be taken into account as capital unless it is disregarded (see p297). As for IS, its value will be based on the current selling price, less any debts secured on it (eg, a mortgage),[18] and less 10 per cent in recognition of the expenses incurred in selling it. Once your home is sold and the capital realised, it is the actual amount of the expenses incurred that are deducted from the proceeds.[19]

If you decide to sell your home in the community, see p296 for what happens while it is for sale.

Adult social care services do not have the power to enforce the sale of your property and they may not withdraw services if your charge is not met, as the duty to make residential provision where there is an assessed need is not conditional upon the payment of the assessed contribution.[20]

If you choose not to sell your property, you may consider entering into a deferred payment agreement with adult social care services (see p272). If you do not have a deferred payment agreement and your charge is not paid, you will be accruing a debt to adult social care services which may be pursued.

Other property

Any other property you own (or jointly own – see p294) will also be taken into account as capital and will be valued in the same way as your home in the community. There is no disregard that can be applied to a property that you did not occupy as your main or only home in the community.

Ownership

In some cases, there may be a difference between the legal and the beneficial ownership of capital such as a property. If another person has been contributing towards the mortgage and/or running costs of your property (including your own home), s/he may be able to establish a beneficial interest in your property, even if it is legally owned by you. If a beneficial ownership is established, the property will be valued as if it is jointly owned.

The size of any beneficial interest in the property may be a complex question and you may need to seek legal advice. How that interest is to be valued will depend on whether the co-owner(s) are in occupation or not (see CPAG's *Welfare Benefits and Tax Credits Handbook*).

Both the DWP and adult social care services value the share that they each determine belongs to you in the same way, by establishing the current market or surrender value – ie, the price a willing buyer would pay to a willing seller for the share, less 10 per cent if there would be costs involved in selling, and less any mortgage or debt secured on the property (see p294).

Jointly owned land or property

Adult social care services and the DWP may treat property that is jointly owned differently. If you own property with one or more people, the DWP usually treats you as owning an equal share, even if your actual share may be more or less than this.[21] The deemed equal share is then valued. However, a Court of Appeal decision[22] makes it clear that this should only apply where the joint owners are joint tenants, and therefore each owner has an equal share of the whole beneficial interest in the property. It does not apply where the joint owners are tenants-in-common and each have a separate share of the property which can be identified separately and may be a 10 per cent or 25 per cent share even where there are only two owners, rather than a 50 per cent share. The DWP has detailed guidance[23] and a special agency, the Valuation Office Agency, which deals with more complex valuations.

Adult social care services value your *actual* share in the jointly owned property.[24] Therefore, if you have more or less than an equal share, the valuation amount may differ from that assessed by the DWP. Unlike the DWP, adult social care services have little guidance on how to proceed in these cases. However, if you dispute a valuation by adult social care services, guidance states that a professional valuation should be obtained.[25] This should not be an expense passed on to you, as there is no provision to charge for such an item.

Official guidance deals with joint beneficial ownership of property.[26] It states that the value of the interest is governed by your 'ability to re-assign the beneficial interest to somebody else' and 'there being a market, ie, the interest being such as to attract a willing buyer for the interest'. The likelihood of there being a willing buyer will depend on the conditions in which the joint beneficial interest has arisen.

The guidance further states that the value would be heavily influenced by whether the other joint owner(s) would be able to buy your share. If the joint owner(s) cannot or does not want to do this, in many cases it would be unlikely that an outsider would be willing to buy into the property. Even if someone was willing to buy into the property, the value of this interest could be very low or effectively nil.

A number of adult social care departments have argued that there will usually be a willing buyer, especially in cases where the jointly owned property is not lived in by the joint owner, on the grounds that a reasonably informed buyer would be aware that after purchase they would have rights as a co-owner which include the right to apply to the court for a sale.

In practice, valuing your share in a jointly owned property is very difficult. It is important to seek advice if you think your share has been overvalued. It is often useful to investigate whether a local estate agent would put your share on the market. In a Local Government Ombudsman case, maladministration was found both in terms of delay in determining the value of a resident's share in a property and in terms of procedure in dealing with valuations of a jointly owned property.[27] The resident jointly owned a property with his son. The son neither wished to purchase his father's share nor sell his own share and a valuation was obtained on the son's behalf which was very low. The Ombudsman found the failures perplexing as there is clear direction in the guidance[28] supporting the view that the real market value of the share of the property was effectively nil. The local authority did not have significant evidence or opinion to disagree and it took no account of the DH guidance or caselaw. As the outcome of this case affects others in similar circumstances, the Ombudsman recommended that if the local authority decided that a nil assessment would normally be expected in such circumstances, it would need to review past assessments as well.

In the Court of Appeal case *Campbell v Griffin*[29] it was held that a long term lodger had acquired an equitable interest in the property because he had provided care over a number of years to an elderly couple prior to their moving to a care home. Although this did not give him a right to remain in the property, the court found entitlement to £35,000 from the proceeds of sale of the property.

In *Kelly v Hammersmith and Fulham LBC*[30] the resident had purchased her council house under the 'right to buy' provisions, but her daughter had funded the whole purchase costs and mortgage repayments. Despite this the court held that the local authority was entitled to maintain a caution on the property in the mother's name for outstanding residential home fees because the daughter was unable to provide evidence to show that her mother had no beneficial interest in the property.

Jointly owned capital (other than property)

If you jointly own capital with another person (except any interest in property or land – see p294), it will be divided in equal shares for financial assessment purposes in order to determine the assessable capital, regardless of what your actual share is.[31] Unlike for IS, this also applies if you are a temporary or permanent resident and you jointly own capital with your partner, as adult social care services have no power to assess a couple according to their joint resources.

This means that if you have, for example, a joint bank account with your sister containing £25,000 of which £10,000 belongs to you and £15,000 belongs to your sister, adult social care services will assess £12,500 as your share. An adviser, anticipating this decision, may recommend that the joint account be closed and two separate accounts opened for each person, so that you would have the £10,000 in an account in your sole name. The notional capital rules (see p301) should not be applied in these circumstances as this would not constitute a deprivation of capital because you are still in possession of your actual beneficial entitlement.[32]

Property owned but rented to tenants

If you let your property to tenants and the value of your property is not disregarded, adult social care services will include its capital value in your financial assessment. If the value takes your capital level to above the capital limit for your country (see p291), you will be charged the full standard rate for your accommodation and care. Guidance states that it will then be for you to agree to pay the rental income (along with any other income) to adult social care services in order to reduce any accruing debt.[33]

3. If your home is up for sale

If you are a permanent resident and the value of your home in the community is not subject to a mandatory or discretionary disregard (see p298), then it will be taken into account after the 12-week disregard period (see p292). Unlike for income support purposes, this applies even if it is up for sale.

If you cannot pay your accommodation and care costs (which will usually be the full standard rate charge – see p265 – if your property plus any other capital to be taken into account is valued at above the capital limit for your country – see p291) until your property is sold and you receive the proceeds of the sale, adult social care services can help meet your accommodation and care costs. You will, however, have to pay back the full amount once your property is sold. This arrangement could be an informal bridging loan or a formalised deferred payment agreement (see p272).

In these circumstances, adult social care services have powers to put a 'legal charge' ('charging order' in Scotland) on your property in order to recover the amount that they have paid towards your costs once your property is sold. The capital limits that are applied when a 'charge' is placed on your property are the capital limits that were in force at the time:

Before April 1996	£8,000
From April 1996	£16,000
From April 2001	£18,500
From April 2002	£19,000 (England and Wales), £18,500 (Scotland)
From April 2003	£19,500 (England), £20,000 (Wales), £18,500 (Scotland)
From April 2004	£20,000 (England), £20,500 (Wales), £19,000 (Scotland)
From April 2005	£20,500 (England), £21,000 (Wales), £19,500 (Scotland)
From April 2006	£21,000 (England), £21,500 (Wales), £20,000 (Scotland)
From April 2007	£21,500 (England), £20,000 (Wales), £20,750 (Scotland)
From April 2008	£22,250 (England), £22,000 (Wales), £21,500 (Scotland)

4. **Capital disregarded indefinitely**

Most capital that is disregarded indefinitely for income support (IS) purposes (see p206) is also disregarded indefinitely for adult social care services financial assessment purposes, *with the important exception that:*

- the 52-week limit on the disregard of arrears and non-payment of compensation of certain benefits that has been lifted for IS purposes in specified circumstances (see p209) remains in force for financial assessment purposes;[34]

and with the addition that:

- adult social care services have discretionary powers to allow a disregard of the value of your former home where you are a **permanent** resident and it is occupied, wholly or in part, if they think it is reasonable to do so (see p298).[35] This is in addition to the mandatory 'defined circumstances', most of which also apply to IS.[36]

The 'defined circumstances' for a disregard of the value of a former home in the community apply where you are a permanent resident are where it is occupied wholly or in part by:

- your partner or former partner or civil partner (except where you are estranged, or divorced from your partner, former partner or civil partner); *or*

- your estranged or divorced partner where s/he is a lone parent with a dependent child; *or*
- a relative of yours or a relative of a member of your family who is:
  - aged 60 or over; *or*
  - incapacitated; *or*
  - aged under 16 and is a child for whom you are responsible.[37]

The property disregard applies only to premises which were occupied as your home.[38] A social security commissioner held that 'premises' was to be interpreted in accordance with the definition of 'dwelling occupied as the home'.[39]

If your partner, children or relatives continue to live in your home, the help they can receive for their housing costs depends on their circumstances. If they are paying the housing costs, even though you are the person liable for them, they can claim housing benefit or IS housing costs instead of you (see pp153 and 163).

Meaning of terms

'Relative' means parent, parent-in-law, brother, sister, son, son-in-law, daughter, daughter-in-law, step-parent, step-son, step-daughter (or the partner of any of these), a grandchild, grandparent, uncle, aunt, niece or nephew.[40]

'Family' includes:
- a married or unmarried couple, a civil partner and any person who is a member of the same household and the responsibility of either or both members of the couple; *or*
- a person who is not a member of a married or unmarried couple or civil partnership and who is - a member of the same household and your responsibility.[41]

'Incapacitated' is not defined in the regulations, but guidance states that it is reasonable to conclude that a relative is incapacitated if s/he is receiving one of the following benefits: incapacity benefit (employment and support allowance is likely to be included in the updated guidance due), severe disablement allowance, disability living allowance, attendance allowance or constant attendance allowance, or an analogous benefit or s/he would satisfy the incapacity conditions for any of these.[42]

Discretion to disregard

Guidance is provided to adult social care services on their discretionary powers to disregard the value of your former home, in which another person continues to live, in circumstances other than those specified in the legislation. This could be where your home is the sole residence of someone who has given up her/his own home in order to care for you.[43] Adult social care services' discretion could also be applied where you were permanently living with an adult son or daughter in your home and s/he is remaining there. Where adult social care services have used their discretion in these types of circumstances, they can review their decision at any time. Guidance suggests that it would be reasonable to begin taking account of the value of a property when the carer dies or moves out.[44]

If you intend to return home

As for IS (see p206), the value of a dwelling normally occupied as your home is disregarded if your stay is temporary (including respite and trial period stays – see p275 for definitions) and you intend to return to your home which is still available to you, or you are taking reasonable steps to dispose of your home in order to acquire another property to return to.[45]

The value of any other property that you own (or jointly own) besides your own home is taken into account as capital.

If your stay is initially thought to be permanent but turns out to be temporary, it is arguable that your home should be treated in the same way as if you had been temporary from the outset.[46] This provision arguably means that the financial assessment undertaken by adult social care services would have to be retrospectively reviewed and any excess payments made refunded or any charges placed on your property lifted. However, this is at variance with other parts of the guidance dealing with temporary residents where it is stated that if a stay turns out to be temporary, adult social care services should not *continue* to treat you as permanent.[47] If this affects you, seek further advice.

5. Capital disregarded for 26 weeks or longer

Most capital that is disregarded for 26 weeks or longer for income support purposes (see p206) is also disregarded for 26 weeks or longer for adult social care services financial assessment purposes, with the important exception that adult social care services do not have the power to disregard property that is up for sale (see p296).

6. Capital disregarded for 52 weeks

Most capital that is disregarded for 52 weeks for income support (IS) purposes (see p206) is also disregarded for 52 weeks for adult social care services financial assessment purposes, with the important addition of:

* arrears and non-payment compensation of certain benefits, even if the amount is £5,000 or over;[48]
* IS being included in the list of benefits for which the balance of any arrears paid or any compensation paid due to non-payment is disregarded as capital for a period of 52 weeks.[49] Any payment of this type should be treated as income over the period for which it is payable and any amount left over after

the period for which it is treated as income has elapsed should be treated as capital.[50]

Example

You are assessed as being able to pay £75 a week towards the cost of your placement on the basis of your current income pending receipt of IS.

It is explained to you that the charge will be reassessed or retrospectively reviewed once IS is received and that back payments will be required.

Although not required to do so, you can choose to make payments of £90 a week.

After six weeks, arrears of IS at £35 a week (£210) are received.

The charges are reassessed/retrospectively reviewed, and you are required to pay £110 a week, from the start of your placement.

As you have been paying £15 a week more than originally required, the arrears payable to the local authority are £120 rather than the full £210 IS arrears.

The remaining £90 becomes capital and is disregarded for 52 weeks.

7. Income treated as capital

As for income support purposes (see p206), any income derived from capital (eg, rental income) is normally treated as capital rather than income, from the date on which it is normally due to be paid,[51] unless it is income derived from capital disregarded – eg, any capital held in trust which is as a result of a personal injury (see below).[52]

Interest paid on capital is treated as capital from the date on which it is paid. However, there is an assumed income from any capital over the capital limit for your country (see p291).[53] See also tariff income, on p285.

8. Trust funds and personal injury payments

The rules about capital placed in a trust fund for adult social care services' financial assessment purposes are the same as for income support (IS) purposes (see p202). If you are a beneficiary of a non-discretionary or absolute entitlement trust, the value of the capital asset and any income derived from the capital is normally taken into account as capital in the calculation of your contribution.[54]

The important exception to this is where the capital held in trust is derived from a personal injury compensation payment, in which case both the capital and the capital value of any right to receive income are fully disregarded.[55] For the treatment of any payments made to you from the capital, see below.

In April 2008, the rules regarding personal injury payments were changed to reflect changes made to the IS rules (currently in England only but due to be amended in Wales and Scotland).[56] Any lump sum personal injury payment held out of court is now disregarded as capital for up to 52 weeks, except where any payment is 'specifically identified' by a court to deal with the cost of providing care. Personal injury trusts remain fully disregarded capital. See p285 for the way in which income from personal injury awards is treated. The Department of Health (DH) is due to update CRAG to reflect these changes in April 2009.

If you are a beneficiary of a trust where the deed directs that you are to receive income produced by the trust capital only, then you only have an absolute entitlement to the income. These trusts are known as life interest or fixed interest trusts. The right to receive the income from a life interest trust has a capital value but it is disregarded for financial assessment purposes.[57] For the treatment of the income from these types of trusts, see p285.

A discretionary trust fund where payments are made wholly at the discretion of the trustees and there is no absolute entitlement to either capital or income will not be treated as a capital asset.[58] For the treatment of payments made from a discretionary trust fund, see p285.

Official guidance explains the different types of trust funds and how they should be treated for financial assessment purposes.[59]

9. **Notional capital**

The notional capital rules are similar to the notional income rules (see p286) and the notional capital rules for income support (see p203). In certain circumstances, you may be treated as possessing a capital asset even where you do not in fact possess it.[60] The important difference is that the notional income rules are mandatory but the notional capital rules for financial assessment purposes are discretionary. You *will* be treated as possessing income of which you have deprived yourself for the purpose of decreasing the amount that you may be liable to pay for your accommodation; but you *may* be treated as possessing capital of which you have deprived yourself for the purpose of decreasing the amount that you may be liable to pay for your accommodation. This means that adult social care services have discretion on whether to apply the rules.

There are three main circumstances in which you *may* be treated as having notional capital:

- where you deliberately deprive yourself of capital in order to reduce the amount of charge you have to pay (see p302);
- where you fail to apply for capital which is available to you (capital payable under a trust derived from a payment made in consequence of a personal injury cannot be taken into account as notional capital);

- where someone else makes a payment of capital to a third party on your behalf, unless it is for an item which was not taken into account when the standard rate was fixed for your accommodation.[61]

---

10. **Deprivation**

The rules on deprivation for financial assessments are similar to the rules for income support (IS – see p204). Any capital which you have disposed of, or deprived yourself of, in order to avoid a charge or to reduce the charge payable towards the cost of your care home, may be considered by adult social care services to be notional capital, and as such may be treated as actual capital and taken into account in the financial assessment.[62]

Adult social care services also have a power to charge a person (or persons) to whom you have given any capital asset if it was within six months before entering a care home under arrangements made by adult social care services (also see p349).[63]

Adult social care services should only consider questions of deprivation of capital when you cease to possess capital which would otherwise be taken into account.[64] As with deprivation of income, it is up to you to prove that you no longer have the resource, otherwise it will be treated as actual capital.

If you have used capital to acquire personal possessions to avoid or reduce the charge, the market value of those personal possessions is not disregarded.[65]

Guidance to adult social care services sets out the questions for consideration when deciding whether the deprivation was in order to *avoid* or *reduce* the charge.

It is important to note that you, as the resident, should not be treated as depriving yourself of capital in order to reduce your charge if you enable your spouse/civil partner to purchase a smaller property by making available to her/him part of your share of the proceeds from the sale of the property you shared as your home.[66]

As with the rules regarding the deprivation of income, the purpose and timing of the deprivation should be considered. The guidance suggests it would be unreasonable to decide that a resident had disposed of an asset in order to reduce her/his charge for accommodation when the disposal took place at a time when s/he was fit and healthy and could not have foreseen the need for a move to residential accommodation.

However, a Scottish Court case (*Yule*)[67] cast some doubt on the use of this argument (see p303), although a more recent case (*Beeson*)[68] in England makes it clear that (at least in England and Wales) the resident's intentions need to be examined using a subjective test not an objective one (see p304).

Another Scottish case (*Robertson*),[69] in which the Outer and Inner House of Sessions adopted the same hard-line approach as in *Yule*, was overturned by the House of Lords,[70] and while the correct application of the deprivation test was not examined, an important principle regarding notional capital and the provision of accommodation was established (see p305).

See p305 for what happens when deprivation has been decided and notional capital has been taken into account in your financial assessment.

Yule v South Lanarkshire Council

In this case, Mrs Yule transferred the ownership of her home to her granddaughter more than a year before there was any significant deterioration in her health. However, the council decided that it was done in order to avoid or reduce the charge. The council dismissed information to the contrary, supplied by the client's granddaughter and solicitor, concluding that the same result could have been achieved had the client left the property to her granddaughter in a will.

The Scottish Outer House of Session did not accept the submission that 'the respondents (ie, the council) could only make the decision which they did if there was evidence that the claimant knew of the existence of a capital limit (an issue considered to be significant by social security commissioners) and that she had foreseen the making of an application for the relevant benefit'. The Court held that 'the respondents were entitled to draw inferences from the information received by them ... The decision on matters of fact is left to the respondents and there is no appeal. Accordingly the weight given by the respondents to particular pieces of evidence is entirely a matter for them and not open to challenge'.

The case was appealed to the Inner House of Session but the decision was upheld.[71] The Court considered that it was not necessary that the applicant should know of the capital limit and that no specific finding is required as to the exact state of knowledge or intention of the applicant if it is a reasonable inference that it must have been a purpose of the transaction to avoid having to pay charges. This is contrary to the judgment in the *Beeson* case (see p304).

In the *Yule* case, the judgment sought to differentiate between the financial assessment/charging regulations and the social security legislation by stating that they have to be looked at differently, 'not least because the purpose of the individual may have been formed possibly some time ahead of the prospect that he or she might require to enter such residential accommodation'.

They also stated that 'we agree with the Lord Ordinary that it is open to a local authority to reach a view as to the purpose of a transaction such as the present, without any specific finding as to the exact state of knowledge or intention of the applicant, so long as the primary facts are such as reasonably to lead to the inference that the purpose was at least in part that specified in regulation 25(1)'.

The approach of the Courts in this case is arguably, in the light of the *Beeson* case (see p304), an objective one, as there was no evidence of the subjective intention of Mrs Yule when she made the gift of her house. Guidance makes it clear that it is the subjective intention and purpose at the time of transfer that needs to be examined[72] and that avoiding the charge must be a **significant** purpose of any transfer.[73]

Beeson v Dorset County Council

The resident in this case had transferred the ownership of his house to his son by deed of gift after he had suffered a stroke but two and a half years before entering a care home. The council decided that he had deprived himself of the capital asset for the purpose of decreasing the amount that he was liable to pay for his accommodation. This decision was upheld following an appeal through the complaints procedure.

In the judgment, the case was distinguished from *Yule* due to the existence of evidence from the resident's family about his and their state of mind at the relevant time. Commenting on the *Yule* judgment, the Judge in *Beeson* states: 'Although the court held that it is not necessary for the claimant to know of 'the' capital limit and that no specific finding is required as to the exact state of knowledge or intention of the applicant, I do not see how an applicant could be found to have the relevant purpose unless he was aware of the possibility that he might be provided with accommodation and that he might be liable to pay for it.'

The resident's son gave evidence to the council that the funding of residential care did not come into his father's thoughts and that the transfer took place at a time when his father intended to live and ultimately die in his home. Although there was evidence to the contrary, this evidence was considered by the Court to be of central importance. It was stated that, if this evidence was accepted, on the basis of the correct subjective test required by regulation 25,[74] it could not be considered that the transfer was for the purpose of decreasing the amount that the resident was liable to pay for his accommodation.[75]

The Court found that the panel that heard the resident's case under the council's complaints procedure had either failed to apply the correct subjective test or if it had applied the subjective test, it failed to give adequate reasons as to why the evidence was rejected. It was concluded that the panel did not direct itself correctly.[76]

This case also considered whether the relevant statutory procedure is incompatible with Article 6(1) of the European Convention on Human Rights. The judgment was that the system used by the council in determining the question of deprivation did not comply with Article 6(1) because the panel established under the adult social care services complaints procedure did not amount to an independent review of the facts and, because there was no such review, judicial review was not an adequate means of appeal.

However, this part of the judgment was overturned on appeal to the Court of Appeal.[77]

The *Beeson* case provides a more helpful examination of the issues involved in deprivation and notional capital cases. It goes into detail on the statutory requirements that councils have to apply themselves to the correct test using the correct procedure, and ultimately to provide an adequately reasoned decision which demonstrates the correct application.

Robertson v Fife Council

In this case, the council had decided that Mrs Robertson had deliberately deprived herself of capital by transferring the ownership of her property to her sons and therefore, as she notionally possessed capital of over the upper capital limit, it did not have any duty to provide her with accommodation.

Although the Scottish Outer and Inner House of Session judgments took the same approach as in *Yule* on the interpretation of the application of the rules regarding the deprivation of capital, the House of Lords[78] overturned the judgments, stating that 'the assessment of need and decisions as to whether they call for the provision of any of the community services comes first. The assessment of means and the requirement to pay what the person can afford, comes afterwards. Notional capital can be taken into account at the stage when charges are being made for the services. But it must be left out of account at the earlier stage when decisions are being taken to provide these services.'[79]

Although this is a Scottish case, the system in England and Wales is similar, especially with regard to the assessment of need and the ability to make payments. Therefore it can be argued that the principle applies and should be followed in all cases.

There may also be an argument that this case would not have been brought in England or Wales because the provision of accommodation was not 'otherwise available' (see p291) to Mrs Robertson. Therefore, adult social care services' duty to provide accommodation still existed.

For enforcement powers (ie, what can happen when deprivation has been established), see pp325–327.

11. **Diminishing notional capital**

Where you have been assessed as having notional capital, adult social care services should reduce the amount of that notional capital each week by the difference between the rate which you are paying for the accommodation and the rate you would have paid if you were not treated as possessing the notional capital (also see p325).[80]

Notes

1 Part III NA(AR) Regs

1. General

2 Sch 4 (capital to be disregarded) NA(AR) Regs

3 Regs 21, 22 and 25 NA(AR) Regs

2. Treatment of capital

4 DH press release 2001/0015, 5 January 2001

5 Reg 21 NA(AR) Regs

6 Reg 28 NA(AR) Regs

7 In Scotland the whole cost means the cost of the accommodation only, for those aged 65 or over where personal care is funded by the local authority. For those in a nursing home aged under 65 in Scotland or any age in England and Wales the whole cost means the cost of accommodation and personal care only, where the nursing care costs are met by the Registered Nursing Care Contribution paid by the NHS.

8 Reg 20 NA(AR) Regs

9 s21 NAA 1948 and *R v Sefton MBC ex parte Help the Aged and Others* [1997] I CCLR 57 CA; para 11 LAC (98)8; WOC 12/98; s12 SW(S)A 1968 and SWSG 6/98

10 *Robertson v Fife* [2002] 25 July UKHL35, HL

11 IS Regs

12 Sch 4 para 1 NA(AR) Regs; para 7.002 CRAG; para 7.002 Scottish CRAG

13 Sch 4 para 1A NA(AR) Regs; para 7.002A CRAG; para 7.002A Scottish CRAG

14 Reg 1 NA(AR) Regs

15 LAC(2001)10

16 The DH plan to issue guidance that will state that Guidance on the 12-week property disregard is published in LAC(2001)10 and LAC(2001)25. The 12-week property disregard applies to the property the resident would otherwise usually occupy as their only or main home from the moment the resident is admitted to permanent residential accommodation provided by a council under Part 3 of the 1948 Act. The disregard applies irrespective of whether the resident was already in a care home as a self-funder. This is because the legislation refers to the provision of accommodation pursuant to Part 3 of the 1948 Act and not to the fact of a person's residence in a care home. If a person makes their own arrangements for residential care (i.e. if they fund their own care), but is subsequently assessed by a council as needing permanent residential accommodation under section 21 of the 1948 Act then the 12-week property disregard should apply. However, if a person has been living in a care home for many years there may be an issue as to whether they would otherwise normally occupy the property in question as their only or main residence.

17 para 7.002B CRAG; para 7.002B Scottish CRAG

18 Reg 23(1)(b) NA(AR) Regs; para 6.011b CRAG; para 6.010B Scottish CRAG

19 Reg 23(1)(a) NA(AR) Regs; para 6.011a and 6.015 CRAG; paras 6.010a Scottish and 6.014 Scottish CRAG

20 ss22(1) and 25(2) NAA 1948

21 Reg 52 IS Regs

22 *James Hourigan on behalf of his mother Mary Hourigan (deceased) v Secretary of State for Work and Pensions,* [2002] EWCA Civ 1890, 19 December 2002 (appeal by Secretary of State against CIS 5906/99)

23 Memo AOG JSA/IS (98)35

24 Reg 27(2) NA(AR) Regs

25 para 7 LAC (97)5; WOC 29/97; para 8 SWSG 7/97

26 paras 7.012 - 7.014A CRAG
27 Complaint no.03/C/09384 against Lincolnshire County Council, August 2004
28 paras 7.012 - 7.014A CRAG
29 [2004] EWHC 435 (Admin)
30 [2001] EWCA Civ 990
31 Reg 27(1) NA(AR) Regs
32 para 6.010 CRAG; para 6.009 Scottish CRAG
33 para 7.017 CRAG; para 7.017 Scottish CRAG

4. Capital disregarded indefinitely
34 Sch 4 para 6 NA(AR) Regs as amended by NA(AR)(A)(No.2)(E) Regs 2002 or in Scotland by NA(AR)(A)(S) Regs 2003. For Scotland, between the rule change for IS on 14.10.02 and the amendment on 28.02.03 such payments should be treated in accordance with the IS Regulations
35 Sch 4 para 18 NA(AR) Regs
36 Sch 4 paras 2 and 2A NA(AR) Regs
37 para 7.003 CRAG; Sch 4 para 2 NA(AR) Regs
38 CIS/767/1993
39 Reg 2(1) IS Regs
40 para 7.004 CRAG; para 7.004 Scottish CRAG
41 para 7.004A CRAG; para 7.004 Scottish CRAG
42 para 7.005 CRAG; para 7.005 Scottish CRAG
43 para 7.007 CRAG; para 7.007 Scottish CRAG
44 para 7.008 CRAG; para 7.008 Scottish CRAG
45 Sch 4 para 1 NA(AR) Regs
46 Note to para 7.002 CRAG; para 7.002 Scottish CRAG
47 para 3.004 CRAG; para 3.004 Scottish CRAG

6. Capital disregarded for 52 weeks
48 Sch 4 para 6 NA(AR) Regs as amended by NA(AR)(A)(No.2)(E) Regs 2002 or in Scotland by NA(AR)(A)(S) Regs 2003. For Scotland, between the rule change for IS on 14.10.02 and the amendment on 28.02.03 such payments should be treated in accordance with the IS Regs

49 Sch 4 para 6 NA(AR) Regs
50 para 6.030 CRAG; para 6.029 Scottish CRAG

7. Income treated as capital
51 Reg 22(4) NA(AR) Regs
52 Sch 3 para 14 NA(AR) Regs
53 Regs 9 and 28 NA(AR) Regs

8. Trust funds and personal injury payments
54 Reg 22(4) NA(AR) Regs
55 Sch 4 para 10 NA(AR) Regs and para 10.025 CRAG; para 10.025 Scottish CRAG
56 Reg 6 SI No.593/2008
57 Sch 4 para 11 NA(AR) Regs and para 10.015 CRAG; para 10.015 Scottish CRAG
58 para 10.020 CRAG; para 10.020 Scottish CRAG
59 Chapter 10 CRAG; Chapter 10 Scottish CRAG

9. Notional capital
60 Reg 25 NA(AR) Regs
61 Reg 25(3) NA(AR) Regs

10. Deprivation
62 Reg 25(1) NA(AR) Regs
63 s21 HASSASSAA 1983
64 para 6.058 CRAG; para 6.057 Scottish CRAG
65 para 6.065 CRAG; para 6.064 Scottish CRAG
66 para 6.063 CRAG
67 *Yule v South Lanarkshire Council*, 12 May 1999
68 *The Queen (on the application of the Personal Representative of Christopher Beeson) and Dorset County Council and the Secretary of State for Health*, Case no. CO/25/2001, 30 November 2001 (Court of Appeal case No. C/2001/2839 18 December 2002)
69 *Robertson v Fife Council*, 12 May 1999
70 *Robertson v Fife Council*, 25 July 2002 HL [2002] UKHL35
71 Court of Session (Inner House) Reclaiming motion in petition of *David Yule v South Lanarkshire Council*, 15 August 2000

72 para 6064 CRAG
73 para 6062 CRAG
74 Reg 25 NA(AR) Regs
75 para 38 of the *Beeson* Judgment
76 para 39 of the *Beeson* Judgment
77 The Secretary of State for Health –
     Appellant and the Personal
     Representative of Christopher Beeson –
     Respondent
78 *Robertson v Fife Council* 25 July 2002
     [2002] UKHL35
79 para 53 *Robertson v Fife Council*

11. **Diminishing notional capital**
80 Reg 26 NA(AR) Regs

Chapter 13

Personal expenses allowance and outgoings

This chapter covers:
1. Personal expenses allowance (below)
2. Outgoings (p312)

1. Personal expenses allowance

Adult social care services are required to allow you to keep a minimum amount of your income after the payment of your care home fees.[1] This personal expenses allowance (PEA) is set by regulations made each year.[2] For 2009/10, the minimum amount is £21.90 a week in England and Scotland and £22 in Wales. However, a different amount may be applied in special or different circumstances (see p310).[3] Where a social security benefit is subject to a reduction (other than a reduction because of voluntary unemployment) – eg, because of an earlier overpayment – the amount taken into account in the assessment is the gross amount of benefit before reduction therefore the amount that you are left with is less than the PEA.[4] You get the same amount whether you are a temporary or permanent resident in a local authority or an independent care home. Guidance states that you will normally be expected to supply your own clothes, but in cases of special need or emergency (eg, if all your clothes are lost in a fire), the local authority may supply replacement clothing.[5]

It is intended that your PEA should be spent as you wish on personal items such as toiletries, stationery or gifts. Neither the care home provider nor adult social care services have any authority to require you to spend your PEA in any particular way, and pressure of any kind to the contrary is extremely poor practice.[6] If you are not able to manage your PEA because of ill health, adult social care services may (subject to your agreement or that of your attorney or appointee) deposit it in a bank account on your behalf and use it to provide for your smaller needs. Many adult social care services departments have set up a savings account system which they administer. Any money that is unspent on your death will form part of your estate.

Adult social care services cannot allow you to use your PEA to help pay for more expensive accommodation, even if you wish to do this.[7] In addition, you should not be expected to use your PEA for aspects of board, lodgings and care that have been contracted for, or assessed as necessary to meet your needs, by adult social care services or the NHS.[8] Guidance reminds councils that the PEA should not be spent in this way and that they should ensure that individual residents' needs for continence supplies or chiropody are fully reflected in their care plan.[9] Guidance also states that you are not precluded from buying extra services from the care home where these are genuinely additional to those services that have been contracted for or assessed as necessary by adult social care services or the NHS.[10]

If you are a permanent resident, the PEA is the amount that you will normally be left with out of your income when you have made your contribution to the cost of your accommodation and care. However, if you are in receipt of or claim disability living allowance (DLA) mobility component[11] or any other disregarded income (eg, the savings disregard for those aged 65 or over[12] or war widow's special pension[13]), this will continue in payment and will be additional income on top of your PEA, whether you are a temporary or permanent resident.

If you are in receipt of attendance allowance or DLA care component, which is normally payable for the first four weeks of your stay (see p346), and you are a temporary resident, you will also have this income in addition to your PEA.[14]

The previous Minister of State for Social Care Services made a commitment in Parliament to 'consult on the stakeholder views which will include consultation on the stakeholders' recommendations on the level of the personal expenses allowance.'[15]

A proposal was put to the Department of Health (DH) to allow for an increase in the PEA to £40 a week, as it is considered that the present amount is 'totally inadequate to enable residents in care homes to remain socially included or able to participate in family and community life by making phone calls, purchase toiletries or buy even the most modest gifts'.[16]

Despite the undertaking, a ministerial statement has been issued announcing that there will not be any consultation on the amount of the PEA afterall.[17] However, the Scottish Government has agreed to launch a review of the PEA.

Increasing the personal expenses allowance

An increase in the PEA is usually called a 'variation'. Adult social care services have discretion to allow more than the minimum amount in 'special circumstances',[18] such as where you:
- need to keep more of your income to help you lead a more independent life. This may be appropriate if you do not qualify as a 'less dependent' resident (see p288) solely because you live in an independent care home or in local authority accommodation where board is provided;

- have a dependent child, the needs of the child (whether or not s/he is placed with you) should be considered in the PEA;
- are in residential accommodation temporarily and you receive income support (IS)/ income-related employment and support allowance (ESA)/pension credit (PC) which includes an amount for a partner, adult social care services should consider the needs of your partner in the PEA. Adult social care services should not request a charge that would leave your partner without enough money to live on;
- are one of an unmarried couple (or unregistered same-sex partnership); adult social care services are not required to disregard 50 per cent of any private pension that you pay to your partner. However, where you are the main recipient of your overall income, adult social care services can use their discretion to increase your PEA to enable you to pass some of your income to your partner. Adult social care services are advised to bear in mind that increasing your partner's income could lead to a reduction in her/his benefits – eg, IS, income-related ESA or PC.
- are responsible for a property that has been disregarded, adult social care services should consider increasing your PEA to meet any resultant costs.[19]

Adult social care services are reminded that they have the power to increase your PEA, particularly where certain activities or services can contribute significantly to your independence and wellbeing.[20]

Further guidance states that if you are temporarily absent from your care home, adult social care services have the discretion to vary the PEA upwards to enable you to have more money while staying with family or friends.[21]

One of a couple temporarily in a care home

If you are one of a couple going temporarily into a care home and you are the claimant of IS/income-related ESA (aged under 60) in respect of both of you, adult social care services usually have a straightforward task of apportioning the IS/ income-related ESA according to your individual incomes because IS/income-related ESA is usually calculated using two single person's applicable amounts added together (see p151). However, if you are one of a couple going temporarily into a care home and you are the claimant of PC (aged 60 or over) in respect of both of you, then the position is far less straightforward because PC is calculated using the couple appropriate minimum guarantee rather than two single person's appropriate minimum guarantees added together (see p160). This means that adult social care services have to decide how to carry out an apportionment. In most cases, it seems that, as a starting point, adult social care services either:

- divide the couple rate standard minimum guarantee equally (ie, £198.45 divided by 2 = £99.23) and add any additional amount included in the appropriate minimum guarantee to the amount for the person for whom it is paid, and then deduct any assessable income received by the partner in order to reach an amount by which to vary the PEA; *or*

- allow the amount that would be paid by way of the guarantee element of PC to the partner as if s/he was a single person and varying the PEA by this amount.

These different approaches produce significant variations across the country in the amounts allowed in charging assessments for partners in the community. As there are no clear rules on how adult social care services should calculate an appropriate variation, you should at least be able to argue for the most favourable treatment. If the amount allowed for your partner leaves her/him without enough money to live on, you should seek advice with a view to using the complaints procedure.

2. **Outgoings**

If you are a temporary resident, adult social care services can disregard a reasonable amount of your income to meet outgoings that you may have for your home in the community. This also includes outgoings on a home you are taking steps to sell in order to acquire another more suitable home to which you will return.[22]

If you are a permanent resident, you are not normally considered to have outgoings as you no longer have a home in the community. However, it may be that you still have outgoings – eg, while your home is up for sale. If this is the case, adult social care services can consider a variation of your personal expenses allowance (PEA) (see p310) to allow you to meet these commitments.

Where income support (IS)/income-related employment and support allowance (ESA)/pension credit (PC), housing benefit (HB) or Supporting People payments are in payment, extra costs not met by benefit might be:

- fixed heating charges;
- water rates;
- mortgage payments or rent not met by IS/income-related ESA/PC/HB;
- service charges not met by IS/income-related ESA/PC/HB;
- insurance premiums;
- housing support charges not met by the local authority.[23]

Where neither IS/income-related ESA/PC, HB or Supporting People payments are being paid, your outgoings might include:

- interest charges on a hire purchase agreement to buy the dwelling you occupy as your home (eg, a caravan);
- interest charges on loans for repairs or improvements to the dwelling;
- ground rent or other rental relating to a long tenancy;
- service charges;

- housing support charges (made under Supporting People);
- insurance premiums;
- standard charges for fuel;
- water rates;
- payments under a co-ownership scheme or tenancy agreement or licence of a Crown tenant.[24]

If you share your home in the community with a partner or other adults, any outgoings allowed are normally divided equally and only your share is included in the extra amount allowed for outgoings in the financial assessment.

Notes

1. **Personal expenses allowance**
   1. s22(4) NAA 1948
   2. NA(SPR)(E) Regs; NA(SPR)(S) Regs; NA(SPR)(W) Regs
   3. s22(4) NAA 1948 states that *'In assessing for the purposes of the last foregoing subsection a person's ability to pay, a local authority shall assume that he will need for his personal requirements such sum per week as may be prescribed by the Minister, or such other sum as in special circumstances the authority may consider appropriate.'*; s22(4A) NAA 1948 states that *'Regulations made for the purposes of subsection (4) of this section may prescribe different sums for different circumstances.'*
   4. Reg 15(3) NA(AR) Regs and para 8.007 CRAG; WOC 29/27; para 8.007 Scottish CRAG
   5. para 5.001 CRAG; para 5.001 Scottish CRAG
   6. para 5 Annex to LAC(2002)11; para 4 Annex to LAC(2003)8; para 4 Annex to LAC(2005)7
   7. para 8.018 CRAG; para 8.018 Scottish CRAG
   8. para 5 Annex to LAC(2002)11; para 4 Annex to LAC(2005)7; para 5.001 CRAG and Scottish CRAG
   9. para 4 Annex to LAC(2003)8 and para 4 Annex to LAC(2005)7
   10. para 6 Annex to LAC(2002)11
   11. Sch 3 para 4 NA(AR) Regs
   12. NA(AR)(A)(No.2)(E) Regs 2003
   13. Sch 3 para 25 NA(AR) Regs; para 8.046 CRAG; para 8.046 Scottish CRAG
   14. Sch 3 para 6 NA(AR) Regs
   15. Hansard 7 January 2008
   16. The majority view (voluntary organisations, LGA and NAFAO) of the CRAG Stakeholders Group expressed by Age Concern in the proposal to the DH October 2008
   17. Written ministerial statement, DH, Personal Expenses Allowance, 27 January 2009
   18. s22(4) NAA 1948
   19. para 5.005 CRAG; para 5.005 SWSG 8/96
   20. para 6 Annex to LAC(2002)11; para 5 Annex to CCD2/2005
   21. para 8 LAC (97)5; WOC 29/27; para 15 SWSG 7/97

2. **Outgoings**
   22. Sch 3 para 27 NA(AR) Regs
   23. para 3.011 CRAG; para 3.011 Scottish CRAG
   24. para 3.012 CRAG; para 3.012 Scottish CRAG

Chapter 14

··

Resident and third party top-ups

This chapter covers:
1. Who can top-up (below)
2. Resident and third party responsibilities (p317)
3. Assessing your charge (p318)

1. Who can top-up

If you are planning to move into, or are already in, a care home which is more expensive than adult social care services would normally pay for someone with your level of needs, you or someone else (ie, a third party) will need to pay the difference. However, you, as the resident, can only pay the difference if you are subject to a 12-week property disregard (see p292) or you have a deferred payment agreement (see p272) and you have certain disregarded income or capital from which to make the payment.[1] For your right to choose your accommodation, see p246.

A third party may be any person, relative, friend or organisation (eg, your employer) willing to make up the difference. Since October 2001, if your spouse makes maintenance payments to your care costs as a liable relative, s/he cannot make third party top-ups. This limitation does not apply to top-up agreements made prior to 1 October 2001 and does not apply to liable relatives who are not making contributions.[2] However, the Health and Social Care Act 2008 provides for the abolishing of the liable relative rules in England and Wales. The relevant part is due to be implemented from April 2009. These provisions have already been abolished in Scotland so you should ask for a review of any existing arrangements.[3]

In addition, you or a third party must reasonably be expected to continue to make top-up payments for the duration of your care arrangements. Adult social care services must be assured that there is every chance that the third party will continue to have the resources to make the payments.[4]

It is important to note that adult social care services should not seek resident or third party top-ups in cases where your placement in more expensive accommodation is because there is no suitable accommodation available to meet your needs within adult social care services 'usual cost'.[5] In these circumstances, adult social care services should meet the whole cost subject to the usual assessment for your contribution (see Chapter 10).

Care home providers should not seek top-ups from you or a third party where your placement is provided under contract with adult social care services. If the care home provider approaches you in this manner, report it to adult social care services.

The question of resident or third party top-ups only arises if you need adult social care services help with funding your care in a care home. It is not an issue if you are able to pay for your own care and do not need to ask adult social care services for help with the fees.

The Office of Fair Trading recommends that adult social care services should make a clear statement that anyone entitled to help with funding from them does not need to secure a top-up to find a care home that is suitable for their needs.[6]

Yourself as a third party

Except in the specific circumstances of where you are subject to the 12-week property disregard or where you have a deferred payment agreement (see p272), you cannot act as your own third party.[7]

In 1994, guidance made it clear that you cannot use your personal expenses allowance to pay for more expensive accommodation.[8] However, it was not until 1998 that misleading information was corrected to make it clear that neither can you use your own resources to pay for more expensive accommodation.[9] A High Court decision held that the revised guidance is correct.[10]

Resident/self top-ups

Since October 2001 you can make your own top-up payment (called 'additional payments' in the legislation) for more expensive accommodation if you are a 'relevant resident'.[11] You are a **'relevant resident'** if you either have a:

- 12-week property disregard on the property that used to be your home in the community (for the duration of the 12-week disregard only) (see p292); *or*
- deferred payment agreement (see p272).

If you have had a 12-week property disregard, it is likely that after 12 weeks you will go on to a deferred payment arrangement if your property is for sale but not sold yet or you have decided not to sell your property. In these circumstances you will be able to continue to top-up yourself as a relevant resident.

As a relevant resident you must also have a **relevant income or capital disregard** applied to you, or other capital resources, before you are allowed to top-up yourself.[12]

If you are subject to a 12-week property disregard you may top-up from:
- disregarded earnings which include:
  - £5 (if you do not qualify for the higher disregard) (see p228);
  - £20 (if you qualify – eg, are entitled to attendance allowance/disability living allowance (DLA) or getting the disability premium or higher pensioner premium in your income support applicable amount) – see p227;
- disregarded income which includes:
  - DLA mobility component (see p215);
  - certain regular charitable or voluntary payments (see p218);
  - up to £10 of war disablement pension (see p215);
- disregarded capital which includes:
  - any payment made under the Macfarlane Trust or the Eileen Trust;
  - arrears payments of certain benefits;

  but *excluding* the value of the property that is disregarded for the first 12 weeks;
- other capital resources, *excluding* your home, but only up to the value of the lower capital limit for your country (see p291).

  Note that where these resources are used to top-up and you have resources above the lower capital limit, the level of tariff income that applies during the 12 weeks of topping-up is the same as it would be if you were not using the capital to top-up – ie, there is no reduction in the tariff income figure applied.[13]

There is currently no legal provision which allows you to defer a self top-up during the 12-week property disregard period to secure your preferred accommodation as the value of your home is specifically excluded from the resources that can be used for a self top-up.[14]

Strictly, if you have a property to sell but no liquid capital or disregarded income, this either prevents you from moving into a care home of your choice or you have to postpone a move into the care home of your choice for 12 weeks. If you are unable to move into the care home of your choice until the 12-week property disregard period has expired, it means that you have to reside in usual cost accommodation during this period (or at least until you have managed to sell your property and realise the proceeds) until a deferred payment agreement with a deferred self top-up can be implemented.

However, recognising the trauma that this may cause to vulnerable people at a difficult time in their lives, many adult social care services consider this to be an accidental oversight in the legislation and allow a resident to defer a top-up during the 12-week property disregard period irrespective of whether they have disregarded income or capital.

A proposal has been submitted to the Department of Health to amend the regulations to allow a relevant resident to defer a self top-up against the value of their property during the 12-week property disregard period in the same way as the deferment provided for during the duration of a deferred payment agreement.

This would be consistent with the policy intention of enhancing the choices that a resident with property has when making her/his choice of care home.[15]

If you have a deferred payment agreement, you may top-up from similar disregarded resources:

- disregarded earnings (see p227);
- disregarded income (see p282);
- disregarded capital (see p206 but without the exclusion of the value of the property);
- other capital resources, *including* the value of your property that is subject to the deferred payment agreement but you must be left with total capital resources under the means test to the value of the lower capital limit.

Note: when the value of property is used as collateral for top-ups, the amount of the top-up is added to your deferred contribution and is eventually repaid when the home is sold (see p272).

Adult social care services should ensure that, if you top-up against the value of your home when it is subject to a deferred payment agreement, you can pay back the deferred contribution and the top-up.[16]

2. Resident and third party responsibilities

Adult social care services must contract to pay the full fees of the care home, and you or the third party, then agree to pay adult social care services (or defer against the value of your property) the difference between what it would normally pay and the cost of the accommodation. This can be done by:

- you or the third party paying adult social care services; *or*
- you or the third party paying the home direct, if the third party and/or you and the home owner agree. In these circumstances, adult social care services remains liable to pay the full costs of the accommodation should you or your third party fail to pay the required amount.[17]

Adult social care services should inform you and your third party that the amounts it is prepared to pay and the home's fees do not necessarily increase at the same rate. If the home's fees rise faster than the level adult social care services will pay, then that increase will fall on you or the third party. Resident and third party contributions should be regularly reviewed.[18]

Any failure by your third party to pay the level of contribution may mean you have to leave the home of your choice (but also see p247). It is suggested that adult social care services should make legally binding contracts with residents or third parties specifying:

- failure to keep up payments may result in the resident having to move to other accommodation unless the assessed needs can only be met in the current accommodation. In these circumstances, adult social care services should make up the cost difference between the resident's assessed contribution and the accommodation fees. Where resident's top-ups are being made against the value of property subject to a deferred payment agreement, adult social care services will have assured themselves from the outset that top-up payments are viable and recoverable when the home is sold;
- an increase in a resident's income will not necessarily lessen the need for a top-up contribution, as the resident's own income is subject to charging in the normal way;
- that a rise in the accommodation fees will not automatically be shared equally between adult social care services, resident (if making a top-up) and third party.[19]

3. Assessing your charge

When you or a third party make a top-up *payment* (rather than a top-up added to any deferred contribution – see p272) to meet the difference between the amount adult social care services will pay and the actual cost of your care home, that payment is treated as your income (if you are making the payment)[20] or notional income (if a third party is making the payment)[21] and is fully taken into account in the assessment for your contribution. Adult social care services retains the liability to pay the full costs of the home, but can recoup more money from you because of the top-up payment.

Example

The home you have chosen costs £420 and adult social care services will normally only pay £380. Your son has agreed to pay the extra £40. Your own assessed income is £290 a week, but you are counted as having £330 because the amount your son pays is notionally treated as your income. Adult social care services charges you £308.10 (leaving you with £21.90 personal expenses allowance). Adult social care services only have to pay the home the difference of £111.90.

Notes

1. Who can top-up

1 s54 HSCA 2001; para 3.2 LAC (2004)20; NA(RAAPAR)(E) Regs

2 para 3.5.10 LAC (2004)20; para 8.018A CRAG

3 s147 HSCA 2008; s62 ASP(S)A 2007

4 paras 3.5.3 and 3.5.4 LAC (2004)20

5 paras 4 2.5.5 and 3.4 LAC (2004)20

6 OFT report published May 2005 in response to 'Super Complaint made by *Which?* In December 2003. See www.oft.gov.uk

7 paras 8.018 and 8.019A CRAG; para 8.018 Scottish CRAG

8 LAC (94)1 (para 13); WOC 4/94; SWSG 5/94

9 para 6 LAC (98)8

10 *R v E Sussex ex parte Ward*, CCLR, June 2000

11 Reg 2 NA(RAAPAR)(E) Regs

12 Reg 4 NA(RAAAR)(E) Regs; para 3.2 LAC (2004)20

13 Reg 28(4) NA(AR) Regs

14 Reg 4(2)(a) of NA(Residential Accommodation) (Additional Payments and Assessment of Resources) (Amendment) (England) Regulations 2001; para 8.019B CRAG

15 One of a number of proposals submitted to the DH by the CRAG Stakeholders Group October 2008

16 para 3.5.4 LAC (2004)20

2. Resident and third party responsibilities

17 para 3.5.2 LAC (2004)20

18 para 3.5.7 LAC (2004)20

19 para 3.5.8 LAC (2004)20

3. Assessing your charge

20 Reg 16A NA(AR) Regs; para 8.019C CRAG

21 Reg 17(4) NA(AR) Regs; para 8.062 CRAG; para 8.062 Scottish CRAG

Chapter 15

Collection of charges and enforcement

This chapter covers:
1. How charges are collected (below)
2. If you cannot or will not pay your charge (p321)
3. Legal charges on your property (p323)
4. Deprivation of assets (p325)
5. Court action that can be used (p327)

1. How charges are collected

When adult social care services arranges your care, either in one of there own homes or in an independent care home, they must establish how much you should pay using the rules described in this *Handbook*. They must ensure you are given a clear explanation, usually in writing, of how your charge has been calculated and how much it will be each week. You should also be informed of why your charge may fluctuate. This is especially important in the first few weeks, when changes to your benefits affect how much you have to pay (see Chapter 16).[1] You should also be told how you will be billed for your charge.

There are two ways to pay if you are in an independent care home:
- adult social care services pays the home the full cost and you pay adult social care services your assessed contribution;[2]
- you pay your assessed contribution direct to the home and adult social care services will pay the difference if you, the home owner and adult social care all agree.[3]

The latter method, sometimes called 'net payment', can only be used with the agreement of all parties. If any of you disagree then adult social care services have to pay the full cost and bill you for your contribution. The Government has indicated that it intends to work with the Commission for Social Care Inspection (now the Care Quality Commission) and local authorities to ensure that net payment arrangements are not imposed upon residents.[4]

Adult social care services have the contractual obligation with the home (if you are council funded but not if you are self-funded), and are responsible for paying the full fees. If you do not pay your contribution, it is adult social care services' responsibility to recover the charge from you,[5] not the home. In practice, some adult social care services use net payments without making it clear that it must be with your agreement and do not explain the alternative.

In Scotland, the local authority can enter into a contract for nursing and/or personal care payments only, paid directly to the home, where you choose to make a private contract with the home to cover accommodation and living costs.

2. If you cannot or will not pay your charge

Adult social care services departments cannot stop providing you with care in a care home purely because you are unable or unwilling to pay the assessed charge.[6] There are a variety of methods they can use for pursuing money owed and it is up to each authority to decide what enforcement actions to take.

Each adult social care department has its own procedures for tracking debts and following them up. Some have early warning signals built into their systems so that as soon as you have missed a few payments you are visited to establish the reason. If you pay the home direct it is likely there will be an arrangement for any non-payment to be reported. Some authorities have panels to monitor debts when they reach a certain level and to decide on any enforcement action.

You do not normally have a contractual relationship with adult social care services when they arrange your accommodation, but the legislation provides that any sum due under the National Assistance Act is recoverable as a civil debt.[7] This allows adult social care services to take the same steps as any creditor to enforce payment of your assessed contributions.

You should normally have enough money to pay your assessed contribution, but there may be times when this is not the case.

- You have been assessed to **pay the full cost because of your capital**, but it is not possible to access it because an application for someone to act as your deputy is with the Court of Protection (or in Scotland an application for a financial guardian is with the Public Guardian's Office – see p261) or an application has been made to register an lasting power of attorney in England and Wales (see p259). Adult social care services should be prepared to wait in these circumstances. The person taking over your affairs may be able to get permission from the Office of the Public Guardian/Public Guardian's Office to enable the fees to be paid in the interim. S/he should contact the customer services section of the Office of the Public Guardian/Guardian's Office for advice. See Chapter 9 for details about the provisions if you cannot manage your financial affairs.

- You have been assessed as **paying the full cost because you have a property,** the value of which is correctly included in the assessment but which has not yet been sold and you have not entered into a deferred payment agreement (see p323).
- You have been assessed as **paying a charge based on the assumption that you receive a means-tested benefit** such as income support (IS) or pension credit (PC). Because adult social care services finance officers are aware of the amount which is usually paid if you are in a care home, the calculation often assumes you receive this amount. Always check your calculation very carefully and see if it tallies with your income, which includes any benefit you get. It may be that you have not applied for IS/PC, or there has been a decision that you are not entitled, but adult social care services are not aware of this. Or the amount that the DWP has paid may be different to what the finance officer thinks should be paid. You should ask for a reassessment. You should not be charged as if you have a benefit if you have not applied for it, unless you have deliberately decided not to apply. In this case it could be considered to be notional income (see p286). If it is necessary to appeal about the level of benefit you get, ask adult social care services to assess your charge based on what you currently receive and reassess you if you win the appeal.

If you do not wish to pay your assessed charge (eg, because you disagree with the amount calculated or you are in dispute about the value of a jointly owned property), seek advice about the subject under dispute and whether you should make any payments and if so how much, while the dispute is resolved. If there is any other reason you are not willing to pay the charges you have been assessed to pay, it is likely that adult social care services will be prepared to consider remedies to enforce payment of the money due.

Actions to avoid debts building up

- If you are becoming forgetful and have difficulty in managing your financial affairs, adult social care services may help you to get a friend or relative to become an appointee (if you do not have much capital and your main income is benefits). If you have already granted a lasting power of attorney (continuing power of attorney in Scotland – see p261) and can no longer manage your affairs, it will need to be registered, so that your attorney can take over your affairs. Or adult social care services may suggest that someone approaches the Court of Protection to become your deputy (or, in Scotland, a financial guardian to manage your financial affairs). For more details, see Chapter 9.
- If your appointee, attorney or deputy does not pay the charges, adult social care services will negotiate with her/him and may inform the relevant authority in order to get her/him removed from dealing with your affairs. If necessary adult social care services may take over this role.

- Some local authorities have money advisers to offer you budgeting advice and ways of making it easier to pay your charge, if this is the problem. If you have other debts, a money adviser may be able to help with negotiating with your creditors. In exceptional circumstances, adult social care services may allow you an extra personal expenses allowance (see Chapter 13). In some cases they may be prepared to write off your debt. Your local Citizens Advice Bureau or National Debtline also offer free debt advice (see Appendix 2).
- If you are getting IS, PC, employment and support allowance or income-based jobseeker's allowance and are not using it to pay your charges, the DWP can pay your benefit direct to adult social care services if it is in your interests and if adult social care services have arranged your accommodation. If you have arranged your own accommodation, the deduction can be paid to the home. In the case of a home run by a voluntary organisation for people dependent on alcohol or drugs, direct payments can be made even if you are not in debt.[8] Your consent is not needed.[9]

3. Legal charges on your property

Adult social care services cannot force you to sell your property in order to pay the assessed charge (which in most cases will be the full cost) without a court order. Instead, if you fail to pay your assessed charge they may create a legal charge on your interest in any land that is in England and Wales[10] (called a charging order in Scotland).[11] A **'legal charge'** means that when you sell your property the local authority will have a call on the proceeds to cover the amount owed, rather like when you have a mortgage which is paid off when the sale goes through. A legal charge can only be created under these rules if you have failed to pay your charge, so unless you have a debt to adult social care services there is no power for it to create a legal charge on your land. If you are willing to pay your charges following the sale of your property at some future time, you can request to enter into a **'deferred payment agreement'** (effectively a loan to pay care fees), which ensures your charges are eventually paid (see p272). This is at the discretion of the local authority.

The charge may be registered against your property ('legal charge' or a 'caution' if the title deeds are in more than one name – see p324) so that adult social care services will know when it is sold. If the title to your property is registered, the charge will be put on the central Land Register. If your property does not yet have a registered title a Class B land charge will be put on the Land Register.[12] If the land is in Scotland then the charging order is recorded in the Register of Sasines or registered in the Land Register as appropriate.[13]

The charge is created by a declaration in writing[14] and guidance in England and Wales says that adult social care services should advise or assist you to consult a solicitor if it is considering creating a legal charge.[15] The Local Government

Ombudsman found that failure to provide sufficiently clear information about the placing of a legal charge was maladministration.[16]

Jointly owned property

In England and Wales local authorities have been advised to register a 'caution' in the cases of jointly owned property.[17] A caution affords local authorities less protection than a legal charge, but would alert them if a sale is going through, so that they could take action (which may include recovery of a civil debt).

Adult social care services should follow the guidance about valuing jointly owned property.[18] An Ombudsman's report criticised a local authority for failing to do so.[19] Before any caution is registered it is important that the value of your interest (if it is established that more than one beneficial owner is entitled to benefit from the sale of a property, or if the legal owner is not a beneficial owner) in the property has been established, as it may have a low or nil value if there is no willing buyer (in the case of beneficial interest, although councils are increasingly including the full face value of a resident's beneficial interest due to the fact that there are an increasing number of ways of realising capital from a property – eg, re-mortgaging and equity release). Complain if you disagree with the valuation of jointly owned property.

Charging interest

Interest on the legal charge or charging order cannot be charged during your lifetime,[20] but will be added from the day after your death.[21] The interest has to be at a 'reasonable rate'. How local authorities set the rate varies around the country, but most use formulas which are within average market rates.

If you have entered into a deferred payment agreement, interest will only be charged from 56 days after your death if the 'loan' has not already been paid back at that time (see p273).

Costs of creating the charge

The law is silent on whether adult social care services or you should bear the cost of creating the legal charge or charging order. Some authorities will pass the cost on to you. If this happens you should establish under what legislation this is done, as the law only relates to the failure to pay the assessed charge. Complain (see p270) if you consider that you should not be charged for the costs, or if you think they are too high.

Calculating the debt accrued

You continue to be charged for the full cost of your care home fees, until such time as your debt means that the value of your property and any other capital you have has reduced to the upper capital limit. From that point charges should be based on your income and tariff income, until the value of your property and other capital is down to the lower capital limit and from then, only based on your income (see pp285 and 291).

In the case of property it can be difficult to calculate the debt, as it is based on a valuation which may or may not reflect the final price you receive. It only becomes a problem if the value of your property after your debt has been taken into account, falls to the upper capital limit.

In practice it appears that most adult social care departments readjust the amount you owe when the property is sold, as they can base the calculation of your debt on the actual sale price of your property. In some cases this will mean that you are asked to pay more if your property is sold for more than expected, or you might be charged less than was estimated if your property sells for less than expected.

A rule of thumb is that you should not be left with total capital (other capital and the proceeds of the sale of your property) of less than the lower capital limit for your country (see p265) unless:

- your debt accrued when the lower capital limit was lower than the current level. Capital limits have increased over the years. If the debt you owe has reduced your capital to the lower limit but that limit is subsequently increased, you could be left with less than the current lower capital limit;
- interest has been charged under the rules explained on p323. As interest is added to the debt, this interest could take capital below the lower capital limit.

4. **Deprivation of assets**

If adult social care services decides that you have given away your assets or not applied for them, in order to avoid or lessen your liability for charges for your care (see p302), then they *will* in the case of income and *may* in the case of capital treat you as if you still possess those assets.[22] This means that your charge will be assessed as if you still have that income or capital (see below and pp286 and 301). Unless you are able to pay the assessed charge you will accrue a debt which can be enforced as a civil debt, or if you still own any land, a legal charge (or charging order in Scotland) on it can be created by the local authority. If you have given away your property then there is no power for a legal charge to be created on it as you no longer have an interest in land. However, if the council decides that the property was transferred to avoid paying care fees, the person the property was transferred to may have the debt for care fees transferred to her/him (see p326).

The local authority should not refuse to make arrangements for you just because you have notional capital (see p301). If you are told that you must make your own arrangements for this reason, you can challenge the authority.

Diminishing notional capital

In the case of capital, if adult social care services decide to treat you as having capital you have given away, you are assessed as notionally having that amount, but it will be reduced each week.[23] The amount of the reduction will be the difference between what you actually pay and the amount you would have paid if you had not been treated as having capital which you have given away.

Example

You have been assessed as having £9,500 actual capital and £21,750 notional capital which you have given away. Your weekly income means you are assessed as having to pay £150 and the home you are in costs £350. The level of your notional capital will be reduced by £200 a week which is what adult social care services has to pay because you gave away your capital. This means that after 45 weeks you will be reassessed as having only £22,250 and your assessed charge will be reduced to the level of your income plus tariff income from capital above £13,500. You will still owe a debt to the local authority which it may try to recoup. (The figures are different for Scotland and Wales.)

Transferring the liability to the person who has received your assets

In addition to deciding whether to treat you as if you still have the assets, adult social care services have the legal power to take enforcement proceedings against the person (or persons) who now owns the assets if you have knowingly and with the intention of avoiding charges, transferred them, either for nothing or at less than their value.[24] Even if the person to whom you transferred those assets was unaware that you did this to avoid paying charges, s/he will still have the liability for your fees transferred to her/him. The question is whether *you* knowingly transferred your assets to avoid charges.

This rule can only be used if you transferred your assets within the six months immediately before you went into residential accommodation. Guidance makes it clear that in this context 'residential accommodation' is where adult social care services have assessed you as needing care in a care home *and* have arranged it for you in an independent or local authority home. Even if you are already in an independent home when you transfer your assets, if you have not been assessed and not had your placement arranged by adult social care services within six months of the transfer, this rule does not apply. The guidance gives an example of a resident who paid for his own accommodation in full for two years, then the following March gave his daughter £20,000 and continued to self-fund until December, when he approached the local authority for support.[25] In this case the six-month rule does not apply, but adult social care services could treat the resident as still possessing the capital (see p325). Time limits only apply to the transfer of liability to pay onto the person who has received the asset. There appear to be no time limits for adult social care services to treat you as still possessing your assets.

Calculating the cost for which the owner is liable

Once adult social care services decides that you have transferred your assets to another person within the six months prior to going into care, knowingly to avoid or lessen the charges, then the owner is liable to pay the difference between what you actually pay adult social care services and what you have been assessed as having to pay.[26]

The amount for which the person who has received the asset is liable should be restricted to the current value of the amount transferred. If the asset has been transferred to more than one person, each person can only be held liable up to the value of her/his share of the asset.[27]

The asset is valued at the amount that would have been realised on the open market at the time it was transferred, and secured debts and reasonable costs of sale will be taken into account.[28]

5. **Court action that can be used**

It is beyond the scope of this *Handbook* to give advice about dealing with any debts you have to adult social care services caused by charges for care (see CPAG's *Debt Advice Handbook*). As with any debt, it is important to negotiate at an early stage and check carefully that you are actually liable for the debt (this is particularly so if someone else is managing your affairs and s/he receives the bills) and that you agree with the calculation of the amount owing. As your debt may have built up over several years, and you will probably have been paying some of the cost out of your income, which will have altered over time, mistakes can be made. You should also establish whether the debt can still be collected as there are time limits. These are normally six years, but in the case of money owed for your care home charges, proceedings for its recovery can only be brought within three years of the sum becoming due.[29] Seek advice if your debt accrued more than three years ago.

Although debt advisers (or money advisers) may have had little experience of dealing with debts for care home charges, they should be very experienced in negotiating and checking whether the debt can be enforced. Your local Citizens Advice Bureau may have a debt adviser, or sometimes local authorities offer money advice, although they may be limited in the amount of advice they can offer if you are in dispute with their employing authority.

This section lists possible action through the courts that adult social care services can use. Although court action has to date rarely been used and there may be concern about taking vulnerable residents to court, the provisions are there. Where there are debts, local authorities have to justify inaction to their auditors. Often the threat of legal action resolves the problem for local authorities because the debt is settled before going to court. Seek advice before agreeing to settle the debt if you have doubts or queries.

Civil debt

Where the assessed charges have not been paid, local authorities can seek to recover the sum as a civil debt.[30] Proceedings under this legislation may be brought at any time within three years of the sum becoming due.[31] If the debt being recovered is older than three years, seek advice.

If the local authority intends to issue proceedings, it is normally its legal department that writes giving you notice and a final chance of settling the debt.

In England and Wales your case is dealt with in the magistrates' court, although there is no rule which would stop a local authority from using county court or bankruptcy proceedings. In Scotland, it is normally the sheriff's court and may be the Court of Session.

It is more likely that adult social care services will be prepared to pursue the person who now owns your assets if you gave them away or sold them for less than their value within six months of needing adult social care services help with paying for care in a care home. If that person who is now liable to pay part of your fees (see p326) does not do so, the local authority could pursue the debt through the courts.

If you have given false information

It is an offence to give information which you know to be false. In England and Wales if you do so, you could be fined up to £5,000 or up to three months in prison or both.[32] Proceedings may be started at any time within three months from the date on which, in the opinion of the local authority, sufficient evidence comes to light to justify a prosecution, or within 12 months of the offence, whichever is longer.

Although this provision has existed since 1948 there is no evidence that it has ever been used. It is more likely that adult social care services would use other enforcement procedures to recover the money owed.

Using insolvency procedures

The Insolvency Act 1986 (England and Wales)

There are two provisions in this Act which adult social care services can consider if you owe more than £750, have transferred your assets and are unable to pay your charge.

- If you have given away your assets at an undervalue and can be declared bankrupt, the local authority can apply to the court for an order to set the 'gift' aside. The time limits are five years before the presentation of the petition, if you were bankrupt at the time of the transaction or became insolvent because of the transaction, and two years in all other cases.[33] The court may make such orders as it thinks fit for restoring the position to what it would have been before the transaction.

- If the local authority can prove that the purpose of giving away your assets at an undervalue was to place them beyond the reach of a possible creditor.[34] There are no time limits on these powers and you do not need to be declared bankrupt.

It may be difficult for the local authority to prove, although if you have used a business which specialises in avoiding assets being taken into account, this could be considered to be useful to the local authority in establishing your motive. Normally solicitors' files are confidential but a case has established that in some cases the court could require disclosure – it has not yet been tested in a case relating to care charges.[35]

Bankruptcy (Scotland) Act 1985

There is provision in the Bankruptcy (Scotland) Act 1985 which might be considered if you owe more than £1,500, whereby you can be declared bankrupt and have your assets transferred when you are unable to pay your charge.

It is possible that proceedings could be taken by the local authority to set aside a transfer which is known under the legislation as a 'gratuitous alienation'. This is where an asset has been transferred, either for no payment or for payment of less than the value of the asset. The time limit for challenging such a transfer is five years before the date of bankruptcy where the person to whom the asset is transferred is an associate and two years for any other person.[36]

Notes

1. How charges are collected
1 para 1.015 CRAG (E&W); para 1.013 CRAG (S)
2 s26(3) NAA 1948
3 s26(3A) NAA 1948; para 1.023 CRAG (E&W); para 1.015 CRAG (S)
4 Government response to *Care homes for older people in the UK*, Office of Fair Trading, 2005
5 para 1.024 CRAG; para 1.016 CRAG (S)

2. If you cannot or will not pay your charge
6 This is because of the mandatory nature of s21 NAA 1948, LAC (93)10 and WOC/35/93. In Scotland it is because of the mandatory nature of s59 SW(S)A 1968 and ss7 and 8 MH(S)A 1984.
7 s56 NAA 1948; s87 SW(S)A 1968
8 Sch 9 para 4 SS(C&P) Regs
9 Sch 9 para 8 SS(C&P) Regs

3. Legal charges on your property
10 s22(1) HASSASSAA 1983
11 CO(RA)(S)O 1993; SWSG 15/93
12 s22(8) HASSASSAA 1983

13 s23(3) HASSASSAA 1983
14 s22(7) HASSASSAA 1983
15 Annex D3.4 CRAG
16 Complaint against Manchester City
    Council, 04/C/4804
17 Annex D3.5 CRAG
18 paras 7.012 – 7.014A CRAG (E, S & W)
19 Complaint against Lincolnshire County
    Council, 03/C/9384
20 Annex D3A CRAG (E&W)
21 s24 HASSASSAA 1983

4. Deprivation of assets

22 Regs 17(1) and 25(1) NA(AR) Regs;
    paras 8.071 and 6.057 CRAG (E&W);
    paras 8.071 and 6.056 Scottish CRAG
23 Reg 26 NA(AR) Regs; para 6.068 CRAG
    (E&W); para 6.067CRAG (S)
24 s21 HASSASSAA 1983
25 Annex D2.1 CRAG (E&W)
26 s21(1) HASSASSAA 1983; Annex D2.6
    CRAG (E&W); para 9 SWSG 7/97
27 s21(4) and (5) HASSASSAA 1983;
    Annexes D2.4 and D2.5 CRAG (E&W);
    SWSG 15/93 para 2.4
28 s21(7) HASSASSAA 1983; Annex D2.3
    CRAG (E&W); SWSG 15/93 para 2.3

5. Court action that can be used

29 s56(2) NAA 1948
30 s56 NAA 1948
31 s56(2) NAA 1948
32 s52 NAA 1948
33 ss339 and 341 IA 1986
34 s423 IA 1986
35 *Barclays Bank v Eustice* [1995]
36 s34 B(S)A 1985

Chapter 16

· ·

Social security benefits in care homes

This chapter covers:
1. Types of care home (below)
2. Types of stay (p337)
3. Social security benefits affected (p338)
4. Self-funding and retrospective self-funding (p350)
5. Temporary absences from care homes (including going into hospital) (p351)
6. Other sources of financial assistance in care homes (p352)
7. Effects on carers (p353)

· ·

All references to income support also apply to income-based jobseeker's allowance.

· ·

---

1. Types of care home

Accommodation and care is usually provided in either:
- local authority care homes (sometimes known as Part III homes or Part IV homes in Scotland); *or*
- independent care homes; *or*
- independent care homes which provide nursing.

Since April 2002, the term **'care home'** is used in the legislation to describe all the above types of accommodation which provide personal an/or nursing care and are required to register with the Care Quality Commission (England), the National Assembly for Wales or the Scottish Commission for the Regulation of Care.[1]

For social security purposes all care homes are treated in the same way unless they are a nursing home which is considered to be a 'hospital or similar institution' (see p351).

In England and Wales, an establishment is a care home if it provides accommodation, together with nursing or personal care, for people who:
- are, or have been, ill; *or*
- have, or have had, a mental disorder; *or*
- are disabled or infirm; *or*
- are, or have been, dependent on alcohol or drugs.

An establishment is *not* a care home if it is:
- a hospital; *or*
- an independent clinic.[2]

In Scotland, an establishment is a care home if it is accommodation in which a care home service is provided – ie, a service providing accommodation with nursing, personal care or personal support for people by reason of their vulnerability or need.

An establishment is *not* a care home if it is:
- a hospital; *or*
- a public, independent or grant-aided school; *or*
- a private psychiatric hospital; *or*
- an independent clinic; *or*
- an independent medical agency.[3]

There are special rules if you receive care in the following types of accommodation:
- hospitals or similar institutions (see below);
- hospices (see p335);
- joint funded accommodation (see p335);
- s256 funded accommodation(see p336);[4]
- aftercare accommodation provided under s117 Mental Health Act 1983 (England and Wales) (see p336).

If you receive care in a registered **Abbeyfield Home** you are treated in the same way as a resident in any other type of registered care home (see p55). If your Abbeyfield Home is not registered then you are treated in the same way as a person in supported accommodation and therefore are eligible to claim HB (see p163).

Hospitals or similar institutions

Special rules apply if you are considered to be an inpatient in a hospital or similar institution. Your accommodation and care are provided free of charge by the NHS (see p239), and disability living allowance (DLA) care and mobility components or attendance allowance (AA) are not normally payable after four weeks (or sooner if you have been in hospital or a care home within the previous 28 days). Other benefits are unaffected until you have been an inpatient for 52 weeks (see p191).[5]

It is usually clear when you are an inpatient in a hospital. However, if you are not actually in a hospital it can be unclear whether these special rules apply. If your care in a care home is fully funded by the NHS under the Continuing Healthcare provisions (see p29), you are treated as an inpatient in a similar institution.

The term 'hospital or similar institution' is not defined in social security legislation,[6] but the test of whether the special rules apply has been considered in a number of decisions of the former social security commissioners[7] and by the courts.[8] Essentially, the test is whether on the particular facts you should be considered to be:

- maintained free of charge;
- undergoing medical or other treatment as an inpatient;[9]
- under the relevant NHS Act;[10]
- in a hospital or similar institution.

If you cannot be considered to be living in a hospital or similar institution it does not matter whether you are being maintained free of charge or undergoing medical treatment as an inpatient.[11]

It has been held that the term **'hospital'** means:

- any institution for the reception and treatment of persons suffering from illness;
- any maternity home; *and*
- any institution for the reception of and treatment of persons during convalescence or persons requiring medical rehabilitation.[12]

It also includes clinics, dispensaries and outpatient departments maintained in connection with any such home or institution.

It has also been held that a **'similar institution'** connotes 'some sort of formal body or structure which controls all aspects of the treatment or care that is provided including the premises in which the treatment is carried out'.[13] In that case a claimant was undergoing medical or other treatment provided by NHS staff at public expense, but because it was provided in a privately rented house where rent was paid and the claimant was responsible for expenditure on food and other outgoings, the claimant could not be considered to be living in an 'institution' at all, let alone a 'similar' one to a hospital.

It has been further held that a crucial test to determine whether an establishment is a 'similar institution' is 'the treatment and care given by the establishment and the similarity between those and the treatment and care which are provided in a hospital,' which will be 'a question of fact and degree in each case'.[14] Another social security commissioner held that what the staff in an establishment do is more important than whether they are employed by the NHS, so that if NHS staff provide social rather than medical care, or supervise residents in a lifestyle which is more typical of a home than a hospital, then it is likely that the establishment cannot be considered to be an institution similar to a hospital.[15]

In other cases, care homes which provide nursing have been held to be similar institutions, where claimants have been discharged from hospital into the homes.[16] This included one person who suffered from a mental disorder, and the hospital rules were considered to apply because this was considered to be an 'illness' for which the treatment was provided.[17] In these cases it was considered relevant that the claimants were undergoing medical or other treatment (which included nursing care) and were 'inpatients' as they received treatment on the premises of an institution and they were maintained free of charge as they were not private fee-paying patients in a NHS or Trust hospital.

Adult social care services and the NHS may have negotiated between themselves who should be responsible for the arrangements and cost of your care. However, social security rules apply independently of any arrangements they may have agreed, and just because the health authorities do not consider that they have any 'NHS Continuing Healthcare' responsibilities (see p29) for you (eg, on moving from a hospital to a care home which provides nursing), you could still be treated as if you are living in a hospital or similar institution. Seek advice if this applies to you (see Appendix 2).

You can only be treated as a hospital inpatient if you are maintained free of charge while undergoing treatment in a NHS hospital or similar institution. You are regarded as being maintained free of charge unless the accommodation and services are provided under legislation which relates to fee-paying patients in NHS hospitals.[18] Caselaw suggests that even where considerable contributions to your maintenance are made you will still be treated as an inpatient.[19] There are conflicting decisions on whether you actually need to be in the hospital for 24 hours a day to be treated as being maintained free of charge as an inpatient, or whether absences for a period within the 24 hours still bring you within the meaning.[20] For DLA care/AA purposes a commissioner held that the equivalent provisions in the DLA Regulations[21] applied so as to make it a condition of entitlement to benefit only for 'complete calendar days throughout which the claimant is not undergoing medical or other treatment as an inpatient' but that what existed at the beginning of the day was presumed to last until the end.[22] But a different commissioner held that a claimant of severe disablement allowance who went home from Friday morning to Monday evening was entitled to receive benefit for Friday and Monday in addition to Saturday and Sunday.[23] The 'full-out' words in the amendment to the legislation deem the condition of being maintained free of charge to be satisfied if you are undergoing treatment as an inpatient unless you are a private patient in a NHS hospital.[24]

A more recent decision[25] held that a person was not 'maintained free of charge' because the NHS was only making a contribution to a *part* of the services provided and the accommodation and care was provided by the local authority under the provisions of Part III (NAA Act 1948). In this case the residents were previously in long-stay NHS mental hospitals and they had severe mental impairment. It was stated that the conditions were developmental disorders, not clinically treatable conditions or 'illnesses', but they needed continuous care and supervision in a care home which provides nursing. Although it was held that the care home was a hospital or similar institution and the residents were receiving treatment, the issue was whether they were maintained free of charge while undergoing the treatment as inpatients in the care home under the defined NHS legislation.[26] The NHS was purchasing some extra day care services for some of the residents but this never extended to the cost of the accommodation or daily maintenance (which was purchased by the local authority). It was held that 'maintained free of charge' refers not only to medical treatment but also to basic maintenance and subsistence needs (accommodation and food) and that arrangements made under the defined NHS legislation must not only be for treatment, but also for maintenance for the hospital inpatient regulations to apply.

A tribunal of commissioners[27] agreed with the approach that the amount of NHS provision may be too slight to bring regulation 8 into play when only incidental or ancillary nursing care were covered by the health authority.

Hospices

You may receive care in a '**hospice**' which is defined as 'a hospital or other institution whose primary function is to provide palliative care for persons resident there who are suffering from a progressive disease in its final stages' (but not an NHS hospital).[28] This is usually arranged via your GP through the NHS. For benefit purposes a hospice is a 'hospital or similar institution', and therefore the hospital rules apply (see p189). However, in these circumstances the law provides for DLA mobility component[29] and care component or AA[30] to continue being paid beyond 28 days.

Joint funded accommodation

If you receive care in a care home which is jointly funded by a local NHS body and adult social care services budget (this arrangement is sometimes called 50/50 funding – see p242), the benefit situation is often unclear. There can be confusion over whether your accommodation is provided by the NHS under the 'similar institution' part of the definition of a 'hospital or similar institution' (see p351), in which case you should receive your care free of charge and the hospital benefit rules apply (see p189); or whether it is provided by adult social care services, in which case the rules for social security benefits in care homes apply. It is important to find out what the terms of the contract with the home are in respect of your placement. Often the NHS funding for your placement is received by adult social care services for them to purchase your accommodation and care rather than by the care home and therefore it is adult social care services who has assessed your need, arranged and contracted with a home for the provision of your accommodation and care[31] and is required[32] to charge you subject to the means tests.

It was held that funding responsibility for residents living in a nursing home lies with adult social care services (under Part III[33]) if the nursing needs are 'incidental and ancillary to other care needs' and with the appropriate health body if the nursing needs are not 'incidental and ancillary to other care needs'.[34]

If you are treated as a hospital inpatient but you are still responsible for paying towards the cost of your accommodation and care, seek advice (see Appendix 4).

Section 256 funded accommodation

You may receive care in a care home that receives an s256 grant from the NHS to help towards the running costs of the home.[35] If you are able to meet the fees of the care home (charged at a reduced rate due to the NHS grant payable) from your benefits (including DLA care/AA) and/or other income and capital, then you may not need, or in fact be able, to be placed in the care home by adult social care services.[36] This is because you are able to organise and pay for your own accommodation and care – ie, it is 'otherwise available'[37] rather than being provided for by adult social care services.

This does not mean that adult social care services cannot help you with finding a suitable care home to meet your needs. However, you, rather than adult social care services would contract with the care home for the provision of your accommodation and care.

This type of arrangement means that for the purposes of DLA care/AA you should, be considered to be self-funding and therefore (subject to the normal conditions of entitlement – see p120) DLA care/AA should be payable. If your DLA care/AA is suspended when you enter a care home under these arrangements, seek advice (see Appendix 2).

Aftercare accommodation provided under s117 Mental Health Act 1983 (England and Wales)

You may receive care in a care home as part of aftercare services provided under s117 Mental Health Act 1983 if you have been previously detained in hospital under a compulsory order (see p368).[38] In these circumstances you should be entitled to income support (IS)/income-related support allowance (ESA)/pension credit (PC) and other benefits (subject to the other conditions of entitlement) in the same way as if you had been placed in a care home under the National Assistance Act 1948 (NAA) even though adult social care services cannot charge for accommodation provided under s117.[39]

Note that other people, placed in the same care home under the provisions of the NAA may be required to make a contribution to the costs which may leave them with only the personal expenses allowance (see Chapter 13).

DLA care/AA are not payable to a person accommodated under s117.[40]

Aftercare accommodation provided under s25 Mental Health (Scotland) Act 2003

This Act places a similar legal duty on social work departments in Scotland to provide aftercare services (see p243). The benefit position is also the same, but social work departments in Scotland **can** charge for aftercare services.

2. Types of stay

There are three basic types of stay in a care home.

- **Permanent stay:** there is no definition of a permanent stay although a working definition that is consistent with the definitions of temporary and trial period (see below) is a stay which is permanent from the day you enter the care home, or if you enter on a temporary or trial period basis, from any subsequent day on which you make the decision that you do not intend to return to the community to live.
- **Temporary stay:** social security legislation defines a temporary stay in terms of a temporary absence from your normal home in the community. In these circumstances income support (IS)/income-related employment and support allowance (ESA)/pension credit (PC) housing costs, housing benefit (HB) and council tax benefit (CTB) can continue to be paid for up to 52 weeks in respect of your home in the community, where:
  - you intend to return to your home in the community; *and*
  - the part of your home normally occupied by you has not been let or sub-let in the meantime; *and*
  - the period of your absence is unlikely to exceed 52 weeks, or, in exceptional circumstances, is unlikely to substantially exceed that period.[41]

A series or planned programme of temporary stays are often referred to as respite stays.

- **Trial period stay:** is a stay in a care home which is treated as a temporary stay but 'for the purpose of ascertaining whether the accommodation suits [your] needs' and 'with the intention of returning to the dwelling which [you] normally occupy as [your] home should, in the event, the residential accommodation prove not to suit [your] needs'. In these circumstances IS/income-related ESA/PC housing costs, HB and CTB can continue to be paid for up to 13 weeks in respect of your home in the community, where:
  - you intend to return to your home (if the care home does not suit your needs); *and*
  - the part of your home normally occupied by you has not been let or sub-let in the meantime; *and*
  - the period of absence is unlikely to exceed 13 weeks.[42]

You are also entitled to these benefits for 13 weeks even if your absence extends beyond 13 weeks as long as your total absence does not exceed 52 weeks.[43]

Unlike for many other aspects of the social security benefits system, there are no linking rules for periods of absence. Therefore, if you are in a care home for a trial period or temporary stay and you genuinely return home for at least 24 hours, you can subsequently receive benefit for a fresh period of absence of either 13 (trial period) or 52 (temporary) weeks.

There is no definition of 'trial period' for financial assessment and charging purposes (see p275) – this can cause problems in ensuring the correct benefit payment.

3. **Social security benefits affected**

If you go into a care home (see p331) either temporarily (including for a trial period) or permanently (see p337 for definitions) the following benefits may be affected:

- income support (IS)/income-based jobseeker's allowance (JSA)/income-related employment and support allowance (ESA) (if you are under 60) (see p339);
- pension credit (PC) (if you are 60 or over) (see p342);
- housing benefit (HB) (see p345);
- council tax benefit (CTB) (see p345);
- social fund payments (see p346);
- disability living allowance care component (DLA care) and attendance allowance (AA) (including constant attendance allowance and exceptionally severe disablement allowance payable with industrial injury disablement benefit or war disablement benefit) (see p346).

The way these benefits are affected depends on whether the resident is:

- a temporary or permanent resident; *and*
- a single person or one of a couple.

See Chapter 18 for example calculations.

All other social security benefits (eg, DLA mobility component – but if your care home is considered to be a hospital or similar institution see p351 – state retirement pension or incapacity benefit/contributory ESA) are claimed and paid in the normal way when you are in a care home, subject to the standard rules (see Chapter 7).

Income support/income-related employment and support allowance

All references to IS also apply to income-based jobseeker's allowance (JSA).

The treatment of residents in either Part III local authority or independent sector care homes is the same for benefit purposes.

Your IS/income-based ESA is calculated in the normal way, with a personal allowance (IS) or prescribed amount and additional component (income-related ESA) and premiums. See Chapter 17 for example calculations.

You may gain or lose entitlement on entering or leaving a care home (see below) and you should always notify the office dealing with your benefit.

If you enter, or are expected to enter, a care home for a period of no more than eight weeks, your IS/income-related ESA can be altered or paid from the day of admission. If your stay is expected to be more than eight weeks, your IS/income-related ESA can only be altered or paid from the start of your benefit week.[44]

Capital limits in care homes

- **Temporary stay:** the IS capital limits that apply during a temporary stay are the same as those that apply in the community:
  - £6,000 lower limit;
  - £16,000 upper limit.
  Capital at the lower limit or below is disregarded. A tariff income is applied to capital between the lower and upper limits of £1 for every £250 or part thereof. There is no entitlement to IS/income-related ESA if you have capital above the upper capital limit.
- **Permanent stay:** the IS capital limits that apply during a permanent stay are:
  - £10,000 lower limit;
  - £16,000 upper limit.
  Capital at or below £10,000 is disregarded. A tariff income is applied to capital between £10,000 and £16,000 of £1 for every £250 or part thereof. There is no entitlement to IS/income-related ESA if you have capital above the upper capital limit.

Single person in a care home

- **Temporary stay:** the amount of any IS/income-related ESA you receive is usually the same as the amount you receive in the community.
- **Permanent stay:** the amount of any IS/income-related ESA you receive is usually the same as the amount you received in the community. However, the amount of any IS/income-related ESA you receive changes in the following circumstances.

- If you have capital between £6,000 and £10,000, there will be an increase in the amount payable as there will no longer be a tariff income applied because of the increased lower capital limit from £6,000 to £10,000 (see p339).
- If you have capital between £10,000 and £16,000, a reduction in the amount of tariff income will be applied (and therefore an increase in IS/income-related ESA due to the increased lower capital limit (see p339).
- If you are a single person living with a non-dependant in the community, or you had a carer in receipt of carer's allowance in the community, you may become entitled to, or there may be a change in, the amount of any IS/income-related ESA payable due to the severe disability premium being included in your applicable amount for the period that any DLA care/AA remains in payment (see p341).
- Housing costs (if any) will no longer be included in your applicable amount.

Note: for temporary and permanent residents, if the severe disability premium and for IS only, the enhanced disability premium (if applicable) are included, they will no longer be included where DLA care has ceased (see p341). The enhanced disability premium will continue to be included in the prescribed amount for income-related ESA if you are in receipt of the support component (see p157).

Couple where both members are in the same room in the same care home

- **Temporary stay:** there is usually no change from the amount of any IS/income-related ESA you receive as a couple in the community. You are both still treated as a couple.
- **Permanent stay:** caselaw suggests that if one or both of you are permanent residents you should not be treated as a couple.[45] This means that you should both be treated as single people with the appropriate single person's applicable amount, personal allowance/prescribed amount and additional component (income-related ESA) and premiums. You and your partner's IS/income-related ESA entitlement is calculated using your individual resources and is paid to each of you separately. Housing costs are no longer included in your applicable amount.

Note: for temporary and permanent residents, if the severe disability premium and for IS only, the enhanced disability premium (if applicable) are included, they will no longer be included where DLA care component has ceased (see p341). The enhanced disability premium will continue to be included in the prescribed amount for income-related ESA if you are in receipt of the support component (see p157).

Couple where one member is in a care home or both are in different care homes or both are in different rooms in the same care home

- **Temporary stay** (ie, temporarily separated): the applicable amount is either:
  - the normal personal allowance (IS) or the prescribed amount and additional component (income-related ESA) for a couple, plus any appropriate premiums at the couple rate, plus housing costs for your home in the community where appropriate; *or*
  - the aggregate of the normal personal allowance (IS) or the prescribed amount and additional component (income-related ESA) for each of you as if you are single people, plus any appropriate premiums for each of you at the single person rate, plus any housing costs for your home in the community where appropriate,

  whichever is the greater.[46]

  In nearly all situations the greater amount is the two single person's applicable amounts. Note that if your stay in care is temporary, even if the single person applicable amounts are used, you and your partner are still assessed as a couple in terms of your resources (capital and income), which are aggregated and IS/income-related ESA is paid to the person who claims in respect of both of you.

- **Permanent stay:** you will no longer be treated as a couple.[47] You are treated as single people with the appropriate single person's applicable amount, personal allowance (IS) or the prescribed amount and additional component (income-related ESA) and premiums. Your IS/income-related ESA entitlement is calculated using your individual resources (capital and income) and is paid to each of you separately. Any jointly held capital is assessed as split equally between the two of you (see p211). Housing costs are not included in the applicable amount of the person(s) in care.

The severe disability premium

Where you are entering a care home on a **permanent** basis and you are still in receipt of the DLA care component (middle or higher rate), the severe disability premium (SDP) should be included in your applicable/prescribed amount as a single person or as one of a couple being treated as a single person.[48]

If you are entering a care home for a **temporary stay** (including respite and trial period stays), there is often confusion about whether or not the SDP should be included in your applicable/prescribed amount.

If you are a **single person** in receipt of DLA care (middle or higher rate) and the SDP is not included in your IS/income-related ESA when you are in your home in the community because there is a 'non-dependant' living with you, or carer's allowance (CA) is in payment to your carer, then you are not entitled to the SDP when you go temporarily into a care home.[49] If you get the SDP in your applicable amount when you are at home in the community then you continue to receive it in the care home for as long as you are in receipt of DLA care (middle or higher rate).

If you are **one member of a couple** and you are temporarily separated from your partner, the SDP can be included in the applicable/prescribed amount for each person in receipt of DLA care (middle or higher rate) even where it was not included in the applicable amount when you were at home (as long as CA is not paid to a person who cares for you). Until June 2002, guidance stated that this applies when you are a joint tenant or joint homeowner with your partner.[50] However, a commissioner's decision held that this guidance was misconceived and it was unlikely that it was intended that entitlement to the SDP should depend on the claimant's property rights.[51] The commissioner further held that where a couple are assessed as single claimants (see p340) it implies that they are being treated as normally living apart for the purposes of calculating the applicable amount, therefore they cannot each be treated as a non-dependant of the other.[52] The commissioner concluded that where a temporary resident's wife was getting AA but the resident's AA had been suspended (because he had been in hospital for more than 28 days prior to his move into a care home), a single SDP should be included in their applicable amount.[53] It would be consistent with the approach in this decision for a single SDP to be included in the applicable amount of a temporary resident who was still in receipt of AA or DLA care (middle or higher rate) where her/his partner in the community (or in hospital) would normally (when they were living together in the community) have prevented its inclusion.

As a result of the decision, guidance issued in June 2002 summarises the 'whichever is the greater' special assessment (see p341) and the commissioner's decision.[54] This guidance, with examples added, has been incorporated in the *Decision Makers Guide*.[55]

Pension credit

During your PC 'assessed income period' you are not required to report any changes in your retirement provision income (see p162). An assessed income period ends if you enter a care home on a permanent basis or if you are no longer entitled to PC – eg, you sell your property and you have capital above the level at which PC continues.[56]

Although PC rules (see p158) are similar to IS rules, especially for the guarantee credit, there are some important differences which affect entitlement when a person goes into a care home.

Capital limits in care homes
- **Temporary stay:** the PC capital limits that apply during a temporary stay are the same as those that apply in the community:
  - £6,000 lower limit;
  - no upper limit.

Capital at the lower limit or below is disregarded. Assumed income from capital (tariff income) is applied to capital above the lower limit of £1 for every £500 or part thereof.[57]

- **Permanent stay:** the PC capital limits that apply during a permanent stay are:
  - £10,000 lower limit;
  - no upper limit.

  Capital at or below £10,000 is disregarded. Assumed income from capital (tariff income) is applied to capital above £10,000 of £1 for every £500 or part thereof.

Single person in a care home

- **Temporary stay:** the amount of any PC you receive is usually the same as the amount you receive in the community.
- **Permanent stay:** the amount of any PC you receive is usually the same as the amount you received in the community. However, the amount of any PC you receive changes in the following circumstances.
  - If you have capital between £6,000 and £10,000, there will be an increase in the amount payable as there will no longer be an assumed income applied due to the increased lower capital limit from £6,000 to £10,000 (see above).
  - If you have capital above £10,000, there will also be a reduction in the amount of assumed income (and therefore an increase in PC) applied due to the increased lower capital limit from £6,000 to £10,000 (see above).
  - If you are a single person living with a non-dependant in the community or you had a carer in receipt of CA in the community, you may become entitled to, or there may be a change in, the amount of any PC payable due to the severe disability additional amount being included in your appropriate amount for the period that any DLA care/AA remains in payment (see p344).
  - Housing costs (if any) are no longer included in your appropriate amount.

  Note: for temporary and permanent residents, if the severe disability additional amount is included, it is no longer included where DLA care/AA has ceased (see below).

Couple – one or both members going into a care home

- **Temporary stay:** there is usually no change from the amount of any PC you receive as a couple in the community. You are both still treated as a couple. Unlike for IS, there is no provision for the treatment of couples as two single people in terms of the appropriate amounts even where you are temporarily separated.[58] See p344 for the effect this has on any severe disability additional amount.

  If you get IS and you are temporarily in a care home on your 60th birthday, you are entitled to a transitional additional amount included in your appropriate amount of PC. This will protect you from a reduction in benefit payable not only during the remainder of your stay in the care home but also when you return to your home in the community. The transitional amount will be reduced by any future increase in the appropriate amount.

- **Permanent stay**: you are no longer treated as a couple.[59] You are treated as single people with the relevant single person's appropriate amount – the standard minimum guarantee and additional amounts. Your PC entitlement is calculated using your individual resources (capital and income) and is paid to each of you separately. Any jointly held capital is assessed as split equally between the two of you (see p211). Housing costs are no longer included in the applicable amount of the person(s) in care.

Note: for temporary and permanent residents, if the severe disability additional amount is included, it is no longer be included where DLA care/AA has ceased (see below).

The severe disability additional amount

Where you are entering a care home on a **permanent** basis and you are in receipt of DLA care (middle or higher rate)/AA, the severe disability additional amount (SDAA) should be included in your applicable amount as a single person or as one of a couple being treated as a single person.

If you are entering a care home for a **temporary stay** (including respite and trial period stays) there is often confusion about whether or not the SDAA should be included in your applicable amount.

If you are a **single person** in receipt of DLA care (middle or higher rate)/AA and the SDAA is not included in your appropriate amount when you are in your home in the community because there is a 'non-dependant' living with you, or CA is in payment to your carer, then you are not entitled to the SDAA when you go temporarily into a care home. If you do receive the SDAA in your applicable amount when you are at home in the community then you continue to receive it in the care home for as long as you are in receipt of DLA care (middle or higher rate)/AA.

If you are **one member of a couple** and you are temporarily separated from your partner, a consequence of there being no provision to treat couples as two single people is that:

- where both of you are in receipt of DLA care/AA; *and*
- have a double SDAA included in your appropriate amount; *and*
- you are in a care home while your partner remains at home,

a suspension of your DLA care/AA after 28 days (or sooner, see p349) not only has the knock-on effect of preventing the SDAA for you from being included in your appropriate amount but also prevents the SDAA for your partner from being included. This is because you, as the resident, are treated as still being in your partner's household and not disregarded for the purposes of qualifying for the SDAA.

A similar situation occurs when one of a couple is temporarily in hospital, but the PC regulations provide for this by allowing a single SDAA to continue in payment for the partner at home. In practice however, the DWP also appears to apply this hospital provision to a care home situation, perhaps because it was not intended to treat one of a couple temporarily in a care home differently in these circumstances to one of a couple temporarily in hospital.

Housing benefit

You are not usually able to get HB (see p163) towards the cost of a registered care home.[60]

As care homes (including local authority care homes) which provide personal an/or nursing care and are required to register with the Care Quality Commission (England), the Care and Social Services Inspectorate Wales or the Scottish Commission for the Regulation of Care even if they do not also provide board, it means that HB is usually not payable. Instead you may receive funding or additional funding for your accommodation from adult social care services subject to the charging assessment (see p264).

If you go into a care home for a **temporary** stay (including respite stays – see p337) you can continue to get HB in respect of your home in the community for up to 52 weeks. If you have entered a care home on a **trial period** basis (see p337), HB is paid for up to 13 weeks in respect of your home in the community.

It has been held that the full 13 weeks continues to be a period of entitlement to benefit irrespective of any decision to become permanent during this period because it is the intention at the beginning of your stay which applies throughout. This means that you will be able to give the appropriate notice of termination of any tenancy as long your liability for rent will come to an end within the 13-week period. If you only become entitled to IS/income-related ESA/PC for the period of your stay in a care home, you will automatically receive HB during this period but you will need to reclaim HB upon your return to your home in the community when your IS/income-related ESA/PC ceases.

If you move to a care home on a permanent basis from a home where you remain liable for the rent because a notice period for the termination of the tenancy is being served, you can be treated as occupying your former home and therefore entitled to HB for up to four weeks, as long as that liability could not reasonably have been avoided.

If you are **one of a couple** and you are going into care permanently while your partner is remaining at home in the community, you need to make sure that your partner claims HB if it was previously claimed under your name.

Council tax benefit

You are able to get CTB if you are liable to pay council tax in respect of your home in the community (see p171). The rules for getting CTB during a **temporary** stay are the same as for HB (see above).

If you are a **permanent** resident, and therefore the care home has become your 'sole or main' home, *and* your home in the community is left unoccupied, you are exempt from council tax.

If you are one of a couple and your partner is now living alone in your home in the community, s/he can get a 25 per cent status discount on her/his council tax as a single person and may qualify for CTB (see p171).

Social fund payments

If you are a permanent resident in a care home (see p337 for definitions) you are excluded from receiving a **crisis loan** from the discretionary social fund unless you are planning to move out within the next two weeks.

For **community care grants** (CCGs) and **budgeting loans** the same rules apply as if you were living in the community (see p185) except that it is unlikely that you would satisfy the criteria for the purpose of a CCG[61] unless it is to help with travel expenses in certain specified situations[62] or you are moving out of the care home into the community.[63]

The same rules as for people living in the community also apply for **funeral expenses** (see p182) and **Sure Start maternity grants** (see p183). However, as a permanent resident in a care or nursing home you are excluded from receiving **cold weather payments**.[64]

You are eligible to receive a **winter fuel payment**, subject to the same rules as if you were living in the community (see p184), if you are a resident in a care home as long as you are *not* in receipt of IS, income-based JSA, income-related ESA or PC.[65] The amount of the payment will be 50 per cent of the annual lump sum.[66]

Disability living allowance care component and attendance allowance

DLA care and AA (including constant attendance allowance and exceptionally severe disablement allowance payable with industrial injury disablement or war disablement benefit) are affected when you are 'resident in a care home' (other than a hospital) on a **temporary or permanent** basis. (For the effect on DLA/AA of a stay in hospital or similar institution, see p189.)

Resident in a care home

DLA care/AA is not payable after a period of 28 days (see p190) of being 'resident in a care home'. You are considered to be 'resident in a care home' when any of the costs of any qualifying services (accommodation, board and personal care) provided for you are paid for out of public or local funds under the following specified legislation:

- Part III of the National Assistance Act 1948;

- Part IV of the Social Work (Scotland) Act 1968;
- the Mental Health (Care and Treatment) (Scotland) Act 2003;
- the Community Care and Health (Scotland) Act 2002;
- the Mental Health Act 1983; *or*
- any other legislation *'relating to persons under disability'* (and, for DLA care only, *'or to young persons or to education or training'*).

'Qualifying services' do not include:
- domiciliary services provided for a person in a private dwelling; *or*
- improvements made to, or furniture and equipment provided for, a person in a private dwelling; *or*
- one-off irregular improvements made to, or furniture and equipment provided for, care homes for which a grant has been made out of public or local funds; *or*
- social and recreational activities provided outside the accommodation for which a grant has been made out of public or local funds; *or*
- the purchase or running of a motor vehicle to be used in connection with the accommodation for which a grant has been made out of public or local funds; *or*
- services provided pursuant to the National Health Service Act 1977 or the National Health Service (Scotland) Act 1978 – eg, free nursing care in care homes which provide nursing (see p22).

You are not considered to be 'resident in a care home' for the purposes of these provisions if you are self-funding or retrospectively self-funding (see p350). In these circumstances you can continue to receive DLA care or AA.

DLA mobility is not affected by residence in a care home (but is affected by stays in hospitals or similar institutions – see p189). For the rules on whether your accommodation may be treated as a hospital or similar institution, see p331.

For the purposes of DLA care/AA, if you go into a care home from the community, the days you enter and leave are counted as days in the community. If you go into hospital from a care home (or vice versa), the days you enter and leave are counted as days in the care home. If your accommodation has been arranged as part of a programme of aftercare under s117 Mental Health Act 1983, see p336.

It is usually clear when you are 'resident in a care home'. Sometimes, however, it is not as the rules can be complicated by many inter-related provisions and exceptions. If the DWP decides you are not entitled to DLA care/AA because it is considered that you are 'resident in a care home' and you have any doubts, seek advice (see Appendix 2).

It should not always be assumed that arrangements made by adult social care services for providing accommodation and care have necessarily been made under Part III of the National Assistance Act 1948 (NAA). Sometimes, adult social care services may use other powers to make payments towards the costs of your care or it may contribute towards the running costs of the home, but is not actually contributing towards the costs of your own placement under Part III of NAA. In such circumstances, there is no reason why DLA care/AA may not continue to be paid to you. Seek advice if your DLA care/AA has been suspended in these circumstances (see Appendix 2).

There are many decisions of the former social security commissioners and court judgments on the issue.

A social security commissioner held that a group home for people with learning disabilities was caught by the rules even though the costs of the home were not borne out of public funds, there were no resident care staff (only visiting carers), and the residents who were paying rent were also responsible for their own meals and paying for their other outgoings. This decision was based on the conclusion that the accommodation must have been provided under Part III of the NAA 1948 because it was not accepted that there could be any other statutory basis for providing the accommodation. In that case the authority was a county council, and as any responsibility for providing housing was instead a district council responsibility, social services must, it was decided, have provided the accommodation under Part III.[67]

However, this decision appears to have been discredited, as another commissioner has taken a more reasoned view, finding that a county council may well have other powers to provide accommodation[68] and that it is not necessary to decide what they are. In this case, there was a lease in the form of a tenancy agreement and this was sufficient to show that the accommodation was not provided under Part III, even though the accommodation was owned and managed by the county council. The commissioner also took the view that it would be unsatisfactory if entitlement to DLA care/AA depended on whether a claimant lived within the boundaries of a county council (which are not housing authorities) or a metropolitan or unitary authority (which are both adult social care services and housing authorities).

Another commissioner's decision has taken a similar approach, stating that 'a home which is mainly used where arrangements have been made under Part III, or which was built for that purpose, could be used to accommodate a person to whom the local authority had no duty under Part III'.[69] In this case the claimant had moved from the respite unit in the local authority care home to a transition unit for the purpose of rehabilitation. During his stay in the transitional unit adult social care services made contributions to the cost of his accommodation and care but it was held that these payments could not be payments under Part III of the NAA as there had been:

- no assessment of need under s47 National Health Service and Community Care Act 1990 which was an essential gateway for the provision of services under Part III; *and*
- no standard charge identified for the accommodation; *and consequently*
- no assessment of individual ability to pay as required by s22 NAA.

The social security commissioner in this case decided that accommodation could have been provided under s137 Local Government Act 1972 (LGA 1972). This is a general power that gives local authorities the power to incur expenditure not authorised by any other enactment.

Under s2 Local Government Act 2000 adult social care services also have the power to provide accommodation which promotes well-being where it exercises this power with regard to its community strategy. Section 2 was introduced in part as a response to what was seen as a restrictive view by the courts of the activities that can be pursued using s137 LGA 1972, which led to uncertainty among local authorities and their potential partners about the extent to which authorities can rely on their general powers to undertake certain activities. Section 2 extends local authorities' general powers to enable them to have 'the freedom to work with other local public, private and voluntary organisations to develop solutions to local problems'.

The linking rule

DLA care/AA is usually payable for the first 28 days of being resident in a care home[70] even if you are not self-funding or retrospectively self-funding (see p350). However, if you were resident in a care home or in a hospital or similar institution within the previous 28 days, that period of stay is linked to your present stay so that benefit is only paid for a total of 28 days including the period of your previous stay. The day you enter a care home and the day you leave do not count as days resident in a care home. If you first claim DLA care/AA when you are already resident in a care home it is not payable until you leave (unless you are self-funding or retrospectively self-funding). If you are resident in a care home again (even within 28 days), your 28-day concession will start from the first day of that stay.

If you are receiving respite care (ie, a planned programme of temporary stays) you may be able to arrange a pattern of stays that allows you to keep your DLA care/AA. The following example illustrates how the 'linking rule' works.

Example

Mr Hammond gets AA and he has respite care every weekend. He goes into a care home on a Friday and leaves on the following Monday. This is counted as two days of respite care (Saturday and Sunday) because the day of entering (Friday) and the day of leaving (Monday) are not counted.

Mr Hammond continues with this pattern of respite care but he is mindful that each of his weekend stays after his first stay are being linked together because they are within 28 days of the previous stay. This means that after 14 weekend stays of two days each he has reached the end of his 28 days' payment of AA while in care. If Mr Hammond spent a 15th weekend in respite care, his AA would stop for the two days in care and only start in payment again when he went home until his next respite care stay, when it would stop again.

However, in order to avoid any break in the payment of his AA, Mr Hammond breaks the 'link' by having shorter respite care stays. For four weekends following the 14th weekend stay he doesn't go into the care home until the Saturday and he leaves on Sunday. As there are no days counted as days in care, he has effectively spent 29 days without a stay in care, thus breaking the link. On the 19th weekend, Mr Hammond goes back to going into the care home on a Friday and leaving on a Monday. If he continues to repeat this pattern his AA will be paid without any break for his stays in the care home.

It is important to inform the Disability Benefits Unit (see Appendix 1), as well as your local DWP office, of any stay in a care home and, if you have a pattern of respite care planned, to advise them of this in advance. If you cannot arrange your respite care to break the link, you will at some point lose your benefit for the period you are in the care home.

4. Self-funding and retrospective self-funding

You are described as '**self-funding**' if you can meet the whole cost of your accommodation and care in a care home from your own resources (or with help from relatives, friends or a charity), without any financial help from adult social care services.[71] Your own resources includes any income support /income-related employment and support allowance/pension credit to which you are entitled. Until 19 June 2000 you could only count as self-funding for benefit purposes if you were in an independent sector care home. Since then the definition also includes those residents in a local authority care home.[72] You are also treated as a self-funder if you receive help from the NHS with the nursing care element of your care in a care home which provides nursing.

You may be required to meet the whole cost of your accommodation and care because of the level of your income or capital (see Chapters 11 and 12). In most cases it is the level of your capital that determines whether you will be required to fund yourself.

If you are making your own arrangements to go into a care home but it is likely that your capital will eventually fall to the upper capital limits for your country (see p291) or less, it is sensible to talk to adult social care services first and perhaps have an assessment of your needs carried out so that there will not be a problem in the future if you ask for financial help from adult social care services.

Disability living allowance care component and attendance allowance

If you are self-funding (see above) you are able to continue receiving any disability living allowance care component (DLA care)/attendance allowance (AA) to which you are entitled beyond the first 28 days in a care home. Even if adult social care

Chapter 16: Social security benefits in care homes
5. Temporary absences from care homes (including going into hospital)

16

services has helped you find the placement and contracted with the home to provide your accommodation and care, you are still able to get DLA care/AA as long as you are meeting the *whole* cost yourself (or with help from relatives, friends or a charity) without funding from adult social care services.[73]

In **Scotland**, if you are aged 65 or over you will not be entitled to DLA care/AA if you are receiving help from the local authority with the cost of your care under the 'free personal care' arrangements. If you are under aged 65, you will still be paid DLA care if the only help you get is for 'free nursing care'.

Retrospective self-funding

If you are required to meet the whole cost of your accommodation and care because you have a property worth more than the upper capital limit for your country (see p291), but you have not sold the property yet or you are awaiting the release of other funds and you do not have additional resources with which to pay the full cost, adult social care services can make payments to the care home for your placement until your property is sold or your funds are released. You must then refund adult social care services. In these circumstances you are considered to be 'retrospectively self-funding'. If you are awaiting the sale of your property or you have chosen not to sell your property, adult social care services has powers to create a legal charge on your property.[74]

Deferred payment agreements can be arranged where adult social care services defers the difference between the full cost and the assessed contribution against the value of your property. The deferred payment is then recouped upon the eventual sale of the property (see p272). You remain entitled to receive DLA care/AA while adult social care services is funding your accommodation and care on an interim, refundable basis – ie, you are retrospectively self-funding.

5. **Temporary absences from care homes (including going into hospital)**

If you are temporarily absent from a care home because you have gone into hospital for less than 52 weeks then your benefits do not usually change unless you are in receipt of disability living allowance (DLA) mobility component which will usually cease after four weeks of a stay in hospital. For how going into hospital effects the payment of care home fees, see p277.[75]

If you are temporarily absent from a care home for any other reason (eg, visiting relatives), the DLA care component or attendance allowance (AA) may become payable.[76] Consequently, you may also become entitled to the severe disability premium in your income support/income-related employment and support allowance applicable amount or the severe disability additional amount in your pension credit appropriate amount. See p277 for how you may be

16

Chapter 16: Social security benefits in care homes
5. Temporary absences from care homes (including going into hospital)

able to keep this benefit for your use during the temporary absence rather than have it included in the amount that you are required to contribute toward the cost of your accommodation and care.

---

6. Other sources of financial assistance in care homes

Health benefits

If you are a permanent resident in a care home and your placement is being wholly or partly funded by adult social care services, you can obtain an HC2 certificate from the Health Benefits Division of the Prescription Pricing Authority for full exemption from NHS charges (eg, prescriptions, dental treatment) and fares to hospital by completing a special short application form HC1(SC).[77] This exemption does not, however, apply to charges for sight tests and glasses, but you may be exempt on other grounds (see p76). Your certificate will last for 12 months and you should make a repeat claim about four weeks before your certificate expires.

If you do not receive any funding for your placement from adult social care services you may still be able to get a full or partial exemption for the same charges under the normal rules that apply for health benefits in the community (see p76).

Special help for war pensioners

If you get a war disablement pension or you have had a gratuity for your disability, you can apply to the Service Personnel and Veterans Agency (previously called the War Pensions Agency) for free medical treatment and services that you need wholly or mainly because of that disability. There is no means test for these services (ie, it does not matter how much income or capital you have), but you must apply before arranging for them.

You may be able to get help for the fees of care homes which provide nursing where you are provided with skilled nursing care if you need permanent care in a care home, or if you need a short break for convalescence, or if you need a respite break in order to give your carer a break.

For a permanent stay in a care home which provides nursing you must need 24-hour nursing care because of your pensioned disability. The Service Personnel and Veterans Agency can pay up to a maximum of £516 (£587 in London) a week for fees provided that adult social care services has not been involved in assessing your nursing needs or arranging a placement. A higher rate can be paid if there is no other care home which provides nursing which is suitable for your needs. In this situation your basic war disablement pension continues to be paid in full while you are in the nursing home but any constant attendance allowance payable will stop after four weeks. Some other extra allowances such as unemployability supplement are reduced or withdrawn after eight weeks.

For a short-term break for convalescence you can claim nursing home fees for a maximum of four weeks a year. However, if you have recently been discharged from hospital or are recovering from an operation, the Service Personnel and Veterans Agency is unlikely to pay as it considers this is an NHS responsibility.

For a respite break you may be able to claim nursing home fees if your carer needs a break from caring for you for medical reasons (medical evidence is required).

Other expenses for medical treatment and services may also be available – ask your local war pensioners' welfare officer to visit you to discuss your needs and help you apply for any services.

7. **Effects on carers**

If you are the carer of a person who goes into a care home for a temporary (including respite or trial periods) or permanent stay, the following benefits are affected:

- carer's allowance (CA – see p131);
- income support (IS), income-related employment and support allowance (ESA) or pension credit (PC) (see p147).

If the person you are caring for receives disability living allowance care component (DLA care) (middle or higher rates) or attendance allowance (AA), you may be claiming CA for caring for her/him. The CA rules allow breaks in care of up to 12 weeks within a 26-week period. Up to four weeks of the 12-week period are allowed for any temporary breaks in care – eg, holidays or if the person you care for goes into a care home for a temporary or respite stay. The remaining eight weeks of the 12-week period allow for either you, as the carer, or the person you care for, to undergo medical or other treatment as a hospital inpatient. However, if the person you care for goes into hospital or into a care home and s/he is not self-funding, her/his DLA care component or AA will stop after four weeks, or sooner if s/he has had a stay in hospital or a care home within the previous 28 days (see p350). This means your CA will also stop.

The person you care for may be able to arrange a pattern of respite care that allows her/him to keep her/his DLA care/AA (see example on p349) thus allowing you to keep your CA. All changes of circumstances (yours or the person you care for) must be reported to the CA Unit. The main rule to remember is that you can be paid CA for any week (Sunday through to Saturday) in which you are caring for the disabled person for at least 35 hours, so odd days or weekends away are unlikely to affect your entitlement.

If the person you care for goes into a care home permanently, and your CA stops, you continue to be eligible for the carer's premium (IS/income-related ESA) or the carer's additional amount (PC) of £29.50 to be included in your applicable/prescribed/appropriate amount/ for a further eight weeks. After this you may need to claim income-based jobseeker's allowance (JSA) instead if you are under 60. The carer's premium is also included in any calculation for housing benefit, council tax benefit, income-based JSA and health benefits for eight weeks after your CA stops (see p153).

If, as a carer, you are also responsible for the disabled person's benefits because s/he cannot manage her/his financial affairs (see p92), you may wish to continue in this role when s/he is living in a care home. In this capacity you may also have the added responsibility of forwarding the contribution to adult social care services for her/his accommodation and care costs and of providing information for the adult social care services financial assessment. If you do not wish to have this responsibility you could choose to relinquish the appointeeship in favour of adult social care services. The adult social care services department responsible for organising the disabled person's placement should be able to give you further information about this.

Notes

1. Types of care home
1 HSCA 2008; s2(3)RC(S)A 2001
2 paras 77005 and 77006 DMG;
3 paras 77007 and 77008 DMG;
4 s256 NHSA 2006
5 SS(HIP&MA) Regs
6 Reg 2(2) SS(HIP) Regs; reg 8(1) SS(DLA) Regs; reg 6(1) SS(AA) Regs; reg 21 IS Regs
7 CP/63/1988; CIS/371/1990; CDLA/7980/95; CDLA/2496/97
8 White and Others v CAO, The Times, 2 August 1993; R(IS) 18/94; Botchett v CAO, The Times, 8 May 1996 (R(IS) 10/96)
9 Reg 2(2) SS(HIP) Regs; reg 8(1) SS(DLA) Regs; reg 6(1) SS(AA) Regs 1991
10 NHSA 2006; NHS(S)A 1978; NHSCCA 1990
11 CIS/371/1990; CDLA/2496/1997; CDLA/7980/1995

12 CP/63/1988; CIS/371/1990; White and Others v CAO, The Times, 2 August 1993 (R(IS) 18/1994); CDLA/7980/1995; CDLA/2496/1997
13 CDLA/7980/1995
14 CIS/371/1990
15 CDLA/2496/1997
16 Botchett v CAO, 8 May 1996, The Times; CIS/371/1990; R(IS) 10/1996; White and Others v CAO, The Times , 2 August 1993; R(IS) 18/1994
17 White and Others v CAO, The Times, 2 August 1993; R(IS) 18/1994
18 s65 NHSA 1977; s58 NHS(S)A 1978 or Sch 2 para 14 NHSCCA 1990; Sch 7A NHS(S)A 1978
19 CS/249/1989 and R(IS) 7/92

20 R(S) 4/84 held that a person was not receiving free inpatient treatment because 'any period' and 'period' must relate to a period of not less than one day. CS/249/1989 held that a person needs to be in hospital 24 hours a day to be treated as maintained free of charge as an inpatient. CIS/192/1991 and CS/94/1992 held that absences during the 24-hour period do not affect inpatient status or that of being maintained free of charge.

21 Reg 8 SS(DLA) Regs 1991

22 CDLA/11099/95

23 CSS/617/97 – looking at reg 2(2) SS(HIP) Regs 1975

24 Reg 2(2) SS(HIP) Regs as amended by reg 11 SS(MP)(No.2) Regs (16 November 1992)

25 CIS/3325/2000 and others

26 Reg 2(2) SS(HIP) Regs as amended by reg 11 SS(MP)(No.2) Regs (16 November 1992)

27 para 73 R(DLA) 2/06

28 Reg 10(7) SS(DLA) Regs; reg 8(5) SS(AA) Regs

29 Reg 12B(9A) SS(DLA) Regs

30 Reg 10(6) SS(DLA) Regs; reg 8(4) SS(AA) Regs

31 s26 NAA 1948

32 s22 NAA 1948

33 NAA 1948

34 R(DLA) 2/06

35 s256 NHSA 2006 payable to housing associations and charitable or voluntary organisations as well as adult social care

36 Under Part III NAA 1948

37 s21 Part III NAA 1948

38 ss3, 37, 47 or 48 MHA 1983

39 *R v Redcar & Cleveland BC ex parte Armstrong; R v Manchester City Council ex parte Stennett; R v Harrow London BC ex parte Cobham* HL 25.7.02

40 Following R(DLA) 6/04 and subsequent amendment (13.02.05) to Appendix 1 to Chapter 61 DMG which now states that s117 MHA is an 'enactment relating to persons under disability' for the purposes of defining those people in 'certain accommodation' for whom DLA care or AA are not payable

41 Sch 3 para 3(11) IS Regs; reg 7(16) HB Regs; reg 8(4) CTB Regs; reg 7 HB(SPC) Regs

42 Sch 3 paras 3(8)-(10) IS Regs; regs 7(11)-(13) HB Regs; reg 7 HB(SPC) Regs; Regs 8(1)-(3) CTB Regs; reg 12 CTB(SPC) Regs

43 CIS/613/1997

3. **Social security benefits affected**

44 Reg 26 and Sch 7 para 7(2)(c) SS(C&P) Regs

45 R(IS) 1/99

46 Sch 7 para 9 IS regs; Sch 5 para 4(a) ESA Regs

47 Reg 16(3)(e) IS Regs; reg 156(1) & (4)(d) ESA Regs

48 para 23230 DMG; reg 3(4) IS regs; reg 71(6) ESA regs

49 para 23229 DMG; reg 3(1) IS regs; 71(1) ESA regs

50 para 23230 DMG; reg 3(4) IS regs; reg 71(6) ESA regs

51 para 13 CIS/1544/2001

52 para 12 CIS/1544/2001

53 para 13 CIS/1544/2001

54 DMG letter 05/02, 14 June 2002

55 DMG vol 4 para 23231-33 amended November 2002

56 s9(4)(c) and (d) SPCA 2002; reg 12(a) SPC Regs

57 s15(2) SPCA 2002; reg 15(6) SPC Regs

58 Reg 5(1)(a) and Sch 2 paras 4(8), (11)(c)(ix) and (12) SPC Regs

59 Reg 5(1)(b) SPC Regs

60 Reg 9(1)(k) & (4) HB Regs; reg 9 HB(SPC) Regs

61 SF Dir 4

62 SF Dir 4(b)

63 SF Dir 4(a)(i)

64 Reg 1A(3) SFCWP Regs

65 Reg 1(2)(3) & (3A) SFWFP Regs

66 Reg 2(b)(ii) SFWFP Regs s72(9)&(10) SSCBA 1992; reg 9 DLA Regs; reg 7 AA Regs Reg 10(8) DLA Regs; reg 8(6) AA Regs

67 CDLA/13479/1996

68 CDLA/1465/1998

69 CDLA/2127/2000

70 Reg 10(1) SS(DLA) Regs; reg 8(1) SS(AA) Regs

4. **Self-funding and retrospective self-funding**

71 Reg 10(8) SS(DLA) Regs; reg 8(6) SS(AA) Regs

72 Reg 10(9) SS(DLA) Regs; reg 8(7) SS(AA) Regs

73 para 61735 DMG

74 s22 HASSASSAA 1983; s55 HSCA 2001

75 Reg 2(9) SS(HIP&MA) Regs

76 para 61752 DMG

6. **Other sources of financial assistance**

77 Reg 4(m) NHS(TERC) Regs

Chapter 17

Calculations – benefits and charges in care homes

This chapter covers:
1. Example income support/income-related employment and support allowance and contribution calculations: aged under 60 (below)
2. Example pension credit and contribution calculations: aged 60 or over (p368)

All examples assume that adult social care services undertakes a financial assessment for any length of stay in a care home (although this is not always the case – see p265). The examples also assume a lower capital limit of £14,000 and an upper capital limit of £23,000 which apply in England from April 2009. For Scotland the capital limits are £13,750 and £22,500 and for Wales the capital limits are £20,750 and £22,000.

---

1. Example income support/income-related employment and support allowance and contribution calculations (aged under 60)

This section includes examples for:
- single person, temporary stay (Example 1 – p368);
- single person, permanent stay (Example 2 – p378);
- couple – one entering a care home, temporary stay, resident claimant (Example 3 – p376);
- couple – one entering a care home, temporary stay, non-resident claimant (Example 4 – p376);
- couple – one entering a care home, permanent stay (Example 5 – p376)

Since 27 October 2008 employment and support allowance (ESA) has replaced incapacity benefit (IB) and income support (IS) on the grounds of incapacity for work for all new claims. The following examples assume that claims were made prior to 27 October 2008 as this is the more likely scenario however, the examples also include what the post 13-week assessment period income-related ESA calculation would be for a new claim.

Example 1: Single person, temporary stay

Mr Singh (50) is a single person living in a rented council house.

His income before entering the care home is made up of long-term incapacity benefit (IB), income support (IS) and disability living allowance (DLA) care and mobility components.

He has no savings.

Mr Singh also receives maximum housing benefit (HB) and council tax benefit (CTB).

He has savings of £7,000.

He goes into the care home for a temporary stay of two weeks.

Income support calculation

Mr Singh's IS was, and continues to be, calculated in the following way:

Income		
	IB (long-term)	£96.35
	Tariff income from savings	£4.00
	Total	**£100.35**

(DLA care component £70.35 disregarded)
(DLA mobility component £49.10 disregarded)

Applicable amount	£64.30	(Personal allowance)
	£27.50	(Disability premium)
	£13.40	(Enhanced disability premium)
	£52.85	(Severe disability premium)
Total	**£158.05**	

Applicable amount (£158.05) *minus* **Income** (£100.35) = **IS** (£57.70)

Mr Singh is entitled to IS of £57.70 a week (paid on top of his IB and DLA).

Income-related employment and support allowance calculation

If Mr Singh was claiming income-related ESA it would be calculated in the following way:

Income		
	Contributory ESA (full rate basic allowance and support component)	£95.15
	Tariff income from savings	£4.00
	Total	**£99.15**

(DLA care component £70.35 disregarded)
(DLA mobility component £49.10 disregarded)

Applicable amount	£64.30	(Prescribed amount)
	£30.85	(Support component)
	£13.40	(Enhanced disability premium)
	£52.85	(Severe disability premium)
Total	**£161.40**	

Applicable amount (£161.40) *minus* Income (£99.15) = Income-related ESA (£62.25)

Mr Singh is entitled to income-related ESA of £62.25 a week (paid on top of his contributory ESA and DLA).

Contribution calculation

Adult social care services calculate his contribution to the cost of his accommodation and care based on his financial assessment.

There are different capital rules that apply for financial assessment purposes. Any capital/savings of £14,000 or less is disregarded so Mr Singh's savings of £7,000 are completely disregarded in the financial assessment.

His contribution to the cost of his accommodation and care is calculated in the following way:

Income		
	IB (long-term)	£96.35
	IS	£57.70
	Total	£154.05

(DLA care component £70.35 disregarded)
(DLA mobility component £49.10 disregarded)

Outgoings		
	Water rates	£5.50
	Standard charges for fuel	£2.50
	Total	£8.00

Personal expenses allowance (PEA) £21.90

Income (£154.05) *minus* Outgoings (£8.00) *minus* PEA (£21.90) = Contribution (£124.15)

Mr Singh's contribution to the cost is £124.15 a week.
Mr Singh will be left with £149.35 a week (DLA, outgoings and PEA).
The full cost of adult social care services residential accommodation is £438.00 a week.
Adult social care services' contribution to the cost is £313.85 a week.

Example 2: Single person, permanent stay

Mr Smith (58) is single. He is a homeowner (without a mortgage) and his sister (70) lives with him. His income before entering the care home is made up of long-term IB, work pension and DLA care and mobility components. He also receives some CTB. Mr Smith is not entitled to IS while he is living in the community.

Usually, for a single person the amount of IS payable in the care home would be the same as that paid in the community. However, an exception is where a person is living with a non-dependant in the community as this has an effect on eligibility for the severe disability premium.

He goes into a care home which provides nursing, on a permanent basis. As he is a permanent resident in the care home, he is no longer liable for council tax.

Mr Smith makes a claim for IS. His home in the community is not taken into account as his elderly sister is still living there.

Income support calculation

Mr Smith's claim for IS is calculated in the following way:

Income	IB (long-term)	£105.45
	Work pension	£7.50
	Total	**£112.95**

(DLA mobility component £49.10 disregarded as income)

(DLA care component £70.35 payable for first four weeks but disregarded as income)

Applicable amount 1	£64.30	(Personal allowance)
(first 4 weeks)	£27.50	(Disability premium)
	£13.40	(Enhanced disability premium)
	£52.85	(Severe disability premium)
Total	**£158.05**	

Applicable amount (£158.05) *minus* Income (£112.95) = IS (£45.10)

Mr Smith is entitled IS of £45.10 a week for the first four weeks of his stay (paid on top of his long-term IB, work pension and DLA).

Applicable amount 2	£64.30	(Personal allowance)
(after 4 weeks)	£27.50	(Disability premium)
Total	**£91.80**	

The severe disability premium and enhanced disability premium are only applicable while Mr Smith continues to receive the qualifying benefit of DLA care component, but this is stopped after 28 days in the care home.

Applicable amount (£91.80) *minus* Income (£112.95) = IS (nil)

Mr Smith is not entitled to IS after four weeks of his stay as he has excess income of £21.15 a week (his only income will be his long-term IB, work pension and DLA mobility component).

Income-related employment and support allowance calculation

If Mr Smith was claiming income-related ESA it would be calculated in the following way:

Income	Contributory ESA (full rate basic allowance and support component)	£95.15
	Work pension	£7.50
	Total	**£102.65**

(DLA mobility component £49.10 disregarded as income)

(DLA care component £70.35 payable for first four weeks but disregarded as income)

Applicable amount 1	£64.30	(Prescribed amount)
(first 4 weeks)	£30.85	(Support component)
	£13.40	(Enhanced disability premium)
	£52.85	(Severe disability premium)
Total	**£161.40**	

Applicable amount (£161.40) *minus* Income (£102.65) = **Income-related ESA (£58.75)**

Mr Smith is entitled income-related ESA of £58.75 a week for the first four weeks of his stay (paid on top of his contributory ESA, work pension and DLA).

Applicable amount 2	£64.30	(Prescribed amount)
(after 4 weeks)	£30.85	(Support component)
	£13.40	(Enhanced disability premium)
Total	**£108.55**	

The severe disability premium is only applicable while Mr Smith continues to receive the qualifying benefit of DLA care component, but this is stopped after 28 days in the care home. The enhanced disability premium continues in payment due to Mr Smith's entitlement to the support component.

Applicable amount (£108.55) *minus* **Income (£102.65) = Income-related ESA (£5.90)**

Mr Smith is entitled to income-related ESA of £5.90 a week after four weeks of his stay (paid on top of his contributory ESA, work pension and DLA mobility component).

Contribution calculation

Mr Smith's IS claim has been decided by the DWP, he informs adult social care services and his financial assessment is amended. His home in the community is not taken into account as capital because his elderly sister is still living there. There are no disregards on Mr Smith's income for 'outgoings' as he is permanently away from his home in the community.

Mr Smith's contribution to the cost of his accommodation and care are calculated in the following way:

Income 1	IB (long-term)	£105.45
(first 4 weeks)	Work pension	£7.50
	IS	£45.10
	DLA care component	£70.35
	Total	**£228.40**

(DLA mobility component £49.10 disregarded as income)

Personal expenses allowances (PEA)	**£21.90**

Income (£228.40) *minus* **PEA (£21.90) = Contribution (£206.50)**

Mr Smith's contribution to the cost for the first four weeks is £206.50 a week.
Mr Smith will be left with £71.00 a week (DLA mobility component and PEA).
The full cost of the nursing home is £538 a week.
Adult social care services' contribution to the cost for the first four weeks is £331.50 a week *minus* the appropriate amount for funded nursing care from the NHS.

Income 2	IB (long-term)	£105.45
(after 4 weeks)	Work pension	£7.50
	Total	**£112.95**

(DLA mobility component £49.10 disregarded as income)

Personal expenses allowances (PEA)   £21.90
Income (£112.95) *minus* PEA (£21.90) = Contribution (£91.05)

Mr Smith's contribution to the cost after four weeks is £91.05 a week.
Mr Smith will be left with £71.00 a week (DLA mobility component and PEA).
The full cost of the care home is £538 a week.
Adult social care services' contribution to the cost after the first four weeks is £446.95 a week *minus* the appropriate amount for funded nursing care from the NHS.

Example 3: Couple – one entering a care home, temporary stay, resident claimant

Mr and Mrs Jones, aged 45 and 50 years respectively, are joint homeowners (without a mortgage). They have no savings. Mr Jones's weekly income before entering the care home is made up of long-term IB, IS and DLA care and mobility components. Mrs Jones receives carer's allowance (CA). Maximum CTB is in payment.
Mr Jones goes into a care home for a temporary stay of three weeks.

Income support calculation
The IS in payment to Mr Jones for Mrs Jones and himself as a couple is recalculated in the following way:

Income		
	IB (long-term) (Mr Jones)	£105.45
	CA (Mrs Jones)	£53.10
	Total	**£158.55**

(DLA mobility component (Mr Jones) £49.10 disregarded as income)
(DLA care component (Mr Jones) £47.10 disregarded as income)

Applicable amount

Mr Jones	£64.30	(Single personal allowance)
	£27.50	(Single disability premium)
Mrs Jones	£64.30	(Single personal allowance)
	£29.50	(Carer premium)
Total	**£185.60**	

Applicable amount (£185.60) *minus* Income (£158.55) = IS (£27.05)

Mr and Mrs Jones are entitled to IS of £27.05 a week payable to Mr Jones as the claimant (on top of Mr Jones's IB (long-term), and DLA, and Mrs Jones's CA).
IS is payable at a higher rate while Mr Jones is staying in a care home than it was when they were both in the community. This is because their applicable amounts are calculated as if they are single people. Their income is still added together because Mr Jones is only a temporary resident in the care home. If Mrs Jones was not getting CA (or she only had an underlying entitlement to it) Mr Jones would also have a severe disability premium in his applicable amount.

Income-related employment and support allowance calculation

If Mr Jones was claiming income-related ESA for Mrs Jones and himself as a couple it would be calculated in the following way:

Income		
	Contributory ESA (full rate basic allowance and support component) (Mr Jones)	£95.15
	CA (Mrs Jones)	£53.10
	Total	**£148.25**

(DLA mobility component (Mr Jones) £49.10 disregarded as income)
(DLA care component (Mr Jones) £47.10 disregarded as income)

Applicable amount		
Mr Jones	£64.30	(Prescribed amount)
	£30.85	(Support component)
	£13.40	(Enhanced disability premium)
Mrs Jones	£64.30	(Prescribed amount)
	£29.50	(Carer premium)
Total	**£202.35**	

Applicable amount (£202.35) *minus* **Income** (£148.25) = **Income-related ESA** (£54.10)

Mr and Mrs Jones are entitled to income-related ESA of £54.10 a week payable to Mr Jones as the claimant (on top of Mr Jones's contributory ESA and DLA, and Mrs Jones's CA).

The enhanced disability premium is in payment due to Mrs Cooper's entitlement to the support component.

Contribution calculation

After Mr and Mrs Jones's IS has been revised by the DWP, they inform adult social care services and Mr Jones's financial assessment is amended. Although Mr and Mrs Jones are a couple, for financial assessment purposes Mr Jones, as the person going into care, is assessed on his income *only*.

However, as Mr Jones receives IS for himself and Mrs Jones based on a calculation of their joint income, adult social care services considers increasing his PEA in order to allow enough for Mrs Jones to meet her living expenses.

If the PEA is increased so that Mr Jones can give Mrs Jones an appropriate amount to meet her living expenses then the 'outgoings' can be shared equally and only half of the total amount disregarded from Mr Jones's income.

(**Note:** if there were any other adults living with Mr and Mrs Jones, the 'outgoings' would be shared between the total number of people sharing the home and only Mr Jones's appropriate share allowed as a disregard on his income.)

Mr Jones's contribution to the cost of his accommodation and care is calculated in the following way:

Income	IB (long-term)	£105.45
	IS	£27.05
	Total	**£132.50**

(DLA mobility component £49.10 disregarded as income)
(DLA care component £47.10 disregarded as income)

Outgoings	Water rates (£4.50 ÷ 2)	£2.25
	Standard charge for fuel (£2.50 ÷ 2)	£1.25
	Building and contents insurance (£10 ÷ 2)	£5.00
	Total	**£8.50**

Personal expenses allowance (PEA)

Normal rate for Mr Jones		£21.90
Amount for Mrs Jones*		£40.70
Total		**£62.60**

*The amount for Mrs Jones is calculated on the basis of her IS applicable amount of £93.80 (£64.30 personal allowance *plus* £29.50 carer premium) *minus* her income of £53.10 CA.

Income (£132.50) *minus* **Outgoings** (£8.50) *minus* **PEA** (£62.60) = **Contribution** (£61.40)

Mr Jones's contribution to the cost is £61.40 a week.
Mr Jones will be left with £167.30 a week (DLA care and mobility components, outgoings and PEA of which he will give £40.70 to Mrs Jones).
The full cost of the care home is £438.00 a week.
Adult social care services' contribution to the cost is £376.60 a week.

Example 4: Couple – one entering a care home, temporary stay, non-resident claimant

Mr and Mrs Harris are aged 58 and 50 years respectively. Mrs Harris is going into a care home for a temporary three-week stay. She receives IB and DLA care and mobility components. Mr Harris receives CA and he claims IS for both of them as a carer. (Since the introduction of ESA on 27 October 2008 Mr and Mrs Harris would be well advised to make a claim for ESA in Mrs Harris's name as the person incapable of work as they would receive more benefit. However, for the purpose of this example Mr Harris remains the claimant of IS as a carer.)

IS is in payment to Mr Harris for Mrs Harris and himself as a couple when they are both in the community. However, when Mr Harris informs the DWP that his wife is going to enter a care home for a temporary stay, it reviews the entitlement.

IS is paid at a higher rate while Mrs Harris is staying in a care home than it was when they were both in the community. This is because their applicable amount is calculated as if they were two single people although their income is still added together and the IS entitlement is still paid to Mr Harris as the claimant. If Mr Harris was not in receipt of CA (or he only had an underlying entitlement to it) Mrs Harris would also have a severe disability premium included in her part of the applicable amount.

Income support calculation

The IS entitlement will be calculated in the following way while Mrs Harris is in a care home for three weeks:

Income:		
	CA (Mr Harris)	£53.10
	IB (Mrs Harris)	£96.35
	Total	**£149.45**

(DLA Mobility Component (Mrs Harris) £49.10 disregarded as income)
(DLA Care Component (Mrs Harris) £70.35 disregarded as income)

Applicable amount:	
	£64.30 (single personal allowance for Mrs Harris)
	£27.50 (disability premium for Mrs Harris)
	£13.40 (enhanced disability premium for Mrs Harris)
	£ 64.30 (single personal allowance for Mr Harris)
	£29.50 (carer premium for Mr Harris)
Total	**£199.00**

Appropriate Amount (£199.00) *minus* **Income (£149.45) = Income Support (£49.55)**

Mr and Mrs Harris are entitled to IS of £49.55 a week (on top of Mr Harris's CA and Mrs Harris's IB and DLA).

Contribution calculation

Adult Social Care Services calculate the charge based on Mrs Harris's financial assessment. Although Mr and Mrs Harris are a couple, for financial assessment purposes Mrs Harris, as the person going into care, is assessed according to her income only.

However, as Mr Harris receives IS for himself and Mrs Harris based on a calculation of their joint income, Adult Social Care Services will ask Mr Harris for an appropriate contribution to the cost of Mrs Harris's accommodation and care from the PC award paid to Mr Harris for both of them.

If Mr Harris makes the appropriate contribution then the 'outgoings' can be shared equally and half of the total disregarded from Mrs Harris's income.

The amount that Mr Harris will be asked to contribute to the cost of her accommodation and care from the IS award will be calculated in the following way:

Single applicable amount:	
	£ 64.30 (single personal allowance)
	£ 29.50 (single carer premium)
Total	**£93.80**

Single applicable amount (£93.80) *minus* Mr Harris's Income (£53.10) = Mr Harris's share of IS (£40.70)

Amount to Contribute:
Total IS award (£49.55) *minus* Mr Harris's share of IS (£40.70) = IS amount to contribute (£8.85)
Mrs Harris's contribution to the cost of her accommodation and care will be calculated in the following way:

Income:		
	IB (Mrs Harris)	£96.35
	IS Contribution from Mr Harris	£8.85
	Total	**£105.20**

(DLA Mobility Component £49.10 disregarded as income)
(DLA Care Component £70.35 disregarded as income)

Outgoings:		
	Water rates	£4.50 ÷ 2 = £2.25
	Building and contents Insurance premium	£10.00 ÷ 2 = £5.00
	Total	**£7.25**

Personal Expenses Allowance **(PEA):** £ 21.90

Income (£105.20) *minus* **Outgoings** (£7.25) *minus* **PEA** (£21.90) = **Contribution** (£76.05)

Mrs Harris's contribution to the cost is £76.05 a week.
Mrs Harris will be left with £148.60 a week (DLA, outgoings and PEA).
The full cost of the care home is £374 a week.
Adult social care services contribution to the cost is £297.95 a week.

Example 5: Couple – one entering a care home, permanent stay
Mr and Mrs Cooper, aged 59 and 55 years respectively, are council tenants. Mr Cooper's weekly income is made up of long-term IB and he has an underlying entitlement to CA. Mrs Cooper's weekly income before entering the care home is made up of severe disablement allowance (SDA) and DLA care and mobility components. They have joint savings of £22,000. They are not entitled to IS as a couple in the community. Mrs Cooper goes into a care home on a permanent basis.
As Mr and Mrs Cooper are now permanently separated they will be treated as single people for IS purposes. Their savings will be divided equally. Mr Cooper's income (£105.45 long-term IB and £20.00 tariff income) is higher than his applicable amount (£64.30 personal allowance, £27.50 disability premium and £29.50 carer premium for eight weeks following the ending of his underlying entitlement to CA); therefore he is not entitled to IS. Mrs Cooper claims IS as a single person. It is calculated in the following way:

Income support calculation

Income	SDA	£73.10
	Tariff income from savings	£4.00
	Total	**£77.10**

(DLA care component: £70.35 payable for first four weeks but disregarded as income)
(DLA mobility component: £18.65 disregarded as income)

Applicable amount 1	£64.30	(Single personal allowance)
(first 4 weeks)	£27.50	(Disability premium)
	£13.40	(Enhanced disability premium)
	£52.85	(Severe disability premium)
Total	**£158.05**	

Applicable amount (£158.05) *minus* Income (£77.10) = IS (£80.95)

Mrs Cooper is entitled to IS of £80.95 a week for the first four weeks of her stay (paid on top of her SDA and DLA).

Applicable amount 2	£64.30	(Single personal allowance)
(after 4 weeks)	£27.50	(Disability premium)
Total	**£91.80**	

Applicable amount (£91.80) *minus* Income (£77.10) = IS (£14.70)

After four weeks Mrs Cooper's DLA care component would stop and therefore the severe disability and enhanced disability premiums would not be included in her applicable amount.

Mrs Cooper is entitled to IS of £14.70 a week after four weeks of her stay (paid on top of her SDA and DLA).

Income-related employment and support allowance calculation

If Mrs Cooper was claiming income-related ESA it would be calculated in the following way:

Income	Contributory ESA (full rate basic allowance & support component)	£95.15
	Tariff income from savings	£4.00
	Total	**£99.15**

(DLA care component: £70.35 payable for first four weeks but disregarded as income)
(DLA mobility component: £18.65 disregarded as income)

Applicable amount 1	£64.30	(Prescribed amount)
(first 4 weeks)	£30.85	(Support component)
	£13.40	(Enhanced disability premium)
	£52.85	(Severe disability premium)
Total	**£161.40**	

Applicable amount (£161.40) *minus* Income (£99.15) = **income-related ESA (£62.25)**

Mrs Cooper is entitled to income-related ESA of £62.25 a week for the first four weeks of her stay (paid on top of her contributory ESA and DLA).

Applicable amount 2	£64.30	(Prescribed amount)
(after 4 weeks)	£30.85	(Support component)
	£13.40	(Enhanced disability premium)
Total	**£108.55**	

Applicable amount (£108.55) *minus* Income (£99.15) = **income-related ESA (£9.40)**

Mrs Cooper is entitled to income-related ESA of £9.40 a week after four weeks of her stay (paid on top of her contributory ESA and DLA).

After four weeks Mrs Cooper's DLA care component would stop and therefore the severe disability premium would not be included in her applicable amount. The enhanced disability premium continues in payment due to Mrs Cooper's entitlement to the support component.

Contribution calculation

After Mrs Cooper's IS claim has been decided by the DWP she informs adult social care services and her financial assessment is amended. Mr and Mrs Cooper's joint savings are divided equally.

There are different capital rules that apply for financial assessment purposes. Any capital/savings of £14,000 or less is disregarded; therefore Mrs Cooper's share of the £11,000 savings are completely disregarded in the financial assessment.

There are no disregards on Mrs Cooper's income for 'outgoings' as she is permanently away from her home in the community.

Mrs Cooper's contribution to the cost of her accommodation and care is calculated in the following way:

Income 1	SDA	£73.10
(first 4 weeks)	IS	£80.95
	DLA care component	£70.35
	Total	**£224.40**

(DLA mobility component: £18.65 disregarded)

Personal expenses allowances (PEA)	£21.90

Income (£224.40) *minus* **PEA** (£21.90) = **Contribution (£202.50)**

Mrs Cooper's contribution to the cost for the first four weeks is £202.50 a week.
Mrs Cooper will be left with £40.55 a week (DLA mobility component and PEA).
The full cost of the care home is £338.00 a week.
Adult social care services' contribution to the cost for the first four weeks is £135.50 a week.

Income 2	SDA	£73.10
(after 4 weeks)	IS	£14.70

	Total	£87.80

(DLA mobility component – £18.65 disregarded)

Personal expenses allowances (PEA)   £21.90

Income (£87.80) *minus* **PEA** (£21.90) = **Contribution** (£65.90)

Mrs Cooper's contribution to the cost after four weeks is £65.90 a week.
Mrs Cooper will be left with £40.55 a week (DLA mobility component and PEA).
The full cost of the care home is £338.00 a week.
Adult social care services' contribution to the cost after four weeks is £272.10 a week.

---

2. Example pension credit and contribution calculations: aged 60 or over

This section includes examples for:
- single person, temporary stay (Example 1 – p368);
- single person, permanent stay (Example 2 – p378);
- couple – one entering a care home, temporary stay, resident claimant (Example 3 – p376);
- couple – one entering a care home, temporary stay, non-resident claimant (Example 4 – p376);
- couple – one entering a care home, permanent stay (Example 5 – p365).

Example 1: Single person, temporary stay

Mr Thomas (86) is a single person living in a rented council house.
His income before entering the care home is made up of state retirement pension, pension credit (PC) and attendance allowance (AA).
Mr Thomas also receives maximum housing benefit (HB) and council tax benefit (CTB). He has savings of £9,000.
He goes into the care home for a temporary stay of two weeks.

Pension credit calculation

Mr Thomas's guarantee credit element of pension credit (PGC) was, and continues to be calculated in the following way:

Income		
	State retirement pension	£110.77
	Tariff income from savings	£6.00
	Total	£116.77

(AA of £70.35 disregarded)

Chapter 17: Calculations – benefits and charges in care homes
2. Example pension credit and contribution calculations: aged 60 or over

17

Appropriate amount	£130.00	(Standard minimum guarantee)
	£52.85	(Severe disability addition)
Total	£182.85	

Appropriate amount (£182.85) *minus* Income (£116.77) = **PGC** (£66.08)

Mr Thomas is entitled to PGC of £66.08 a week (paid on top of his state retirement pension and AA).

Mr Thomas is also entitled to the savings credit of pension credit (PSC) of £12.46.

Contribution calculation

Adult social care services calculates his contribution to the cost of his accommodation and care based on his financial assessment.

There are different capital rules for financial assessment purposes. Any capital/savings of £14,000 or less (in England) is disregarded so Mr Thomas's savings of £9,000 are completely disregarded in the financial assessment.

His contribution to the cost of his accommodation and care are calculated in the following way:

Income	State retirement pension	£110.77
	PGC	£66.08
	PSC minus disregard of £5.65	£6.81
	Total	**£183.66**

(AA of £70.35 disregarded)

Outgoings	Water rates	£4.00
	Standard charges for fuel	£2.50
	Total	**£6.50**
Personal expenses allowance (PEA)		£21.90

Income (£183.66) *minus* Outgoings (£6.50) *minus* PEA (£21.90) = **Contribution** (£155.26)

Mr Thomas's contribution to the cost is £155.26 a week.
Mr Thomas will be left with £104.40 a week (AA, savings disregard, outgoings and PEA).

The full cost of adult social care services residential accommodation is £374.00 a week. Adult social care services' contribution to the cost is £218.74 a week.

Example 2: Single person, permanent stay

Mr Davidson (72) is single. He is a homeowner (without a mortgage) and his sister (70) lives with him. His income before entering the care home was made up of state retirement pension, the savings credit element of PC (PSC), work pension and AA. He also receives some CTB. Mr Davidson is not entitled to PGC while living in the community.

Usually, as a single person the amount of PGC payable in the care home would be the same as that paid in the community. However, an exception is where a person is living

17

Chapter 17: Calculations – benefits and charges in care homes
2. Example pension credit and contribution calculations: aged 60 or over

with a non-dependant in the community as this has an effect on eligibility for the severe disability addition.

He goes into a care home which provides nursing, on a permanent basis. As he is a permanent resident in the care home, he is no longer liable for council tax.

Mr Davidson makes a claim for PC. His home in the community is not taken into account as his elderly sister is still living there.

Pension credit calculation

Mr Davidson's claim for the PGC is calculated in the following way:

Income		
	State retirement pension	£100.76
	Work pension	£36.16
	Total	**£136.92**

(AA £70.35 payable for the first four weeks but disregarded as income)

Appropriate amount 1	£130.00	(Standard minimum guarantee)
(first 4 weeks)	£52.85	(Severe disability addition)
Total	**£182.85**	

Appropriate amount (£182.85) *minus* **Income (£136.92) = PGC (£45.93)**

Mr Davidson is entitled to PGC of £45.93 a week for the first four weeks of his stay (paid on top of his state retirement pension, work pension and AA).

He is also entitled to PSC of £20.40.

Appropriate amount 2	£130.00	(Standard minimum guarantee)
(after 4 weeks)		
Total	**£130.00**	

The severe disability addition is only applicable while Mr Davidson continues to receive the qualifying benefit of AA but this is stopped after 28 days in the care home.

Appropriate amount (£130.00) *minus* **Income (£136.92) = PGC (nil)**

Mr Davidson is not entitled to PGC after four weeks of his stay as he has excess income of £6.92 a week (his only income will be his state retirement pension, work pension and AA).

Mr Davidson is also entitled to PSC of £17.64

Contribution calculation

Mr Davidson's PC claim has been decided by the DWP, he informs adult social care services and it amends his financial assessment. His home in the community is not taken into account as capital because his elderly sister is still living there. There are no disregards on Mr Davidson's income for 'outgoings' as he is permanently away from his home in the community.

Chapter 17: Calculations – benefits and charges in care homes
2. Example pension credit and contribution calculations: aged 60 or over

17

Mr Davidson's contribution to the cost of his accommodation and care is calculated in the following way:

Income 1	State retirement pension	£100.76
(first 4 weeks)	Work pension	£36.16
	PGC	£45.93
	PSC minus disregard of £5.65	£14.75
	AA	£70.35
	Total	**£267.95**

Personal expenses allowances (PEA)   **£21.90**

Income (£267.95) *minus* **PEA (£21.90) = Contribution (£246.05)**

Mr Davidson's contribution to the cost for the first four weeks is £246.05 a week.
Mr Davidson will be left with £27.55 a week (savings disregard and PEA).
The full cost of the care home is £476.00 a week.
Adult social care services' contribution to the cost for the first four weeks is £229.95 a week *minus* the appropriate amount for funded nursing care from the NHS.

Income 2	State retirement pension	£100.76
(after 4 weeks)	PSC *minus* disregard of £5.65	£11.99
	Work pension	£36.16
	Total	**£148.91**
Personal expenses allowances (PEA)		**£21.90**

Income (£148.91) *minus* **PEA (£21.90) = Contribution (£127.01)**

Mr Davidson's contribution to the cost after four weeks is £127.01 a week.
Mr Davidson will be left with £27.55 a week (savings disregard and PEA).
The full cost of the care home is £476.00 a week.
Adult social care services' contribution to the cost after the first four weeks is £348.99 a week minus the appropriate amount for funded nursing care from the NHS.

Example 3: Couple – one entering a care home, temporary stay, resident claimant

Mr and Mrs Gill, aged 65 and 61 years respectively, are joint homeowners (without a mortgage). Mr Gill's weekly income before entering the care home is made up of state retirement pension, PC and DLA care and mobility components and he has an underlying entitlement to carer's allowance (CA). Mrs Gill receives state retirement pension and DLA care component; she also has an underlying entitlement to CA. Maximum CTB is in payment. Mr Gill goes into a care home for a temporary stay of 13 weeks.

Pension credit calculation

The PGC in payment to Mr Gill for Mrs Gill and himself as a couple is calculated in the following way:

17

Chapter 17: Calculations – benefits and charges in care homes
2. Example pension credit and contribution calculations: aged 60 or over

Income	State retirement pension (Mr Gill)	£104.96
	State retirement pension (Mrs Gill)	£57.05
	Work pension (Mr Gill)	£6.52
	Total	**£168.53**

(DLA mobility component (Mr Gill) £49.10 disregarded as income)

(DLA care component (Mr Gill) £47.10 payable for the first four weeks but disregarded as income)

(DLA care component (Mrs Gill) £47.10 disregarded as income)

Appropriate amount 1	£198.45	(Couple standard minimum guarantee)
(first 4 weeks)	£105.70	(Couple severe disability addition)
	£29.50	(Carer addition)
	£29.50	(Carer addition)
Total	**£363.15**	

Appropriate amount (£363.15) *minus* Income (£168.53) = PGC (£194.62)

Mr and Mrs Gill are entitled to PGC of £194.62 a week for the first four weeks payable to Mr Gill as the claimant (on top of Mr Gill's state retirement pension, work pension and DLA, and Mrs Gill's state retirement pension and DLA).

Mr and Mrs Gill are also entitled to PSC of £9.08 a week.

Appropriate amount 2	£198.45	(Couple standard minimum guarantee)
(weeks 5 to 12)	£29.50	(Carer addition)
	£29.50	(Carer addition)
Total	**£257.45**	

After four weeks Mr Gill is no longer entitled to DLA care component therefore he no longer qualifies for the severe disability addition in the appropriate amount. Mrs Gill still gets DLA care component but because they are still treated as a couple living together, Mr Gill's presence without being in receipt of DLA care component also prevents Mrs Gill from qualifying for the severe disability addition.

Appropriate amount (£257.45) *minus* Income (£168.53) = PGC (£88.92)

Mr and Mrs Gill are entitled to PGC of £88.92 a week during weeks 5 to 12 of Mr Gill's stay, payable to Mr Gill as the claimant (on top of Mr Gill's state retirement pension, work pension and DLA mobility component and Mrs Gill's state retirement pension and DLA care component).

Chapter 17: Calculations – benefits and charges in care homes
2. Example pension credit and contribution calculations: aged 60 or over

17

Mr and Mrs Gill are also entitled to PSC of £9.08 a week.

Appropriate amount 3	£198.45	(Couple standard minimum guarantee)
(after 12 weeks)		
Total	**£198.45**	

As Mr Gill is no longer receives DLA care component, Mrs Gill no longer qualifies for the underlying entitlement to CA and therefore after eight weeks her carer addition is no longer included in the appropriate amount. Mr Gill also no longer qualifies for the underlying entitlement to CA as he has had a break of more than four weeks in the care of Mrs Gill therefore after eight weeks his carer addition is no longer included in the appropriate amount.

Appropriate amount (£198.45) *minus* **Income** (£168.53) = **PGC** (£29.92)

Mr and Mrs Gill are entitled to PGC of £29.92 a week after 12 weeks of Mr Gill's stay, payable to Mr Gill as the claimant (on top of Mr Gill's state retirement pension, work pension and DLA mobility component and Mrs Gill's state retirement pension and DLA care component).

Mr and Mrs Gill are also entitled to PSC of £9.08 a week.

Contribution calculation

Adult social care services calculates Mr Gill's charge based on his financial assessment. Although Mr and Mrs Gill are a couple, for financial assessment purposes Mr Gill, as the person going into care, is assessed on his income *only*.

However, as Mr Gill receives PGC for himself and Mrs Gill based on a calculation of their joint income and Mrs Gill has provided her financial details to adult social care services, adult social care services will consider increasing his PEA in order to allow enough for Mrs Gill to meet her living expenses.

If the PEA is increased so that Mr Gill can give Mrs Gill an appropriate amount to meet her living expenses then the 'outgoings' can be shared equally and only half of the total amount disregarded from Mr Gill's income.

(Note: if there were any other adults living with Mr and Mrs Gill, the 'outgoings' would be shared between the total number of people sharing the home and only Mr Gill's appropriate share allowed as a disregard on his income.)

Mr Gill's contribution to the cost of his accommodation and care is calculated in the following way:

Income 1	State retirement pension	£104.96
(first 4 weeks)	Work pension	£6.52
	PGC	£194.62
	PSC minus disregard of £8.43	£0.63
	Total	**£306.73**

(DLA mobility component £49.10 disregarded as income)

17

Chapter 17: Calculations – benefits and charges in care homes
2. Example pension credit and contribution calculations: aged 60 or over

(DLA care component £47.10 disregarded as income)

Outgoings		
	Water rates (£4.50 ÷ 2)	£2.25
	Standard charge for fuel (£2.50 ÷ 2)	£1.25
	Building and contents insurance (£10 ÷ 2)	£5.00
	Total	**£8.50**

Personal expenses allowance (PEA)

Normal rate for Mr Gill	£21.90
Amount for Mrs Gill*	£155.30
Total	**£177.20**

*The amount for Mrs Gill is calculated on the basis of a single person's appropriate minimum guarantee of £212.35 (standard minimum guarantee plus the severe disability and carer additions) minus her income of £57.05 state retirement pension.

Income (£306.73) *minus* **Outgoings (£8.50)** *minus* **PEA (£177.20) = Contribution (£121.03)**

Mr Gill's contribution to the cost is £121.03 a week for the first four weeks.

Mr Gill will be left with £281.90 a week (DLA care and mobility components, outgoings and PEA, £155.30 which he will give to Mrs Gill).

The full cost of the care home is £338.00 a week.

Adult social care services' contribution to the cost is £216.97 a week.

Income 2		
(weeks 5 to 12)	State retirement pension	£104.96
	Work pension	£6.52
	PGC	£88.92
	PSC minus disregard of £8.45	£0.63
	Total	**£201.03**

(DLA mobility component £49.10 disregarded as income)

Outgoings		
	Water rates (£4.50 ÷ 2)	£2.25
	Standard charge for fuel (£2.50 ÷ 2)	£1.25
	Building and contents insurance (£10 ÷ 2)	£5.00
	Total	**£8.50**

Personal expenses allowance (PEA)

Normal rate for Mr Gill	£21.90
Amount for Mrs Gill*	£102.45
Total	**£124.35**

*The amount for Mrs Gill is calculated on the basis of a single person's appropriate minimum guarantee of £159.50 (standard minimum guarantee plus the carer addition only as she no longer qualifies for the severe disability addition because under current law

Chapter 17: Calculations – benefits and charges in care homes
2. Example pension credit and contribution calculations: aged 60 or over

17

she is still treated as living with Mr Gill and Mr Gill no longer receives DLA care component. However she still qualifies for the carer addition for a further eight weeks after her underlying entitlement to CA ceases) minus her income of £57.05 state retirement pension.

Income (£201.03) *minus* **Outgoings** (£8.50) *minus* **PEA** (£124.35) = **Contribution** (£68.18)

Mr Gill's contribution to the cost in weeks 5 to 12 is £68.18 a week.
Mr Gill will be left with £181.95 a week (DLA mobility component, outgoings and PEA, £102.45 of which he will give to Mrs Gill).
The full cost of the care home is £338.00 a week.
Adult social care services' contribution to the cost is £269.82 a week.

Income 3	State retirement pension	£104.96
(after 12 weeks)	Work pension	£6.52
	PGC	£29.92
	PSC minus disregard of £8.43	£0.63
	Total	**£142.03**

(DLA mobility component £49.10 disregarded as income)

Outgoings	Water rates (£4.50 ÷ 2)	£2.25
	Standard charge for fuel (£2.50 ÷ 2)	£1.25
	Building and contents insurance (£10 ÷ 2)	£5.00
	Total	**£8.50**

Personal expenses allowance (PEA)

Normal rate for Mr Gill	£21.90
Amount for Mrs Gill*	£72.95
Total	**£94.85**

*The amount for Mrs Gill is calculated on the basis of a single person's appropriate minimum guarantee of £130.00 (standard minimum guarantee only as she no longer qualifies for the carer addition after eight weeks of her underlying entitlement to CA ceasing due to the suspension of Mr Gill's DLA care component) minus her income of £57.05 state retirement pension.

Income (£142.03) *minus* **Outgoings** (£8.50) *minus* **PEA** (£94.85) = **Contribution** (£38.68)

Mr Gill's contribution to the cost after 12 weeks is £38.69 a week.
Mr Gill will be left with £152.45 a week (DLA mobility component, outgoings and PEA, of which he will give £72.95 to Mrs Gill).
The full cost of the care home is £338.00 a week.
Adult social care services' contribution to the cost is £299.32 a week.

17

Chapter 17: Calculations – benefits and charges in care homes
2. Example pension credit and contribution calculations: aged 60 or over

Example 4: Couple – one entering a care home, temporary stay, non-resident claimant

Mr and Mrs Harvey are aged 65 and 61 years respectively. Mrs Harvey is going into a care home for a temporary three-week stay. She receives state retirement pension and DLA care component. Mr Harvey receives state retirement pension, AA and he claims PC for both of them. Mr and Mrs Harvey care for each other and they both have an underlying entitlement to CA.

Pension credit calculation

The guarantee credit element of PC in payment to Mr Harvey for Mrs Harvey and himself as a couple is calculated in the following way:

Income:	State retirement pension (Mr Harvey)	£100.81
	State retirement pension (Mrs Harvey)	£57.05
	Total	**£157.86**

(AA (Mr Harvey) £70.35 disregarded as income)
(DLA care component (Mrs Harvey) £70.35 disregarded as income)

Appropriate Amount:	£198.45 (couple standard minimum guarantee)
	£105.70 (couple severe disability addition)
	£29.50 (CA)
	£ 29.50 (CA)
Total	**£363.15**

Appropriate amount (£363.15) *minus* income (£157.86) = **guarantee credit (£205.29)**

Mr and Mrs Harvey are entitled to PGC of £205.29 a week (on top of Mr Harvey's state retirement pension, and AA and Mrs Harvey's state retirement pension and DLA).

Mr and Mrs Harvey are also entitled to pension savings credit of £2.68 a week.

Contribution calculation

Adult social care services calculate the charge based on Mrs Harvey's financial assessment. Although Mr and Mrs Harvey are a couple, for financial assessment purposes Mrs Harvey, as the person going into care, will be assessed according to her income only.

However, as Mr Harvey receives PC for himself and Mrs Harvey based on a calculation of their joint income, adult social care services will be asking Mr Harvey for an appropriate contribution to the cost of Mrs Harvey's accommodation and care from the PC award paid to Mr Harvey for both of them.

Single Appropriate Amount:	£130.00 (Single SMG)
	£52.85 (Single SDAA)
	£29.50 (Carer addition)
Total	**£212.35**

Chapter 17: Calculations – benefits and charges in care homes
2. Example pension credit and contribution calculations: aged 60 or over

17

Single Appropriate Amount (£212.35) *minus* **Mr Harvey's Income** (£100.81) = **Mr Harvey's share of PGC** (£111.54)
Amount to contribute
Total PGC Award (£205.29) *minus* Mr Harvey's share of PGC (£111.54) = **PGC Amount to Contribute** (£93.75)

Note: Mr Harvey also receives PSC of £2.68. As this is below £8.45 (couple savings disregard) it will be ignored in any contribution calculation. If the PSC amount payable was more than £8.45 then it would be appropriate to divide the difference between the PSC payable and £8.45 in order to establish the amount in respect of the partner in a care home. This PSC amount would then be requested from Mr Harvey on top of the PGC amount to contribute for Mrs Harvey's care and accommodation.

Mrs Harvey's contribution to the cost of her accommodation and care will be calculated in the following way:

Income:	State Retirement Pension (Mrs Harvey)	£57.05
	PGC Contribution from Mr Harvey	£93.75
	Total	**£150.80**

(DLA Care Component £70.35 disregarded as income)

Outgoings:	Water rates	£4.50 ÷ 2 = £2.25
	Building and contents Insurance premium	£10.00 ÷ 2 = £5.00
	Total	**£7.25**

Personal Expenses Allowance (PEA):   £ 21.90

Income (£150.80) *minus* **Outgoings** (£7.25) *minus* **PEA** (£21.90) = **Contribution** (£121.65)

Mrs Harvey's contribution to the cost is £121.65 a week.
Mrs Harvey will be left with £99.50 a week (DLA Care, outgoings and PEA).
The full cost of the care home is £374.00 a week.
Adult social care services contribution to the cost is £252.35 a week.

Example 5: Couple – one entering a care home, permanent stay
Mr and Mrs Sahota, aged 70 and 68 years respectively, are council tenants. Mr Sahota's weekly income is made up of state retirement pension and a work pension and he has an underlying entitlement to CA. Mrs Sahota's weekly income before entering the care home is made up of severe disablement allowance (SDA) and AA. They have joint savings of £22,000. They are not entitled to PGC as a couple in the community although PSC is in payment.

17

Chapter 17: Calculations – benefits and charges in care homes
2. Example pension credit and contribution calculations: aged 60 or over

Mrs Sahota goes into a care home on a permanent basis. As Mr and Mrs Sahota are now permanently separated they are treated as single people for PC purposes and their joint savings are divided equally.

Mr Sahota's income (£109.48 state retirement pension, £40.68 work pension and £10.00 tariff income) is higher than his appropriate amount therefore he is not entitled to PGC although he is entitled to PSC of £20.40. Mrs Sahota claims PC as a single person.

Pension credit calculation
Mrs Sahota's claim for the PGC is calculated in the following way:

Income	SDA	£73.10
	Tariff income from savings	£2.00
	Total	**£75.10**

(AA £70.35 payable for the first four weeks but disregarded as income)

Appropriate amount 1	£130.00	(Single standard minimum guarantee)
(first 4 weeks)	£52.85	(Single severe disability addition)
Total	**£182.85**	

Appropriate amount (£182.85) *minus* **Income (£75.10) = PGC (£107.75)**

Mrs Sahota is entitled to PGC of £107.75 a week for the first four weeks of her stay (paid on top of her SDA and AA).

Mrs Sahota is not entitled to PSC.

Appropriate amount 2	£130.00	(Single standard minimum guarantee)
(after 4 weeks)		
Total	**£130.00**	

After four weeks Mrs Sahota's AA stops and therefore the severe disability addition will not be included in her appropriate amount.

Appropriate amount (£130.00) *minus* **Income (£75.10) = PGC (£54.90)**

Mrs Sahota is entitled to PGC of £54.90 after four weeks of her stay (paid on top of her SDA).

Mrs Sahota is not entitled to PSC.
Contribution calculation
After Mrs Sahota's PC claim has been decided by the DWP, she informs adult social care services and her financial assessment is amended. Mr and Mrs Sahota's joint savings are divided equally.

Any capital/savings of £14,000 or less are disregarded, therefore Mrs Sahota's share of the savings of £11,000 are completely disregarded in the financial assessment.

Chapter 17: Calculations – benefits and charges in care homes
2. Example pension credit and contribution calculations: aged 60 or over

17

There are no disregards on Mrs Sahota's income for 'outgoings' as she is permanently away from her home in the community.

Mrs Sahota's contribution to the cost of his accommodation and care is calculated in the following way:

Income 1	SDA	£73.10
(first 4 weeks)	PGC	£107.75
	AA	£70.35
	Total	**£251.20**
Personal expenses allowances (PEA)		**£21.90**

Income (£251.20) *minus* **PEA** (£21.90) = **Contribution** (£229.30)

Mrs Sahota's contribution to the cost for the first four weeks is £229.30 a week.

Mrs Sahota will be left with £21.90 a week (PEA).

The full cost of the care home is £374.00 a week.

Adult social care services' contribution to the cost for the first four weeks is £144.70 a week.

Income 2	SDA	£73.10
(after 4 weeks)	PGC	£54.90
	Total	**£128.00**
Personal expenses allowances (PEA)		**£21.90**

Income (£128.00) *minus* **PEA** (£21.90) = **Contribution** (£106.10)

Mrs Sahota's contribution to the cost after four weeks is £106.10 a week.

Mrs Sahota will be left with £21.90 a week (PEA).

The full cost of the care home is £374.00 a week.

Adult social care services' contribution to the cost after the first four weeks is £267.90 a week.

Appendices

Appendix 1

Useful addresses

Government departments/agencies UK wide

The Tribunals Service
5th floor
Fox Court
14 Grays Inn Road
London WC1X 8HN
Tel 020 7712 2600
www.appeals-
service.gov.uk

**Department for Work
and Pensions
(benefits)**
Quarry House
Quarry Hill
Leeds LS2 7UA
Tel: 0113 232 4000
www.dwp.gov.uk

**Department for Work
and Pensions (policy)**
The Adelphi
1-11 John Adam Street
London WC2N 6HT
Tel: 020 7962 8000
www.dwp.gov.uk

**Disability Benefits
Unit**
Warbreck House
Warbreck Hill Road
Blackpool
Lancashire FY2 0YE
Tel: 0845 712 3456
Textphone: 0845 722
4433

**HM Revenue and
Customs (child benefit
and guardian's
allowance)**
Child Benefit Office
Newcastle upon Tyne
NE88 1AA
Tel: 0845 302 1474
www.hmrc.gov.uk

**HM Revenue and
Customs (tax credits)**
Tax Credits Office
Preston
PR1 0SB
Tel: 0845 300 3909
www.hmrc.gov.uk

**Independent Review
Service for the Social
Fund**
Centre City Podium
5 Hill Street
Birmingham B5 4UB
Tel: 0121 606 2100
www.irs-review.gov.uk

**The Parliamentary
Ombudsman**
Millbank Tower
Millbank
London SW1P 4QP
Tel: 0845 015 4033
www.ombudsman.org.uk

The Pension Service
Tel: 0845 60 60 265
Textphone:
0191 218 2160
www.pensionservice.gov.uk

Regional Disability Benefits Centres

Bootle DBC
St Martin's House
Stanley Precinct
Bootle L69 9BN
Tel: 0151 934 6000
Covers: Merseyside,
Central and North West
Lancashire, Cumbria,
North, South and West
Cheshire

Bristol DBC
Government Buildings
Flowers Hill
Bristol BS4 5LA
Tel: 0117 971 8311
Covers: Cornwall,
Devon, Wiltshire,
Gloucestershire, Bristol,
Somerset, Dorset

Edinburgh DBC
Argyle House
3 Lady Lawson Street
Edinburgh EH3 9SH
Tel: 0131 222 5467
Minicom: 0131 222
5494
Covers: the eastern part
of Scotland, including
Edinburgh, Perth,
Dundee and Aberdeen

Glasgow DBC
29 Cadogan Street
Glasgow G2 7BN
Tel: 0141 249 3500
Covers: West of
Scotland including
Glasgow, Strathclyde,
Ayrshire, Oban, part of
the Western Isles and
Outer Hebrides

Leeds DBC
Government Buildings
Otley Road
Leeds LS16 5PU
Tel: 0113 230 9000
Covers: Derbyshire
(High Peak), East
Cheshire, Yorkshire,
East Lancashire, part of
Tyne and Wear

Manchester DBC
Albert Bridge House
Bridge Street
Manchester
M60 9DA
Tel 0161 831 2000
Covers: Greater
Manchester and
surrounding areas

Midlands DBC
Five Ways Complex
Edgbaston
Birmingham B15 1SL
Tel: 0121 626 2000
Covers: West Midlands,
Shropshire, Hereford
and Worcester,
Staffordshire,
Leicestershire,
Warwickshire,
Northamptonshire,
Derbyshire,
Nottinghamshire,
Lincolnshire

Newcastle DBC
Arden House
Regent Centre
Regent Farm Road
Newcastle-upon-Tyne
NE3 3JN
Tel: 0191 223 3000
Covers: Tyne and Wear,
Durham,
Northumberland,
Cleveland

Sutton DBC
Sutherland House
29-37 Brighton Road
Sutton
Surrey SM2 5AN
Tel: 020 8652 6000
Covers: postal districts
WC1 and WC2, SE1-
SE28, SW1-SW20, W1,
W6, W8 and W14, Kent,
Berkshire, Hampshire,
Surrey, East Sussex,
West Sussex, Isle of
Wight, Kingston,
Woking, Hounslow,
Twickenham

Wales DBC
Government Buildings
St Agnes Road
Cardiff CF14 4YJ
Tel: 029 2058 6002
Covers: Wales

Wembley DBC
Olympic House
Wembley HA9 0DL
Tel: 020 8795 8400
Covers: postal districts
EC1-EC4, E1-E18, N1-
N27, NW1-NW11, W2-
W5, W7, W9-W13,
Buckinghamshire,
Bedfordshire, Essex,
Cambridgeshire,
Hertfordshire,
Middlesex (except
Hounslow and
Twickenham),
Oxfordshire, Suffolk,
Norfolk

Government departments/agencies nationally based

England

Department of Health
Richmond House
79 Whitehall
London SW1A 2NL
Tel: 020 7972 2000
www.doh.gov.uk

**Upper Tribunal
(Administrative
Appeals)**
11th Floor Cardinal
Tower
12 Farringdon Road
London EC1M 3HS
Tel: 020 7549 4660
www.osscsc.gov.uk

Scotland

**Scottish Government
Health Department**
St Andrew's House
Regent Road
Edinburgh
EH1 3DG
Tel: 0131 566 8400
www.scotland.gov.uk

**Upper Tribunal
(Administrative
Appeals)**
George House
126 George Street
Edinburgh EH2 4HH
Tel: 0131 271 4310
www.ossc-
scotland.org.uk

Wales

**Welsh Assembly
Government**
Public Information
Cardiff Bay
Cardiff CF99 1NA
Tel: 029 2089 8200
www.wales.gov.uk

As England

Health Service Ombudsman
Millbank Tower
London SW1P 4QP
Helpline: 0845 015 4033
www.ombudsman.org.uk.

Scottish Public Services Ombudsman
4 Melville Street
Edinburgh
EH2 1EN
Tel: 0870 011 5378
www.scottish
ombudsman.org.uk.

Public Services Ombudsman for Wales
1 Ffordd yr Hen Gae
Pencoed
CF35 5LJ
Tel: 01656 641150
www.ombudsman-wales.org.uk

Local Government Ombudsman
Millbank Tower
Millbank
London SW1P 4QP
phone
www.lgo.org.uk

Scottish Public Services Ombudsman
4 Melville Street
Edinburgh
EH2 1EN
Tel: 0870 011 5378
www.scottish
ombudsman.org.uk.

Public Services Ombudsman for Wales
1 Ffordd yr Hen Gae
Pencoed
CF35 5LJ
Tel: 01656 641150
www.ombudsman-wales.org.uk

Mental Health Act Commission
Maid Marian House
56 Houndsgate
Nottingham NG1 6BG
Tel: 0115 943 7100
www.mhac.org.uk

Mental Welfare Commission for Scotland
Floor K Argyle House
3 Lady Lawson Street
Edinburgh EH3 9SH
Tel: 0131 222 6111
www.mwcscot.org.uk

As England

Care Quality Commission
New Kings Beam House
22 Upper Ground
London SE1 9BW
Tel: 03000 616161
www.cqc.org.uk

Scottish Commission for the Regulation of Care (Care Commission)
Compass House
11 Riverside Drive
Dundee DD1 4NY
Tel: 01382 207 300
www.carecommission.com

Care Standards Inspectorate for Wales
4/5 Charnwood Court
Heol Billingsley
Parc Nantgarw
Nantgarw CF15 7QZ
Tel: 01443 848450
www.cssiw.org.uk

Public Guardianship Office Archway Tower 2 Junction Road London N19 5SZ Tel: 0845 330 2900 www.public guardian.gov.uk	**Office of the Public Guardian** Hadrian House Callendar Business Park Callendar Road Falkirk FK1 1XR Tel: 01324 678 300 www.publicguardian- scotland.gov.uk	As England

Government-based phonelines

Benefit Enquiry Line 0800 88 22 00 Textphone: 0800 243 355 Specialises in benefit advice for disabled people, their carers and representatives.	**Disability Benefits Customer Care Helpline** 0845 712 3456 Textphone: 0845 722 4433 For general enquiries on disability benefits.	**NHS Direct** (England & Wales) Tel: 0845 4647

Major voluntary organisations nationally based

Space precludes listing all but the major organisations which offer information and advice about paying for care and other aspects of community care.

England	Scotland	Wales
Age Concern England Astral House 1268 London Road London SW16 4ER Information line: 0800 00 99 66. www.ageconcern.org.uk	Age Concern Scotland Causewayside House 160 Causewayside Edinburgh EH9 1PR Information line: 0800 00 99 66. www.ageconcern scotland.org.uk	Age Concern Cymru Ty John Pathy 13/14 Neptune Court Vanguard Way Cardiff CF24 5PJ Tel: 029 2043 1555 www.accymru.org.uk

Alzheimer's Society
Gordon House
10 Greencoat Place
London SW1P 1PH
Helpline: 0845 300 0336
www.alzheimers.org.uk

**Alzheimer Scotland –
Action on Dementia**
22 Drumsheugh
Gardens
Edinburgh EH3 7RN
Helpline: 0808 808
3000.
www.alscot.org

Alzheimer's Society

Baltic House
Mount Stuart Square
Cardiff CF10 5FH
Helpline: 0845 300 0336
www.alzheimers.org.uk

CarersUK
20 Great Dover Street
London SE1 4LX
Tel: 020 7378 4999
Advice Line: 0808 808
7777
www.carersuk.org

Carers Scotland
91 Mitchell Street
Glasgow G1 3LN
Tel: 0141 221 9141
www.carerscotland.org

Carers Wales
River House
Ynsbridge Court
Gwaelod-y-Garth
Cardiff CF15 9SS
Tel: 029 2081 1370
www.carerswales.org

Help the Aged
207-221 Pentonville
Road
London N1 9UZ
Senior Line
020 7278 1114
www.helpthe
aged.org.uk

Help the Aged
11 Granton Square
Edinburgh EH5 1HX
Tel: 0131
www.helptheaged.org.uk

Help the Aged
12 Cathedral Road
Cardiff CF11 9LJ
Tel: 02920 346 550
www.helptheaged.org.uk

MENCAP
123 Golden Lane
London EC1Y 0RT
Tel: 020 7454 0454
www.mencap.org.uk

ENABLE
146 Argyle Street
Glasgow G2 8BL
Tel: 0141 226 4541
www.enable.org.uk

MENCAP Cymru
31 Lambourne Crescent
Cardiff CF14 5GF
Tel: 029 2074 7588
www.mencap.org.uk

Mind (The National
Association of Mental
Health)
Granta House
15-19 The Broadway
London E15 4BQ
Infoline: 0845 766 0163
www.mind.org.uk

Mind Cymru
Quebec House
Castlebridge
5-19 Cowbridge Road
East
Cardiff CF11 9AB
Tel: 029 2039 5123
Infoline: 0845 766 0163
www.mind.org.uk

Royal National
Institute for the Blind
105 Judd Street
London WC1H 9NE
Helpline: 0845 766 9999
www.rnib.org.uk

Royal National
Institute for the Blind
(Scotland)
Dunedin House
25 Ravelston Terrace
Edinburgh EH4 3TP
Tel: 0131 311 8500
www.rnib.org.uk

Royal National
Institute for the Blind
(Cymru)
Trident Court
East Moors Road
Cardiff CF24 5TD
Tel: 029 2045 0440
www.rnib.org.uk

Royal National
Institute for Deaf
People
19-23 Featherstone
Street
London EC1Y 8SL
Helpline: 0808 808 0123
Textphone:
0808 808 9000
www.rnid.org.uk

RNID Scotland
Empire House
131 West Nile Street
Glasgow G1 2RX
Tel: 0141 341 5330
Text: 0141 341 5347
www.rnid.org.uk

RNID Cymru
16 Cathedral Road
Cardiff CF11 9LJ
Tel: 029 2033 3054
Textphone: 029 2033
3036
www.rnid.org.uk

Major voluntary organisations – UK wide

Space precludes listing all but the major organisations which offer information
and advice about paying for care and other aspects of community care.

Citizens Advice
Myddelton House
115-123 Pentonville
Road
London N1 9LZ
Tel: 020 7833 2181
www.citizens
advice.org.uk

Counsel and Care
Twyman House
16 Bonny Street
London NW1 9PG
Tel: 0845 300 7585
www.counsel
andcare.org.uk

Dial UK (Disability
information)
St Catherine's
Tickhill Road
Doncaster DN4 8QN
Tel: 01302 310 123
www.dialuk.info

Disabled Living
Centres Council
Red Bank House
4 St Chad's Street
Manchester M8 8QA
Tel: 0870 770 2866
www.dlcc.org.uk

Independent Age
6 Avonmore Road
London W14 8RL
Tel: 020 7605 4200
www.independent
age.org.uk

National Centre for
Independent Living
Hampton House
Albert Embankment
London SE1 7TJ
Tel: 020 7587 1663
www.ncil.org.uk

The Patients
Association
PO Box 935
Harrow HA1 3YJ
Helpline: 0845 608
4455
www.patients-
association.org.uk

RADAR (Royal
Association for
Disability and
Rehabilitation)
12 City Forum
250 City Road
London EC1V 8AF
Tel: 020 7250 3222
Minicom: 020 7250
4119
www.radar.org.uk

United Kingdom
Homecare
Association
Group House
52 Sutton Court Road
Sutton SM1 4SL
Tel: 020 8288 5291
www.ukhca.co.uk

Appendix 2

Information and advice

Independent advice and representation

If you want advice or information, the following may be able to assist.

- Citizens Advice Bureaux (CAB). You can find out where your local CAB is from the Citizens Advice website at www.citizensadvice.org.uk (England and Wales) or www.cas.org.uk (Scotland).
- Law centres. You can find your nearest law centre at www.lawcentres.org.uk.
- Other independent advice centres.
- Local authority welfare rights services.
- Local organisations for particular groups of claimants may offer help. For instance, there are unemployed centres, pensioners groups and centres for people with disabilities.
- Solicitors can give free legal advice to people on low incomes under the 'Legal help' scheme. This does not cover the cost of representation at an appeal hearing but can cover the cost of preparing written submissions and obtaining evidence such as medical reports.

You can find details of advice centres and lawyers in the phone book either under 'advice' or in the 'community' section at the front of the book. Your library or community centre may have details of where to get advice in your area. Community Legal Advice has a list of many organisations who provide advice in different areas of law including welfare benefits and community care. You can phone them on 0845 345 4345 or visit www.clsdirect.org.uk and search the 'directory' for advisers and lawyers within.

Advice from CPAG

Unfortunately, CPAG is unable to deal with enquiries directly from members of the public, but if you are an adviser you can phone the advice line from 2pm to 4pm, Monday to Friday on 020 7833 4627.

Organisations based in Scotland can contact CPAG in Scotland at Unit 9, Ladywell, 94 Duke Street, Glasgow G4 0UW or email advice@cpagscotland.org.uk. A phone line is open for advisers in Scotland on Monday to Thursday from 10am to 12 noon on 0141 552 0552.

Advice from the DWP

The phone book should list contact details for your local DWP office. See also Appendix 1 of this *Handbook* for contact details for the DWP and the Revenue. If you are disabled, you can obtain free telephone advice on benefits on 0800 882 200; minicom: 0800 243 355 (in Northern Ireland 0800 220 674; minicom: 0800 243 787). This is for general advice and not specific queries on individual claims.

Finding help on the Internet

CPAG's online subscription services (aimed at advisers) contain comprehensive in-depth information on welfare benefits, tax credits and child support. The text of the *Welfare Benefits and Tax Credits Handbook* is updated on a rolling basis throughout the year and is available with direct links to all of the relevant updated legislation, commissioners' and Upper Tribunal decisions. Information on this and other online information packages is at http://onlineservices.cpag.org.uk.

Some information about benefits and tax credits, including a selection of leaflets and forms is available on the DWP website at www.dwp.gov.uk and the Revenue website at www.hmrc.gov.uk. The DWP website also has links to the executive agencies of the DWP. You may also find some useful information at www.direct.gov.uk.

CPAG's website (www.cpag.org.uk) has some articles and briefings, and information about its publications, training and campaigning activities.

The RightsNet website (aimed at advisers) at www.rightsnet.org.uk has details of new legislation, some caselaw and guidance. It also has links to other useful sites.

Most Acts and regulations can be found on the government information website at www.opsi.gov.uk. You can find decisions of the Social Security Commissioners at www.osscsc.gov.uk.

Appendix 3

Useful publications

Many of the books listed here will be in your local public library. Stationery Office books are available from Stationery Office bookshops or ordered by post, telephone, fax or email from The Stationery Office, Post Cash Department, PO Box 29, Norwich NR3 1GN (tel: 0870 600 5522; fax: 0870 600 5533; email: customer.services@tso.co.uk; web: www.tso.co.uk). Many publications listed are available from CPAG.

1. Textbooks

From poor law to community care, Means and Smith, 1998 (second edition). Policy Press. A history of the development of welfare services for older people.
Community Care and the Law, Luke Clements and Pauline Thompson, 2007 (fourth edition). Legal Action Group. An overview and analysis of the legislation.
Community Care Practice and the Law, Michael Mandelstam, 2008 (fourth edition). Jessica Kingsley Publishers. A guide to law and practice, containing digests of legal judgements and ombudsman investigations.
Finding the right care home, Rosemary Hurtley and Julia Burton-Jones, 2008, Age Concern England.

2. Caselaw and legislation

Social Security Case Law – Digest of Commissioners' Decisions
D Neligan (Stationery Office, looseleaf in two vols).

CPAG's Welfare Benefits and Tax Credits Law Online
Includes all social security and tax credits legislation updated and consolidated throughout the year; over 3,000 commissioners' decisions, some with commentary; the *Welfare Benefits and Tax Credits Handbook* updated throughout the year with links to the relevant legislation, decisions and caselaw. Annual subscription £51 + VAT per concurrent user (bulk discounts available). More information and free seven-day trial from http://onlineservices.cpag.org.uk

CPAG's Child Support Law Online
Includes all child support legislation updated and consolidated throughout the year; the *Child Support Handbook* updated once a year in line with the print edition, with links to the relevant legislation, commissioners' decisions and caselaw. From summer 2009 it incorporates commentary from *Jacobs*. Annual subscription £65 + VAT per concurrent user (bulk discounts available). More information at http://onlineservices.cpag.org.uk

CPAG's Housing Benefit and Council Tax Benefit Law Online
Includes complete housing benefit and council tax benefit legislation, updated and consolidated throughout the year; commentary from *CPAG's Housing Benefit & Council Tax Benefit Legislation (Findlay)*, updated twice a year in line with the print edition, with links to commissioners' decisions, court cases and other relevant material. Annual subscription £105 + VAT per concurrent user (bulk discounts available). More information at http://onlineservices.cpag.org.uk

CPAG's Benefits for Migrants Law Online
Includes full text of the *Benefits for Migrants Handbook*, with links to online legislation, commissioners' decisions, court cases and other relevant material. Annual subscription £30 + VAT per concurrent user (bulk discounts available). More information at http://onlineservices.cpag.org.uk

The Law Relating to Social Security
(Stationery Office, looseleaf, 12 vols) All the legislation but without any comment. Known as the 'Blue Book'. Also available at www.dwp.gov.uk/advisers.

Social Security Legislation, Volume I: Non-Means-Tested Benefits
D Bonner, I Hooker and R White (Sweet & Maxwell) Legislation with commentary. 2009/10 edition (October 2009): £89 for the main volume, reduced to £80.20 if you are a CPAG member and order from CPAG before 30 June 2009, or at full price from July.

Social Security Legislation, Volume II: Income Support, Jobseeker's Allowance, State Pension Credit and the Social Fund
J Mesher, P Wood, R Poynter, N Wikeley and D Bonner (Sweet & Maxwell) Legislation with commentary. 2009/10 edition (October 2009): £89 for the main volume, reduced to £80.20 if you are a CPAG member and order from CPAG before 30 June 2009, or at full price from July.

Social Security Legislation, Volume III: Administration, Adjudication and the European Dimension
M Rowland and R White (Sweet & Maxwell) Legislation with commentary. 2009/10 edition (October 2009): £89 for the main volume, reduced to £80.20 if you are

a CPAG member and order from CPAG before 30 June 2009, or at full price from July.

Social Security Legislation, Volume IV: Tax Credits, Child Trust Funds and Employer-Paid Social Security Benefits
N Wikeley and D Williams (Sweet & Maxwell) Legislation with commentary. 2009/10 edition (October 2009): £89 for the main volume, reduced to £80.20 if you are a CPAG member and order from CPAG before 30 June 2009, or at full price from July.

Social Security Legislation – updating supplement to Volumes I, II, III & IV
(Sweet & Maxwell) The spring 2010 update to the 2009/10 main volumes: £55, reduced to £50 if you are a CPAG member and order from CPAG before 30 June 2009, or at full price from July.

CPAG's Housing Benefit and Council Tax Benefit Legislation
L Findlay, R Poynter, S Wright and C George (CPAG) Legislation with detailed commentary. 2009/10 (22nd) edition (December 2009): £99 including Supplement. Reduced to £92 per set if ordered before 30 June 2009. The 21st edition (2008/09) is still available, £97 per set. Available as part of *CPAG's Housing Benefit and Council Tax Law Online* (see p394).

Child Support: The Legislation
E Jacobs (CPAG) Legislation with commentary. 9th edition main volume (summer 2009): £87.

3. Official guidance

See Appendix 2 for community care guidance.

Decision Makers Guide
(14 volumes, memos and letters) Available at www.dwp.gov.uk/advisers

Handbook for Delegated Medical Practitioners
(Stationery Office, 1988)

Housing Benefit and Council Tax Benefit Guidance Manual
(Stationery Office, looseleaf) Available at www.dwp.gov.uk/advisers

Industrial Injuries Handbook for Adjudicating Medical Authorities
(Stationery Office, looseleaf)

Income Support Guide
(Stationery Office, looseleaf, 8 vols) Procedural guide issued to DWP staff.

Notes on the Diagnosis of Prescribed Diseases (except pneumoconiosis and related occupational diseases and occupational deafness)
(Stationery Office, 1991)

Tax Credit Technical Manual
Available at www.hmrc.gov.uk/manuals/

The Social Fund Guide
(Stationery Office, looseleaf 2 vols) Available at www.dwp.gov.uk/advisers/guides

4. Leaflets

The DWP publishes many leaflets which cover particular benefits or particular groups of claimants. They are free from your local DWP Jobcentre Plus office or at www.dwp.gov.uk. The Department of Health also produces information, much of which can be found at www.dh.gov.uk. Most local authorities also produce a range of leaflets on the services they provide.

5. Periodicals

The *Welfare Rights Bulletin* is published every two months by CPAG. It covers developments in social security law and updates the *Welfare Benefits and Tax Credits Handbook* between editions. The annual subscription is £32 but is sent automatically to CPAG rights and comprehensive members. For subscription and membership details contact CPAG.

Articles on social security and social welfare can also be found in *Legal Action* (Legal Action Group, monthly magazine), the *Journal of Social Security Law* (Sweet & Maxwell, quarterly), and the *Adviser* (Citizens Advice, every 2 months). More specialist publications include:

- *Journal of Social Welfare and Family Law*, quarterly, Routledge.
- *Community Care Magazine*, weekly.
- *Elderly Client Adviser*, bi-monthly, Ark Publishing.
- *Elderly Law and Finance*, quarterly, Jordan Press.
- *Disability Rights Bulletin*, 3 times a year, Disability Alliance.

6. Other publications – general

CPAG's Welfare Benefits and Tax Credits Handbook
£37.00 (11th edition, April 2009) £8.50 for claimants). Also available as part of
CPAG's Welfare Benefits and Tax Credits Law Online.

Child Support Handbook
£26 (17th edition, summer 2009) (£6.50 for claimants). Also available as part of
CPAG's Child Support Law Online.

Personal Finance Handbook
£16.50 (3rd edition, autumn 2009)

Student Support and Benefits Handbook: England, Wales and Northern Ireland
£13 (7th edition, autumn 2009)

Benefits for Students in Scotland Handbook
£13 (7th edition, October 2009). Available free online at:
www.scottishhandbooks.cpag.org.uk, funded by the Scottish Government.

Homeowners' Rights Handbook
£15 (1st edition, late 2009)

Council Tax Handbook
£17 (8th edition, summer 2009)

Debt Advice Handbook
£20 (8th edition, December 2008)

Fuel Rights Handbook
£17 (14th edition, March 2008)

Benefits for Migrants Handbook
£23 (5th edition, summer 2009)

Children's Handbook Scotland: benefits for children living away from their parents
£12.50 (2nd edition, autumn 2009). Available free online at:
www.scottishhandbooks.cpag.org.uk, funded by the Scottish Government.

Guide to Housing Benefit and Council Tax Benefit
£25 (summer 2009)

Disability Rights Handbook
£25 (May 2009)

The Young Persons Handbook
£15.95 (4th edition, 2009)

Welfare to Work Handbook
£22 (4th edition, April 2009)

For CPAG publications and most of those in sections 2 and 6 contact:
CPAG, 94 White Lion Street, London N1 9PF, tel: 020 7837 7979, fax: 020 7837 6414. Enquiries: email bookorders@cpag.org.uk. Order forms are available at www.cpag.org.uk/publications. Postage and packing: free for online subscriptions and orders up to £10 in value; for order value £10.01–£100 add a flat rate charge of £3.99; for order value £100.01–£400 add £5.99; for order value £400+ add £9.99.

Appendix 4
....
Key legislation

Reproduced in this appendix is some of the key legislation governing some of the powers and duties of social services departments (and health authorities) relevant to this *Handbook*. It contains the following legislation which applies in **England and Wales**:
1. ss21, 22, 26 and s29 National Assistance Act 1948 (p400)
2. ss45 and 65 Health Services and Public Health Act 1968 (p404)
3. ss7–7D Local Authority Social Services Act 1970 (p405)
4. ss1 and 2 Chronically Sick and Disabled Persons Act 1970 (p406)
5. ss17, 21, 22 and 24 Health and Social Services and Social Security Adjudications Act 1983 (p407)
6. s117 Mental Health Act 1983 (p410)
7. ss4, 8 and 16 Disabled Persons (Services, Consultation and Representation) Act 1986 (p410)
8. ss46 and 47 National Health Service and Community Care Act 1990 (p411)
9. s1 Carers (Recognition and Services) Act 1995 (p413)
10. ss1, 2 and 3 Carers and Disabled Children Act 2000 (p413)
11. s2 Local Government Act 2000 (p414)
12. s49 Health and Social Care Act 2001 (p415)
13. s254 National Health Service Act 2006 (p416)
14. s192 National Health Service (Wales) Act 2006 (p416)
15. ss1, 3, 4, 10 and 20 Health and Social Care Act 2008 (p417)

It also reproduces the following legislation which applies in **Scotland**:
16. ss4–5B, 12–12B, 13-14 and 86A–87 Social Work (Scotland) Act 1968 (p419)
17. ss1, 36 and 37 NHS (Scotland) Act 1978 (p425)
18. s2 Regulation of Care (Scotland) Act 2001 (p426)
19. s1 and Sch 1 Community Care and Health (Scotland) Act 2002 (p426)
20. Mental Health (Care and Treatment) (Scotland) Act 2003 (p428)

The full legislation can be found at www.opsi.gov.uk.

1. National Assistance Act 1948

Duty of local authorities to provide accommodation

21.–(1) Subject to and in accordance with the provisions of this Part of this Act, a local authority may with the approval of the Secretary of State, and to such extent as he may direct shall, make arrangements for providing–

(a) residential accommodation for persons aged 18 or over who by reason of age, illness, disability or any other circumstances are in need of care and attention which is not otherwise available to them; and

(aa) residential accommodation for expectant and nursing mothers who are in need of care and attention which is not otherwise available to them.

[(1A) and (1B) omitted]

(2) In making any such arrangements a local authority shall have regard to the welfare of all persons for whom accommodation is provided, and in particular to the need for providing accommodation of different descriptions suited to different descriptions of such persons as are mentioned in the last foregoing subsection.

(2A) In determining for the purposes of paragraph (a) or (aa) of subsection (1) of this section whether care and attention are otherwise available to a person, a local authority shall disregard so much of the person's resources as may be specified in, or determined in accordance with, regulations made by the Secretary of State for the purposes of this subsection

(2B) In subsection (2A) of this section the reference to a person's resources is a reference to his resources within the meaning of regulations made for the purposes of that subsection.'

(3) [*repealed*]

(4) Subject to section 26 of this Act, accommodation provided by a local authority in the exercise of their functions under this section shall be provided in premises managed by the authority or, to such extent as may be determined in accordance with the arrangements under this section, in such premises managed by another local authority as may be agreed between the two authorities and on such terms as to the reimbursement of expenditure incurred by the said other authority, as may be so agreed.

(5) References in this Act to accommodation provided under this Part thereof shall be construed as references to accommodation provided in accordance with this and the five next following sections, and as including references to board and other services, amenities and requisites provided in connection with the accommodation except where in the opinion of the authority managing the premises their provision is unnecessary.

(6) References in this Act to a local authority providing accommodation shall be construed, in any case where a local authority agree with another local authority for the provision of accommodation in premises managed by the said authority, as references to the first-mentioned local authority.

(7) Without prejudice to the generality of the foregoing provisions of this section, a local authority may–

(a) provide, in such cases as they may consider appropriate, for the conveyance of persons to and from premises in which accommodation is provided for them under this Part of the Act;

(b) make arrangements for the provision on the premises in which accommodation is being provided of such other services as appear to the authority to be required.

(8) Nothing in this section shall authorise or require a local authority to make any provision authorised or required to be made (whether by that or by any other authority) by

or under any enactment not contained in this Part of this Act, or authorised or required to be provided under the National Health Service Act 1977.

Charges to be made for accommodation

22.–(1) Subject to section 26 of this Act, where a person is provided with accommodation under this Part of this Act the local authority providing the accommodation shall recover from him the amount of the payment which he is liable to make.

(2) Subject to the following provisions of this section, the payment which a person is liable to make for any such accommodation shall be in accordance with a standard rate fixed for that accommodation by the authority managing the premises in which it is provided and that standard rate shall represent the full cost to the authority of providing that accommodation.

(3) Where a person for whom accommodation in premises managed by any local authority is provided, or proposed to be provided, under this Part of this Act satisfies the local authority that he is unable to pay therefore at the standard rate, the authority shall assess his ability to pay, and accordingly determine at what lower rate he shall be liable to pay for the accommodation.

(4) In assessing for the purposes of the last foregoing subsection a person's ability to pay, a local authority shall assume that he will need for his personal requirements such sum per week as may be prescribed by the Minister, or such other sum as in special circumstances the authority may consider appropriate.

(4A) Regulations made for the purposes of subsection (4) of this section may prescribe different sums for different circumstances.

(5) In assessing as aforesaid a person's ability to pay, a local authority shall give effect to regulations made by the Secretary of State for the purposes of this subsection except that, until the first such regulations come into force, a local authority shall give effect to Part III of Schedule 1 to the Supplementary Benefits Act 1976, as it had effect immediately before the amendments made by Schedule 2 to the Social Security Act 1980.

(5A) If they think fit, an authority managing premises in which accommodation is provided for a person shall have power on each occasion when they provide accommodation for him, irrespective of his means, to limit to such amount as appears to them reasonable for him to pay the payments required from him for his accommodation during a period commencing when they begin to provide the accommodation for him and ending not more than eight weeks after that.

(6)-(7) [*repealed*]

(8) Where accommodation is provided by a local authority in premises managed by another local authority, the payment therefore under this section shall be made to the authority managing the premises and not to the authority providing the accommodation, but the authority managing the premises shall account for the payment to the authority providing the accommodation.

(9)[*repealed*]

Provision of accommodation in premises maintained by voluntary organisations

26.–(1) Subject to subsections (1A) and (1B) below, arrangements under section 21 of this Act may include arrangements made with a voluntary organisation or with any other person who is not a local authority where–

(a) that organisation or person manages premises which provide for reward accommodation falling within subsection (1)(a) or (aa) of that section, and

(b) the arrangements are for the provision of such accommodation in those premises.

(1A) Subject to subsection (1B) below, arrangements made with any voluntary organisation or other person by virtue of this section must, if they are for the provision of residential accommodation with both board and personal care for such persons as are mentioned in section 1(1) of the Registered Homes Act 1984 (requirement for registration), be arrangements for the provision of such accommodation in a residential care home which is managed by the organisation or person in question, being such a home in respect of which that organisation or persons–

(a) is registered under Part 1 of that Act, or

(b) is not required to be so registered by virtue of section 1(4)(a) or (b) of that Act (certain small homes) or by virtue of the home being managed or provided by an exempt body;

and for this purpose 'personal care' and 'residential care home' have the same meaning as in that Part of that Act.

(1B) Arrangements made with any voluntary organisation or other person by virtue of this section must, if they are for the provision of residential accommodation where nursing care is provided, be arrangements for the provision of such accommodation in premises which are managed by the organisation or persons in question, being premises–

(a) in respect of which that organisation or person is registered under Part 11 of the Registered Homes Act 1984, or

(b) which, by reason only of being maintained or controlled by an exempt body, do not fall within the definition of a nursing home in section 21 of that Act.

(1C) Subject to subsection (1D) below, no such arrangements as are mentioned in subsection (1B) above may be made by an authority for the accommodation of any person without the consent of such Health Authority as may be determined in accordance with regulations.

(1D) Subsection (1C) above does not apply to the making by an authority of temporary arrangements for the accommodation of any person as a matter of urgency; but, as soon as practicable after any such temporary arrangements have been made, the authority shall seek the consent required by subsection (1C) above to the making of appropriate arrangements for the accommodation of the person concerned.

(1E) [repealed]

(2) Any arrangements made by virtue of this section shall provide for the making by the local authority to the other party thereto of payments in respect of the accommodation provided at such rates as may be determined by or under the arrangements and subject to subsection (3A) below the local authority shall recover from each person for whom accommodation is provided under the arrangements the amount of the refund which he is liable to make in accordance with the following provisions of this section.

(3) Subject to subsection (3A) below, a person for whom accommodation is provided under any such arrangements shall, in lieu of being liable to make payment therefore in accordance with section twenty–two of this Act, refund to the local authority any payments made in respect of him under the last foregoing subsection:

Provided that where a person for whom accommodation is provided, or proposed to be provided, under any such arrangements satisfies the local authority that he is unable to make refund at the full rate determined under that subsection, subsections (3) to (5) of section twenty–two of this Act shall, with the necessary modifications, apply as they apply where a person satisfies the local authority of his inability to pay at the standard rate as mentioned in the said subsection (3).

(3A) Where accommodation in any premises is provided for any person under any arrangements made by virtue of this section and the local authority, the person concerned and the voluntary organisation or the other person managing the premises (in this subsection referred to as 'the provider') agree that this section shall apply–

(a) so long as the person concerned makes the payments for which he is liable under paragraph (b) below, he shall not be liable to make any refund under subsection (3) above and the local authority shall not be liable to make any payment under subsection (2) above in respect of the accommodation provided for him;

(b) the person concerned shall be liable to pay to the provider such sums as he would otherwise (under subsection (3) above) be liable to pay by way of refund to the local authority; and

(c) the local authority shall be liable to pay to the provider the difference between the sums paid by virtue of paragraph (b) above and the payments which, but for paragraph (a) above, the authority would be liable to pay under subsection (2) above.

(4) Subsections (5A), (7) and (9) of the said section 22 shall, with the necessary modifications, apply for the purposes of the last foregoing subsection as they apply for the purposes of the said section 22.

(4A) Section 21(5) of this Act shall have effect as respects accommodation provided under arrangements made by virtue of this section with the substitution for the references to the authority managing the premises of a reference to the authority making the arrangements.

(5) Where in any premises accommodation is being provided under this section in accordance with arrangements made by any local authority, any person authorised in that behalf by the authority may at all reasonable times enter and inspect the premises

(6) [*repealed*]

(7) In this section the expression 'voluntary organisation' includes any association which is a housing association for the purposes of the Housing Act 1936, 'small home' means an establishment falling within section 1(4) of the Registered Homes Act 1984 and 'exempt body' means an authority or body constituted by an Act of Parliament or incorporated by Royal Charter.

Welfare arrangements for blind, deaf, dumb and crippled persons, etc

29.–(1) A local authority may, with the approval of the Secretary of State, and to such extent as he may direct in relation to persons ordinarily resident in the area of the local authority shall make arrangements for promoting the welfare of persons to whom this section applies, that is to say persons aged eighteen or over who are blind, deaf or dumb or who suffer from mental disorder of any description, and other persons aged eighteen or over who are substantially and permanently handicapped by illness, injury, or congenital deformity or such other disabilities as may be prescribed by the Minister.

(2) [*repealed*]

(3) [*repealed*]

(4) Without prejudice to the generality of the provisions of subsection (1) of this section, arrangements may be made thereunder–

(a) for informing persons to whom arrangements under that subsection relate of the services available for them thereunder;

(b) for giving such persons instruction in their own homes or elsewhere in methods of overcoming the effects of their disabilities;

(c) for providing workshops where such persons may be engaged (whether under a contract of service or otherwise) in suitable work, and hostels where persons engaged in the workshops, and other persons to whom arrangements under subsection (1) of this section relate and for whom work or training is being provided in pursuance of the Disabled Persons (Employment) Act 1944 or the Employment and Training Act 1973 may live;

(d) for providing persons to whom arrangements under subsection (1) of this section relate with suitable work (whether under a contract of service or otherwise) in their own homes or elsewhere;

(e) for helping such persons in disposing of the produce of their work; for providing such persons with recreational facilities in their own homes or elsewhere;

(f) for providing such persons with recreational facilities in their own homes or elsewhere;

(g) for compiling and maintaining classified registers of the persons to whom arrangements under subsection (1) of this section relate.

(4A) Where accommodation in a hostel is provided under paragraph (c) of subsection (4) of this section–

(a) if the hostel is managed by a local authority, section 22 of this Act shall apply as it applies where accommodation is provided under s21;

(b) if the accommodation is provided in a hostel managed by a person other than a local authority under arrangements made with that person, subsections (2) to (4A) of section 26 of this Act shall apply as they apply where accommodation is provided under arrangements made by virtue of that section; and

(c) sections 32 and 43 of this Act shall apply as they apply where accommodation is provided under sections 21 to 26;

and in this subsection references to 'accommodation' include references to board and other services, amenities and requisites provided in connection with the accommodation, except where in the opinion of the authority managing the premises or, in the case mentioned in paragraph (b) above, the authority making the arrangements their provision is unnecessary.

(5) [repealed]

(6) Nothing in the foregoing provisions of this section shall authorise or require–

(a) the payment of money to persons to whom this section applies, other than persons for whom work is provided under arrangements made by virtue of paragraph (c) or paragraph (d) of subsection (4) of this section or who are engaged in work which they are enabled to perform in consequence of anything done in pursuance of arrangements made under this section; or

(b) the provision of any accommodation or services required to be provided under the National Health Service Act 1977.

(7) A person engaged in work in a workshop provided under paragraph (c) of subsection (4) of this section, or a person in receipt of a superannuation allowance granted on his retirement from engagement in any such workshop, shall be deemed for the purposes of this Act to continue to be ordinarily resident in the area in which he was ordinarily resident immediately before he was accepted for work in that workshop; and for the purposes of this subsection a course of training in such workshop shall be deemed to be work in that workshop.

2. Health Services and Public Health Act 1968

Promotion, by local authorities, of the welfare of old people

45.–(1) A local authority may with the approval of the Secretary of State, and to such extent as he may direct shall, make arrangements for promoting the welfare of old people.

(2) [*repealed*]

(3) A local authority may employ as their agent for the purposes of this section any voluntary organisation or any person carrying on, professionally or by way of trade or business, activities which consist of or include the provision of services for old people, being an organisation or person appearing to the authority to be capable of promoting the welfare of old people.

(4) No arrangements under this section shall provide–

(a) for the payment of money to old people except in so far as the arrangements may provide for the remuneration of old people engaged in suitable work in accordance with the arrangements;

(b) for making available any accommodation or services required to be provided under the National Health Service Act 1977.

Financial and other assistance by local authorities to certain voluntary organisations

65.–(1) A local authority may give assistance by way of grant or by way of loan, or partly in the one way and partly in the other, to a voluntary organisation whose activities consist in, or include, the provision of a service similar to a relevant service, the promotion of the provision of a relevant service or a similar one, the publicising of a relevant service or a similar one or the giving of advice with respect to the manner in which a relevant service or a similar one can best be provided, and so may the Greater London Council.

(2) A local authority may also assist any such voluntary organisation as aforesaid by permitting them to use premises belonging to the authority on such terms as may be agreed, and by making available furniture, vehicles or equipment (whether by way of gift, or loan or otherwise) and the services of any staff whoa re employed by the authority in connection with the premises or other things which they permit the organisation to use.

(3) In this section–...

(c) 'relevant service' means a service the provision of which must or may, by virtue of the relevant enactments, be secured by the local authority. . .

---

3. Local Authority Social Services Act 1970

Local authorities to exercise social services functions under guidance of Secretary of State

7.–(1) Local authorities shall, in the exercise of their social services functions, including the exercise of any discretion conferred by any relevant enactment, act under the general guidance of the Secretary of State.

Directions by the Secretary of State as to exercise of social services functions

7A–(1) Without prejudice to section 7 of this Act, every local authority shall exercise their social services functions in accordance with such directions as may be given to them under this section by the Secretary of State.

(2) Directions under this section–

(a) shall be given in writing; and

(b) may be given to a particular authority, or to authorities of a particular class, or to authorities generally.

Complaints procedure

7B–[repealed]

Inquiries

7C–(1) The Secretary of State may cause an inquiry to be held in any case where, whether on representations made to him or otherwise, he considers it advisable to do so in connection with the exercise by any local authority of any of their social services functions (except in so far as those functions relate to persons under the age of eighteen).

(2) Subsections (2) to (5) of section 250 of the Local Government Act 1972 (powers in relation to local inquiries) shall apply in relation to an inquiry under this section as they apply in relation to an inquiry under that section.

Default powers of Secretary of State as respects social services functions of local authorities

7D–(1) If the Secretary of State is satisfied that any local authority have failed, without reasonable excuse, to comply with any of their duties which are social services functions (other than a duty imposed by or under the Children Act 1989), he may make an order declaring that authority to be in default with respect to the duty in question.

(2) An order under subsection (1) may contain such directions for the purpose of ensuring that the duty is complied with within such period as may be specified in the order as appear to the Secretary of State to be necessary.

(3) Any such direction shall, on the application of the Secretary of State, be enforceable by mandamus.

---

4. Chronically Sick and Disabled Persons Act 1970

Information as to need for and existence of welfare services

1(1) It shall be the duty of every local authority having functions under section 29 of the National Assistance Act 1948 to inform themselves of the number of persons to whom that section applies within their area and of the need for the making by the authority of arrangements under that section for such persons.

(2) Every such local authority–

(a) shall cause to be published from time to time at such times and in such manner as they consider appropriate general information as to the services provided under arrangements made by the authority under the said section 29 which are for the time being available in the area; and

(b) shall ensure that any such person as aforesaid who uses any of those services is informed of any other service provided by the authority (whether under any such arrangements or not) which in the opinion of the authority is relevant to his needs and of any service provided by any other authority or organisation which in the opinion of the authority is so relevant and of which particulars are in the authorities' possession.

Provision of welfare services

2.–(1) Where a local authority having functions under s29 National Assistance Act 1948 are satisfied in the case of any person to whom that section applies who is ordinarily resident in their area that it is necessary in order to meet the needs of that person for that authority to make arrangements for all or any of the following matters, namely:–

(a) the provision of practical assistance for that person in his home;

(b) the provision for that person of, or assistance to that person in obtaining, wireless, television, library or similar recreational facilities;

(c) the provision for that person of lectures, games, outings or other recreational facilities outside his home or assistance to that person in taking advantage of educational facilities available to him;

(d) the provision for that person of facilities for, or assistance in, travelling to and from his home for the purpose of participating in any services provided under arrangements made by the authority under the said section 29 or, with the approval of the authority, in any services provided otherwise than as aforesaid which are similar to services which could be provided under such arrangements;

(e) the provision of assistance for that person in arranging for the carrying out of any works of adaptation in his home or the provision of any additional facilities designed to secure his greater safety, comfort or convenience;

(f) facilitating the taking of holidays by that person, whether at holiday homes or otherwise and whether provided under arrangements made by the authority or otherwise;

(g) the provision of meals for that person whether in his home or elsewhere;

(h) the provision for that person of, or assistance to that person in obtaining, a telephone and any special equipment necessary to enable him to use a telephone,

then, subject to the provisions of section 7(1) of the Local Authority Social Services Act 1970 (which requires local authorities in the exercise of certain functions, including functions under the said section 29, to act under the general guidance of the Secretary of State) and to the provisions of section 7A of that Act (which requires local authorities to exercise their social services functions in accordance with directions given by the Secretary of State) it shall be the duty of that Authority to make those arrangements in exercise of their functions under the said section 29.

5. Health and Social Services and Social Security Adjudications Act 1983

Charges for local authority services in England and Wales

17.–(1) Subject to subsection (3) below, an authority providing a service to which this section applies may recover such charge (if any) for it as they consider reasonable.

(2) This section applies to services provided under the following enactments–

(a) section 29 if the National Assistance Act 1948 (welfare arrangements for blind, deaf, dumb, and crippled persons etc.);

(b) section 45(1) of the Health Services and Public Health Act 1968 (welfare of old people);

(c) Schedule 8 to the National Health Service Act 1977 (care of mothers and young children, prevention of illness and care and after-care and home help and laundry facilities);

(d) section 8 of the Residential Homes Act 1980 (meals and recreation for old people); and

(e) paragraph 1 of Part II of Schedule 9 to this Act other than the provision of services for which payment may be required under section 22 or 26 of the National Assistance Act 1948.

(3) If a person–

(a) avails himself of a service to which this section applies, and

(b) satisfies the authority providing the service that his means are insufficient for it to be reasonably practicable for him to pay for the service the amount which he would otherwise be obliged to pay for it,

the authority shall not require him to pay more for it than it appears to them that it is reasonable practicable for him to pay.

(4) Any charge under this section may, without prejudice to any other method of recovery, be recovered summarily as a civil debt.

Recovery of sums due to local authority where persons in residential accommodation have disposed of assets

21.–(1) Subject to the following provisions of this section, where–

(a) a person avails himself of Part III accommodation; and

(b) that person knowingly and with the intention of avoiding charges for the accommodation–

(i) has transferred any asset to which this section applies to some other person or person not more than six months before the date on which he begins to reside in such accommodation; or

(ii) transfers any such asset to some other person or persons while residing in the accommodation; and

(c) either–

(i) the consideration for the transfer is less than the value of the asset; or

(ii) there is no consideration for the transfer,

the person or persons to whom the asset is transferred by the person availing himself of the accommodation shall be liable to pay to the local authority providing the accommodation or arranging for its provision the difference between the amount assessed as due to be paid for the accommodation by the person availing himself of it and the amount which the local authority receive from him for it.

(2) This section applies to cash and any other asset which falls to be taken into account for the purpose of assessing under section 22 of the National Assistance Act 1948 the ability to pay for the accommodation of the person availing himself of it.

(3) Subsection 1(1) above shall have effect in relation to a transfer by a person who leaves Part III accommodation and subsequently resumes residence in such accommodation as if the period of six months mentioned in paragraph (b)(i) were a period of six months before the date on which he resumed residence in such accommodation.

(3A) If the Secretary of State so directs, subsection (1) above shall not apply in such cases as may be specified in the direction.

(4) Where a person has transferred an asset to which this section applies to more than one person, the liability of each of the persons to whom it was transferred shall be in proportion to the benefit accruing to him from the transfer.

(5) A person's liability under this section shall not exceed the benefit accruing to him from the transfer.

(6) Subject to subsection (7) below, the value of any asset to which this section applies, other than cash, which has been transferred shall be taken to be the amount of the

consideration which would have been realised for it if it had been sold on the open market by a willing seller at the time of the transfer.

(7) For the purpose of calculating the value of an asset under subsection (6) above there shall be deducted from the amount of the consideration–

(a) the amount of any incumbrance on the asset; and

(b) a reasonable amount in respect of the expenses of the sale.

(8) In this Part of this Act 'Part 111 accommodation' means accommodation provided under sections 21 to 26 of the National Assistance Act 1948, and, in the application of this Part of this Act to Scotland, means accommodation provided under the Social Work (Scotland) Act 1968 or section 7 (functions of local authorities) of the Mental Health (Scotland) Act 1984.

Arrears of contributions charged on interest in land in England and Wales

22.–(1) Subject to subsection (2) below, where a person who avails himself of Part 111 accommodation provided by a local authority in England, Wales or Scotland–

(a)   fails to pay any sum assessed as due to be paid by him for the accommodation; and

(b)   has a beneficial interest in land in England and Wales;

the local authority may create a charge in their favour on his interest in the land.

(2) In the case of a person who has interests in more than one parcel of land the charge under this section shall be upon his interest in such one of the parcels as the local authority may determine.

(2A) In determining whether to exercise their power under subsection (1) above and in making any determination under subsection (2) above, the local authority shall comply with any directions given to them by the Secretary of State as to the exercise of those functions.

(3) [repealed]

(4) Subject to subsection (5) below, a charge under this section shall be in respect of any amount assessed as due to be paid which is outstanding from time to time.

(5) The charge on the interest of an equitable joint tenant in land shall be in respect of an amount not exceeding the value of the interest that he would enjoy in the land if the joint tenancy were severed but the creation of such a charge shall not sever the joint tenancy.

(6) On the death of a joint tenant in the proceeds of sale of land held upon trust for sale whose interest in the proceeds is subject to a charge under this section–

(a)   if there are surviving joint tenants, their interests in the proceeds; and

(b)   if the land vests in one person, or one person is entitled to have it vested in him, his interest in it,

shall become subject to a charge for an amount not exceeding the amount of the charge to which the interest of the deceased joint tenant was subject by virtue of subsection (5) above.

(7) A charge under this section shall be created by a declaration in writing made by the local authority.

(8) Any such charge, other than a charge on the interest of an equitable joint tenant in land, shall in the case of unregistered land be a land charge of Class B within the meaning of section 2 of the Land Charges Act 1972 and in the case of registered land be a registrable charge taking effect as a charge by way of legal mortgage.

Interest on sums charged on or secured over interest in land

24.–(1) Any sum charged on or secured over an interest in land under this Part of this Act shall bear interest from the day after that on which the person for whom the local authority provided the accommodation dies.

(2) The rate of interest shall be such reasonable rate as the Secretary of State may direct or, if no such direction is given, as the local authority may determine.

6. Mental Health Act 1983

Aftercare

117.–(1) This section applies to persons who are detained under section 3 above, or admitted to a hospital in pursuance of a hospital order made under section 37 above, or transferred to a hospital in pursuance of a transfer direction made under section 47 or 48 above, and then cease to be detained and (whether or not immediately after so ceasing) leave hospital.

(2) It shall be the duty of the Health Authority and of the local social services authority to provide, in co–operation with relevant voluntary agencies, aftercare services for any person to whom this section applies until such time as the Health Authority and the local social services authority are satisfied that the person concerned is no longer in need of such services but they shall not be so satisfied in the case of a patient who is subject to aftercare under supervision at any time while he so remains subject.

(2A) [repealed]   (2B) Section 32 above shall apply for the purposes of this section as it applies for the purposes of Part II of this Act.

(3) In this section 'the Health Authority' means the Health Authority and 'the local social services authority' means the local social services authority for the area in which the person concerned is resident or to which he is sent on discharge by the hospital in which he was detained.

7. Disabled Persons (Services, Consultation and Representation) Act 1986

4. When requested to do so by–
(a)   a disabled person ...
(c)   any person who provides care for him in the circumstances mentioned in section 8,
a local authority shall decide whether the needs of the disabled person call for the provision by the authority of any services in accordance with section 2(1) of the 1970 Act (provision for welfare services).

8.–(1) Where–
(a)   a disabled person is living at home and receiving a substantial amount of care on a regular basis from another person (who is not a person employed to provide such care by any body in the exercise of its functions under any enactment), and
(b)   it falls to a local authority to decide whether the disabled person's needs call for the provision by them of any services for him under any of the welfare enactments,
the local authority shall, in deciding that question, have regard to the ability of that other person to continue to provide such care on a regular basis.

16.   In this Act–
. . .
'disabled person'–
(a) in relation to England and Wales, means

(i) in the case of a person aged 18 or over, a person to whom s29 of the National Assistance Act 1948 applies. . .

8. National Health Service and Community Care Act 1990

Local authority plans for community care services

46.–(1) Each local authority–

(a) shall, within such period after the day appointed for the coming into force of this section as the Secretary of State may direct, prepare and publish a plan for the provision of community care services in their area;

(b) shall keep the plan prepared by them under paragraph (a) above and any further plans prepared by them under this section under review; and

(c) shall, at such intervals as the Secretary of State may direct, prepare and publish modifications to the current plan, or if the case requires, a new plan.

(2) In carrying out any of their functions under paragraphs (a) to (c) of subsection (1) above, a local authority shall consult–

(a) any Health Authority the whole or any part of whose district lies within the area of the local authority;

(b) [*repealed*]

(c) in so far as any proposed plan, review or modifications of a plan may affect or be affected by the provision or availability of housing and the local authority is not itself a local housing authority, within the meaning of the Housing Act 1985, every such local housing authority whose area is within the area of the local authority;

(d) such voluntary organisations as appear to the authority to represent the interests of persons who use or are likely to use any community care services within the area of the authority or the interests of private carers who, within that area, provide care to persons for whom, in the exercise of their social services functions, the local authority have a power or a duty to provide a service;

(e) such voluntary housing agencies and other bodies as appear to the local authority to provide housing or community care services in their area; and

(f) such other persons as the Secretary of State may direct.

(3) In this section–

'local authority' means the council of a county, a county borough, a metropolitan district or a London borough or the Common Council of the City of London;

'community care services' means services which a local authority may provide or arrange to be provided under any of the following provisions–

(a) Part III of the National Assistance Act 1948;

(b) section 45 of the Health Services and Public Health Act 1968;

(c) section 21 of and Schedule 8 to the National Health Service Act 1977; and

(d) section 117 of the Mental Health Act 1983; and

'private carer' means a person who is not employed to provide the care in question by any body in the exercise of its function under any enactment.

Assessment of needs for community care services

47.–(1) Subject to subsections (5) and (6) below, where it appears to a local authority that any person for whom they may provide or arrange for the provision of community care services may be in need of any such services, the authority–

(a)   shall carry out an assessment of his needs for those services; and

(b)   having regard to the results of that assessment, shall then decide whether his needs call for the provision by them of any such services.

(2) If at any time during the assessment of the needs of any person under subsection (1)(a) above it appears to a local authority that he is a disabled person, the authority–

(a)   shall proceed to make such a decision as to the services he requires as is mentioned in section 4 of the Disabled Persons (Services, Consultation and Representation) Act 1986 without his requesting them to do so under that section; and

(b)   shall inform him that they will be doing so and of his rights under that Act.

(3)   If at any time during the assessment of the needs of any person under subsection (1)(a) above, it appears to a local authority–

(a)   that there may be a need for the provision to that person by such Health Authority as may be determined in accordance with regulations of any services under the National Health Service Act 1977, or

(b)   that there may be the need for the provision to him of any services which fall within the functions of a local housing authority (within the meaning of the Housing Act 1985) which is not the local authority carrying out the assessment,

the local authority shall notify that Health Authority or local housing authority and invite them to assist, to such extent as is reasonable in the circumstances, in the making of the assessment; and, in making their decision as to the provision of services needed for the person in question, the local authority shall take into account any services which are likely to be made available for him by that Health Authority or local housing authority.

(4) The Secretary of State may give directions as to the manner in which an assessment under this section is to be carried out or the form it is to take but, subject to any such directions and to subsection (7) below, it shall be carried out in such manner and take such form as the local authority consider appropriate.

(5) Nothing in this section shall prevent a local authority from temporarily providing or arranging for the provision of community care services for any person without carrying out a prior assessment of his needs in accordance with the preceding provisions of this section if, in the opinion of the authority, the condition of that person is such that he requires those services as a matter of urgency.

(6) If, by virtue of subsection (5) above, community care services have been provided temporarily for any person as a matter of urgency, then, as soon as practicable thereafter, an assessment of his needs shall be made in accordance with the preceding provisions of this section.

. . .

9. Carers (Recognition and Services) Act 1995

Assessment of ability of carers to prow de care: England and Wales

1.–(1) Subject to subsection (3) below, in any case where–

(a)   a local authority carry out an assessment under section 47(1)(a) of the National Health Service and Community Care Act 1990 of the needs of a person ('the relevant person') for community care services, and

(b)   an individual ('the carer') provides or intends to provide a substantial amount of care on a regular basis for the relevant person,

the carer may request the local authority, before they make their decision as to whether the needs of the relevant person call for the provision of any services, to carry out an assessment of his ability to provide and continue to provide care for the relevant person; and if he makes such a request, the local authority shall carry out such an assessment and shall take into account the results of that assessment in making that decision.

(2) Subject to subsection (3) below, in any case where–

(a)   a local authority assess the needs of a disabled child for the purpose of Part III of the Children Act 1989 or section 2 of the Chronically Sick and Disabled Persons Act 1970, and

(b)   an individual ('the carer') provides or intends to provide a substantial amount of care on a regular basis for the disabled child,

the carer may request the local authority, before they make their decision as to whether the needs of the disabled child call for the provision of any services, to carry out an assessment of his ability to provide and continue to provide care for the disabled child; and if he makes such a request, the local authority shall carry out such an assessment and shall take into account the results of that assessment in making that decision.

(3) No request may be made under subsection (1) or (2) above by an individual who provides or will provide the care in question–

(a)   by virtue of a contract of employment or other contract with any person; or

(b)   as a volunteer for a voluntary organisation. . .

10. Carers and Disabled Children Act 2000

1.–(1) If an individual aged 16 or over ('the carer')–

(a)   provides or intends to provide a substantial amount of care on a regular basis for another individual aged 18 or over ('the person cared for'); and

(b)   asks a local authority to carry out an assessment of his ability to provide and to continue to provide care for the person cared for,

the local authority must carry out such an assessment if it is satisfied that the person cared for is someone for whom it may provide or arrange for the provision of community care services.

(2) For the purposes of such an assessment, the local authority may take into account, so far as it considers it to be material, an assessment under section 1(1) of the Carers (Recognition and Services) Act 1995.

(3) Subsection (1) does not apply if the individual provides or will provide the care in question–

(a)   by virtue of a contract of employment or other contract with any person; or

413

(b)   as a volunteer for a voluntary organisation.

(4) The Secretary of State (or, in relation to Wales, the National Assembly for Wales) may give directions as to the manner in which an assessment under subsection (1) is to be carried out or the form it is to take.

(5) Subject to any such directions, it is to be carried out in such manner, and is to take such form, as the local authority considers appropriate.

(6) In this section, 'voluntary organisation' has the same meaning as in the National Assistance Act 1948.

2. (1) The local authority must consider the assessment and decide–

(a) whether the carer has needs in relation to the care which he provides or intends to provide;

(b) if so, whether they could be satisfied (wholly or partly) by services which the local authority may provide; and

(c) if they could be so satisfied, whether or not to provide services to the carer.

(2) The services referred to are any services which–

(a)   the local authority sees fit to provide; and

(b)   will in the local authority's view help the carer care for the person cared for,

and may take the form of physical help or other forms of support.

(3) A service, although provided to the carer–

(a)   may take the form of a service delivered to the person cared for if it is one which, if provided to him instead of to the carer, could fall within community care services and they both agree it is to be so delivered; but

(b)   if a service is delivered to the person cared for it may not, except in prescribed circumstances, include anything of an intimate nature.

(4) Regulations may make provision about what is, or is not, of an intimate nature for the purposes of subsection (3).

3. (1) Regulations may make provision for the issue of vouchers by local authorities.

---

11. Local Government Act 2000

2. (1) Every local authority are to have power to do anything which they consider is likely to achieve any one or more of the following objects–

(a)   the promotion or improvement of the economic well-being of their area,

(b)   the promotion or improvement of the social well-being of their area, and

(c)   the promotion or improvement of the environmental well-being of their area.

(2) The power under subsection (1) may be exercised in relation to or for the benefit of–

(a)   the whole or any part of a local authority's area, or

(b)   all or any persons resident or present in a local authority's area.

(3) In determining whether or how to exercise the power under subsection (1), a local authority must have regard to their strategy under section 4.

(4) The power under subsection (1) includes power for a local authority to–

(a)   incur expenditure,

(b)   give financial assistance to any person,

(c)   enter into arrangements or agreements with any person,

(d)   co-operate with, or facilitate or co-ordinate the activities of, any person,

(e)   exercise on behalf of any person any functions of that person, and

(f)   provide staff, goods, services or accommodation to any person.

(5) The power under subsection (1) includes power for a local authority to do anything in relation to, or for the benefit of, any person or area situated outside their area if they consider that it is likely to achieve any one or more of the objects in that subsection.

(6) Nothing in subsection (4) or (5) affects the generality of the power under subsection (1).

Limits on power to promote well-being.

3. (1) The power under section 2(1) does not enable a local authority to do anything which they are unable to do by virtue of any prohibition, restriction or limitation on their powers which is contained in any enactment (whenever passed or made).

(2) The power under section 2(1) does not enable a local authority to raise money (whether by precepts, borrowing or otherwise)

(3) The Secretary of State may by order make provision preventing local authorities from doing, by virtue of section 2(1), anything which is specified, or is of a description specified, in the order.

(4) Before making an order under subsection (3), the Secretary of State must consult such representatives of local government and such other persons (if any) as he considers appropriate.

(5) Before exercising the power under section 2(1), a local authority must have regard to any guidance for the time being issued by the Secretary of State about the exercise of that power.

(6) Before issuing any guidance under subsection (5), the Secretary of State must consult such representatives of local government and such other persons (if any) as he considers appropriate.

(7) In its application to Wales, this section has effect as if for any reference to the Secretary of State there were substituted a reference to the National Assembly for Wales.

(8) In this section 'enactment' includes an enactment comprised in subordinate legislation (within the meaning of the Interpretation Act 1978).

12. **Health and Social Care Act 2001**

49 Exclusion of nursing care from community care services

(1) Nothing in the enactments relating to the provision of community care services shall authorise or require a local authority, in or in connection with the provision of any such services, to–

(a)   provide for any person, or

(b)   arrange for any person to be provided with,

nursing care by a registered nurse.

(2) In this section 'nursing care by a registered nurse' means any services provided by a registered nurse and involving–

(a)   the provision of care, or

(b)   the planning, supervision or delegation of the provision of care,

other than any services which, having regard to their nature and the circumstances in which they are provided, do not need to be provided by a registered nurse.

13. National Health Service Act 2006

Local social service authorities

254–(1) Subject to paragraphs (d) and (e) of section 3(1), the services described in Schedule 20 in relation to–

    (a)   care of mothers,

    (b)   prevention, care and after-care,

    (c)   home help and laundry facilities,

are functions exercisable by local social services authorities.

(2) A local social services authority which provides premises, furniture or equipment for any of the purposes of this Act may permit the use of the premises, furniture or equipment by–

    (a)   any other local social services authority,

    (b)   any of the bodies established under this Act, or

    (c)   a local education authority.

(3) The permission may be on such terms (including terms with respect to the services of any staff employed by the authority giving permission) as may be agreed.

(4) A local social services authority may provide (or improve or furnish) residential accommodation for officers–

    (a)   employed by it for the purposes of any of its functions as a local social services authority, or

    (b)   employed by a voluntary organisation for the purposes of any services provided under this section and Schedule 20.

(5) In this section and Schedule 20 'equipment' includes any machinery, apparatus or appliance, whether fixed or not, and any vehicle.

14. National Health Service (Wales) Act 2006

Local social service authorities

192–(1) Subject to paragraphs (d) and (e) of section 3(1), the services described in Schedule 15 in relation to–

    (a)   care of mothers,

    (b)   prevention, care and after-care,

    (c)   home help and laundry facilities,

are functions exercisable by local social services authorities.

(2) A local social services authority which provides premises, furniture or equipment for any of the purposes of this Act may permit the use of the premises, furniture or equipment by–

    (a)   any other local social services authority,

    (b)   any of the bodies established under this Act, or

    (c)   a local education authority.

(3) The permission may be on such terms (including terms with respect to the services of any staff employed by the authority giving permission) as may be agreed.

(4) A local social services authority may provide (or improve or furnish) residential accommodation for officers–

    (a)   employed by it for the purposes of any of its functions as a local social services authority, or

    (b)   employed by a voluntary organisation for the purposes of any services provided under this section and Schedule 15.

(5) In this section and Schedule 15 'equipment' includes any machinery, apparatus or appliance, whether fixed or not, and any vehicle.

15. **Health and Social Care Act 2008**

The Care Quality Commission

1–(1) There is to be a body corporate known as the Care Quality Commission (referred to in this Part as 'the Commission').

(2) The Commission for Healthcare Audit and Inspection, the Commission for Social Care Inspection and the Mental Health Act Commission are dissolved.

(3) Schedule 1 (which makes further provision about the Care Quality Commission) has effect.

The Commission's objectives

3–(1) The main objective of the Commission in performing its functions is to protect and promote the health, safety and welfare of people who use health and social care services.

(2) The Commission is to perform its functions for the general purpose of encouraging—

(a) the improvement of health and social care services,

(b) the provision of health and social care services in a way that focuses on the needs and experiences of people who use those services, and

(c) the efficient and effective use of resources in the provision of health and social care services.

(3) In this Chapter 'health and social care services' means the services to which the Commission's functions relate.

Matters to which the Commission must have regard

4–(1) In performing its functions the Commission must have regard to—

(a) views expressed by or on behalf of members of the public about health and social care services,

(b) experiences of people who use health and social care services and their families and friends,

(c) views expressed by local involvement networks about the provision of health and social care services in their areas,

(d) the need to protect and promote the rights of people who use health and social care services (including, in particular, the rights of children, of persons detained under the Mental Health Act 1983, of persons who are deprived of their liberty in accordance with the Mental Capacity Act 2005 (c. 9), and of other vulnerable adults),

(e) the need to ensure that action by the Commission in relation to health and social care services is proportionate to the risks against which it would afford safeguards and is targeted only where it is needed,

(f) any developments in approaches to regulatory action, and

(g) best practice among persons performing functions comparable to those of the Commission (including the principles under which regulatory action should be transparent, accountable and consistent).

(2) In performing its functions the Commission must also have regard to such aspects of government policy as the Secretary of State may direct.

(3) In subsection (1)(c), 'local involvement network' has the meaning given by section 222(2) of the Local Government and Public Involvement in Health Act 2007 (c. 28).

Requirement to register as a service provider

10–(1) Any person who carries on a regulated activity without being registered under this Chapter in respect of the carrying on of that activity is guilty of an offence.

(2) The Secretary of State may by regulations make provision for the purposes of this Chapter for determining, in relation to a regulated activity carried on by two or more persons acting in different capacities, which of those persons is to be regarded as the person who carries on the activity.

(3) In the following provisions of this Part, the registration of a person under this Chapter in respect of the carrying on of a regulated activity by that person is referred to as registration 'as a service provider' in respect of that activity.

(4) A person guilty of an offence under this section is liable—
- (a) on summary conviction, to a fine not exceeding £50,000, or to imprisonment for a term not exceeding 12 months, or to both;
- (b) on conviction on indictment, to a fine, or to imprisonment for a term not exceeding 12 months, or to both.

(5) In relation to an offence committed before the commencement of section 154(1) of the Criminal Justice Act 2003 (c. 44), the reference in subsection (4)(a) to 12 months is to be read as a reference to 6 months.

Regulation of regulated activities

2–(1) Regulations may impose in relation to regulated activities any requirements which the Secretary of State thinks fit for the purposes of this Chapter.

(2) Regulations under this section may in particular make provision with a view to—
- (a) securing that any service provided in the carrying on of a regulated activity is of appropriate quality, and
- (b) securing the health, safety and welfare of persons for whom any such service is provided.

(3) Regulations under this section may in particular—
- (a) make provision as to the persons who are fit to carry on or manage a regulated activity;
- (b) make provision as to the manner in which a regulated activity is carried on;
- (c) make provision as to the persons who are fit to work for the purpose of the carrying on of a regulated activity;
- (d) make provision as to the management and training of persons who work for the purpose of the carrying on of a regulated activity;
- (e) make provision as to the fitness of premises;
- (f) impose requirements as to the keeping of records and accounts;
- (g) impose requirements as to the provision of information;
- (h) impose requirements as to the financial position of a person registered as a service provider;
- (i) impose requirements as to the making available to the public of information as to any charges made for the provision of any services provided in the carrying on of a regulated activity;
- (j) impose requirements as to the review of the quality of any services provided in the carrying on of a regulated activity, as to the preparation of reports of such reviews, and as to the making available to the public of such reports;

(k)   make provision as to the handling of complaints and disputes and the application of lessons learnt from them.

(4) Regulations made under this section by virtue of subsection (3)(b) may in particular include provision as to the control and restraint, in appropriate cases, of persons receiving health or social care or other services in connection with the carrying on of a regulated activity.

(5) Regulations made under this section may make provision for the prevention and control of health care associated infections and may include such provision as the Secretary of State considers appropriate for the purpose of safeguarding individuals (whether receiving health or social care or otherwise) from the risk, or any increased risk, of being exposed to health care associated infections or of being made susceptible, or more susceptible, to them.

(6) In this Chapter 'health care associated infection' means any infection to which an individual may be exposed or made susceptible (or more susceptible) in circumstances where—

(a)   health or social care is being, or has been, provided to that or any other individual, and

(b)   the risk of exposure to the infection, or of susceptibility (or increased susceptibility) to it, is directly or indirectly attributable to the provision of that care.

(7) But 'health care associated infection' does not include an infection to which the individual is deliberately exposed as part of any health care.

(8) Before making regulations under this section, except regulations which amend other regulations under this section and do not, in the opinion of the Secretary of State, effect any substantial change in the provision made by those regulations, the Secretary of State must consult such persons as the Secretary of State considers appropriate.

(9) Consultation undertaken by the Secretary of State before the commencement of this section is as effective for the purposes of this section as consultation undertaken after that time.

---

16. **Social Work (Scotland) Act 1968–**

Provisions relating to performance of functions by local authorities

4. Where a function is assigned to a local authority under this Act or section 7 (functions of local authorities) or 8 (provision of after-care services) of the Mental Health (Scotland) Act 1984 or Part II of the Children (Scotland) Act 1995 and a voluntary organisation or other person, including another local authority is able to assist in the performance of that function, the local authority may make arrangements with such an organisation or other person for the provision of such assistance as aforesaid.

Powers of Secretary of State

5.–(1) Local authorities shall perform their functions under this Act. . . under the general guidance of the Secretary of State.

(1A) Without prejudice to subsection (1) above, the Secretary of State may issue directions to local authorities, either individually or collectively, as to the manner in which they are to exercise any of their functions. . .and a local authority shall comply with any direction made under this subsection.

Local authority plans for community care services

5A.–(1) Within such period after the day appointed for the coming into force of this section as the Secretary of State may direct, and in accordance with the provisions of this section, each local authority shall prepare and publish a plan for the provision of community care services in their area.

(2) Each local authority shall from time to time review any plan prepared by them under subsection (1) above, and shall, in the light of any such review, prepare and publish–

(a) any modifications to the plan under review; or

(b) if the case requires, a new plan.

(3) In preparing any plan or carrying out any review under subsection (1) or, as the case may be, subsection (2) above the authority shall consult–

(a) any Health Board providing services under the National Health Service (Scotland) Act 1978 in the area of the authority;

(b) [*repealed*]

(c) such voluntary organisations as appear to the authority to represent the interests of persons who use or are likely to use any community care services within the area of the authority or the interests of private carers who, within that area, provide care to persons for whom, in the exercise of their functions under this Act or any of the enactments mentioned in section 5(1B) of this Act, the local authority have a power or a duty to provide, or to secure the provision of, a service;

(d) such voluntary housing agencies and other bodies as appear to the authority to provide housing or community care services in their area; and

(e) such other persons as the Secretary of State may direct.

(4) In this section–

'community care services' means services, other than services for children, which a local authority are under a duty or have a power to provide, or to secure the provision of, under Part II of this Act or section 7 (functions of local authorities), 8 (provision of after-care services) or 11 (training and occupation of the mentally handicapped) of the Mental Health (Scotland) Act 1984; and

'private carer' means a person who is not employed to provide the care in question by any body in the exercise of its functions under any enactment.

Complaints procedure

5B.–(1) Subject to the provisions of this section, the Secretary of State may by order require local authorities to establish a procedure whereby a person, or anyone acting on his behalf, may make representations (including complaints) in relation to the authority's discharge of, or failure to discharge, any of their functions. . .in respect of that person.

(2) For the purposes of subsection (1) of this section, 'person' means any person for whom the local authority have a power or a duty to provide, or to secure the provision of, a service, and whose need or possible need for such a service has (by whatever means) come to the attention of the authority.

(3) An order under subsection (1) of this section may be commenced at different times in respect of such different classes of person as may be specified in the order.

(6) A local authority shall comply with any directions given by the Secretary of State as to the procedure to be adopted in considering representations made as mentioned in subsection (1) of this section and as to the taking of such action as may be necessary in consequence of such representations.

(7) Every local authority shall give such publicity to the procedure established under this section as they consider appropriate.

General social welfare services of local authorities

12.–(1) It shall be the duty of every local authority to promote social welfare by making available advice, guidance and assistance on such a scale as may be appropriate for their area, and in that behalf to make arrangements and to provide or secure the provision of such facilities (including the provision or arranging for the provision of residential and other establishments) as they may consider suitable and adequate, and such assistance may, subject to subsections (3) to (5) of this section, be given in kind or in cash to, or in respect of, any relevant person.

(2) A person is a relevant person for the purposes of this section if, not being less than eighteen years of age, he is in need requiring assistance in kind or, in exceptional circumstances constituting an emergency, in cash, where the giving of assistance in either form would avoid the local authority being caused greater expense in the giving of assistance in another form, or where probable aggravation of the person's need would cause greater expense to the local authority on a later occasion.

(3) Before giving assistance to, or in respect of, a person in cash under subsection (1) of this section a local authority shall have regard to his eligibility for receiving assistance from any other statutory body and, if he is eligible, to the availability to him of that assistance in his time of need.

(4) Assistance given in kind or in cash to, or in respect of, persons under this section may be given unconditionally or subject to such conditions as to the repayment of the assistance, or of its real value, whether in whole or in part, as the local authority may consider reasonable having regard to the means of the person receiving the assistance and to the eligibility of the person for assistance from any other statutory body.

(5) Nothing in the provisions of this section shall affect the performance by a local authority of their functions under any other enactment

(6) For the purposes of subsection (2) of this section 'person in need' includes a person who is in need of care and attention arising out of drug or alcohol dependency or release from prison or other form of detention.

Duty of local authority to assess needs

12A.–(1) Subject to the provisions of this section, where it appears to a local authority that any person for whom they are under a duty or have a power to provide, or to secure the provision of, community care services may be in need of any such services, the authority–

(a)   shall make an assessment of the needs of that person for those services; and

(b)   having regard to the results of that assessment, shall then decide whether the needs of that person call for the provision of any such services.

(2) Before deciding, under subsection (1)(b) of this section, that the needs of any person call for the provision of nursing care, a local authority shall consult a medical practitioner.

(3) If, while they are carrying out their duty under subsection (1) of this section, it appears to a local authority that there may be a need for the provision to any person to whom that subsection applies–

(a)   of any services under the National Health Service (Scotland) Act 1978 by the Health Board–

(i)   in whose area he is ordinarily resident; or

(ii)   in whose area the services to be supplied by the local authority are, or are likely, to be provided; or

(b)   of any services which fall within the functions of a housing authority (within the meaning of section 130 (housing) of the Local Government (Scotland) Act 1973) which is not the local authority carrying out the assessment, the local authority shall so notify that Health Board or housing authority, and shall request information from them as to what services are likely to be made available to that person by that Health Board or housing authority; and, thereafter, in carrying out their said duty, the local authority shall take unto account any information received by them in response to that request.

(3A) Subject to subsection (3B) below, in any case where–

(a) a local authority make an assessment of the needs of any person ('the relevant person') under subsection (1) (a) above, and

(b) a person ('the carer') provides or intends to provide a substantial amount of care on a regular basis for the relevant person,

the carer may request the local authority, before they make their decision under subsection (1)(b) above, to make an assessment of his ability to provide and to continue to provide care for the relevant person; and if he makes such a request, the local authority shall make such an assessment and shall have regard to the results of that assessment in making that decision.

(3B) No request may be made under subsection (3A) above by a person who provides or will provide the care in question–

(a) by virtue of a contract of employment or other contract; or

(b) as a volunteer for a voluntary organisation.

(3C) Section 8 of the Disabled Persons (Services, Consultation and Representation) Act 1986 (duty of local authority to take into account ability of carers) shall not apply in any case where an assessment is made under subsection (3A) above in respect of a person who provides the care in question for a disabled person.

(4) Where a local authority are making an assessment under this section and it appears to them that the person concerned is a disabled person, they shall–

(a) proceed to make such a decision as to the services he requires as is mentioned in section 4 of the Disabled Persons (Services, Consultation and Representation) Act 1986 without his requesting them to do so under that section; and

(b) inform him that they will be doing so and of his rights under that Act.

(5) Nothing in this section shall prevent a local authority from providing or arranging for the provision of community care services for any person without carrying out a prior assessment of his needs in accordance with the preceding provisions of this section if, in the opinion of the authority, the condition of that person is such that he requires those services as a matter of urgency.

(6) If, by virtue of subsection (5) of this section, community care services have been provided for any person as a matter of urgency, then, as soon as practicable thereafter, an assessment of his needs shall be made in accordance with the preceding provisions of this section.

(7) This section is without prejudice to section 3 of the said Act of 1986.

(8) In this section–

'community care services' has the same meaning as in section 5A of this Act;

'disabled person' has the same meaning as in the said Act of 1986;

'medical practitioner' means a fully registered person within the meaning of section 55 (interpretation) of the Medical Act 1983; and

'person' means a natural person.

Direct payments in respect of community care services

12B.–(1) Where, as respects a person in need–

(a) a local authority have decided under section 12A of this Act that his needs call for the provision of any service which is a community care service within the meaning of section 5A of this act, and

(b) the person is of a description which is specified for the purposes of this subsection by regulations,

the authority may, if the person consents, make to him, in respect of his securing the provision of the service, a payment of such amount as, subject to subsection (2) below, they think fit.

(2) If–

(a) an authority pay under subsection (1) above at a rate below their estimate of the reasonable cost of securing the provision of the service concerned, and

(b) the person to whom the payment is made satisfies the authority that his means are insufficient for it to be reasonably practicable for him to make up the difference,

the authority shall so adjust the payment to him under that subsection as to avoid there being a greater difference than that which appears to them to be reasonable practicable for him to make up.

Power of local authorities to assist persons in need in disposal of produce of their work

13. Where, by virtue of section 12 of this Act, a local authority make arrangements or provide or secure the provision of facilities for the engagement of persons in need (whether under a contract of service or otherwise) in suitable work, that local authority may assist such persons in disposing of the produce of their work.

Residential accommodation with nursing

13A.–(1) Without prejudice to section 12 of this Act, a local authority shall make such arrangements as they consider appropriate and adequate for the provision of suitable residential accommodation where nursing is provided for persons who appear to them to be in need of such accommodation by reason of infirmity, age, illness or mental disorder, dependency on drugs or alcohol or being substantially handicapped by any deformity or disability.

(2) The arrangements made by virtue of subsection (1) above shall be made with a voluntary or other organisation or other person, being an organisation or person managing premises which are–

(a) a nursing home within the meaning of section 10(2)(a) of the Nursing Homes Registration (Scotland) Act 1938 in respect of which that organisation or person is registered or exempt from registration under that Act; or

(b) a private hospital registered under section 12 of the Mental Health (Scotland) Act 1984,

for the provision of accommodation in those premises.

(3) The provisions of section 6 of this Act apply in relation to premises where accommodation is provided for the purposes of this section as they apply in relation to establishments provided for the purposes of this Act.

Provision of care and aftercare

13B.–(1) Subject to subsection (2) below, a local authority may with the approval of the Secretary of State, and shall, if and to the extent that the Secretary of State so directs, make arrangements for the purpose of the prevention of illness, the care of persons suffering from illness, and the after-care of such persons.

(2) The arrangements which may be made under subsection (1) above do not include arrangements in respect of medical, dental or nursing care, or health visiting.

Home help and laundry facilities

14.–(1) It shall be the duty of every local authority to provide on such scale as is adequate for the needs of their area, or to arrange for the provision on such a scale as is so adequate of, domiciliary services for households where such services are required owing to the presence, or the proposed presence, of a person in need or a person who is an expectant mother or lying-in, and every such authority shall have power to provide or arrange for the provision of laundry facilities for households for which domiciliary services are being, or can be, provided under this subsection.

(2) [repealed]

(3) [repealed]

(4) On the coming into operation of the provisions of this and the last two foregoing sections, the provisions of sections 13, 44 and 45 of the Health Services and Public Health Act 1968 shall cease to have effect.–

Exclusion of powers to provide accommodation in certain cases

86A.–(1) Subject to subsection (3) below, no accommodation may be provided under this Act for any person who, immediately before the date on which this section comes into force, was ordinarily resident in relevant premises.

(2) In subsection (1) above 'relevant premises' means–

(a) any establishment in respect of which a person is registered under section 62 of this Act;

(b) any nursing home within the meaning of the Nursing Homes Registration (Scotland) Act 1938 in respect of which a person is registered or exempt from registration under that Act;

(c) any private hospital registered under section 12 of the Mental Health (Scotland) Act 1984; and

(d) such other premises as the Secretary of State may by regulations prescribe.

(3) The Secretary of State may by regulations provided that in such cases and subject to such conditions as my be prescribed subsection (1) above shall not apply in relation to such classes of persons as may be prescribed in the regulations.

(4) The Secretary of State shall by regulations prescribe the circumstances in which persons are to be treated as being ordinarily resident in any premises for the purposes of subsection (1) above.

(5) This section does not affect the validity of any contract made before the date on which this section comes into force for the provision of accommodation on or after that date or anything done in pursuance of such as contract.

Charges that may be made for services and accommodation

87.–(1) Subject to. . . the following provisions of this section, a local authority providing a service under this Act or section 7 (functions of local authorities) or 8 (provision of after-care services) of the Mental Health (Scotland) Act 1984. . . may recover such charge (if any) for it as they consider reasonable.

(1A) If a person–

(a) avails himself of a service provided under this Act or section 7 or 8 of the said Act of 1984. . . ; and

(b) satisfies the authority providing the service that his means are insufficient for it to be reasonably practicable for him to pay for the service the amount which he would otherwise be obliged to pay for it,

the authority shall not require him to pay more for it than it appears to them that it is reasonably practicable for him to pay.

(2) Persons. . ., for whom accommodation is provided under this Act or section 7 of the said Act of 1984, shall be required to pay for that accommodation in accordance with the subsequent provisions of this section.

(3) Subject to the following provisions of this section, accommodation provided under this Act or section 7 of the said Act of 1984 shall be regarded as accommodation provided under Part III of the National Assistance Act 1948, and sections 22(2) to (8) and 26(2) to (4). . . and sections 42. . . and 43 of the said Act of 1948 (which make provision for the mutual maintenance of wives and husbands and the maintenance of their children by recovery of assistance from persons liable for maintenance and for affiliation orders, etc.) shall apply accordingly.

(4) In the application of the said section 22, for any reference to the Minister there shall be substituted a reference to the Secretary of State, and in the application of the said section 26, any references to arrangements under a scheme for the provision of accommodation shall be construed as references to arrangements made by a local authority with a voluntary organisation or any other person or body for the provision of accommodation under this Act or section 7 of the said Act of 1984.

(5) The Secretary of State may, with the consent of the Treasury, make regulations for modifying or adjusting the rates at which payments under this section are made, where such a course appears to him to be justified, and any such regulations may provide for the waiving of any such payment in whole or in part in such circumstances as may be specified in the regulations.

---

17. NHS (Scotland) Act 1978

Secretary of State

1.–(1) It shall continue to be the duty of the Secretary of State to promote in Scotland a comprehensive and integrated health service designed to secure–

(a)improvement in the physical and mental health of the people of Scotland, and

(b)the prevention, diagnosis and treatment of illness,

and for that purpose to provide or secure the effective provision of services in accordance with the provisions of this Act.

(2) The services so provided shall be free of charge, except in so far as the making and recovery of charges is expressly provided for by or under any enactment, whenever passed.

Other Services and Facilities

36.–(1) It shall be the duty of the Secretary of State to provide throughout Scotland, to such extent as he considers necessary to meet all reasonable requirements, accommodation and services of the following descriptions–

(a) hospital accommodation, including accommodation at state hospitals;

(b)premises other than hospitals at which facilities are available for any of the services provide under this Act;

(c) medical, nursing and other services, whether in such accommodation or premises, in the home of the patient or elsewhere.

(2) Where accommodation or premises provided under this section afford facilities for the provision of general medical, general dental or general ophthalmic services, or of pharmaceutical services, they shall be made available for those services on such terms and conditions as the Secretary of State may determine.

37. The Secretary of State shall make arrangements, to such extent as he considers necessary to meet all reasonable requirements, for the purposes of the prevention if illness, the care of persons suffering from illness or the aftercare of such persons.

18. s2 Regulation of Care (Scotland) Act 2001

(28) In this Act, unless the context otherwise requires–

'someone who cares for' (or 'a person who cares for') a person, means someone who, being an individual, provides on a regular basis a substantial amount of care for that person, not having contracted to do so and not doing so for payment or in the course of providing a care service;

'vulnerability or need', in relation to a person, means vulnerability or need arising by reason of that person–

(a) being affected by infirmity or ageing;

(b) being, or having been, affected by disability, illness or mental disorder;

(c) being, or having been, dependent on alcohol or drugs; *or*

(d) being of a young age;

'personal care' means care which relates to the day to day physical tasks and needs of the person cared for (as for example, but without prejudice to that generality, to eating and washing) and to mental processes related to those tasks and needs (as for example, but without prejudice to that generality, to remembering to eat and wash); *and*

'personal support' means counselling, or other help, provided as part of a planned programme of care.

19. Community Care and Health (Scotland) Act 2002

Regulations as respects charging and not charging for social care

1(1) Subject to subsection (2)(a) below, a local authority are not to charge for social care provided by them (or the provision of which is secured by them) if that social care is–

(a) personal care as defined in section 2(28) of the Regulation of Care (Scotland) Act 2001 (asp 8);

(b) personal support as so defined;

(c) whether or not such personal care or personal support, care of a kind for the time being mentioned in schedule 1 to this Act; or

(d) whether or not from a registered nurse, nursing care.

(2) The Scottish Ministers may (either or both)–

(a) by regulations qualify the requirements of subsection (1) above in such way as they think fit;

(b) by order amend schedule 1 to this Act.

(3) In paragraph (d) of subsection (1) above, 'nursing care' does not include such social care as falls within any of paragraphs (a) to (c) of that subsection.

(4) Subject to subsection (1) above, the Scottish Ministers may by regulations-

(a) require a local authority–

(i) to charge; or

(ii) not to charge,

for such social care provided by (or the provision of which is secured by) the authority as may be specified in the regulations;

(b) where a requirement is made under paragraph (a)(i) above, specify the amount to be charged or factors which the authority must (either or both)-

(i) take into account;

(ii) not take into account,

in determining any such amount; and

(c) where a requirement is made under paragraph (a)(ii) above, qualify that requirement in such way as they think fit.

(5) Regulations under subsection (4) above may–

(a) specify, as a factor which the authority must take into account by virtue of paragraph (b) of that subsection, the maximum amount which may be charged for the social care in question or for that and such other social care (being social care provided to the same person by the authority) as may be specified in the regulations; *or*

(b) provide that a person who, in such manner and by reference to such factors as may be specified in the regulations, is assessed by the authority as unable to pay the amount falling to be charged by virtue of that paragraph is required to pay only so much as appears from the assessment to be reasonably practicable for that person.

(6) In section 87 of the 1968 Act (charges that may be made for services and accommodation), after subsection (1A) there is inserted the following subsection–

'(1B) Subsections (1) and (1A) above do not apply as respects any amount required not to be charged by subsection (1) of section 1 of the Community Care and Health (Scotland) Act 2002 (asp 5) (charging and not charging for social care) or required to be charged or not to be charged by virtue of subsection (4) of that section.'

(7) Regulations under this section may make such transitional provision as the Scottish Ministers consider necessary or expedient, modifying either or both of subsections (1) and (2) of section 12A of the 1968 Act (duty of local authority to assess needs of certain persons for community care services) in their application to persons who, immediately before the date of coming into force of this section, were receiving such services in residential accommodation and for whom the local authority were not, at that time, providing or securing the provision either of the services or the accommodation.

SCHEDULE 1

Social care not ordinarily charged for

1. As regards the personal hygiene of the person cared for–

(a) shaving;

(b) cleaning teeth (whether or not they are artificial) by means of a brush or dental floss and (in the case of artificial teeth) by means of soaking;

(c) providing assistance in rinsing the mouth;

(d) keeping finger nails and toe nails trimmed;

(e) assisting the person with going to the toilet or with using a bedpan or other receptacle;

(f) where the person is fitted with a catheter or stoma, providing such assistance as is requisite to ensure cleanliness and that the skin is kept in a favourable hygienic condition;

(g) where the person is incontinent–

(i) the consequential making of the person's bed and consequential changing and laundering of the person's bedding and clothing; and

(ii) caring for the person's skin to ensure that it is not adversely affected.

2. As regards the person's eating requirements–

(a) assisting with the preparation of food;

(b) assisting in the fulfilment of special dietary needs.

3. If the person is immobile or substantially immobile, dealing with the problems of that immobility.

4. If the person requires medical treatment, assisting with medication, as for example by–

(a) applying creams or lotions;

(b) administering eye drops;

(c) applying dressings in cases where this can be done without the physical involvement of a registered nurse or of a medical practitioner;

(d) assisting with the administration of oxygen as part of a course of therapy.

5. With regard to the person's general well-being–

(a) assisting with getting dressed;

(b) assisting with surgical appliances, prosthesis and mechanical and manual equipment;

(c) assisting with getting up and with going to bed;

(d) the provision of devices to help memory and of safety devices;

(e) behaviour management and psychological support.

20. Mental Health (Care and Treatment) (Scotland) Act 2003

25 Care and support services etc.

(1) A local authority–

(a) shall–

(i) provide, for persons who are not in hospital and who have or have had a mental disorder, services which provide care and support; or

(ii) secure the provision of such services for such persons; and

(b) may–

(i) provide such services for persons who are in hospital and who have or have had a mental disorder; or

(ii) secure the provision of such services for such persons.

(2) Services provided by virtue of subsection (1) above shall be designed to–

(a) minimise the effect of the mental disorder on such persons; and

(b) give such persons the opportunity to lead lives which are as normal as possible.

(3) In subsection (1) above, 'care and support'–

(a) includes, without prejudice to the generality of that expression–

   (i)   residential accommodation; and
   (ii) personal care and personal support (each of those expressions having the meaning given by section 2(28) of the Regulation of Care (Scotland) Act 2001 (asp 8)); but
   (b)   does not include nursing care.
(4) In section 59(1) of the Social Work (Scotland) Act 1968 (c. 49) (duty of local authorities as respects provision and maintenance of residential or other establishments), for the words 'or under' there shall be substituted 'sections 25 and 26 of the Mental Health (Care and Treatment) (Scotland) Act 2003 (asp 13) or'.

26 Services designed to promote well-being and social development

(1) A local authority–
   (a)   shall–
   (i)   provide, for persons who are not in hospital and who have or have had a mental disorder, services which are designed to promote the well-being and social development of those persons; or
   (ii) secure the provision of such services for such persons; and
   (b)   may–
   (i)   provide such services for persons who are in hospital and who have or have had a mental disorder; or
   (ii) secure the provision of such services for such persons.
(2) Services provided by virtue of subsection (1) above shall include, without prejudice to the generality of that subsection, services which provide–
   (a)   social, cultural and recreational activities;
   (b)   training for such of those persons as are over school age; and
   (c)   assistance for such of those persons as are over school age in obtaining and in undertaking employment.
(3) Subsection (1) above is without prejudice to the operation of–
   (a)   section 1 of the Education (Scotland) Act 1980 (c. 44) (duties and powers of education authorities in relation to the provision of social, cultural and recreative activities and vocational and industrial training); and
   (b)   section 1 of the Further and Higher Education (Scotland) Act 1992 (c. 37) (duty of Scottish Ministers in relation to the provision of further education).
(4) In subsection (2)(b) and (c) above, 'school age' has the same meaning as in section 31 of the Education (Scotland) Act 1980 (c. 44).

27 Assistance with travel

A local authority–
   (a)   shall–
   (i)   provide, for persons who are not in hospital and who have or have had a mental disorder, such facilities for, or assistance in, travelling as the authority may consider necessary to enable those persons to attend or participate in any of the services mentioned in sections 25 and 26 of this Act; or
   (ii) secure the provision of such facilities or assistance for such persons; and
   (b)   may–
   (i)   provide such facilities or assistance for persons who are in hospital and who have or have had a mental disorder; or
   (ii) secure the provision of such facilities or assistance for such persons.

Appendix 5

Key guidance

The following are some of the key circulars issued to adult social care services which are useful for establishing whether or how much you pay for your care. These and other circulars mentioned in the text can be obtained from:

- **England**: Department of Health, www.dh.gov.uk/en/Publicationsandstatistics/Lettersandcirculars.
- **Wales**: Welsh Assembly Government, http://wales.gov.uk/publications/circular/?lang=en.
- **Scotland**: Scottish Government, www.show.scot.nhs.uk/sehd.

	England	Wales	Scotland
Charges **Includes the full guidance for charges with previous circulars annexed**	At the time of writing the latest final version is CRAG amendment 26 is with LAC(2007)4. However, there is a draft CRAG April 2008 on the DH website but it is doubtful whether a April 2008 version will be available before the April 2009 regulations and guidance. References in the *Handbook* are appropriate to the April 2008 Draft CRAG - available at http://www.dh.gov.uk/en/Publications andstatistics/Publications/Publications PolicyAnd Guidance/DH_086008	Welsh CRAG has been amended with WAGC 11/2008 and is available at http:/ /new.wales. gov.uk/topics/ health/ publications/ socialcare/ guidance/2008/ cragamend ment24?lang =en	Scottish CRAG has been amended with CCD 2/2008 and is available at http:// www.sehd. scot.nhs.uk/ publications/ CC2008_02.pdf

	England	*Wales*	*Scotland*
Covers discretionary charges for adult services	LAC (01)32 *Fairer charging policies for home care and other non-residential social services*	NAfWC 17/2003 interim guidance and NAfWC 28/2002	SWSG1/97 and guidance on charging policies for non-residential services that enable older people to remain in their own home issued by COSLA 2002. Free personal care guidance CCD 4/2002

Other Important Circulars

Choice of Accommodation	LAC (93)18 LAC (04) 20	WOC12/93 WOC47/93 NAfWC 21/2003	SWSG5/93 SWSG6/94
Ordinary residence	LAC(93)7	WOC35/93	SWSG1/96
NHS responsibilities for meeting continuing health care needs	*The National Framework for NHS Continuing Healthcare and NHS-funded Nursing Care*	*National Framework for Continuing NHS Health Care,* Welsh Assembly Government	CEL 6 (2008)
Guidance on the Community Care (Residential Accommodation) Act 1998	LAC (98)19	WOC 27/98	SWSG2/99 CCD 3/2002
Guidance on free nursing care (and personal care in Scotland)	LAC (2001)26 HSC 2001/1 And LAC 2003 (7)	NAfWc 34/2001 and NAfWC 12/2003	CCD4/2002
Guidance on intermediate care	LAC (2001)01 LAC (2003)14	NAfWC 05/2002 NAfWC 43/2002	CCD2/2001

Appendix 6

Abbreviations used in the notes

AC	Appeal Cases
All ER	All England Reports
CA	Court of Appeal
CAO	Chief Adjudication Officer
CCLR	Community Care Law Reports
DC	Divisional Court
ECHR	European Convention on Human Rights
ECtHR	European Court of Human Rights
EWHC	England and Wales High Court
HC	High Court
HL	House of Lords
HLR	Housing Law Reports
NAB	National Assistance Board
para(s)	paragraph(s)
QBD	Queen's Bench Division
reg(s)	regulation(s)
s(s)	section(s)
SBC	Supplementary Benefits Commission
Sch(s)	Schedule(s)
TLR	Times Law Reports
WLR	Weekly Law Reports

Acts of Parliament

ASP(S)A 2007	Adult Support and Protection (Scotland) Act 2007
B(S)A 1985	Bankruptcy (Scotland) Act 1985
CA 1989	Children Act 1989
CC(DD)A 2003	Community Care (Delayed Discharges etc) Act 2003
CCDPA 1996	Community Care (Direct Payments) Act 1996
CCH(S)A	Community Care and Health (Scotland) Act 2002
CDCA 2000	Carers and Disabled Children Act 2000
CPA 2004	Civil Partnership Act 2004
CRSA 1995	Carers (Recognition and Services) Act 1995

CSA 2000	Care Standards Act 2000
CSDPA 1970	Chronically Sick and Disabled Persons Act 1970
CSPSSA 2000	Child Support, Pensions and Social Security Act 2000
DPSCRA 1986	Disabled Persons (Services, Consultation and Representation) Act 1986
H(S)A 1987	Housing (Scotland) Act 1987
HA 1985	Housing Act 1985
HA 1996	Housing Act 1996
HA 1999	Health Act 1999
HASSASSAA 1983	The Health and Social Services and Social Security Adjudication Act 1983
HCPA 1995	Hospital Complaints Procedure Act 1995
HGCRA 1996	Housing Grants, Construction and Regeneration Act 1996
HSCA 2001	Health Service Commissioners Act 2001
HSCA 1993	Health Service Commissioners Act 1993
HSCA 2008	Health and Social Care Act 2008
HSPHA 1948	Health Services and Public Health Act 1948
IA 1986	Insolvency Act 1986
JSA 1995	Jobseekers Act 1995
LASSA 1970	Local Authority Social Services Act 1970
LG(S)A 1975	Local Government (Scotland) Act 1975
LGA 1974	Local Government Act 1974
LGA 2000	Local Government Act 2000
LGFA 1992	Local Government Finance Act 1992
LGHA 1989	Local Government and Housing Act 1989
MH(CT)(S)A 2003	Mental Health (Care and Treatment) (Scotland) Act 2003
MH(S)A 1984	Mental Health (Scotland) Act 1984
NAA 1948	National Assistance Act 1948
NHSA 2006	National Health Service Act 2006
NHS(S)A 1978	National Health Service (Scotland) Act 1978
NHS(W)A 2006	National Health Service (Wales) Act 2006
NHSCCA 1990	National Health Services Act and Community Care Act 1990
PA 2004	Pension Act 2004
RHA 1984	Registered Homes Act 1984
SPCA 2002	State Pension Credit Act 2002
SSA 1998	Social Security Act 1998
SSAA 1992	Social Security Administration Act 1992
SSCBA 1992	Social Security Contributions and Benefits Act 1992
SW(S)A 1968	Social Work (Scotland) Act 1968
TCA 2002	Tax Credits Act 2002
WRA 2007	Welfare Reform Act 2007
WRPA 1999	Welfare Reform and Pensions Act 1999

Regulations

APS(E) Regs	The Adult Placement Schemes (England) Regs 2004 No.2071
ARP Regs	The Age-Related Payments Regulations 2005 No.1983
C(LC)SSB Regs	The Child (Leaving Care) Social Security Benefits Regulations 2001 No.3074
CC(DD)(QS)(E) Regs	The Community Care (Delayed Discharge etc) Act (Qualifying Services) (England) Regulations 2003 No. 1196
CCDP Regs	Community Care (Direct Payments) Regulations 1997 No.734
CCSCCS(DP)(E) Regs	The Community Care, Services for Carers and Children's Services (Direct Payment) (England) Regulations 2003 No 762
CDC(V)(E) Regs	Carers and Disabled Children (Vouchers) (England) Regulations 2003 No.1216
CO(RA)(S)O 1993	The Charging Order (Residential Accommodation) (Scotland) Order 1993
CT(ED)O	The Council Tax (Exempt Dwellings) Order 1992 No.558 as amended: 1994 No.539
CT(RD) Regs	The Council Tax (Regulations for Disabilities) Regulations 1992 No.554
CT(RD)(Amdt) Regs	The Council Tax (Reductions for Disabilities) (Amendment) Regulations 1999
CT(RD) Regs	The Council Tax (Reductions for Disability) Regulations 1992 No. 554
CTB Regs	The Council Tax Benefit Regulations 2006 No.215
CTB(SPC) Regs	The Council Tax Benefit (Persons who have Attained the Qualifying Age for State Pension Credit) Regulations 2006 No.216
DFA Regs	The Discretionary Financial Assistance Regulations 2001 No.1167
DP(BMV) Regs	The Disabled Persons (Badges for Motor Vehicles) Regulations 1982
DWA Regs	The Disability Working Allowance (General) Regulations 1991 No.2887
ESA Regs	The Employment and Support Allowance Regulations 2008 No.795
ESA(TP) Regs	The Employment and Support Allowance (Transitional Provisions) Regulations 2008 No.795
HB Regs	The Housing Benefit Regulations 2006 No.213
HB(SPC) Regs	The Housing Benefit (Persons who have Attained the Qualifying Age for State Pension Credit) Regulations 2006 No.214
HB&CTB(DA) Regs	The Housing Benefit and Council Tax Benefit (Decisions and Appeals) Regulations 2001 No.1002
HEES(E)	The Home Energy Efficiency Scheme (England) Regulations
HEES(W)	The Home Energy Efficiency Scheme (Wales) Regulations
HRA Regs	The Home Repair Assistance Regulations 1996
HRG Regs	The Housing Renewal Grants Regulations 1996

IL(2006)FO	Independent Living (2006) Fund Order
IRBS(Amdt2) Regs	The Income-related Benefits Schemes (Miscellaneous Amendments) (No.2) Regulations 1995 No.1339
IS Regs	The Income Support (General) Regulations 1987 No.1967
JSA Regs	The Jobseeker's Allowance Regulations 1996 No.207
LA(CSWS)(E) Regs	Local Authority (Charges for Specified Welfare Services) (England) Regulations 2003 No.907
LASSNHSC(E) Regs	The Local Authority Social Services and National Health Service Complaints (England) Regulations 2009 No.309
N(RA)(RC)(E) Regs	The National Assistance (Residential Accommodation) (Relevant Contributions) (England) Regulations 2001 No. 3069
NA(AR) Regs	The National Assistance (Assessment of Resources) Regulations 1992 No.2977
NA(AR)(A)(E) Regs	The National Assistance (Assessment of Resources) (Amendment) (England) Regulations 2002 No.410
NA(AR)(Amdt2) Regs	The National Assistance (Assessment of Resources) (Amendment) (No.2) Regulations 1998 No.1730
NA(AR)(Amdt2) Regs	The National Assistance (Assessment of Resources) (Amendment) (No.2) Regulations 2001 No.1066
NA(RAAPAR)(E) Regs	The National Assistance (Residential Accommodation) (Additional Payments and Assessment of Resources) (Amendment) (England) Regulations 2001 No.3441
NA(RADR)(E) Regs	The National Assistance (Residential Accommodation) (Disregarding of Resources) (England) Regulations 2001 No.3067
NA(SPR)(E) Regs	The National Assistance (Sums for Personal Requirements) (England) Regulations 2001 No.411
NHS(C) Regs	The National Health Service (Complaints) Regulations 2004
NHS(CDA) Regs	The National Health Service (Charges for Drugs and Appliances) Regulations 2000 No.620
NHS(CDA)(S) Regs	The National Health Service (Charges for Drugs and Appliances) (Scotland) Regulations 2001 No.430
NHS(CDA)(W) Regs	The Nationla Health Service (Charges for Drugs and Appliances) (Wales) Regulations 2001 No.1358(W86)
NHS(DC) Regs	The National Health Service (Dental Charges) Regulations 1989 No.394
NHS(DC)(S) Regs	The National Health Service (Dental Charges) (Scotland) Regulations 1989 No.363
NHS(GOS) Regs	The National Health Service (General Ophthalmic Services) Regulations 1986 No.975
NHS(OCP) Regs	The National Health Service (Optical Charges and Payments) Regulations 1997 No.818
NHS(OCP)(S) Regs	The National Health Service (Optical Charges and Payments) (Scotland) Regulations 1998 No.642

Appendix 6: Abbreviations used in the notes

NHS(TERC) Regs	The National Health Service (Travelling Expenses and Remission of Charges) Regulations 1988 No.551
NHS(TERC)(S) Regs	The National Health Service (Travelling Expenses and Remission of Charges) (Scotland) Regulations 1988 No.546
RR(CA)O	The Regulatory Reform (Carer's Allowance) Order 2002
SFCWP Regs	The Social Fund Cold Weather Payments (General) Regulations 1988 No.1724
SFM&FE Regs	The Social Fund Maternity and Funeral Expenses (General) Regulations 1987 No.481
SFWFP Regs	The Social Fund Winter Fuel Payment Regulations 2000 No.729
SMP Regs	The Statutory Maternity Pay (General) Regulations 1986 No.1960
SPC Regs	The State Pension Credit Regulations 2002 No. 1792
SS(AA) Regs	The Social Security (Attendance Allowance) Regulations 1991 No.2740
SS(AA/DLA) Regs	The Social Security (Attendance Allowance and Disability Living Allowance) (Amendment) Regulations 2002 No.208
SS(C&P)A Regs	The Social Security (Claims and Payments) Amendment Regulations 2005 No.455
SS(C&P) Regs	The Social Security (Claims and Payments) Regulations 1987 No.1968
SS(CE) Regs	The Social Security (Computation of Earnings) Regulations 1996 No.2745
SS(DLA) Regs	The Social Security (Disability Living Allowance) Regulations 1991 No.2890
SS(GB) Regs	The Social Security (General Benefits) Regulations 1982 No.1408
SS(HIP) Regs	The Social Security (Hospital In-Patients) Regulations 1975 No.555
SS(HIP&MA) Regs	The Social Security (Hospital In-Patients and Miscellaneous Amendments) Regulations 2003 No.1195
SS(IB) Regs	The Social Security (Incapacity Benefit) Regulations 1994 No.2946
SS(IB-ID) Regs	The Social Security (Incapacity Benefit – Increases for Dependants) Regulations 1994 No.2945
SS(IB)T Regs	The Social Security (Incapacity Benefit) (Transitional) Regulations 1995 No 310
SS(ICA) Regs	The Social Security (Invalid Care Allowance) Regulations 1976 No.409
SS(IFW) Regs	The Social Security (Incapacity for Work) (General) Regulations 1995 No.311
SS(IIPD) Regs	The Social Security (Industrial Injuries) (Prescribed Diseases) Regulations 1985 No.967
SS(MA) Regs	The Social Security (Miscellaneous Amendments) Regulations 1998 No.563
SS(ME) Regs	The Social Security (Medical Evidence) Regulations 1976 No.615

SS(MP)(No.2) Regs	The Social Security (Miscellaneous Provisions) Amendment (No.2) Regulations 1992 No.2595
SS(OB) Regs	The Social Security (Overlapping Benefits) Regulations 1979 No.597
SS(PAOR) Regs	The Social Security (Payments on account, Overpayments and Recovery) Regulations 1988 No.664
SS(WB&RP) Regs	The Social Security (Widow's Benefit and Retirement Pensions) Regulations 1979 No.642
SS(WTCCTC)(CA) Regs	The Social Security (Working Tax Credit and Child Tax Credit) (Consequential Amendments) Regulations 2003 No.455
SSA(CLED) Regs	The Social Security Amendment (Capital Limits and Earnings Disregards) Regulations 2000 No.2545
SSA(RCNH) Regs	The Social Security Amendment (Residential Care and Nursing Homes) Regulations 2001 No.3767
SSB(Dep) Regs	The Social Security Benefit (Dependency) Regulations 1977 No.343
SSB(PRT) Regs	The Social Security Benefit (Persons Residing Together) Regulations 1977 No.956
SS&CS(DA) Regs	The Social Security and Child Support (Decisions and Appeals) Regulations 1999 No.991
SSCP Regs	The Social Security Commissioners Procedure Regulations 1987 No.214
TC(A)(No 2) Regs	The Tax Credits (Claims and Notifications) Regulations 2002 No. 2014
TC(CN) Regs	The Tax Credits (Claims and Notifications) Regulations 2002 No. 2014
TC(DCI) Regs	The Tax Credit (Definition and Calculation of Income) Regulations 2002 No. 2006
TC(NA) Regs	The Tax Credits (Notice of Appeal) Regulations 2002 No. 3119
WRPA(No 9)O	The Welfare Reform & Pensions Act 1999 (Commencement No 9 and Transitional and Savings Provisions) Order 2000 No. 2958

Other information

AOG	The Adjudication Officers' Guide now superseded by the DMG
CRAG	Charging for Residential Accommodation
DD(CC)	The Delayed Discharge (Continuing Care) Directions 2007
DMG	The Decision Makers Guide; vols1-7 and 9-12
GM	The Housing Benefit and Council Tax Benefit Guidance Manual
LGOR	Local Government Ombudsman's Report
SFDir	Directions on the Discretionary Social Fund

References like CIS/142/1990 and R(SB) 3/89 are references to commissioners' decisions.

Index

. . . .

How to use this Index

Entries against the bold headings direct you to the general information on the subject, or where the subject is covered most fully. Sub-entries are listed alphabetically and direct you to specific aspects of the subject.